THE

DAYS OF MAKEMIE;

OR,

THE VINE PLANTED.

A. D. 1680–1708.

WITH AN APPENDIX.

BY THE
REV. L. P. BOWEN, D. D

"For my own part I have ever observed in all the Writings of men Ignorance, Infirmity and Imperfection, to magnifie the Excellency of the Scriptures above all Books of men's Composure."—MAKEMIE.

PHILADELPHIA:
PRESBYTERIAN BOARD OF PUBLICATION,
1334 CHESTNUT STREET

PREFACE.

THE name has lived, but has Francis Makemie been much more than a myth in the dim twilight of the past? With sure instinct the Church has always *felt* that a debt of gratitude was owed by her to the Apostle of the Chesapeake, but how little she has known about him!

Dr. Miller's *Memoir of John Rodgers*, published in 1813, attracted some attention to our pioneer. He is spoken of as coming to America *about the year 1700*. The conflict between the Old and the New School parties, and the attempt to trace back their distinctive principles to the origin of the American Presbyterian Church and place them upon a historical basis, aroused a new interest in the founder of the Peninsula churches.

Irving Spence, in his *Letters on the Early History of the Presbyterian Church*, published in 1838, embodying the results of his own investigations among the traditions and court records of the lower Eastern Shore of Maryland, gave new impulse to inquiry and did more than any one before to clear away the thick mists. Dr. Hill and Dr. Hodge in their controversies widened the interest, resulting in the publication of the *Constitutional History* of the latter in 1839. Neither Dr. Hill's *Sketches* nor Dr. Hodge's *History* added materially to our knowledge of Makemie. Hill's mistakes are glaring. A slight step forward was taken when Foote's *Sketches* were published, in 1850, containing a very interesting account of our pioneer. In 1857 appeared Webster's *History*, giving the most satisfactory sketch of Makemie yet published, and adding more than any one since the days of Spence to our knowledge of our founder. His dates are valuable, but sometimes erroneous. No original researches seem to have been attempted since Webster wrote, later writers depending for material upon Webster and Spence. Makemie remains almost as much a myth as ever.

The present writer has been engaged for seven years in direct personal investigations, critically questioning all that has been published before, taking nothing for granted, authenticating dates, plodding through records covered with the dust of two centuries, securing transcripts of all of Makemie's writings, studying his character from his own utterances, and sparing no pains, time nor expense in these patient researches. Born upon that historic ground, familiar with the name of "Parson Makemie" from infancy, having for two years occupied the pulpit of some of the oldest churches founded by him, it has been the author's ambition to know all that could be known of the old worthy, and to make him again a living, breathing, speaking personality in ecclesiastical history.

The result is the present work. Effort is made to give a picture of the times and scenes in which Makemie was so prominent an actor. The thin thread of fiction introduced to keep up the flow of narrative will not obscure the historical facts which are definitely fixed in the notes. The setting of extracts from records and from the writings of Makemie and his contemporaries, when of any length, in a smaller type than that used in the narrative, will aid the reader who desires especially to note them. The colonists of the Eastern Shore of Chesapeake Bay, among whom our pioneer lived and died, have never before had a historian.

The writer has taken special pleasure, too, in rescuing from utter oblivion a few names, the customs and a few specimens of the language of the Indians then inhabiting the Eastern Shore, and who, along with their dialect, have wholly disappeared from the earth

It must be distinctly noted that in the severe strictures upon the Quakers and the adherents of the Church of England, there is no purpose to reflect upon those churches of the present day. The picture is painted from *the standpoint of a Presbyterian of that age* denounced by the one and persecuted by the other; as such, the picture is historical and reflects the spirit of Makemie's own writings.

The author does not care to press his claim that many of his most important discoveries, embraced in this volume, have been of late put in print by others without credit given to the discoverer. His great purpose has been to vindicate the fame of the pioneer. This has been a labor of love, and he rejoices in the wider honor accorded to Makemie during the last two years, whoever may have assisted in proclaiming the results of these researches.

In Europe valuable assistance has been given the author by the Rev. Dr. Killen of Belfast, Prof. Witherow of Londonderry and the Rev. Dr. Robert Anderson of Glasgow.

It would be ungrateful not to mention, also, Mr. William H. Brown of Princess Anne, Maryland, who has rendered most efficient aid as an enthusiastic antiquarian.

As the manuscript is passing from the writer's hands news comes of the death of the Rev. John C. Backus, D D , LL.D , of Baltimore, whose sympathy and encouragement have helped to inspire the long-continued labor. That the completed book might have been read and approved by that great and good man was a reward pleasantly contemplated, now never to be enjoyed. But his words of good cheer will still seem to linger about its pages.

MARSHALL, MISSOURI,
November 1, 1884.

THE DAYS OF MAKEMIE.

CHAPTER I.

A. D. 1680.

"A Country capable of superlative Improvement."—MAKEMIE.

AND yonder at last is Maryland! The mysterious New World, long dreamed of, is now
dawning upon our view under the slanting beams of
the rising May sun. Before we retired to sleep last
night in our sea-cradle the captain promised a pleasant
surprise to early risers, and just as the round orb of
day is about to roll up out of the horizon of waters,
we are hurried on deck to take our first look at the
scene of many hazy hopes and untried possibilities.
Here we sit upon the prow of the brigantine and
drop into silence, gazing upon the moving shores
and feeling as only flying exiles can feel.

Slowly from the crest of breakers emerges the low
coast. Long arrays of white hills chase one another to
the north and the south like snowdrifts beyond the blue
billows, but as we draw nearer and see the tumbling
waves bursting into foam, their shining spray throws
into dimmer shade the sunny sands. Beyond the
hills we discover an interior sheet of placid waters
lying in serene beauty between the beach and the
main, expanding and contracting in graceful curves

9

up and down the view. On the other side of this inner sound the eye is gladdened with the sight of green woodlands, their variegated hues contrasting pleasantly with the intervening sparkle of snow and silver, and by their repose of beauty resting the tired gaze from the incessant ocean-motion of days and weeks.

So, I am told, one hundred and eighty-two years ago, the great voyager Sebastian Cabot passed southward along the coast from Newfoundland, looking upon these same hills and the lands over yonder, gazing through the inlets with curiosity sublime, then turning away his helm from the thirty-eighth parallel and carrying home to England the sure announcement of a new continent. The first European that ever beheld the white beaches of Maryland, the brave navigator was dreaming of the Indies and their spices and gold with all the romance of 1498; but he did not know how Jehovah's hand was at the helm, preparing a refuge for the suffering and oppressed of the Old World in the years of great need.

From the captain's map I find that we have had glimpses of Fenwick's and Assateague islands, and that "Sinepuxent" is the name of the arborescent grounds beyond. The inner sheet of beautiful waters is now called "New Haven Bay," but I hope that the rightful aboriginal name will finally prevail and displace the foreign intruder. Assateague—Sinepuxent: the unaccustomed sounds point to the people who inhabit these wilds and whose acquaintance we must make ere long. In the distance, across the bay, do we not discover the little cabins and the smoke of a town of the natives? Oh, I wonder what our life

among those strange people is to be? Can the Amer-
can tomahawk prove more cruel than the English mitre?
Somewhere between these ocean-waves and the magnificent Chesapeake of which we have heard so much,
our lot is to be cast and new graveyards are to be
made. Here and there we seem to see indications of
settlement upon the main by the whites (1*). Who are
these that are ahead of us as pioneers? Are they content? Is the virgin soil more prolific of thorns or flowers? So I sit upon the advancing prow and pry over
into the profound unknown, and wonder and wonder.

Sail on as lightly and hopefully as you can toward
the contemplated harbor, my graceful caravel, and
remember what a frail cargo you are bearing of girl-
hood's fancies and visions of the improbable. Yes,
and you are freighted with the past as well.

Far backward over this waste of billows, nestled
behind the cliffs of Albion, I see a dear little cottage
embowered in vines and fragrant with the odors of
springtime. The hedge is green, the trees are leafy and
tremulous, the sky is smiling in sunshine. The rich
English landscape widens away, dotted with houses,
checkered with wheat-fields and adorned at intervals
with temples of the Most High God.

Ah! why should the bright scene have been clouded?
Why make it a crime to worship the good Lord as the
pious soul believes to be right? Especially hard is it
for the conscience to be dominated by king and courtiers who have no conscience of their own—men wicked and corrupt, whose religion is a hatred of those who
love the Saviour.

There! I have bravely put upon my page a solemn

* Figures in brackets refer to the Appendix.

truth which on the other side of the sea would have
been treason. My reckless goosequill, thou art dis-
loyal to the Stuart! The breath of May floats out
from the Maryland shore redolent already with inspi-
rations of freedom.

My honored sire joins us, his well-worn Bible in
hand. When leaving our old home for ever, we all
had our especial treasures from which we could not
part—mother's embroidered family-tree; John's gun,
with its wheel-lock; Martha's *Book of Martyrs*, by
John Foxe; and my own theorbo, with which I hope
" to sooth a savage breast," as Mr. William Shakespeare once said—but my father's one treasure is the
Holy Book so beautifully translated under King James
seventy years ago, and which comprises for my sire
his sweetest music, his grandest martyrology, his
armory of defence and his family record, all in one
In the times of our increasing troubles it had been
his bosom-companion, his daily solace. If new nations
are ever to arise upon this Western continent, he firmly
believes that all their greatness is to grow from the
teachings of the Book divine.

For a while my thoughtful sire turns his eyes to
the shore, and then, the household all gathered, he
opens the sacred pages and reads: " By faith Abraham,
when he was called to go out into a place which he
should after receive for an inheritance, obeyed, and
he went out not knowing whither he went. By faith
he sojourned in a strange country, dwelling in taber-
nacles with Isaac and Jacob, the heirs with him of
the same promise; for he looked for a city which
hath foundations whose maker and builder is God."
Then we all kneel, and we know that the roar of

the billows does not drown his words from the Ear in the heavens :

"Thou Mightiest One, who hast measured the waters in the hollow of thy hand and meted out heaven with a span and comprehended the dust of the earth in a measure and weighed the mountains in scales and the hills in a balance, thou art God, and thou alone. The Old World and the New are alike thy handiwork. The centuries gone and the centuries to come are thy vassals. In august sovereignty, through persecution and wrong, but in righteousness infinite, thou art so ruling as to cast many exiles upon yonder wilderness. May truth and rectitude and religious liberty take root upon every hill and plain and valley! May the continent be occupied for God! In yonder province, through the rivalry of two cruel churches, thy sceptre has evolved the boon of equal toleration to all. Surely thy ways are marvelous. Be thou our Maryland's Lord Proprietary. Shape thou the destinies of those who have gone, and of those who are yet to come. The wilderness blossoming as the rose, may it blossom with thy glory! May the New World teach the Old the lesson of the rights of man and the rights of God!"

My father always reminded me of what they tell us of the stauncher Puritan days.

As we rose from our knees, the heavy burst of the breakers along the Maryland beach seemed to swell heavenward the response, "Amen, and amen!"

Chingoteague, Matompkin, Watchapreague, Matchapungo, the names imitating the roll and tumble of the surges along the shore,—so we pass on down the coast of the sister-colony named for the Virgin Queen. Entering the broad Chesapeake—said to mean, in the Indian language, "the Mother of Waters"—my heart leaps back once more across the great ocean whose billows wash the shore of Britain, and, thinking of the days departed, two or three pictures rise before me which I wish to perpetuate upon the pages of my journal.

FIRST PICTURE.—A plain room in the city of Bath; a little girl of four years entering the door, her hand in her father's, her timid heart beating in awe, her eyes looking around for the good man of whom she has often heard. Driven from his pulpit at Taunton, hunted, imprisoned, maltreated, until now his health is gone, he is lingering only a little this side the gate of heaven; for no iniquitous Five-Mile Act can keep him at a distance from the Celestial City. When the child sees him worn and emaciated, she would shrink away; but his gentle eye seems to melt into hers and his voice sounds like the voice of an angel. She hears him tell of holy joys and heavenly ravishments, and of patient waiting to be borne away. Speaking of the sweet love of Jesus for the little ones, his transparent saintly face seems to light with more than human beauty, and his arm draws gently around her waist, as if to lift her with him to the bosom of God The child could never forget the year 1668 and the godly Joseph Alleine. The day was to come when this memory and his book, *The Alarm to the Unconverted*, were to lead her to Christ. Little did the child know that during the same year, 1668, was born in far America a baby-girl who was to be her friend and companion in the after-days.

SECOND PICTURE.—Eight years have passed. The same maiden, grown large, but still a child, is playing in their pleasant cottage-yard with neighbor Winston's younger son—the boy four years her senior and her favorite playmate from infancy His family are of the Established Church, good people and tolerant; for such were found even in those evil times. No week passes without many romps by William and the child in the pretty trellised enclosure. To-day they are happy, as usual, and too absorbed to notice the highway, until a rude voice exclaims,

"You had better be gone, young sir, and leave that Presbyterian wench alone."

Before she has time to think, William flings back to the gay troup of cavaliers the angry reply,

"You had best be gone yourselves and learn better breeding before you ride this way again!"

They dismount and dash through the gate to seize the boy, but he stands his ground, defying them and giving back taunt for taunt. She sees them growing more enraged; and when one of them draws his sword upon her playmate, she rushes recklessly in between. Then one of the cavaliers strikes heavily with his hand, and she is thrown upon the grass. The blow is not so hard but she can understand the harder words ·

"Take that, you Puritan whelp!"

The boy catches up a stone to hurl at her assailant, when they seize him and, cursing, carry him off. She hears him say as they drag him away,

"If the Church must have such base defenders as you, I too will be a Puritan!"

William's father had too much influence at court for his son to suffer harm, but he has been my ideal hero ever since.

Those were sad days in the British Isles.

THIRD PICTURE.—A lovely Sabbath morning not long ago. Last year occurred the slaying of Archbishop Sharp in Scotland and the battle of Bothwell Bridge, and the redoubled hatred against Presbytery in Scotland and everywhere. Our king had lately reproached his illegitimate son, Monmouth, with sparing so many lives at Bothwell and troubling the government with prisoners. Our pastor was impoverished and banished. A few neighbors and their children are collected in our little parlor, my dear father reading the Scriptures and talking of God's promises. Then, amid the hush of the day, the company are led in prayer by the deep tones of my sire. Suddenly loud knocks and boisterous voices at the door, and then my loved father is hurried away to lie six months in a dungeon under charge of convening a riotous assembly, his real crime being that he did not use prescribed prayers and frequent the parish church. The Conventicle Act of 1664 had forbidden any one over sixteen years of age to attend any other than the Established worship in any place where five or more persons were present.

And so we are here. We pass Naswadox, Occahannock, Pungoteague, Matchatank, Onancock, Chessonessex, Mosongo, and find ourselves steering through a narrowing sound toward the mouth of a little river about one hundred miles up this great bay. Space around for scores of mighty navies, our brave craft floats solitary and alone upon the bosom of the vast inland sea. Will the day ever come when this wide stretch of waters shall be busy with the commerce of the world?

The view around is far from unattractive, though

there is nothing grand or startling in its effects—no rocky coasts, no towering mountains. The absence of these, leaves here a charm of quietude and serenity. Brooding softly over all we see, is an indescribable *something* which falls most genially into harmony with the yearning of tired souls. Our lives have already had enough of the harsh and the boisterous.

Green marshes hanging out like beautiful floating frills from the drapery of mainland; dunes of clean sand spotted over with flocks of sea-birds; hundreds of interjacent coves and lakes and miniature bays, placid, multiform, bringing heaven and earth as closely mated as two friends looking into the same mirror; evergreen forests rising slowly from the broad levels, as if loth to break the repose of some great millennium,—all possessing a soft picturesqueness of their own, comporting happily with the moods of a heart that would have sung to it a lullaby of peace. I look at these many graceful indentations around the Maryland coast, these outstretched arms of welcome, and I seem to see a perpetual hospitality offering itself to all who have been struck by earth's storms and are yearning for a tranquil home.

Martha smiles at my enthusiasm.

Passing up within the banks of the dark-watered Pocomoke, two incidents from its past remind me that the little river already has a history. The first time its ripples were ever stirred by the keel of the civilized was in 1608, when Captain John Smith entered the stream with his exploring-party in search of fresh water, and when, as he tells us, "at first the people with great fury seemed to assault us, yet at last with songs and dances and much mirth became very tract-

2

able." These were the tribes among whom we are to live. Perhaps, while I write, we are sailing over the very spot where Virginia's truest knight bargained with the savages for water and obtained "such puddle that never till then we ever knew the want of good water. We digged and searched in many places, but before two days were expired we would have refused two barricoes of gold for one of that puddle water of Wighcocomoco." So he called the Pocomoke.

Suddenly, from the shore, where we see a cluster of rude cabins and banks of sea-shells, two or three boats hollowed out of trees shoot out and paddle to meet us. The children, affrighted, run below. Brother John hurries after his wheel-lock gun. The captain smiles and assures us there is no danger, the red men are peaceable and friendly. Our brigantine was fitted out for trade with the natives and with the farmers along the shore. The savages are holding up oysters, crying, "Kaw-sheh;" fish, crying, "Wammass;" beavers, shouting, "Nataque;" turkeys, advertising them as "Pah-quun;" and maize or Indian corn, calling aloud, "Cawl-naa-woop;" uttering harsh gutturals as of beasts. I distinguish but one English word, "Beads! Beads!" For these gaudy ornaments they clamor more loudly than for anything else, although the scarcity of clothing is lamentable (2).

Our captain tells us that these Indians are of the one chief Eastern Shore nation of the Nanticokes, whom Captain Smith pronounces "the best marchants of all the salvages." Each tribe is designated by the name of the stream on which it mostly dwells. Hence I hear already of the Choptanks, the Wicomicoes, the Monokins, the Chingoteagues, the Assawamans, the

Pocomokes—uncouth words to the unaccustomed ear, but possessed of a wild music of their own which, it is to be hoped, shall go on sounding with the roar of the waves and the sighs of the pines for ever.

So much has been written of the proud, stately red men of America that I must confess a little disappointment at the comparatively diminutive appearance of these Indians. Martha smiles again, as she has a way of smiling whenever my romantic notions are disconcerted. Our philosophic father wonders if there is anything in the climate to produce this dwarfing of stature, and if in the course of centuries the same causes will superinduce like results in the descendants of the white settlers (3).

I record my second historical item Forty-five years ago—only a year after the settlement of St. Mary's, and six years after the occupation of Kent Island by the troubler William Clayborne—Lieutenant Ratcliff Warren, an adherent of Clayborne, enters the stream, in command of the pinnace Longtail, with a crew of thirteen men. Soon two pinnaces, the St Margaret and the St. Helen, fitted out by Governor Calvert, pursue and assault the other. The quiet of these scenes is broken by the hoarse voice of conflict, and four dying men—three Virginians and one Marylander—dye the dark waters darker with their blood. There, upon the modest bosom of the little Pocomoke, was fought one of the first naval battles waged by white men upon American waters.*

Marshes upon right and left, and sweet smells of the hay; thick forests occasionally crowding to the water's

* April 23, 1635 *Founders of Maryland*, Rev E D Neill, D.D, p. 52

edge; patches of wild flowers; a plantation gladden-
ing the eye now upon one bank, and now upon the
other, suggesting thoughts of neighborhood and neighbors in days to come,—thus slowly with favoring
breezes we ascend the tortuous river.

Another boat puts off from the right bank, and,
dropping anchor, we await its coming. Through the
cedars and maples a brick building is discovered about
one hundred yards from the shore, looking homelike
amid its setting of trees, wearing the comfortable as-
pect of scenes left far behind and contrasting strikingly
with the wigwams of the buyers of the beads.

In the approaching boat—called the Ark—my eye
singles out a gentleman of distinguished appearance
who rises from his seat. He must be about fifty years
of age * and is evidently in full vigor of body and mind.
No one need mistake the mien of a born leader of
men. His face is full of intelligence, and underlying
all is the unmistakable impress of manly character.

As he arose from his seat I noticed that my father
rose also, and that a gesture of recognition passed between them. The pleasant explanation soon follows.
This is Colonel William Stevens, judge of the county
court since its organization in 1666, and the incumbent
of other high offices in the province (4).

He comes on board, helped by my father's hand.
They knew each other in boyhood, my sire visiting at
the house of his father, John Stevens, in the parish of
Mealemore, Buckinghamshire. The judge was one of
the earliest settlers in this county, and he has been
very active in giving information to the oppressed in
Europe and opening up to them this asylum from per-

* Born in 1630

secution. When my father began to look abroad for a place of refuge, it was natural to apply to his old friend for advice with regard to the selection of our Transatlantic home. He came out to-day for supplies, nor did we know we were so near him; so that the surprise is mutually pleasant. I look upon our first friend in America, and the wilderness begins to brighten.

Under his kind invitation, our family are for a while the judge's guests. It is Friday, and our friend insists that we cannot become comfortably domiciled in our strange home before the Sabbath, and that we can far better enjoy the rest of God's holy day with him. Thus it comes about that on my sixteenth birthday we have first set foot upon American soil and under the auspices of hospitality as delightful as heart can wish. The thought suddenly possesses me, and, stooping down, I lay my hand upon the soft cool earth and devote this land of the Eastern Shore to such hospitality through all her future generations.

The Sabbath! Glorious day! Was there ever a brighter sunrise, a bluer sky? Breathing is rapture.

> "Hail, bounteous May, that dost inspire
> Mirth and youth and warm desire!
> Woods and groves are of thy dressing,
> Hill and dale doth boast thy blessing;
> Thus we salute thee with our early song,
> And welcome thee and wish thee long!"

So sang the old blind bard whom I saw worn and wrinkled, looking upon him with childish wonder and reverence during the month of his death, six years ago. If Mr. Milton ever saw such a May as smiles upon me now, he must have seen it in Italy, not in England.

I sit in the shade, flat on the grass, with the lazy

river at my feet.   They tell me that this little stream
is essentially Southern in its features, reminding one
of the bayous along which De Leon sought the fountain of immortal youth.   Wild violets bloom around
me, mingling their odors with the spicy perfumes of
sassafras and myrtle.   And this is our Maryland—soft,
breezy, dreamy, balmy, halcyon Maryland !

The judge and my father come down from the house
and take their seats near me, beneath a large wild-
cherry which overhangs the river.

"Yes," said our friend, "we call our province the
'Land of the Sanctuary.'   No ostracism here for religious sentiment, no denial of the rights of conscience
to any faith.   While to the north and south the settlers
have brought over with them the Old World's intolerance, here no man can dictate to another his creed.
Would that we could welcome all victims of ecclesiastical despotism to this favored clime !   After trying
the experiment of religious liberty, the idea seems
unmistakably divine."

I was intensely interested.   My father's prayer was
remembered in which he adored God's sovereignty in
accomplishing these blessed results through the instrumentality of two persecuting churches.   I listened for
an explanation.

"Through a charter jealously worded for the purpose of guarding the religion of an Episcopal kingdom
and the religion of a Catholic Proprietary from im-
pinging upon each other, the wisdom of the Infinite
One prepared a refuge for those oppressed by both
churches.   To no colony would England have granted
the Papists authority to harass her Protestant subjects,
and Lord Baltimore was willing to surrender the power

to persecute others if thereby he could save his own faith from persecution. Then, the ascendency of Cromwell resulted to our greater security here, bringing about the enactment at St Mary's, in 1649, under a Protestant governor and council and legislature, of the celebrated act concerning religion. Governor Stone was from this Shore, having been sheriff of Northampton county, and was an earnest partisan of the Parliament" (5).

At the desire of my father, I jot down everything bearing upon the religious history of the colony. Afterward I asked our host for a copy of this famous act, and I here transcribe the noble words:

WHEREAS, the enforcing of the conscience in matters of religion hath frequently fallen out to be of dangerous consequence in those Commonwealths where it hath been practiced ; and for the more quiet and peaceable government of this Province, and the better to preserve mutual love and unity amongst the inhabitants here. Be it, therefore, by the Lord Proprietary, with the advice and assent of this Assembly, ordained and enacted, that no person or persons whatsoever within this Province, or the islands, ports, harbors, creeks or havens thereunto belonging, professing to believe in Jesus Christ, shall from henceforth be any ways troubled, molested or discountenanced, for or in respect of his or her religion, nor in the free exercise thereof within this Province or the islands thereunto belonging, nor any way compelled to the belief or exercise of any other religion against his or her conscience.

"These words," continued the judge, "deserve an immortality of honor, containing the first explicit statement of toleration by any government in the history of the world. Let us praise God rather than the men who made it. In the events of the times he has so ruled that the Catholic Proprietary should be glad to approve such a law in self-defence and for the protection of his own Church. In the condition of affairs in England any other policy would have lost him the province and the liberty of his Catholic subjects. The spirit of our present king, Charles II., may be understood from the fact that at that time, from his exile at Breda, he denounced Baltimore for yielding to the Parliament and 'admitting all kinds of sectaries and schismatics and ill-affected persons into that plantation'" *

Said my father,

"If the Presbyterian settlers had been in numbers sufficient to have ministers and public worship of their own, do you think they would have been treated until now with the same leniency as in the past? Our Church has never yet been strong enough in the province to awaken the jealousy of others."

"The point is not without force," answered our host; "for the special hatred of ritualistic churches to your own is historical. But, under the circumstances, our Proprietaries have been aware that they had most to fear from the Church of England. In addition to this, the planting of this colony by the Baltimores was largely a commercial speculation; and, wishing to see their province fill with population, they have known that the protection of all religions would invite immigration and sooner bring prosperity. I may say further that this has never been in any true sense a Catholic province. Of those originally coming over in the Ark and Dove, the majority were Protestants, and since then the Protestant immigration has far outstripped the Catholic (6) I wish to say, further, that, from personal acquaintance with the

* *Terra Mariæ*, Rev. E D. Neill, D D , Philadelphia, p 88.

present Lord Baltimore—who succeeded his father
in 1675, and who during the year following approved
the re-enactment of the law of 1649—I believe that he
sincerely desires the happiness of all his colonists.
We feel better content when he is in the province,
and are rejoicing that he returned to us from Europe
four months ago."

"Possessed of this rare treasure of religious liberty,
why have the Presbyterians been content to remain
shepherdless? How long are the beautiful Sabbaths
to come and go over a land so sadly needing an orthodox ministry?"

"The Presbyterian settlers are widely separated and
very poor. Our county was at first principally occupied by Quakers and Episcopalians from the adjoining province. It is only in the few later years that
your people have been coming from Scotland, the
North of Ireland and France to this part of the colony.
My own efforts have contributed zealously to this end.
My intrepid friend Colonel Ninian Beall came over
from Fifeshire some ten years ago, and has effected a
considerable Scotch settlement between the Patuxent
and Potomac. There have been a few scattering Presbyterians elsewhere. In the year 1669 the Rev. Matthew Hill, one of the two thousand ejected ministers
in England, and a Presbyterian in preference, after the
loss of almost everything at home, reached the province and settled for some years in Charles county.
He may be said to be the first Presbyterian minister
that ever sailed upon the Chesapeake. He was a good
scholar, a serious, warm and lively preacher, and of a
free and generous spirit. He began to hope for great
usefulness, when the clouds darkened and he went

away   No church was planted, no permanent effect produced (7).

"Most of our Presbyterians have come from amid the fines and confiscations of Europe stripped of all their earthly possessions. Their simple lives could barely be supported but for Nature's generous supplies from the woods and the waters. Some are yet serving their four years as indentured servants in payment of the fare across the ocean; others, condemned by their persecutors to slavery, given to favorites or purchased by speculators, have been sold in America for a term of years. We could not expect ministers to come from Europe for the mere pittance they were able to contribute, and they had to be content with the preaching of the Quakers. These strange people have had some of their strongest preachers among us, and have done much good in our county.

"At other times, in a primitive way, we have had services of our own, calling out some unordained teacher to break unto us the bread of life. Eight years ago—1672—while Justices Henry Smith, James Jones, John Winder, George Johnson, William Colburn and myself were upon the bench, the grand jury, through their Scotch foreman, Mr. David Brown, called one of our neighbors to preach stately at four points in the county. As guardians of law and morals, the jury felt that they could do nothing which would better contribute to the good of the people. Mr. Brown is still living, and a Presbyterian. Such was our device for securing regular gospel services. Our records will bear to future generations the following testimony to the desire of the hearts of the destitute for the word of life: 'It is the opinion of us grand

jurors that sermon be taught four several places
in the county—viz., one the first Sunday, at the house
of Mr. William Stevens, at Pocomoke; one the second
Sunday, at the house of Daniel Custis, in Annamessex;
one the third Sunday, at the house of Christopher Nut-
ter, in Monokin; and one on the fourth Sunday, at the
house of Thomas Roe, at Wicomico. And it is our
desire that Mr. Matix should here preach'" (8).

"And yet," persisted my father, "I am sure there
are ministers of ours, men of God, who would be
willing, for the good of souls and the honor of the
Master, to share the poverty of the colonists and
encounter the utmost stringency of self-denial."

This was the beginning of many conversations upon
that subject.

Now behold us settled in our new home. The
house, built of logs and covered with cypress shingles,
stands upon the southern bank of the Pocomoke in
sight of Stevens's Ferry. We have succeeded in
making our four rooms marvelously comfortable,
for my dear mother could transform the bark wigwam
of an Indian into a thing of beauty. The country
being almost a perfect level, we are rather proud of
our little hill and its gentle slope to the river. Across
the stream rise the green cypresses, straight as arrows
and covered with foliage fringe. Back of our plantation the pines form a wall of evergreen, filling the air
with their resinous breath and incessant whisperings.

While I write a sweet trill of music attracts my eye
to the lawn hickory, where a cheerful neighbor seems
to recognize me as his fellow-denizen of the wilds—a
little creature all black and golden perched near the
curious nest that hangs pendent to its twig and swings

in the wind. Dressed in the same colors with the
decorations of the Lord Proprietary, the colonists
have loyally bestowed the title of the Baltimore
oriole. Sing on, happy songster, and may the worship of the Marylander be ever as hearty as thine,
and as independent of the dictation of men!

Though late in planting, the July suns and showers
have brought our maize on finely. Expecting no
sudden wealth through discovery of gold or idle
chance, and knowing that prosperity can come only
by honest industry, John has taken off his coat and
is very proud of his straight rows. Until now specimens of this new plant have been to us the greatest
of curiosities.

But, ah! the pones—the delicious pones! My in-
genious mother has caught the high art. Golden
meal scalded through its every atom, enveloped in
oak leaves, enthroned in the great oven, warming and
seasoning and sweetening all night, and then the rich,
mellow, yellow, smoking slices brought upon the table
in the morning hungry for the butter or the honey!
King Charles himself, amid all his French gluttony,
tastes no more dainty morsel than that. I put on
the gift of prophecy and predict for the Eastern Shore
pone an eternity of fame.

Our acquaintance is gradually extending. August
has brought my heart a jewel. The kind judge had
told us of an interesting family down in Accomack
and promised me much pleasure in knowing one of
the daughters. Yesterday, sitting in the door at my
spinning-wheel, I saw the Ark—named for one of
the ships which brought the first colonists to St.
Mary's, forty-six years ago—winging its way up the

river. The coming of the Ark is always an event
in the household. As they land I notice among the
judge's family a bright young creature who captures
my heart at first sight Who can help loving what is
lovable ? So, when I saw the girlish eyes that looked
for affection, complexion brown with the sunshine of
Virginia, a native atmosphere of good-breeding resting all over the little woman, and pretty pouting lips
ready to be kissed, I went and kissed them. That
was our introduction.

The name came afterward very charmingly : Naomi
—"pleasantness." I did not love her less for the
musical Bible syllables full of pastoral memories. I
always wanted a younger sister, and this twelve-year-
old maiden corresponds precisely with my ideal. Little did I know that I was coming all the way to this
Western world to find her (9).

We maidens always fall into a feeling of motherly
interest in *something*, and the difference in our ages of
four years settles me into a delightful sense of proprietorship in my friend. On my solicitation, seconded
by the prompt acquiescence of the little Virginian, the
judge consents to leave her with us a few days. My
special guest, I set myself to the responsible task of
entertaining her.

First I take Naomi to my garden, where I am endeavoring to coax some of the indigenous Maryland
flowers to grow under culture in contact with our imported civilization. The brilliant laurel seems unwilling and coy. One of my wild roses is blooming
rarely, and I put my arm around the tiny waist of my
friend and call her my own sweet wild rose of America

Now we stroll along the river-banks, now bravely

off into the woods; for why should we two heroines
be afraid of the red men or the beasts of prey? An
unknown flower is discovered, and transplanted to my
garden as a remembrancer of our blossoming friendship. Farther out we venture, intrepid explorers of
the boundless wilderness, until in the distance we certainly hear an ominous howl, and we retire from the
expedition.

We wander up to the ferry to watch chance colonists,
of all grades of society and in all varieties of costumes,
passing from one part of the large county to another,
and to see the Indians who come there to sell their
poultry and buy trinkets. We are not afraid, for we
know it has been part of our county's glory to treat well
these children of the forest. To one with rather a
pleasant face we give some beads and some sweet
bread from our pockets, and he seems very grateful
and assures us that he will bring us a "noose-atq" in
return. We like his name—Matchacoopah*—and we
go back home wondering what the gift will be.

Naomi Anderson slept in my arms every night
until the Ark came back—all too soon—and bore
my treasure away, while I return to my spinning-
wheel.

Oh the gorgeous autumn woods! Surely there was
never such profusion of colors, such marvelous com-
binations of tints—scarlet, purple, crimson, amethyst,
pearl, sapphire and ruby; canopies of gold fringing the
green of the pines, flashes of flame blazing out here
and there as from woods on fire. With no prema-
ture frosts to blight and kill, the foliage quietly passes

* The name of this Indian, and those of all others mentioned hereafter, are taken from the court records.

through all the stages of a gentle dying, and, like the dying saint, puts on new glories to the end.   With her Indian summer haze and her regal drapery, verily the Eastern Shore is the queenliest of climes.

Amid the tenderness and pathos of the season a letter reaches me by my father's hand from William. Letters arrive at long intervals by trading-vessels and chance travelers.   This came in a sloop of Mr Anderson's, and in forwarding it to me a childlike pen had written upon the back, "From one dearer than Naomi, perhaps."   Is the darling jealous of William?

The son of our old neighbor expresses the fear that we may all be scalped by the Indians, but intimates that this could be no worse than what the Presbyterians have had to endure, and are yet to endure, from professed Christians of England   He misses his playmate, but is glad that we can now worship as we please. As an index to the state of affairs from which we have escaped, he speaks of two expressive words just introduced into the language—"mob" and "sham;" also two other terms which sound almost as uncouth and meaningless as the harsh Indian jargon—"Whig" and "Tory," the rustics of the western lowlands of Scotland supplying the one term, the Popish outlaws of the bogs of Ireland supplying the other.*   A tempest rages over the proposal to exclude the Duke of York from the succession because of his being a Papist. The bitter conflict between Popery and Prelacy affords some temporary relief to the Protestant Nonconformists.   The latter, however, have little to expect while subjected in turn to the power of two foes who both hate Presbytery worse than they hate each other.

* Macaulay, 1 p. 200

Meanwhile, William tells me that the cruelties increase in poor Scotland. The country overrun with
brutal soldiery, the curates acting as informers, the
Sanquhar Declaration has been issued by the hunted
people of God, full of brave truth and amounting
almost to a declaration of independence Cameron
has fallen at Airdmoss, and his hands and head, after
being shown to his poor old father in prison, have
been fixed up in public places to the gaze of Edinburgh. Hackston, already wounded and bleeding,
has had his hands cut off one after the other ; then he
is hung, and while yet conscious his bosom is ripped
open, his heart is torn out and held up quivering to
the view of the friends standing around. The Duke
of York has gone to Scotland and is hounding on
these enormities, giving sad evidence of the spirit
that is in him by lately being present at and enjoying
the tortures of a victim of the horrible iron boot, the
other noblemen hurrying away, unable to bear the
brutal sight. This is the man who is likely to be
our future king !*

Thus from our Maryland asylum we still get
glimpses of the tribulations of God's saints in the
Old World My correspondent hopes that he will
not be forgotten, and thinks that we shall not always
be parted by the wide ocean.

In our little boat—called the Dove, from the other
of Lord Baltimore's pilgrim fleet—my father has just
returned from down the river with good news. Wherever a Presbyterian heart is found, it is found beating
with deep longing for the courts of the Lord. In

* Hetherington's *History of the Church of Scotland*, pp. 260, 261 ;
also Wodrow, *passim*

the midst of abounding wickedness and Sabbath desecration saddened souls are crying more and more
loudly for our own official expounders of the word,
and for the holy sacraments as of old. Colonists of
our faith are still arriving.   While Europe groans, has
not God his eye upon this continent for good?   Colonel Stevens is in full sympathy with the praying
ones whom he has invited to this county, and of
late a letter has started from his hand to the North
of Ireland pleading for a preacher. He addresses
the Presbytery of Laggan, a body of men full of mar-
tyr-spirit, laying before them the claims of this great
country and begging in the name of the Presbyterian
exiles for some man of apostolic mould to raise the
standard of sound doctrine and scriptural polity upon
these Western shores.

May the good providence of Him who owns both
the Old World and the New, further that letter on
its way and prosper it in its quest!

3

CHAPTER II.

A. D. 1681.

"All may see how free Grace is expected and desired with Gifts to qualifie for the Ministerial Office."—MAKEMIE.

M Y father is pleased with my plan for keeping a journal, thinking it will be interesting to the family in the future to read over some record of our first impressions and early experiences in this strange land. His hand is unsteady from his labors in the fields or he would write himself. I see, indeed, that this is likely to be my father's journal rather than my own. Whatever is sensible in it must be attributed to him ; the rest, to me.

The feeling of distance, exile, isolation, is at times oppressive, at other times romantic and fascinating. The people are settling almost entirely along the streams, while interminable forests stretch gloomily away in all directions. To the imagination these boundless wilds seem fit haunts for goblins and demons No wonder that the superstitious colonists tremble sometimes under dread of witchcraft and the power of the evil one. They have even called one of our Chesapeake islands "Diel's," or the devil's.

Matchacoopah has redeemed his promise. The other day his copper features suddenly appeared near the house, his coarse black hair ornamented with the feathers of the red-bird, and leading a brown creature

34

tied with a string made of the inner bark of a tree. Martha could not restrain her smile.

The Indian pointed to the broad leaves floating upon the river and made signs for "Water-Lily." Finding me last summer paddling my canoe through one of our swamps hunting this most beautiful of flowers, he has insisted ever since that this shall be my name.

Beckoning him nearer, what was my delight to find Matchacoopah's gift was a tame fawn! and this was the meaning of the word over which we had wondered— "noose-atq." At first the pretty creature was timid and shy, but she readily yielded to kindness, looking with her lustrous eyes into mine and laying her head upon my shoulder. The Indian was pleased at the appreciation of his gift, and doubled my joy by signifying that he had one for Naomi also. I think that the friendship between Matchacoopah and myself is assured.

The Indian dialect will supply our future dictionaries with another undying word—the wholesome *hominy*. Its mellowness seems to run through the soft Indian syllables—"Ahuminea" (10). The handmill and hominy-mortar are important articles of household equipment in this new land.

It is full time to mention three neighbors gained from Europe this year.

A Scotch family from the fields of Ayrshire, from the banks of the Clyde. In broad accents they tell us of the scenes from which they have escaped in their native land. In January two of Scotia's daughters died upon the scaffold for the double crime of hearing Cargill preach and expressing womanly sympathy for the sufferers from the bloody moss-troopers. "So I lay down my life," said Isabel Anderson, "for owning and adhering to Jesus Christ his being a free King in his own house. I have looked greedy-like to such a lot as this, but still thought it was too high for me." She passed away crying, " Welcome, everlasting love, joy and light!"

The same day Marion Harvey, twenty years of age, telling of her ungodly life while a hearer of curates, and of the blessed change under the true gospel, also sealed her fidelity in a triumphant death, lauding the power of grace and proclaiming, " I bless the Lord that the snare is broken and we are escaped" (11).

I look at the Scotch lassies among our immigrant families and almost envy them their birthplace.

Cargill's head is beaten by the rains and blackened by the sun upon the gates of Edinburgh, but nothing satiates the barbarity of the oppressor. The vile test-oath has been devised, by which conscience, the Covenant, the Scriptures, and everything sacred to a Scotchman's heart, must be forsworn in abject subordination to the supremacy of a profligate king. Many are relinquishing the dreary struggle and going into voluntary exile. Thus, our neighbors have turned away from their bloody home-hearths and are bringing the Catechism and the Covenant to Maryland's free Eastern Shore.

Another family hails from the county of Derry, in the North of Ireland. Disheartened under the renewed stringency of the government and the more unconscionable bitterness of the prelates, our own ministry silenced, and seeing no promise of religious freedom in the Green Isle, they have made the salt waters of the Atlantic salter with the tears of exile. The ardent faith of Ulster has come with them over the billows, and the plaintive Celtic tones which uttered God's praises upon the shores of Lough Foyle now speak the honors of Jesus on the banks of the Pocomoke.

The third family come from among the vineyards of Languedoc, bringing with them the traditions of an ancestry who fought under the prince of Condé and Henry of Navarre, and who have handed down from father to son stories of the horrors of St. Bartholomew's Day. Louis XIV., growing more superstitious as he grows older, and falling more and more under the influence of Madame de Maintenon, has been steadily deepening his despotism over the Huguenots, and is evidently contemplating a revocation of the Edict of Nantes. To escape present hardships and more terrible probabilities, our friends fled first to London, but, seeing intolerance and wrong reigning there too, they set sail for the New World The soft accent, broken but sweet, has sounded very charmingly to John and myself to-day while comparing Maryland's balmy evenings to the skies and breezes of Southern France. Then we listen to the entrancing voice of Margaret—named for the good Queen Margaret of Navarre—while she sings to us some sad ballad concerning the persecutions of the Albigenses or the heroism of Roger Raymond. Now, again, the sweet Southern voice sings a selection from the *Holy Song-Book* of Clement Marot, written one hundred and forty-six years ago under the auspices of Beza and Calvin and set to an air composed by the martyr-musician Gaudemel.

My philosophic father has been speculating upon the future characteristics of the Presbyterianism settling upon our soil from so many various tributaries.

Immediately around us here the sturdy conscientiousness of English Nonconformity, the Scot's undying
loyalty to the crown-rights of Jesus, the generous
fervor of Irish piety, the enthusiastic devotion of the
countrymen of Farel and Jean Claude,—he sees in
the commingling of these noble types the promise of
a new and mighty evangelization.

If my brother John continues to listen as he did to-
day to those troubadour canzos, I see some possibilities, too.

However all that may be, I am delighted to include
among my American friendships Mary, the rosy Scotch
lassie; Peggy, the blue-eyed maid of Ulster; and Margaret, the sweet-toned singer of the Vincennes.

In the very midst of our welcomes to these fugitives
from the harassments of the established religions of
Europe, startling reports burst upon us. Rebellion
in the province! A plot against the Proprietary!
Bloodshed imminent!

We wait and listen. John is thinking of Roger
Raymond and polishing his gun. New colonists are
always excitable. Without mails, the rumors may
be exaggerated or they may not equal the truth.
Oh, why will not wicked men permit the province
to enjoy the peace which tranquil Nature breathes
around?

The Eastern Shore is almost wholly Protestant,
and Lord Baltimore and his Church have never disturbed us. But there is a growing restlessness and
agitation abroad not confined wholly to the other
side of the bay. The domination and state support
long enjoyed in Europe are still lusted after by our
prelatic neighbors. Many from Virginia long to

bring with them across the line a right to supremacy and to the tithes.

Five years ago—May, 1676—one of their Western Shore clergymen, John Yeo, wrote to the archbishop of Canterbury invoking direct interference by the English authorities. He said, " Here are in this province ten or twelve thousand souls, and but three Protestant ministers of us that are conformable to the doctrine and discipline of the Church of England." He begs " that a maintenance for a Protestant ministry may be established as well in this province as in Virginia. I think that the generality of the people may be brought by degrees to a uniformity, provided we had more ministers that were truly conformable to our mother the Church, *and none but such were suffered to preach among us.*"

Ah, yes, John Yeo! and to prevent them from preaching among us I suppose you are ready to use the same appliances of thumb-screw and gunpowder as in bleeding Scotland. Until you are permitted to do that you will still continue to call our Maryland " a Sodom of uncleanness and a pesthouse of iniquity."

To that mournful statement of grievances the Lord Proprietary, then in England, replied, " The act of 1649, confirmed in 1676, tolerates and protects every sect. Four ministers of the Church of England are in possession of plantations which afford them a decent subsistence. From the various religious tenets of the members of the Assembly, it would be extremely difficult to induce it to consent to a law that shall oblige any sect to maintain other ministers than its own " (12).

Plantations would not satisfy these grasping clergy-

men without a tax upon all who differ with them, and
without the prohibition of all other worship except
their own.   Thus failed that attempt to override the
noble policy of the colony and to force Episcopacy
upon the necks of an unwilling people.   But the agitations and contentions have continued, until Governor
Culpeper of Virginia has just written to the home-gov-
ernment: " Maryland is now in a ferment, and not only
troubled with our disease, poverty, but in very great
danger of falling in pieces; whether it be that the old
Lord Baltimore's politic maxims are not followed by
the son or that they will not do in the present age."
The difficulty was not in the policy of the Proprietary,
except as it conflicted with the designs of ecclesiastical factionists.   It is said that it was this growing tur-
bulence which discouraged the good Matthew Hill
and lost him to our province.

This Rev. John Yeo—a man of little culture, and as
little Christian charity—after making his appeal for the
tithes in vain, left for Hoarkil (Lewes), at the capes of
the Delaware, where he was the cause of constant disturbance, and at length was arrested and prosecuted.
Lately he has returned to the Western Shore to contribute his influence to the disaffection of the people
there.

Suddenly the news flashes along the Pocomoke of
an insurrection on the other side of the bay against
the Proprietary government.   His life once forfeited
and spared, the chronic revolutionist Fendal has been
joined in new plots by the characterless clergyman
John Coode.   The name of the latter accomplice
throws some light upon the actuating motive.   Without respectability, but dignified by the imposition of a

bishop's hands, his zeal for the Church, inspired by her emoluments, fits him to trample upon all rights that conflict with his own aggrandizement. Earth's worst embodiments of malevolence have been draped in soiled clerical robes (13).

Better news at last. John has put away his gun.

Our Proprietary has not been caught napping. The two leaders have been brought to trial and convicted. We expected that they must atone for their crimes with their lives, but the clemency of our Proprietary has spared them. Colonel Stevens thinks it will result in new troubles in the future. We often rejoice that our grand Chesapeake Bay separates us from these Western Shore turmoils, but there are others around us whose countenances wear the shadows of poorly-concealed disappointment.

> " 'Tis said the Gods lower down that chain above
> That tyes both Prince and Subject up in love ;
> And if this fiction of the Gods be true,
> Few, Mary-Land, in this can boast but you.
> Live ever blest and let those Clouds that do
> Eclipse most States be always Lights to you ;
> And dwelling so, you may for ever be
> The only Emblem of Tranquillity !"

So sang in our province the rollicking indentured servant George Alsop eighteen years ago, and so we would ever sing.

After the anxiety was over and the exquisite Indian-summer days again had come, we went upon a notable excursion of thirty miles to our sister-colony. To the favoring breezes our little Dove spreads her pinions, and in less than a day we fly down the river, waving salutations to the Stevens and Jenkins families

as we pass, then out into the sound, now southward
about three miles to the creek which seems to invite
our coming.   The dreamy attractiveness of our water-
scenery breathes over us as we go.

Behind a little wooded tributary which enters the
creek about a half-mile from its mouth we notice a
pleasant-looking house standing back a short distance
upon the bank; and just as the round sun halves himself in the blazing waves of the Chesapeake, Naomi
and her father await us upon the shore, two little
white hands throwing kisses as we come.

Mr. Anderson is an industrious merchant and planter, vigilant, energetic, determined to make the New
World take shape under the blows of manly enterprise.
A sloop unloading at the wharf, over nine hundred
broad acres lying around his house, another thousand
between the Onancock and the Matchatank, another
large estate, called "Occocomson," east of us, on the
seaboard, at Wollop's, with other possessions elsewhere,
attest his prosperity.   He is about building at Onancock, made a port of entry last year.*   A year ago he
was made justice of the peace by Governor Chichely.

My friend Naomi and her younger sister, Comfort,
were left motherless at a tender age.   Sad fate for
young girls anywhere—especially sad in this new
country.   Three years ago Mr. Anderson married
Mrs. Mary Renny, widow of John Renny, a woman
who has had a rough experience in her American
life, having once been indicted in court for abusing a
woman's privilege of telling her mind (14).   Through
her Mr. Anderson acquired his Occocomson and

* *Sketches of Virginia,* Foote, p 44; for other facts, the Accomack records.

Pocomoke plantations. We find here such evidences of wealth as we have found nowhere else on our peninsula.

Mrs Anderson came down the lawn attired in a flowered silk gown and silver-lace petticoat, a girdle clasped with gold buckles, an imposing headdress, a black silk scarf flowered with gold, a set of double ruffles about her neck, and gold rings on her fingers, to welcome us to their home. After a while supper was announced, the display of silver on the table again reminding us of the great contrasts of riches and poverty already found on the new continent. At a late visit to one of our good neighbors, wooden trenchers, wooden platters, wooden spoons and wooden forks formed the table service, and this is so common that no one less relished the hospitable meal A pewter service is a luxury afforded by the better classes alone.

From our host we learn that the Eastern Shore of Virginia, to the south of us, contains a population of one thousand whites; that it had one hundred English settlers within its bounds as long ago as 1620 He read to us Master John Pory's interesting account of his expedition during that year to visit the plantations on the lower peninsula, and of his meeting Kiptopeke, "the laughing king of Accowmake." This king was kind and hospitable, the one named characteristic particularly notable, inasmuch as the Indians even smile but seldom. He tells them that on this narrow strip of country "inhabit many people; so that by the narrowness of the land there is not many deare, but most abundant of fish and fowle." We were also told of another chief, Kickotanke, who in 1649 cared for, and conducted to safety on the mainland, Colonel Norwood and his crew, who had been cast away on one of the islands on the coast. At the time of Smith's expeditions he speaks of two tribes occupying the country—the Occohannocks and the Accomacks, the former with forty warriors, the latter with eighty. They are described as fine-looking men, the subjects of Powhatan, speaking his language and numbering two thousand. Their "werowance," or chief, he represents to be the "comeliest proper civill salvage we incountered."

Naomi and I have turned philosophers, theorizing upon the problem whether there is not something in this genial atmosphere to beget civility and hospitality even in a savage, and are wondering who will be the laughing kings of Accomack two hundred years hence.

There seem to be considerable pride of wealth, high social position of the gentry, and the maintenance of all the formal courtesies of the day. I hear already of a number of prominent families—Scarborough, Robins, Littleton, West, Wise, Middleton, Custis, Ratcliffe, Poulson, Bowman, Jenifer, Corbin, Drummond, Upshur, Finney, Taylor, Tully Robinson, Andrew Hamilton and others Of many of these Mr Anderson speaks highly.

The early title of the colony was that of *Virginia and Accomack.* Accowmake was one of the original shires of 1634 and retained the old Indian name until 1642, when, to please the Robins family, who came from Northamptonshire, England, it was changed to "Northampton." Afterward, in 1662, the county was divided into two, the upper one taking back the former name of "Accomack," although the ancient Indian town of that name was on the southern end of the peninsula.

The first settlements and the first churches were in what is now the lower county. Rev. Robert Bolton became their minister before the year 1623. During that year Governor Wyatt ordered "that Mr. Bolton shall receive for his salary this year, throughout all the plantations at the Eastern Shore, ten pounds of tobacco and one bushel of corn for every planter and tradesman above the age of sixteen years alive at the crop." Bolton was followed by William Cotton. In 1642 the parish was divided into two—Hungar's and Nuswattocks—and since then the following clergymen have officiated in one or the other: John Rogers, Thomas Higby, Francis Doughty, Thomas Palmer, John Almoner, a Mr. Richardson, a Mr. Key and Thomas Teackle. The latter is still living. He came to Virginia in 1656 and has had his home at Cradock He is a man of culture and owns a large and valuable library. Accomack has two parishes —Accomack and St. George's

The population is mostly of the Established Church. Soon after the year 1650 the Quakers appeared on the Shore, made some converts and built themselves a log meeting-house ten feet square. Some of them were accused of slandering the clergy, of defying the laws and of blasphemy; were arrested and banished. The judicial records show evidence against them of denying the incarnation of Christ, and of some of them speaking of God as "a foolish old man." It must be admitted that among this peculiar people there are those, illiterate and fanatical, who are entirely too

abusive of all that differ with them, seeming to take
delight in shocking the religious sensibilities of others
and in virtually inviting persecution. The Quakers
are now seldom molested, some of them highly re-
spected, neither disturbing others nor being disturbed.
Among these are Mr. Thomas Browne and wife, living at the family-seat, called " Brownsville," on the
seashore, and enjoying the honor of having it placed
on record that, "although Quakers, they are yet of
such known integrity that their affirmation is received
instead of an oath."

The reign of Episcopacy upon this seagirt shore
has not been without its internal tempests. The court
records are full of suits by the clergy against their
vestry for the tithes. In 1633, Henry Charlton called
the Rev. Mr. Cotton " a black-coated rascal," and the
court ordered that the traducer of the cloth " make a
pair of stocks and sit in them several Sabbath days
during divine service, and then ask Mr. Cotton's forgiveness." On the other hand, in 1652, Rev. Mr.
Higby is presented to court charged with slanders
against Major Robins. In 1664, Major Robins obtains
judgment against a woman for scandalous speeches
about Rev. Mr. Teackle, and she is condemned to receive twenty lashes on her bare shoulders and be banished from the county. Then, again, Colonel Scarborough, one of high position socially and in the church,
has not hesitated to assail the moral character of Mr.
Teackle. Dominating over others, the Church has
not been able to keep the peace within its own
fold (15).

Meanwhile, the few Presbyterians are shepherdless
and too weak to arouse jealousy. Here and there a

true heart is found patiently awaiting the hour when the Church of its love may plant its own vine and fig tree in this lovely clime and raise its voice for truth and holiness

Another conversation which occurred during this visit interested us exceedingly. A gentleman lately from the North of Ireland came in with Mr. Anderson from the store and took supper with us. My father soon inquired about God's saints in Ulster.

Our informant tells us that the treatment of the Presbyterians is becoming almost intolerable. The soldiers of Laggan—a district of country lying between Lough Foyle and Lough Swilly and along their tributaries—refused to take the hated oath of supremacy (the supremacy of the king over religion and conscience), and the ministers have been accused of encouraging them. The resistance in Scotland, resulting in the battle of Bothwell Bridge, two years ago, having aroused in the government fears of similar movements in Ulster, the prelates seized upon this opportunity for deepening these fears to the injury of our Church. The air is full of accusations of disloyalty and rebellion. When the king is disposed to relax and the civil authorities tire of severity, the bishops and their tools arouse constantly to new devices of oppression.

Said the gentleman,

" One word uttered or the least sympathy suspected in behalf of civil or religious liberty is a crime. The bishops are Charles Stuarts in gowns. Ulster's noble witnesses for the truth have borne almost everything, but sometimes it looks as if they must be crushed and the cause go down."

" Never !" said my father.   " When the present sufferers shall fade and fail, other witnesses will be raised
up to grasp the Bible and hold aloft God's banner."

The fields and forests of Accomack seemed to take
up the loud " Never !" and send it echoing to the
stars

Noticing my father's prophecy, our informant said,

"So severe are the hardships of our ministry—in-
digent, pursued, harassed—that one might reasonably
expect a dearth of candidates for positions which
bring constant exposure to want and wrong; yet
during these very two years of darkening persecution
I have been looking in upon the meetings of the Presbytery of Laggan in my native place of St. Johnstown,
a little village on Lough Foyle, five miles south of
Londonderry, and I have seen two young men deliberately facing the clouded future, challenging its dangers and preparing themselves to share hard toil and
jeopardy with those now in the midst of the fires.

"One of these I especially noted.   On the 28th of
January last year (1680) he appeared upon the floor and
asked to be received under care of Presbytery as a probationer for the gospel ministry.   On inquiry, I learned
that the blue-eyed, brown-haired youth was born of
Scotch lineage in county Donegal and was a graduate
of the University of Glasgow.   In native talent and by
culture he seemed fitted for eminence in any of the
learned professions.   Nor was he ignorant of the dangers he was challenging.   While yet a lad playing upon
the hill which slopes from his childhood's home down
to the eastern margin of Lough Swilly, or strolling
with his brothers John and Robert or hand in hand

with his younger sister, Anne, to enjoy their diversions around the old water-mill at Ramelton, or to look upon the ancient castle scarred by the Catholic fires of 1641, or to wander in childish dread over toward the castle of Ramullan, where the bishop of Raphoe lived in princely state,—the boy's heart was already stirred by stories of the hardships of God's heroic ministry, the noble sixty-one of the province of Ulster, thirteen of them of this brave Presbytery of Laggan, who in 1661 refused to enslave their consciences to the demands of the tyrant Church, were ejected from their places, forbidden to baptize or preach and driven forth from their livings to penury and want. One of these was the boy's own pastor, Thomas Drummond, expelled from i 's pulpit, the true gospel prohibited in Ramelton. The lad had witnessed the flames in which the Solemn League and Covenant was burned that summer by act of Parliament in all the cities and towns through the kingdom (16).

"In the year 1664, still but a stripling, he had known of the excommunication, arrest and imprisonment of four ministers by the persecuting bishop Leslie of Raphoe, son of the persecuting bishop of Down. Inheriting the spirit of an ecclesiastical despot, this primate of Raphoe, a gourmand and a drunkard so bloated that he could not walk under his own weight unsupported, kept the four godly men John Hart, William Semple, Adam White and the boy's pastor Drummond in confinement at Lifford for six dreary years, only released at last, against the bishop's wish, by the king's positive command.

"Somewhere in the midst of these stormy events, while the enemies of the cross were trying to suppress

4

the gospel work, the Master put it into the heart of a pious schoolmaster to talk to the lad about the love of Jesus, and won him to Christ at fifteen years of age. Who can predict the results of that early conversion ?

"In the year 1675 the young man left the banks of the Swilly for the banks of the Clyde, and at Glasgow his university studies were pursued among scenes even more sad and terrible. That year he saw garrisons placed all over the land in the houses of Presbyterians for the suppression of God's worship in the fields and everywhere, the praises of Jesus interdicted alike in our churches and on moor and mountain Next he saw issued the order forbidding all persons, under severest penalties, to supply the necessaries of life to the proscribed or to hold any communication with them—even fathers and mothers or wives or husbands to be treated as felons and traitors if they gave food or shelter or a word of comfort to any loved one under the ban of the oppressor. As long as he remained he saw these barbarities increasing in virulence, until finally, the English garrisons not brutal enough, the half-civilized marauders of the Highlands were let loose upon their defenceless victims and Scotia's streams ran blood

"Yes, the young man knew perfectly well what he was braving when last year, with Dalziel and Claverhouse still raging across the Channel and the hand of tyranny stretched out over Donegal, he stood before Presbytery vouched for by the old veteran Drummond. This hero of the days of the ejectment, the unyielding prisoner of six years, would hardly have vouched for this youthful probationer if he had not known him to be fitted for troublous times. We all felt this while we saw these brave sufferers of the past sitting around him, and heard his application to be received as a candidate for the office which would bring with it the hatred of mighty and heartless men.

"Solemnly he answered the questions as to his personal reliance from boyhood upon that saving blood which he hopes to preach to others. Satisfying themselves that the constraining love of Christ was the power that caused him to face the solemnities of the sacred calling, they appointed Mr. Robert Rule of Derry and Mr. John Hart of Taboyn—another of the Lifford prisoners—to confer with the candidate with regard to his attainments and studies. As a spectator of all there occurring, I was naturally more interested in his appearance and conduct than you can possibly be these thousands of miles away."

The company urged him to go on. In these Western wilds we get hungry for news, and there are few pleasanter hours than when we meet with a good talker from the old country. Naomi and Comfort were listening as intently as the oldest.

"I will prophesy," continued our informant, "that he will make his mark upon the world. He has good natural parts, zeal, piety, courage, and the Presbytery is doing all it can to develop what is in him. I attended six or seven more of their meetings at St. Johnstown, continuing at intervals until May of the present year, and have witnessed their persistent care to ground him thoroughly in our doctrines and make him a workman that needeth not to be ashamed. Committees frequently appointed to examine and encourage and superintend his studies reported that he was diligent Even after the committee was ready to recommend him for trial, he was not himself satisfied, setting his standard higher and asking for more time.

"On the continued 'good report' made to the Presbytery, they assigned him as the text for a trial sermon 1 Tim. 1. 5: 'Now the end of the commandment is charity out of a pure heart, and of a good conscience and of faith unfeigned'—an excellent text for these uncharitable days. On the 25th of this past April (1681) we heard him preach upon it, the discourse in treatment and manner meeting the approval of his brethren and giving promise of no ordinary pulpit power in the days to come. Another sermon was assigned, on the sweet invitation, 'Come unto me, all ye that labor and are heavy laden, and I will give you rest.' Last May, the 25th, we heard him tell of the yearnings of the heart of Jesus in that beautiful text It was pleasant to think of his going forth to talk upon such themes to the tried ones of the Redeemer's kingdom. In these two texts—characteristic of those who assigned them and creditable to him who so treated them as to secure the approval of such Presbyters—the keynote of a blessed ministry was seemingly struck.

"On the 29th of last December (1680) there came an interesting communication to the Presbytery from America, from your neighboring province. It contained a statement of the spiritual destitution existing in these regions and an urgent plea for a godly minister. The sympathies of those good men were drawn out to their countrymen yearning in distant climes for the word of life. Mr. Hart was instructed to write to the Rev. William Keyes of Belfast about the matter ; Mr. Rule, to correspond with the Presbyteries of Route and Tyrone; and Mr. William Trail, to correspond with the Presbyteries of Down and Antrim. Such an interest did the appeal of your fellow-citizen Colonel William Stevens awaken that day at St. Johnstown."

This, then, was the letter, freighted with so many hopes and prayers, which had taken flight from the banks of our own little Pocomoke, borne on under the ordination of the Almighty.

" To that letter I noticed our young candidate listening attentively. Was there a new depth in his blue eyes and a new thoughtfulness upon his fine brow ? I could not help thinking what substantial material there was in this young man himself for a missionary.

" The ' common-head ' assigned the candidate was very suggestive, ' De Antichristo '—' concerning the Antichrist ' For illustrations of his subject he need not go far At this very day is not the civil power claiming to sit in the temple of God as God, usurping the crown-rights of Jesus and denying that he is the supreme Ruler in his own Church? The meeting of May 25th of the present year was to be the last that could be openly attended. Before the time came to present the ' common-head ' the leading ministers were so pursued and harassed that there could be no more public meetings of the Presbytery. Four of its members were subjected to arrest after arrest, until sentence was finally secured against them from a packed jury, and they are now suffering imprisonment at Lifford at the will of their oppressors.

"Against one of these, Mr. William Trail, there seems to be an especial hatred—perhaps because of his being an influential member of Presbytery and its clerk, and because of his faithfully visiting the incarcerated soldiers who had refused to take the oath of supremacy. He is a Scotchman born, not likely to forget that he is a fellow-countryman of John Knox.

"Our young Donegal friend is pressing his studies and awaiting ordination at the hands of his brethren. The youth who hears and obeys the call of God in the face of such obstacles must be starting in life at an elevation above all that is little or mean or cowardly."

"Certainly, certainly!" replied our host. "I will answer for such a man in the day of trial!"

That night, after I thought my bedfellow sleeping, Naomi said,

"Was not that a noble young man?" And again, after a while, "I wonder what is the young minister's name?" (17).

CHAPTER III.

A. D. 1682.

"The World was involved in such a Labyrinth of Darkness and Corruption, man would not have known, without the Bible, what was to be done."—MAKEMIE.

AS early as 1658 a few patents of land had been granted along the Pocomoke, and a few white adventurers were to be found at points here and there. In 1661, in answer to a petition from the outlawed Quakers in Accomack, Governor Calvert issued a commission to Colonel Edmund Scarborough, Randal Revell and John Elzey to grant lands to as many as wished to settle on the lower Eastern Shore of Maryland.* Revell himself soon made his home in what was therefore called "Revell's Neck," and Elzey on the Monokin, most of the Quakers from below removing into the country around. In May, 1662, Revell reports to the governor that fifty tithable persons are settled on the Monokin and Annamessex. Here the followers of George Fox have never been disturbed except by the Virginia raider, Scarborough himself.

During the year 1657, Lord Baltimore had declared that he "would never give his assent to the repeal of the law established in Maryland whereby all persons professing to believe in Jesus Christ have freedom of

* *Report of Commission on Boundary of Virginia and Maryland,* 1873, p. 23.

conscience there," and in that very year this strange
sect appeared on the Western Shore with their women-
preachers, Elizabeth Harris and others.   Their refusal
to take the oath of fidelity, and their apparently contemptuous persistence in wearing their hats in the
presence of the courts, were naturally construed into
political disloyalty rather than religious scruples.
The rash tongues of indiscreet zealots often confirmed
these damaging impressions.   Many still say that they
would not defend the province against an invader, but
would feel in conscience bound to supply provisions to
public enemies.*   Such declarations were easily misunderstood.   The accusations against these people on
the Accomack records, and on the Western Shore of
our own province, were not so much on account of
their religious theories as for contempt of the civil
law.   For a while Maryland began to arrest and whip
and banish.   In 1660 there was published in London
a complaint from one of them, saying, " The Indians
whom they judged to be brethren exceeded in kindness, in courtesies, in love and mercy unto them who
were strangers; which is a shame to the mad, rash
rulers of Mariland who have acted so barbarously to
our people." †

As soon as it became apparent that the Quakers
meant no disloyalty, and that their peculiarities were
harmless, the Western Shore oppressions ceased   In
1666, George Alsop said, " Quakerism is the only
opinion that bears the bell away."   During the past
twenty years they have been by far the most zealous
and active of all the Protestants in the province, itin-

* Bishop Meade' *Old Churches*, i. 427.
† Neill *Founders of Maryland*, p 131

erants of both sexes frequently passing through the settlements and heard by nearly all the people.

The only time these settlers of our own county were ever molested was from Accomack in 1663, and then not for their religion. The occupation of this territory having been effected by encouraging immigration from the Virginia counties, the dashing Colonel Scarborough now laid claim to it in the name of his own province and with about forty horsemen proceeded to establish her authority over its inhabitants. His progress through the fields of the Annamessex and the Monokin was that of a haughty, domineering Cavalier, arresting, threatening, denouncing and proscribing, by the "broad arrow" marked upon their doors, all who would not submit. The Quakers refused to swerve from their allegiance to Lord Baltimore. The governor of Virginia disowned these high-handed measures, and in 1668 a "divisional line" was arranged, leaving these lands under the jurisdiction of Maryland. Henceforth the Quakers were free.*

Suddenly, in 1672, their great apostle, George Fox, landed on the banks of the Patuxent and began to preach In December he left the Cliffs of Calvert and crossed the great bay. It was the same year that the grand jury, interpreting the cry of the wilderness for the Gospel, had called out Mr. Maddux to preach at four points in the county. Now this famous Quaker revivalist, this weird, wild, anomalous mystic of the century, goes thundering through our own Eastern Shore settlements. Of course he strikes for the Rehoboth plantation, one of the chief centres, with its motto, "Room for All." There the leading men of

* Accomack records, 1663; Scarborough's report.

both whites and Indians, with many others, congregated to hear him. With the hearty consent of the owner of the grounds, he established a general monthly meeting for the whole county. The lips of the people are full of reminiscences of the wonderful man— how woods and streams rang with his appeals ten years ago, his denunciations of ritualism, his laudations of the mysterious Inner Light.

Our friend Colonel Stevens has been describing the scene He says:

"I imagine I hear him still. That day the house and yard were crowded with people flocking after him from the whole country around If Paul or John the Baptist had reappeared, the excitement in the province could not have been greater. Fox's followers believed him certainly under the inspiration of Heaven; and when he came through these forests and swamps, defying the wild beasts and the rigors of winter, they looked and listened with awe almost idolatrous He who had faced the power of England and never faltered, wearing that strange hat in the presence of his angry judges, triumphing in spirit in a dozen prisons, seeing visions, casting out devils, receiving revelations from the eternal throne, arousing thousands of disciples to the wildest zeal,—here he was, in all his marvelous fascination, in my own house and on the banks of our little river. The plantations poured out their inhabitants to see His fellow-zealots regarded him with reverence, the ignorant with superstitious awe, all of us with intense curiosity

"There at my door he stood in his leather breeches and preached to the eager auditors That indescribable face, those unearthly, tremulous intonations, the abrupt, broken, inverted, almost unintelligible sentences, the terrific earnestness while his body shook and quaked, quivering like an aspen-leaf, produced an impression not soon to be forgotten. The literal in the Scriptures was spiritualized into the most unexpected meanings, the figurative interpreted literally. Old beliefs were thrown scornfully away; new constructions were forced upon the Bible at every point. Scathing invectives were hurled at the learned and the powerful, while the Inner Light and the privilege of immediate fellowship with almighty God were held forth as possible glories to the poorest and meanest. Analyzed afterward, many of his utterances were the veriest jargon, but his not being understood seemed to increase his power over his hearers.*

" Yonder sat the old Indian emperor with his dusky group, the dark upturned faces of these sons of our forests adding to the impressiveness of the scene. In the wild oratory of the preacher there seemed something near akin to the weird chants of their own medicine-men " (18).

Matchacoopah remembers the great day when the emperor came home escorting the wonderful teacher up the river. A boy then, he sat among his people beneath the trees and listened to the awful voice, while the interpreter took his words and turned them into meaning.

" He came talking out of the sea," says Matchacoopah, "and went talking back into the sea. His voice was the voice of the night-wind when it shrieks and wails among the cypresses along the river-shore."

I grow constantly more interested in the natives of

* Macaulay, iv. 19.

the wilds.   Who are they?   Whence came they?
What shall be their destiny?

These thoughts are inspired by an event with which
the opening of the present year has been crowned.
We had heard how the daughter of Powhatan—
the " Little Wanton," as her father called her—was
instructed in the Scriptures, embraced Christianity,
was baptized and married John Rolf sixty-nine years
ago.   Forty-two years ago, in our own province, at
his capital, Kittamaquindi, a chief named Tayac and
his wife and daughter were baptized by the zealous
Father White, the chief declaring that he regarded
above every other benefit the true knowledge of the
one God.*   Now, on the 25th of January, we have
had a baptism on our own shore.   An Indian by the
name of Poocum has been for some while attending the
ministrations of our Church of England clergyman, Rev.
John Hewett.   Mr. Hewett has been preaching in the
county, living on the Wicomico.   After instruction in the
principles of our religion, the baptismal rite was administered to the young man in the 'name of the Holy Trinity.
The Indian took the Christian name of the minister.

Now follows another sensation—one quite romantic.
Rumors of a matrimonial alliance between the blood
of England and the blood of the Nanticokes pass from
neighborhood to neighborhood.   The black eyes of
the Christianized savage have dwelt in love upon
the pale-faced daughter of Europe, and she has
not repelled him.   She cannot marry a pagan:
the Church could not solemnize such a marriage; but
now that barrier is removed, and only a month elapses
when, on the 25th of February, Mr. Hewett performs

* Annal of Annapolis. McSherry' Maryland, p. 49.

another ceremony, mating together the Christian Nanticoke and the willing bride, Miss Jane Johnson.
Henceforth the Indians of the Eastern Shore and
the colonists from across the sea have their wedded
representatives in the same forest-cabin, where white
hands prepare for the original proprietor of the soil
his own pone and hominy.*

This reminds me of a discovery I have lately made
Somewhere on the green fields of Derry there is one
who writes pretty verses to the smiling Peggy, my
warm-hearted maid of Ulster.   In the last letter received from him there were some things not requiring
secrecy, and I transcribe them.   The writer says:

On the 2d of April I was in Burt, and went up to Mr William
Hempton's church.   In the pulpit was a young man who
would have attracted attention anywhere. Under his clear utterances you felt that there was in him a wonderful reserve of force
and will-power.   His text was the third verse of the thirteenth
chapter of Luke "I tell you, Nay, but except ye repent, ye shall
all likewise perish " In the afternoon I returned to hear him
again ; his text and theme were the same The call to repentance, with which both John the Baptist and the Saviour himself had
entered upon their public ministry, was now sounded aloud at
the beginning of his.   Such is the preaching which the prelates
of Ireland would keep from the ears of the people

The young minister's training has been thorough, the Presbytery using the utmost circumspection "that in the worst of times
able and fruitful ministers may be continued amongst us," and
requiring " distinct and positive answers to the questions usually
proposed for showing soundness in the faith and adhering to the
truth professed in the Reformed Churches against Popery, Arminianism, Prelacy, Erastianism, Independency, and whatsoever
else is contrary to sound doctrine and the power of godliness, and
a resolution to adhere to the Covenant."   I give the very words
of the rules of the Presbyteries Now, in the face of the manifold dangers surrounding the perilous office, he was standing

---

* Somerset records, the name is there spelled " Puckam." People of
that name, evidently of Indian blood, are still in the county.

boldly forth crying to the nation, "Repent !" The name of the
young man is Makemie There is some talk of his going
abroad and carrying the gospel to foreign parts.*

From other sources of information we know that at
the very time the young licentiate was preaching at
Burt, but a little distance away, at Lifford, the Rev.
William Trail, pastor of the latter church, the Rev.
James Alexander of Raphoe, the Rev Robert Campbell
of Ray and the Rev. John Hart of Taughboyne were
lying in confinement These were the men who had
helped to train the youthful preacher. On the 3d of
last May (1681) they had been summoned before
the magistrates at Raphoe under charge of holding a
fast at the beginning of the year and recommending
it to the people

Presiding over the assizes was Sir William Steward
of Ramelton, Makemie's own townsman, an unworthy
son of a noble Presbyterian father and grandfather,
both brave soldiers of the Covenant The grandfather
had planted the Scotch colony at Ramelton as long
ago as 1610, three years after the settlement of Jamestown, in Virginia, and the family have been staunch
and true to their hereditary faith, until now this degenerate scion has renounced the principles of his ancestry
and leagued himself with the persecutor for reward.

The keeping of the fast and the authorship of the
reasons assigned, were promptly admitted by the four
ministers. The magistrates seemed to have been
ashamed to convict upon so foolish a charge, and
the brethren were discharged for the time. It was
only to be pursued in another form In a month

* Reid, ii 567, 570, 342. The sermon at Burt and its date—the last
mention of Makemie in Ireland

they were cited to appear before the lord lieutenant and council at Dublin.   There, in the castle, two of these ministers were questioned separately and closely upon the charges   There are good reasons why I transcribe some parts of the examination of one of them :

"Are you Mr. Trail ?" said the duke of Ormond, present lord lieutenant.
" Yes."

Here one of the counsel said to him,

" Be not afraid, be not surprised."
" I am not, for why should I ?" was the answer.

In the presence of the great of earth there was no tremor.

" Were you at that meeting at St. Johnstown when the causes of your late fast were drawn up ?"
" Yes "
" Who was with you there ?"
" I am not free to declare that   I confess my own accession to it, but I am not clear to tell of others, to bring them into trouble."
" What do you mean in these causes of your fast," said the lord chancellor, " by apostasy and perjury and breach of our solemn covenants and vows ?"
" The breach of all our lawful vows and covenants, which are many ; for we came under vows and covenants at baptism and at our partaking of the Lord's Supper, and upon other occasions."
" Whom do you mean by the Antichristian party ?"
" By the Antichristian party we mean the Popish party."
" But do you mean none other but only the Popish party by the Antichristian party ?"

Here Mr. Trail remained silent—that silence more eloquent than words.

" Did you ever take the oath of supremacy ?"
" No ; I was never put to it."
" But will you now take it ?"
" I am not free to take it.   I acknowledge that it is capable of

a sound sense, and that there is a sound sense put upon it by law."

"Why, then, do you not take it?"

"Because I think it were a juggling with the king, and much more with God, to take an oath that is capable of a sound sense, and yet to keep that sound sense in my mind."

During an interval, while they were examining papers, Mr. Trail said,

"I hope Your Grace and this honorable board will pardon and excuse my freedom and boldness in speaking if I speak not with that reverence and respect that is due?"

The lord lieutenant answered, smiling,

"I like you very well, Mr. Trail; you may speak what you please."

His perfect candor and manly bearing had made an impression.

"How long is it since you came to Ireland?"

"Ten years." *

"As to the nature of a fast," said Mr. Trail, "we do not make the time holy when we keep a fast, but the day is our own when the fast is over. It is not so on the Lord's day, for that is holy."

"It is even so on the Lord's day, and is all one," said the archbishop. "The time is no more holy upon the Lord's day than upon a fast-day."

"If this were a fit place for dispute, I would endeavor to prove the contrary," was the answer.

Neither in Dublin Castle nor anywhere else, before prince nor primate, would this Ulster Presbyterian admit that human forms and appointments stand upon the same footing with the divine.

Lord Lanesborough said,

* Mr. Trail was not quite forty years old   Born in Scotland in 1642; laureated at Edinburgh University in 1658; licensed to preach in 1670, in London; went to Ireland in 1671, and was ordained at Lifford in 1672. He is the eldest son of Rev. Robert Trail of Edinburgh, and had a younger brother, Robert, undergoing persecution also.

"Would you take it if they would give you a good benefice?"
"No, My Lord; I have not said that yet.   I am content to be
as I am without that."

This feeling of contentment and independence was
maintained upon a salary of twenty-one pounds a year.
He was not to be bought.

Again the archbishop:

"Do you use to ride through the country with arms, swords
and pistols?"

Trail answered, smiling,

"I came to Dublin without a sword.   There is neither sword nor
gun about my house.   I think I am one of the greatest cowards
in His Majesty's dominions, and that they are all fools that fight."

In reporting this examination Mr Trail explains by
telling us that he could never look upon blood, neither
his own nor that of others, without falling into a swoon
at the sight.   Yet this is the man, constitutionally
timid, whose inflexible moral bravery will not yield
one hair's-breadth to the oppressor, and now stands
unabashed, playing pleasant humor in the presence
of his judges!

When leaving the room, he said,

"I would entreat this honorable board to believe that we are
loyal subjects."

Lord Lanesborough replied,

"I believe that of you, Mr. Trail."

Yet these four ministers were bound over, at their
cost and on bail, to appear for trial before the assizes
at Lifford!   An indictment was found, and they were
tried before a packed jury of Trail's own neighbors
who were anxious to close his lips.   Of course the
verdict was "Guilty."   The sentence was a fine of

twenty pounds and security not to offend again, or to go to jail. Determined by no act of theirs to admit the legality of the sentence, on the 11th of August last year (1681) they went to prison for Christ's sake.

People assembling to listen to the word of life from the lips of the prisoners were often driven away by the authorities.

For over eight months these men remained in duress, until, on the 20th of April of this year, they have at length been released by act of the sheriff.

Balked for the time in their triumph, Mr. Trail's enemies have been venting their spite in an act of childish malice. On the 29th of May following his release, a mob of drunken gentry and justices of the peace worked themselves into such a passion that they made an effigy of the good minister and burned it in a great public *auto-da-fé*. Side by side with the effigy of the Presbyterian clergyman they burned one of the earl of Shaftsbury, the leader of the popular party in England and the author of the famous Habeas Corpus Act passed three years ago. Did they mean that Prelacy would gladly destroy Presbyterianism and the liberties of the people in the same fires?*

The successful prosecution of Mr. Trail and his friends has encouraged the enemies of our cause. The verdict which declared it illegal for the Presbytery to enjoin a fast means that it is a crime for them to perform any other function of an ecclesiastical court.

Looking across the Channel to the Mother-Church in Scotland, they see their friends in even a worse

* Reid, ii 338, etc., 574, etc. Other facts about Mr Trail I get from Dr Robert Anderson of Glasgow and Prof. Witherow of Londonderry.

condition.   Sycophantic prelates are applauding the
cruel Duke of York for his rancor "against the most
unreasonable schism ;" and he, on leaving for England,
advises more violent measures against the Presbyterians and declares that " Scotland will never be at peace
till the whole country south of the Forth is turned
into a hunting-field."   The curates lend themselves
zealously to the work, supplying the military murder-
ers with lists of victims.   Observance of family worship is conclusive evidence of Presbyterianism and
treason.   Hume of Hume, a gentleman of high
standing, is accused, condemned without proof and
executed, a full pardon from London reaching the
authorities two days before, but kept concealed.[*]

Meanwhile, an event of some importance to us takes
place in England.   The Quaker William Penn, son of
an admiral, secured from King Charles, on the 5th of
March last year, the grant of a large tract of land to
the north of us.   The name first selected was " New
Wales," then " Sylvania," to which the king has pre-
fixed the name of the grantee, making it " Pennsylvania."   On the 27th of October of the present year
Penn arrives and lands at New Castle from the ship
Welcome, bringing the small-pox with him.   Farther
up, at a place called " Wicacoa," at the junction of two
rivers, on three hundred and sixty acres obtained from
three Swede brothers Swaenson,[†] a city called " Philadelphia " has just been laid out, with boundaries large
enough to accommodate many people.

The Quakers around us are elated at this new
movement, for they know that the Proprietor has in-

---

[*] Macaulay. Knight, Wodrow, *passim*.
[†] Acrelius, *Hist. New Sweden*, p. 111.

fluence at the English court. Much is said of his
fairness in dealing with the Indians, but it is a fact,
about which there has been no boasting, that our
own province is nearly a half century ahead of Penn
in setting the example. At St. Mary's no land was
taken but was paid for, and the pleasantest relations
of amity were established between the two races. The
village of Yowacomaco was sold to the whites and
became their capital, and there the English and Indians lived side by side in the rude huts constructed
by savage hands, the one teaching the art of hunting
the deer and planting the maize and preparing the suc-
cotash and hominy, the other teaching the lessons of
civilized life and religion.*

Twenty years ago, when the commissioners were
bringing settlers to this county from Virginia, a treaty
of amity was formed with the emperor of the Nanticokes, and that treaty has never been infringed. The
Indians have been protected in their rights by our
county officials; and if molested by the whites, the
red men have a fair hearing before our courts, and
their wrongs are carefully redressed.† Peace and justice
to the children of the wilderness reigned by the Pocomoke through twenty uninterrupted years before Penn
but the other day made his noted treaty under the
shade of the elm on the banks of the Delaware.

In the year 1669 an act of Assembly owns the
Indians on the Choptank as "our neighbors and
confederates" and confirms to them a strip of land
three miles wide along its south bank. When, in
1675, Major Trueman and his troops executed certain

* *Annals of Annapolis;* McSherry's *Maryland,* p. 36.
† McMahon, p 19, Somerset records

Indian chiefs on the Western Shore in retaliation for murders committed upon the whites, the province was shocked and demands were made for his punishment. The next year our own Colonel Stevens, who had lived here on friendly terms with our Indians so long, was appointed by the Lower House one of the committee to conduct the impeachment of Trueman.*

In December of this year our Proprietary and Mr. Penn met to confer about the pending difficulties concerning boundary-lines. Our colonists fear that our Quaker neighbor, where his personal interests are at stake, is not disposed to deal so fairly by his white rival as he claims to have done toward his copper-colored brethren. Colonel Stevens was present at the conference, and he and others testify that " Mr. Penn declared in a very florid manner his real and hearty inclination to maintain and keep a neighborly and friendly correspondence with His Lordship," but, notwithstanding his many professions, they believe that he is bent upon getting all the territory from Maryland he can† (19).

Still we yearn and wait upon our Shore for the coming of the true gospel. Now and then there are rumors of the probability of securing a minister; then, again, the hope dies away. Forty-six years ago (1636) Livingston, Hamilton, Blair, McClelland and their friends set sail in the Eagle Wing from Loch Fergus for America, but were driven back by adverse winds to new persecutions. May fair breezes fill the sails of the next ship that starts from the harbors of Ulster!

* McSherry's *Maryland; Annals of Annapolis,* p. 89.
† *Report of Virginia and Maryland Boundary Laws, 1873,* Appendix 80.

CHAPTER IV.

A. D. 1683.

"Our mission was from Jesus Christ and warrented from the Scriptures."—MAKEMIE.

SOMEWHERE in the midst of these months, at a place unknown, on a day never to be named on the page of history, a circle of God's servants is gathered in the country of the Laggan. The doors are closed; no eye but that of the All-Seeing beholds them. In his name they meet; by his authority they act. The spies of the persecutor are abroad.

In the midst of that well-tried band a young man kneels. He has been tested and not found wanting. Solemnly he is set apart to the perilous office with fasting and prayer and the laying on of hands. He rises under sanction of Presbytery and of the God of Presbytery to preach the gospel wherever the Master may appoint.

No record is made of this solemn ceremony except on the registry by the eternal throne. Future historians will search in vain to learn the time and place. Some time in the midst of God's months, somewhere in the land of the faithful and true, ordaining hands rested upon his brown locks, and Francis Makemie rose up an accredited herald of the cross.

We turn again from the Old World to the New. I

have been reading an important paper issued seventeen years ago—the act of incorporation of our large county.*

Thus the white man lays his hand upon the continent and carves it as he will   But has not God his own purpose to subserve and a use for this quiet domain of forests and streams in the days yet to be ?   The virgin county is just two years older than my friend Naomi.

Judge Stevens is well acquainted with the family of Lord Baltimore, and speaks very pleasantly of the Lady Mary Somerset, for whom our county is named, as a woman of many quiet virtues and great benevolence, feeding the sick, clothing the naked, a favorite with all and much beloved by the young people—the true Lady Bountiful of St Mary's.† So that we are not ashamed of the county's name and feel something of a chivalric love toward our lady-patroness across the bay.

Several of the commissioners appointed at the organization of the county were Quakers—none of them Catholics—our Proprietary selecting his officers irrespective of sect.   Here are portraits of three of them as painted three years before the organization by the imperious Scarborough :

Stephen Horsey, ye ignorant yet insolent officer , a cooper by profession, who lived long in ye lower parts of Accomack, once elected a burgess by ye comon crowd, and thrown out by ye Assembly for a factious tumultuous person , a man repugnant to all government of all sects, yet professedly none , constant in nothing but opposing church government , his children at great ages yet unchristened ; that left the lower parts to head

*Comprising now the three counties Somerset, Worcester and Wicomico   See Appendix 19

† J P Kennedy's historical romance, *Rob of the Bowl*, p. 71.

rebellion at Anamessecks, where he now liveth, and stands arrested, but bids defiance until by stricter order dealt with.

George Johnson, ye Proteus of heresy, who hath been often wandering in this county, where he is notorious for shifting schismatical pranks; at length pitched at Anamessecks, where he hath bin this year and made a plantation; a known drunkard, and reported by ye neighbors to be a man of dissolute habits and guilty of many evil deeds, and withstands government for fear of justice. He now professeth quaking and to instruct others who is himself to learn good manners, calling ye obedient subjects villains, rogues and foresworne persons for subscribing; stands arrested to appear before ye hon'ble gov'ner, and bids defiance untill stricter course be taken.

Henry Boston, an unmannerly fellow, that stands condemned on our records for slighting and condemning ye laws of ye county, a rebel to government and disobedient to authority, for which he received a late reward with a rattan, and hath not subscribed; hid himself, and so escaped arrest.*

The pen of the Cavalier was as insolent as his presence.

George Fox speaks of being at the house of James Jones, "a Friend and a justice of the peace, where we had a large and very glorious meeting." John White Gent., another of the original commissioners, is a brother-in-law of Colonel Stevens.

As yet there have been no "witchcrafts, inchantments, sorcerys and magick arts" this side of the Chesapeake for these commissioners to inquire into. Henry Corbin, founder of the Corbin family in Virginia, reported to our governor that Mary Lee had been hung as a witch on board the ship Charity during her voyage from England to Maryland in 1654. John Washington, father of the Virginia Washingtons, testified that Elizabeth Richardson was hung on a ship on her way to our province from England in 1659.

* Scarborough's report, Accomack records.

Those concerned in both of these executions were prosecuted.* But, nine years ago (1674), John Cowman was found guilty at St. Mary's of witchcraft on the body of Elizabeth Goodall, and was reprieved on condition that the sheriff carry him to the gallows with rope about his neck, and he there confess his indebtedness for the sparing of his life solely to the mercy of the Lower House of Assembly in securing him a pardon.† All this was on the Western Shore, and I pray that our Somerset courts may be for ever spared from this terrible business. Sometimes, when I look out into these dark forests and hear the hooting owls and feel the awe of our American wilderness, and think of women all around us bad enough to sell themselves to Satan, I almost shudder.

Judge Stevens tells us that his Rehoboth plantation was patented in 1665, the year before the county was organized. For the old Bible name he points to Gen xxvi. 22: "And he removed from thence and digged another well, and for that they strove not; and he called the name of it Rehoboth; and he said, For now the Lord hath made *room* for us and we shall be fruitful in the land." Elsewhere, both in Europe and on this continent, there had been enough Ezeks and Sitnahs, fountains of contention and hatred : *this* he would dedicate as an ever-welling spring of living waters, abundant space all around and freedom unfettered for every faith to come and drink of the streams of peace and good-will to men.

It was a memorable day which we spent together at this Rehoboth home—Mary, the rosy Scotch lassie ;

* Neill's *Founders of Maryland*, pp. 128. 137
† *Annals of Annapolis*; McSherry's *History of Maryland*

Peggy, the blue-eyed maid of Ulster; Margaret, the soft-toned singer of the Vincennes; Naomi, our dark-eyed Virginia friend; and myself, the important representative of the Nonconformity of England.

I must tell of an imposing ceremony in which we all took part. Our host, interested in whatever concerns the prosperity of this Shore, showed us a choice variety of grape sent him by a correspondent in the North of Ireland; and now he would have us assist in planting it.

" It stood," he said, " where the strong winds from old Scotia's glens and heaths fanned and fed its growth, and where the rich sod of Erin supplied its juices.   It has crossed the ocean as a very little thing, but who knows, when watered by the dews and showers from the American sky, how widely it may spread and where its branches may reach ?   Rehoboth—there is room ! The Bible speaks of the Church as a vine of God's planting, and I have not yet relinquished my hope of an answer to the letter that went to St. Johns-town wafted by so many prayers."

" But," said some one, "the grapevine is not a native of Ireland."

" Neither is the Presbyterian Church," he answered " But exotics frequently do well by transplanting—are sometimes improved."

We see his meaning, and are suddenly taken with a great enthusiasm. Our Scottish Mary seizes the hoe and cuts the weeds away; our Ulster Peggy, spade in hand, makes the opening and sets in the scion ; our Huguenot Margaret, humming a song from Clement Marot, fills in the soil and mellows it about the plant; our Accomack Naomi props and trains it for graceful

growing; my own English hands hasten to dip the
water from the shimmering Pocomoke and pour it
about the roots; while the judge, just home from St.
Mary's, representing to our thought the genius of the
Maryland government and the fairness of the courts,
looks on, smiling and encouraging these workers from
many lands.   In the yard, gazing without a word, were
the judge's three sons—John, fourteen years old; William, eleven; and James, seven—all born on this plantation   Thereupon the fancy took me that through
their eyes future generations of American birth were
watching the planting and awaiting the results.

Just as we finished, the youngest pet, little three-year-
old Jane, came toddling into the circle and threw her
dimpled arms around the laborers' necks and kissed
us every one.*

"The womanhood of the days to come is cheering the planting of the vine," said her father.—"Now,
boys, bring the cypress-rails of Eastern-Shore growth
and fence it well.   Foot of man nor beast must tread
it down."

We took a label and wrote upon it the figures
" 1683."

Just then a new burst of sunshine broke through
the clouds and beamed in showers of light upon the
infant vine.

We went home, Naomi with me, full of the little
drama we had enacted.   That night my father said,

"We want the purest and best   Northward of us are
churches with Presbyterians in them—in the Jerseys,
on Long Island and in New England—but the inter-

* Somerset records give names of children and dates and place of
birth as above.

mixture of laxer systems is too great for the organization of any Church in the full power of our faith and polity. In such partnership with the looser, there must always be a letting down in the compromise until that which is distinctive in the genius of Presbyterianism is almost eliminated. There have been Congregational ministers over societies where there were some Presbyterians, and there have been Presbyterian ministers over flocks largely Congregational, but in all such cases so much had to be conceded to peace and prejudice that what was peculiarly our own has been surrendered. In new, weak, mixed fields it could not be otherwise. In alliances between the laxer and the stricter, the former will prevail in reducing the latter to its own level, sensitive and rebellious if the more rigid views are asserted. In Presbyterianism adulteration is death.

"The difficulty in the North at present is not so much in doctrine as in government. Three years ago (1680) the Westminister Confession of Faith was adopted by the Synod at Cambridge, Independents as zealous for it as anybody. And there are elders in name found here and there, but without true ecclesiastical authority and without authoritative Church courts. Calvinism so poorly guarded is not likely to last.

"May God send us the staunch and genuine! That which came into life under the preaching of Knox and grew into power amid the storms of its native heaths—that which has passed through one transplanting and proved its vitality upon the fields of Ulster—seems fitted of God, by parentage and training, for taking root upon a foreign shore. In these American wilds it would be bracing to listen to those who, under the strict usages of the Ulster Presbyteries, are required before ordination to give positive assurances of 'adhering to the truth professed in the Reformed churches against Popery, Arminianism, Prelacy, Erastianism, Independency, and whatever else is contrary to sound doctrine and the power of godliness.'"

A few days, and stirring news strikes us and goes reverberating from plantation to plantation. A sail has entered the Pocomoke bringing cargo more precious than ever ploughed its waters before. A Presbyterian minister has arrived from Europe, is at the house of Judge Stevens and will preach next Sabbath. The riders along the narrow horse-roads carry the tidings everywhere. The boats upon the little rivers bear the good news to every landing. Traders at the farm-stores forget their purchases and hurry home. Word flies by the county road over to the Annamessex, up to the Monokin, there strengthens for further flight, and hurries on to the Wicomico. Another rumor starts for Accomack, and another for the seaboard. Every Presbyterian plantation is moved as winds from the ocean move the fields of silken maize. The arrival of George Fox caused no greater enthusiasm among the Quakers.

The holy day has come, the whippoorwills—the first, probably, that the new preacher ever heard—announcing the dawn with gladness. The Dove spreads her canvas and goes down the river. Other boats begin to dot the bosom of the winding Pocomoke.

When we draw near the Rehoboth plantation, we see colonists arriving from below—the Andersons and Taylors and others from Accomack. The groves are full of horses with saddles and pillions. And still they come—the Jenkinses, the Browns, the Whites, the Howards, the Kings, the Spences, the Fassetts, the Layfields, the Covingtons, the Wilsons, the Joneses, the Dents, the Winders, the Colbourns, the Whittingtons, the Erskines, the Dashiels, the Hendersons, the Galbraiths, the Sangsters, the Handys, the Pipers, the Drydens, the Bostons, the Horseys, the Aydelotts, the Franklins, the Hopkinses, the Beauchamps, the Dennises, the Madduxes, the Fontaines, the Elzeys, the Stevensons, the Alexanders, the Bowens, the Flemingses, the Venables, the Stewarts, the Baynums, the Brays, the Hudsons, the Clarkes, the Schofields, the Dickinsons, the Everndons, the Fentons, and many more.*

Already are the colonists presenting the usual contrasts of riches and poverty—of the higher and lower grades of social position—some maintaining the pomp and circumstance of the gentry of England, others humbly clad and excluded from the circle of the great. Here is the costume of light-green cloth trimmed with lace, the doublet, the ruff, the short cloak, the parti-colored stockings, the conical and broad-brimmed hat, showing the lingering fashions of the days of Cromwell. Not far off are some habited in coarse buff jerkins, with belt and heavy buckle, leggins of rough leather and caps of undressed rabbit-skins—the hunters of the forest. Here, again, are hints of the tawdry dress of the period since the Restoration —embroidered velvet coats with wadded skirts, wristbands of fine lace, the large full vests, the embroidered breeches, the shoes with their showy silver buck-

* Names from contemporaneous records

les, and the jaunty three-cornered hats. Yet more are
seen in coarse blue-and-gray frocks of Scotch cloth or
home-spun and home-woven, wearing moccasins of un-
tanned skins and leggins tied above the knees and over
the shoes like a buskin. These are, of course, the
poorer classes, many of them indentured servants.
Yet let it be understood that some of these are
among the most intelligent and excellent people in
the province—men who have been impoverished and
banished by the persecutor and are now paying their
passage-money by four years of service.*

We are pleasantly seated with one of our favorite
families. Madam Mary Jenkins, the daughter of Robert King, Gent, who lives over on the Monokin, is just
nineteen years old and in the prime of her beauty.
Her husband, Francis Jenkins, is one of the justices and
a member of the governor's council, and therefore honored with the title of "Colonel." The youthful Madam
Mary is elegantly dressed and very fascinating—a hat
of green silk with a graceful pinner, a closely-fitting
jacket, also of green silk, a scarlet silk petticoat and
silk shoes with very high heels. Lace floats about
her like fleecy clouds over the moon.

All around us are women in kersey waistcoats and
linsey-woolsey petticoats, heavy stockings of their own
knitting, shoes bought for the occasion, the shoes and
stockings brought in their hands and put on within a
mile of the house.

All is expectancy. Now the door opens and the
minister appears, wearing the black Genevan gown
and the white bands. We recognize the description
which had preceded him—the intellectual forehead

* Costumes adapted from Kennedy.

crowned with brown locks, the fair complexion, the expressive blue eyes, and, over all, the mien of a true Irish gentleman. This is the pupil of Drummond and Hart and Trail—he who in boyhood played by the shores of Lough Swilly and who now stands upon the banks of our own Pocomoke. This is Francis Makemie (20).

How the ears and the hearts of the Scotch and Scotch-Irish exiles thrill under the familiar tones of their countryman, vibrating with memories of home! Need we wonder if the tears flow while his plaintive accent reminds them of martyred pastors over the sea? Nor will the most fastidious, in their embroidered velvets and Persian silks, find anything to offend the cultured ear. In its first utterances to the American continent, Presbytery speaks through an educated ministry.

Yonder, too, sit King Daniel of the Pocomokes and our friend Matchacoopah. Over to the other side are the black-skinned children of Africa, their gaze fixed upon Mr. Makemie and listening. I see the preacher's eyes again and again resting upon these natives of Africa and America. He has never seen either of them before. Two mighty race-problems are there before him, unsolved.

It is pleasant to hear our minister take position firmly and emphatically by the Holy Scriptures. The American Presbyterian Church is talking of her great charter. Note his words:

"The Christian religion has so full, so complete, and so perfect a Rule, or Canon, for its guide and direction, that there is nothing deficient that is necessary for the Christian's counsel, and for advancing his accomplishment, in every state and condiuon, in every station, capacity or relation, men may be placed in of God in the world ; whether for instructing blinded and dead sinners what glory and perfection they were originally created in and willfully forfeited and lost by Adam's apostasy ; or for detecting the enormities and irregularities, both of heart and life, as a clear looking-glass wherein we view both the inward and outward man. And it not only points out to sinners the true way of life and salvation, but most particularly instructs us how to think, how to speak and how to act, both toward God and toward one another. And this is the Word of life, the Revelation of Heaven, the Rule and Test both of faith and life

" Lives are orderly or disorderly as they are guided and governed by that Rule or not conformed thereto. For every sin is nothing else but a transgression of the law, a violation or deviation from that Rule   And by this Rule our actions shall be detected and conversations judged and tried. It is termed from the Spirit of God a walking according to rule. Gal. vi. 16. It is called a walking in the law of the Lord. Ps. cxix. 1. It is called a taking heed to our ways according to God's Word. Ps. v. 9. And this rule and canon is the revealed will, law and mind of God, which is a clear, a perfect, universal and extensive rule and canon, directing us in the management of our very thoughts and intentions of our souls, beyond the power and virtue of all human laws It is a bridle and gives check to our unruly tongues and regulates our very words without which all religion is judged vain. James i. 26.

" How little regard is had hereunto by this licentious age who glory in oaths and curses, exercise their wits and parts in all obscenities, ribaldry and profaneness, mocking and ridiculing and hissing at all conversation any way tending to the honor of God and edification of our neighbor ; and even this by such as make no small pretence to religion and devotion !

" It is a rule and guide for our lives and actions, instructing and guiding all men how to demean themselves toward God, our neighbor and ourselves ; both what we are to forbear and abstain from, and in doing our duty. Tit. ii. 11, 12. ' For the grace of God that bringeth salvation hath appeared unto all, teaching us that denying ungodliness and worldly lusts, we should live soberly, righteously and godly in this present world.' " *

The flutter of the leaves of the old Bibles in the

* Makemie's New York sermon.

6

hands of our North Britons whenever the minister quoted a text was refreshing to hear and to see   His preaching was as full of Scripture as Peter's on the day of Pentecost, keeping God's word prominent as authority for all he said.   A man of attractive presence, a speaker of considerable oratorical power, his chief strength lay in the honor which he placed upon the Holy Bible.

Before sermon the preacher had read and commented upon the chapter, for he does not practice the "dumb-reading" common in the ritualistic churches. Oh how the old psalm from Rouse swelled out that day up and down the banks of the Pocomoke!   That all might sing, the minister read it out line by line :

> " By Babel's streams we sat and wept,
>   when Zion we thought on.
> In midst thereof we hanged our harps
>   the willow trees upon
> For there a song required they
>   who did us captive bring ;
> Our spoilers called for mirth and said,
>   'A song of Zion sing.'
> Oh, how the Lord's song shall we sing
>   within a foreign land ?
> If thee, Jerus'lem I forget,
>   skill part from my right hand !"

The worship continued until after two o'clock and did not seem long.   Mary, our rosy Scotch lassie, Peggy, the blue-eyed maid of Ulster, Margaret, the sweet voiced-singer of the Vincennes, and Naomi, the Virginia beauty, looked happier and holier than I had ever seen them before.

After service the judge presented us to the minister, saying that we represented the various types of Presbyterianism on the Shore, and we felt greatly honored. Thinking then of her native Ireland, Peggy was prouder than any of us.

My father came to the group and said,

" Young maidens, the vine has taken root."

We looked at the enclosed scion, and the buds were alive and swelling.

I was glad that I had written so much about the county and its inhabitants, for who knows what great interests for future generations may be germinating to-day in these lands south of the Nanticoke? I was glad that we had heard of Ramelton, too, and the little home back upon the hill which rises away from Lough Swilly, and of what we knew of the young man's fearlessly braving the perils of a consecration to the ministry in such troublous times.

It was not long before my father had Mr. Makemie home with us. The pone had been mellowing all night, and was yellow and luscious; Matchacoopah had captured the great wild turkey and brought us a new supply of oysters: His Turkeyship was brown and tender; brother John had found the bee tree and secured its treasures; Martha and I had been gathering the myrtle-berries, and the candles made from their wax were straight and firm and as fragrant as the spices of the Indies; the sassafras-root supplied us with a beverage no less palatable than the costly tea of China; our pewter dishes had been rubbed until bright as silver. The Eastern Shore was doing her best for her pioneer minister, and his cordial appreciation of it all proved that God had formed him for the land to which he had come.

It was soon noticeable that Mr. Makemie manifested

an interest in whatever concerned the temporal prosperity of the people as well as in their religious culture. He wished to know all about the condition of the country and what was doing for its advancement. My father spoke of the act of Assembly this year for the establishment of towns of import and export. Five have been designated for our county—the first on the Wicomico, by the bay-side, on the land next above the property belonging to the orphans of Charles Ballard; the second on the north side of Mudford Creek, on Smith's and Glannil's island; the third on Horsey's land, in Annamessex; the fourth on Morgan's land, commonly called "Burrow's," toward the head of the Pocomoke; and the fifth on the land between Mr. Francis Jenkins's plantation and Mr. Edmund Howard's, on the north side of our river. This is about to take the name of "Rehoboth," from Colonel Stevens's plantation. In each of these, one hundred acres are to be divided into one hundred lots, any person to have a lot free of cost who will build on it a house twenty feet square by the last of August, 1685.* Virginia also has been trying to effect the establishment of towns. On their plan Mr. Anderson built last year at Onancock †

Mr Makemie seems already in sympathy with the spirit of public improvement, and speaks as if he were one of us. Besides other benefits to arise from coming together into these trading posts, he says,

"Our fishery would be advanced and improved highly by encouraging many poor men to follow that calling. Our vast plenty of oysters would make a beneficial trade, both with the town and foreign traders, believing we have the best oysters

---

* Acts of Assembly 1683.   † Accomack records.

for pickling and transportation, if carefully and skillfully managed. So that it is not to be doubted but if towns were promoted, many poor people would produce more, by selling sundry things which now turn to little account, than they now make
of whole tobacco crops." *

It was natural that he and my father should talk
together of the sad state of affairs in the British Isles
and in France. The Stuart is a bribed underling of
the Catholic king Louis, and both are tyrants—our
own the baser of the two.

We learn from Mr. Makemie that many ministers
and thousands of others are looking to this country
and awaiting reports from himself as to homes in
America. He has come not only to bring the gospel
to God's scattered people here, but to explore the land
and send back word to those who are gazing anxiously across the deep.†

To have a minister of God again by our household
altar, as in other days, was indeed a pleasure. He
questioned us all upon his last sermon, and then from
the Westminster Catechism. After reading and ex-
plaining the Scriptures and leading us in prayer that
we might love the truth and embody it in our lives,
he said to us,

" Neglect of family religion promotes as much irreligion as
any one thing beside. Many parents will labor hard, rise up
early and sit up late, to provide for the backs and bellies of
their children ; and he is worse than an infidel that does not ;
but what must they be that take no care of, and make no provision for, their souls, but ruin them by sinful indulgence and so
train up vassals for the Devil instead of training up servants for
the living God ? And as youth and tender years are fittest for
bearing the yoke of religion, so they are the most suitable for

* From Makemie's *Perswasive for Promoting Towns, etc.*
† Makemie's letter from Elizabeth River, quoted hereafter.

receiving impressions of divine knowledge and habits of right living   For want of which early Christian education, many run naturally, as the sparks fly upward, to a thousand disorders and all excess of riot." *

In answer to a question from my father, Mr. Makemie was led into some account of God's gracious dealings with his own soul   We felt deep interest in whatever concerned his personal history.   He told us of the old school-house on the hills of Donegal, and of the good man who was there teaching for eternity as well as in the sciences of earth   I shall never forget how modestly and how solemnly the minister spoke :

"Ere I received the imposition of hands in that Scriptural and orderly separation unto my holy and ministerial calling, I gave enquiring satisfaction to godly, learned and judicious men, of a work of grace and conversion wrought on my heart, at fifteen years of age, by and from the pains of a godly schoolmaster who used no small diligence in gaining tender souls to God's service and fear.   Since which time, to the glory of his free grace be it spoke, I have had the sure experiences of God's various dealings with me, according to his infinite and unerring wisdom, to my unspeakable comfort." †

Very early had God begun the preparation of heart and life for some great work.   I thought of my friend Naomi being now just fifteen years old, and I wished that she could have heard him

The months that followed were privileged seasons in the lives of our Presbyterian colonists.   Mr. Makemie was *everywhere*, cheering the hearts of the scattered Calvinists, preaching on the Annamessex, preaching on the Monokin, preaching on the Wicomico, preaching up toward the head of navigation on the Poco-

* New York sermon.   † From Makemie's *Answer to Keith*

moke, preaching over on the seaboard, preaching down on the Virginia line, carrying God's comforting messages wherever the lonely Presbyterian heart yearned for the gospel in its purity. In the young man we witness a zeal and energy which cannot rest while he sees the great destitutions in America.

Before the year is past we learn of the execution of the patriots Russell and Algernon Sidney, wholly innocent of the conspiracy charged against them, their standing in the way of the despotism of the tyrant being their only crime. The brutal tool, Judge Jeffreys, dances in glee over the judicial murder of Sidney.* This same "Rye-House Plot" is charged against the Presbyterians of Scotland and made the pretext for more terrible persecutions there. Ministers fly thither from Ireland, to find their condition worse than at home. The distress deepens everywhere, and many more are talking of emigrating.

Meanwhile, there is hilarity at court. Seven days after the noble Lady Russell is made a widow, Anne, the king's niece, marries amid great rejoicings. The king publicly parades his sins. The wicked riot in iniquity, while the godly are oppressed in the name of religion.

But above all interests now to us, is the presence of our minister with us and the great gospel privileges that are ours. My father says that Mr. Makemie is already giving evidence of capacity as an organizer, bringing our people together for co-operation in a common purpose, and exerting himself to place our cause upon a permanent basis. It needs a strong man to represent our Church here properly at this

* Evelyn's *Diary*, December 5

juncture, standing as it does between two widely-contrasted systems. On the one extreme is Episcopacy, subordinating the spiritual to its Laudian externals, making its sacraments saving, very careless in morals and unchurching all who will not subscribe to the apostolic virtue of a diocesan's hands. On the other extreme is the Quakers' hate of all visible forms, discarding the sacraments, ridiculing the ordination of the ministry, demeaning the Sabbath, believing that there is no religion where their mysterious divine afflatus is not claimed, and subordinating the Bible to this Inner Light. These two are not only violently antagonistic to each other, but to all who would avoid their widely diverse errors. To maintain a firm and scriptural stand between the two demands a leader of vigorous intellect, acknowledged piety and great decision of character. So says mine honored sire.

This year, while the Turks were pressing Vienna and the Austrian king had fled and hope was almost gone, John Sobieski appeared with his valiant Poles upon the mountain of Holimburg, and the beleaguered people, weary, waiting, watching, saw the lances and the banners, took heart, renewed the struggle and soon were free. This same year, while latitudinarianism and immorality abound, and while Prelacy and Mysticism are doing but little here to stay the foe, a timely leader has come to our help against the prevailing errors, and we too are cheered and feel that deliverance is at hand.

Matchacoopah has taught us the art of another dish made from the Indian corn—a dish which has already found its way into poetry. The dough, spread upon boards and baked before the large open fires, is called "johnny-cake," already contracted into "jonakin." So long ago as the year 1675—the year that Mr. Makemie entered the University of Glasgow—the poetic schoolmaster of Boston, Mr. Benjamin Thomson, wrote as follows:

> " The times wherein old Pompion was a saint—
> When men fared hardly, yet without complaint,
> On vilest cates—the dainty Indian maize
> Was eat with clamp shells out of wooden trays,
> Under thatched huts without the cry of rent,
> And the best sauce to every dish—content.
> When Cimnels were accounted noble blood
> Among the tribes of common herbage-food—
> 'Twas in those days an honest grace would hold
> Till an hot pudding grew at heart a-cold,
> And men had better stomachs to religion
> Than I to capon, turkey-cock or pigeon.
> When honest sisters met to pray, not prate
> About their own, and not their neighbor's, state—
> Then times were good; merchants cared not a rush
> For other fare than jonakin and mush " (21).

CHAPTER V.

A. D. 1684.

"My compassion over tender souls in an American desert"—MAKEMIE

THE tutelary saint chosen for Maryland by the Romanists is no other than the famous founder of the Jesuit order, Ignatius Loyola While Luther (born A. D. 1483—just two centuries before the arrival of our Makemie upon these shores) was rising in the might of the great Reformation to shake the papal throne, another great movement, under another great leader—born only eight years after Luther—was rising in its might to prop that throne against the heavy blows of the new Protestantism. When the Ark and Dove started from Europe, Father White, himself a Jesuit, tells us that they implored the intercession "of the Blessed Virgin, of St. Ignatius, and of all the guardian angels of Maryland." The beautiful St Inigoe's Creek perpetuates the Spanish name of the patron saint, and there, on the side of St. Mary's nearest the creek, is a chapel devoted to Loyola and held in great esteem.

Here, upon our own Pocomoke, we now raise our little wilderness sanctuary, dedicating the cypress temple and the soil it adorns to no saint in Romish calendar, but to the blessed Redeemer alone, invoking his presence and favor as our one glorious Patron and Helper

Mr. Makemie warns against dissensions among fellow-Protestants, showing that their uncharitableness toward one another only strengthens the power of Rome and encourages her schemes of evil. He says:

" It has been too notorious what diabolical designs and base plots the emissaries of Rome have contrived, promoted and attempted, to overthrow that glorious work and cause of Reformation, or to lead or cajole us back into our anti-Christian slavery, idolatry and superstition ; and for effectuating thereof they have not been wanting, neither have stuck at anything to widen our breaches, augment our differences, hinder our mutual condescensions and our endeavored accommodations, raising implacable heats and keeping us asunder by distinguishing names, setting up contrary interests, and often raising violent storms of bitter persecutions, instigating the ascendant party still to trample upon the Nonconformists and by all means to render them black and odious. And all this, and much more, to ruin Protestants and weaken the Protestant interest."

It is believed that the present king * is a Papist in disguise, and there is no doubt about his probable successor, the Duke of York, being a Papist of deepest dye. Under these circumstances, those who are exposed to the hatred of the common foe ought to be too wise to prey upon one another. Yet there are many in Virginia, and Maryland too, as well as in the British Isles, who are ready to war upon their fellow-Protestants and play indirectly into the hands of Rome. Mr. Makemie continued:

" I wish there may not be found among us still too many incendiaries to raise dissentions and stir up unchristian heats among Reformed Protestants that we may become a prey to the common enemy." †

There are Yeos and Coodes yet in our province, watchfully awaiting their opportunity. Our side of

---

* Charles II.   † Makemie's *Truths in a True Light.*

the bay is peaceful. Mr. John Hewctt, our Episcopal clergyman, seems inclined to give us no trouble.
Colonel Stevens, a man of affairs, appreciates Mr.
Makemie's magnanimity, sound judgment and practical common sense. He knows that these are gifts
which mould possibilities into prosperity, building up
commonwealths and churches. Deeply interested in
developing this Shore, he is tolerant in his feelings
toward all sects and opposed to any contentions between them. Rehoboth! On this vast continent
there ought to be room enough for all.

In our county are several centres of increasing
population. At these, the churches naturally gather
and take form. One of these centres for religious
gatherings, now for a number of years, has been
the Rehoboth plantation. There the grand jury
invited Mr. Maddux to preach in 1672, there George
Fox preached at the Quakers' monthly meetings in
1672 and 1673, and there the Church of England
clergy have been equally welcome. Mr. Hewett
and the Richardsons have warm friends along our
river (22). The Assembly having now located one
of its towns of export and import in this section,
just below the plantation, the gathering of the people for business and otherwise will be more and more
in this direction. The few Virginia Presbyterians, not
tolerated on their own soil, will be better accommo-
dated at Rehoboth than almost anywhere else as yet;
boat-travel being the most pleasant of all in these days
of poor roads, undrained swamps and bad bridges. In
tender compassion for God's scattered sheep, Mr. Makemie goes everywhere seeking out the exiled Presbyterians and breaking to them the bread of life.

I want to describe one of these journeys as a specimen of many others. Colonel Stevens and his brother-in-law, Sheriff White, were going over into Bocketenorton Hundred and then up the bay to look after their purchases, and our religious pioneer—as enterprising in his work as they in theirs—decides to accompany them. Now I hear that my father is going too, and a strong fancy takes possession of me to be one of the party. The judge calls me a true Maryland girl and secures my father's consent. Ever since the bright May morning, four years ago, when the rising sun blazed over the beaches upon the beautiful inland bay and the green woodlands beyond, giving us the first glimpse of the great New World, the desire has remained with me to explore those fair regions.

It looks strange to see our minister with holster and pistols strapped to his saddle, as fully armed as the others. This is a reminder that there are bad Indians as well as good, that there are dangerous men among the white colonists too, and that we are in a land of wolves and bears. These wild beasts, and the wilder men of the times, would not respect the officers of the law nor our minister more than any one else. Matchacoopah guides us as far as the coast, leading us carefully through the unsettled lands and to points where streams are fordable—"unna-tah-quit-timps," as he calls the shallow places.

Southward from our ferry we travel upon the Virginia road, meaning to strike the inhabited part of the coast in the Chingoteague settlements. Entering the low grounds near a little stream, suddenly several arrows (*kullah-ow*) speed in rapid succession from his bow (*all-ontz*), and a large animal falls dead at our feet from the thick branches overhead. "Winquipim" ("A bear"), says the Indian, with great satisfaction; and soon a fine steak is dangling at his side. While he secures his prize on that little elevation near the junction of two branches of the stream, Mr Makemie speaks of it as a fit location for a temple of the living God; and we all felt its retired solemnity, its picturesque environment of venerable trees and its convenient nearness to the Virginia line. God had planted these old forests long before the keel of Columbus had sought the Indies, and the gray mosses seemed to hang like tabernacle curtains around the site for a sacred shrine to the Most High God.

Mr Stevens intimates that the bells are already ringing for the congregations to assemble. Chimes of frogs' voices, in all keys of the gamut, are rising from the waters around us. The explanation is made to the new immigrant that these merry harbingers of the springtime are currently called "the Virginia bells" in the parlance of the colonists (23). All smile at my admission that for me these choruses are full of music. Somebody speaks of the similarity between these cadences and the Indian names of our streams and rivers—Pocomoke, Quindocqua, Aricoco, Morumsco, Rockawakin, Nassiongo, Quepongo.

Not many months afterward we would remember Mr. White's remark: "These Virginia bells were sounding here long before we heard them, and they will be ringing long after our ears shall hear them no more." No one then knew how soon the body of the speaker was to be laid near our river where Nature's requiems should go on singing down the centuries the memories of the pioneers of the wilderness.

Mr. Stevens tells me that the stream we are fording is named " Pitts's Creek," for a resident of the counties below—Mr. Robert Pitts, who has patented thousands of acres through these sections. It remained uncertain to which province the lands belonged until the divisional line was run by Scarborough and Calvert in 1668. In memory I marked well the site of that little hill, and wondered if the day would come when the praises of God would there be sung by human voices where now the choirs of woods and waters were honoring the Great Jehovah

Matchacoopah is a wary guide; and where the dim horse-roads fail us, he leads through the more open forests and finds the easiest paths for me. Soon the breezes grow more refreshing, and the air seems to be full of heavy sound as of distant thunder. I hear Mr. Stevens speak from time to time of traversing lands patented from 1666 to 1678 by Daniel Selby, Colonel Wallop, Colonel Littleton and Major Edward Robins. Suddenly the beautiful silver bay opens before us, and the scene enchants me.

Mr. Makemie is equally moved. He loves the seashore and its voices, and I think we saw the sparkle of the waves of Lough Swilly in his face that bright day. My father says that no one born beside the sea ever loosens from the embrace of its great arms about the heart

Night beside the waters, the deep roll of the breakers booming along the beaches of Assateague. Mr. Stevens patented a part of its southern end and is well known in these parts. He has no difficulty in securing hospitable entertainment and the use of a boat for our expedition. Everywhere Mr. Makemie is more careful in inquiring for Presbyterians than for food and comfort.

Just as the rising sun shines over the beaches, filling the bay with millions of dancing diamonds, we embark upon our pinnace with the prow northward. Beneath us, in their many native coves, we see the fat oysters "laying on the ground as thick as stones," as said John Pory in his gay picture of the colonists' first month in Virginia in 1607—perhaps the oldest mention of the oyster in American history. Chingoteague and Pope's islands are left to the south of us. Gliding by many low green islands or shining stretches of sand, occasionally we touch at points on the mainlands in which these patentees are interested, and where Mr. Makemie would hunt for Presbyterians—beautiful indentations of seaboard, graceful little crystal lagoons. Indian wigwams alternate more frequently than the cabins of the whites, and their canoes are often seen fishing on the clam-banks

Toward evening a point of land seems to approach from the north, cleaving in twain the expanse of waters. Gradually it grows into a low emerald promontory clad in woodland, and not far from its southern cape we notice a residence shaded by native groves, with children playing about the yard. Thither we move and disembark—a romantic spot for a home, the New Haven, or Sinepuxent, Bay on the east, with the great ocean beyond; the Newport Bay on the west.

Our county officers know the proprietor—Mr. Edward Wale, a resident of our own part of the county until 1679, Judge Stevens having there married him to Miss Elizabeth Ratcliff on the 29th of January,

1669. He and his brother-in-law, Charles Ratcliff, patented twenty-two hundred acres on this end of "the neck" in 1679, and divided it between them in 1681. Seven children, ages varying from fifteen years to two—little Sinepuxoners, as their father calls them—are making South Point ring with childhood's gladness.

We are warmly welcomed. The colonists are always glad to see new guests—perhaps especially so in this region, since our own communication with other parts of the world is more frequent. And is there not something in the very air to inspire to kindliness? A large drum-fish upon the supper-table regales appetites sharpened by the fresh atmosphere breathed all day and still blowing about us.

My attention is attracted from everything else to an old gentleman whom we have not seen until we meet him at the table. He seems much worn with age and care. Certainly seventy years old, but there is a stateliness and dignity about him which is very marked. He is habited in a faded costume of the days of the Protector and bears himself with a military air, reminding us of the soldiers of England. His face and forehead are full of intelligence, and his eye now and then glows with flashes almost electric. He looks like a man of grand experiences—one used to command.

When presented to this Mr. Middleton, we were received by him with a silent bow. I could not help watching him, and, though apparently taking but little notice of us or of the conversation, there were occasional flashes of the eye which showed that we were not unobserved. Finally I saw that grand old

7

face beam with expression and the soul within seem
to arouse like a lion from sleep. Mr Makemie had
just said

"It is the superlative excellency of the Christian religion,
and a demonstration of the fulness of the Scriptures, that there
are duties for all ranks and stations prescribed and taught there;
for the sins incident to all degrees and ranks of men and women,
are detected and reproved there. Magistrates and rulers in the
government and state, have the work cut out to their hands and
are limited and bounded by the Supreme Law of an Universal
Sovereign, to whom the greatest of them must be accountable.
The subject oweth subjection, loyalty and obedience to his just
and lawful commands, for he is the minister of God for good;
and this is due by virtue of a divine command and appointment.
But if he exceeds his power and require anything sinful and repugnant to the laws of God, the Apostle's rule is still observable:
God is to be obeyed rather than man." *

It was pleasant to witness the admiration with which
the old man was regarding our youthful minister. I
thought he was on the point of speaking—the fire
blazing into words; but it was suppressed, and he
was silent. Did Mr. Wale appear uneasy, appre-
hensive? The topic was certainly soon changed.

The old man continued to observe Mr. Makemie
very closely. As we passed from the table he took
our minister's arm and asked him if he were a clergyman of the Church of England; then how long he
had been in America; and then, again, something
about the present Stuart king.

Who was this remarkable man, here upon this obscure neck of land? The rough Western world is
not a place for the aged, unless driven from European
homes by the tyranny that spares not old or young.
Even after I went to bed his impressive bearing re-

* Makemie's New York sermon.

mained with me like a presence. I dreamed of him, my vision mixing him up strangely with ancient heroes who seemed to come and go among phantom islands and estuaries of a coast like this. Frequently I was startled into wide wakefulness by the shock of battle and the flight and pursuit of armies. The roar of the surf along the beach continued the cannonading of my dream.

Our judge and sheriff says there is a mystery connected with the old man which no one can explain, that he came from Virginia into the province about the time Mr. Wale moved from the Pocomoke settlements up to Sinepuxent, and that he had kept aloof from the colonists, evidently avoiding all familiarity. This trip has given me another romance, at which sister Martha enjoyed her usual smile. But I knew that this rude Western wilderness has been the asylum of many a noble exile.

Sailing on up the eastern fork of the bay next morning, and passing along the tract of land called " Goshen," patented by Mr. Makemie's friend Colonel Jenkins, in one of its green groves bordered by its white fringe of sand we see a little town of the aborigines, their canoes strowing the banks. A larger cabin indicates the palace of majesty, and, veering our course nearer, we see Queen Weocomoconus sitting in state at the door and her son Knusonum at her side with the plumes of the sea-gull in his hair. Her leading men approach the shore, making their trade-signs and inviting us closer. We hear one of them speaking intelligible English and offering for sale fancy shells (*peake* and *roenoke*) and the luxurious soft crabs. We made some purchases, and I secured

from Robin, the interpreter, the names of other leading men of the tribe—Wasposson, Tanguawton,
Squifortum, Young Robin and Rintaughton (24).

The crabs were cooked, and we enjoyed a feast
worthy of royalty, wishing long life to Queen Weocomoconus and centuries of prosperous growth to these
rare delicacies of her dominions.

Passing the estate called " Neighborhood," we come
to the tract of two thousand acres owned by Judge
Stevens, patented by him, under the name of " Carmel," in the year 1679. The bay here narrows into
what is called "The Thoroughfare," and, looking
northward, we see it widening and then narrowing
up to the country claimed by William Penn. Above
and below, the water-view is beautiful. To this point
the judge had come to see after the interests of his
lands. Horses are obtained, the pinnace going back
to meet us at the head of Newport Bay, with orders
to stop on the way and send a guide from the Indian
town.

Wasposson came promptly, refusing any horse and
keeping pace with us on a long quick trot westward
through the woods and over the heads of streams.
Mr. Ambrose White had joined us, coming from his
estate called " Happy Entrance," north of St. Martin's
River, owned by him through Mr. Stevens since 1679.
The meeting with these widely-scattered Presbyterians
was delightful The sight of a godly minister of their
own in these far wilds melted their souls to thankful-
ness and their eyes to tears. Together we went on to
Kelsey Hill—another of Mr. Stevens's tracts, taken
up but a year ago—thence on a mile farther to his
land called " Burley," of three hundred acres, granted

him in 1677 (25). Coyes's Folly, belonging to Mr. Wale, lies to the north, and Mount Pleasant between the two. On the Burley tract a gentle quiet hill covered with venerable oaks and gemmed with wild-flowers, offered a quiet resting-place for our midday repast.

There we sat during the hour of noon, while Mr. Makemie lined the twenty-third psalm from dear old Rouse, and we sang together:

> "The Lord's my Shepherd, I'll not want;
> 　he makes me down to lie
> In pastures green; he leadeth me
> 　the quiet waters by.
> My soul he doth restore again,
> 　and me to walk doth make
> Within the paths of righteousness,
> 　ev'n for his own name's sake.
> Goodness and mercy all my life
> 　shall surely follow me,
> And in God's house for evermore
> 　my dwelling-place shall be."

We went on southward to Sheriff White's lands of fifteen hundred acres—a tract granted to Colonel Stevens in 1668 and conveyed to Mr. White in 1681. In memory of the judge's native county in England, it took the name of "Buckingham." Crossing a "branch" and ascending another hill, some one said,

"While making these land-surveys, why not watch out for the sites patented in the counsels of the Almighty for churches yet to be?"

I was bold enough to say,

"Why not just here, upon grounds taken up by one who represents so well the genius of Maryland in her tolerance of all religions?"

As we were soon to part from Mr. Ambrose White,

it was proposed to hold a little season of prayer. I
well remember Mr. Makemie's paraphrase of the divine
promise :

"I will show the salvation of God. That is, I will discover
and manifest this salvation which was hid and concealed from
ages and the past generations ; yea, even from the wise and
prudent, and will shew it unto babes Yea, which is more, I will
particularly and in a more special manner instruct and direct
you, by my word and Spirit, effectually and savingly, to this
necessary and great salvation. But more than all this is implied
in the promise ; I will most freely and fully give, impart, bestow
upon and apply this salvation unto you, Unspeakable promise !
Unparalleled blessing ! Desired by most, obtained by few, and
fully known by none but such as are swallowed up in the eternal
enjoyment thereof." *

The voices of the pines seemed hushed while our
minister led us to the throne of grace and dedicated
these territories anew to the God that made them.
Wasposson looked on in silence. Then we rode on
eastward, through the length of the Buckingham
plantation, down to Newport Creek, where our pinnace was awaiting us (26).

At South Point we touched again, to put Wasposson
on shore and exchange salutations with our late host.
In one of the denser hummocks I saw the venerable
man walking thoughtfully, erect and slow ; but if he
noticed us at all, it was only to retire farther into the
recesses of the grove What is the secret of this life
buried here amid the shadows of the New World ?

This was only one of many journeys of Mr. Makemie to seek and cheer the scattered sheep of the
Good Shepherd—now up the Pocomoke, now down to
the Annamessex, now over to the Monokin, now on
beyond to the Wicomico. He is awake to everything

* Makemie's New York sermon

that concerns the needs of the colonists. Other Presbyterian ministers have been upon this continent before —have come and gone. Mr. Makemie has cast his lot with these brave exiles for life, resolved to become an American

And yet we are uneasy. The persecutions of his friends in Europe hang heavily upon his heart, every letter that crosses the ocean showing their condition to be worse, the cry of their afflictions louder. Their churches are closed, their lives in danger; the entire Presbytery of Laggan are pursued with such implacable fury that a majority of the ministers of Donegal and Derry have made known to the Presbytery of Antrim their intention of coming to America "because of persecutions and general poverty abounding in these parts, and on account of their straits and little or no access to their ministry." * Some have fled to Scotland, only to find the situation worse. There the year has opened with four judicial murders, and the South and the West flow with blood.† This year is called by preeminence "the killing-time." It is difficult to imagine how malignity and cruelty can reach a wilder riot.

Mr. Makemie is burdened with these increasing horrors, and longs to find homes to which he may invite the sufferers. Here there is too great poverty among the Presbyterians to support even one minister. He refuses to contract for any stipulated salary, accepting only voluntary offerings from those whom he knows to be able to give.‡ He is evidently purposing to visit the other colonies and see if there may not be wider fields and a surer support for the

---

* Reid, ii. 341.   † Wodrow, iv., chap. viii.
‡ Makemie's *Answer to Keith.*

refugees. My father says he has a mind and heart comprehensive enough to embrace the continent in his plans. But what shall *we* now do without the bread of life from his lips? How lonely the Eastern Shore without him!

This year our Assembly at St. Mary's have again been at work upon the towns, changing the one on Wicomico River—of which the space was too limited —to a point "at or near a parcel of land in that river on the land which was formerly William Wright's." Another has been located "at or near Tipquin, south side of the Nanticoke," and still another "at some convenient place between the going in of Selby's Bay and Cornelius Jones's land in Assateague Bay on the seaboard side."* The legislature seems to expect that our county will be crowded with cities some day and full of the world's commerce. Already in the autumn and early winter the little sloops and ketches are seen threading the many streams, trafficking for tobacco, furs and pork, and bringing to the plantation-stores goods from Europe, New England and the West Indies.

Mr. Makemie watches all these public movements carefully, regarding them not only from a commercial but a missionary standpoint. He says:

" In remote and scattered settlements we can never enjoy so fully, frequently and certainly those privileges and opportunities as us to be had in all Christian towns and cities. For by reason of bad weather or other accidents, ministers are prevented and people are hindered to attend and so disappoint one another. But in towns congregations are never wanting and children and servants never are without opportunity of hearing, who cannot travel many miles to hear and be catechised."

*Law of the province for 1684

It is pleasant to note Mr. Makemie's interest in the religious culture of children and servants. The catechising of Scotland and Ulster he longs to see transplanted to American soil. He continues:

"It is a melancholy consideration how many came very ignorant of religion to the plantations and by removing to remote settlements have been neglected by others and, careless of themselves, continue grossly ignorant of many necessary parts of the Christian religion. And many natives, born in ignorant families, and by distance, seldom hear a sermon." *

Mr. Makemie is gathering the people at every available centre, encouraging and compacting them for permanent organization. The boundary-troubles with Mr. Penn take Lord Baltimore to Europe this year, and he appoints Colonel Stevens one of his deputy lieutenants. This promotion secures the judge still wider influence and gives greater prominence to the plantation and the new town. The wealth and character of Colonel Jenkins, Sheriff White and others in that section, will help to make Rehoboth the leading church—the Mecca—of Presbyterianism.

The sweet Maryland springtime is all about us—the woods glad with blossoms, the air pulsating with bird-songs. The river is strewn with boats, the horse-roads with riders. The breezes come all the way from the salt waters, gathering the balms of the forests in their censers.

> "The gummy Pine
> Does cheerful with unsully'd verdure shine;
> The Dogwood flowers assume a snowy white,
> The Maple blushing gratifies the light;
> No verdant leaves the lovely Red Bud grace,
> Carnation blossoms now supply their Place;

* Makemie's *Plain and Friendly Perswasive.*

The Sassafras unfolds its fragrant Bloom,
The Vine affords an exquisite Perfume ;
These grateful Scents wide wafting through the air
The swelling Sense with balmy Odors cheer.
And now the birds sweet singing stretch their Throats
And in one choir unite their various Notes ;
Nor yet unpleasing is the Turtle's voice
Though he complains while other Birds rejoice.
These vernal Joys all restless thoughts controul
And gently soothing calm the troubled soul " (27).

There *are* troubled souls, for we cannot forget that the time has come at last and our minister is going away. " Only for a while," says the deputy lieutenant, who seems determined to cheer us. " Only for a while," says my father, whose trust in God never fails. The faith of some of us is not so strong, for we remember the former months of waiting, and are sad.

The interest of the occasion is intensified by the last administration of both sacraments before our minister leaves us. While the Quakers reject and denounce the two holy ordinances as copied from Rome, and while our friends can celebrate them in Europe only at the risk of having their own blood mingled with the water and the wine, it is a blessed boon for these ends of the earth to be able to sit around the table of our Lord without molestation, and to bring the children of the covenant and offer them to Jesus through the appointed symbol.

The woods-paths echo with the prattle of the Maryland babies. Are these to be the founders of a new empire ? Yes ; the household covenant is taking root —the promises sure to a thousand generations. What fantastic garbs ! What wise little faces ! and how important these pioneers of millions yet to be! Mr. Makemie said :

"It is the same baptism the disciples and apostles performed in all and every church where they preached the gospel according to that last command of our Lord's immediately before his ascension—'Go teach and baptize all nations,' and 'Lo, I am with you alway.'

"Three things are observable in this text. First, That teaching of nations, yea, all nations, by external means and instruments is a standing and perpetual ordinance in the Church of Christ to the end of the world. Second, That as many as are called ministers of the gospel are also commissionated to baptize also—'Go teach all nations, baptizing them.' Third, That water baptism or the external ordinance, is that enjoined or commanded in the words, and not the baptism with the Holy Ghost and with fire. For it is enjoined to mere men who can do no more than John could do who professed he baptized with water. The outward mean, ordinance and administration was from John; and the fruit, efficacy and blessing was from Jesus Christ. It is bold impudence and arrogant presumption for any to pretend to baptize with the Holy Ghost and with fire, which is Christ's peculiar work and prerogative."

Rejecting and assailing all outward rites, the disciples of John Fox claim to confer the spiritual baptism. Our minister proceeded ·

"We who use the outward mean, instrument and ordinance, may be—through the blessing of God and efficacious presence of Christ's Spirit—and undoubtedly are, made instruments of the inward grace, life and advantage of that ordinance. But how those can be instruments of baptizing spiritually who are opposite to and ridicule the outward ordinance which is the only proper means and instrument of God's own appointment, I can not resolve unless they take God's place, by working without means and contrary to means; or unless they imagine to work effects by unsuitable causes and attain an end by improper means. As if a man intend to merchandize by laboring in the ground, or intend for Europe from America and yet steer to the South, or by planting tobacco to imagine to reap corn." *

* Makemie's *Answer to Keith.*

The young Marylanders are brought forward, and out of a bowl of clear water taken from the Pocomoke, the beautiful symbol falls upon their infant brows. I hear the names of two little boys called for the deputy lieutenant—Stevens White and William Stevens Howard, the former a nephew of our friend, and the latter a son of his nearest neighbor.*

After a precious sermon of two hours' length—only too short to those who know not when they may hear another—the Supper of our Lord is spread, and the communicants, their tokens in hand, gather about the table. We thought of fellow-communicants in the dens and caves of the Old World. It is sad that, while Prelacy would there wrest it from them by sword and duress vile, fanaticism in this free land should depreciate and despise the holy rite.

" Christian experience witnesseth against them," said Mr. Makemie, " and confutes all their quibbling arguments and sophistical quirks."

Our minister seldom speaks of himself We watch for any word throwing light upon the inner life of the man—this new voice crying in the wilderness. Many hearts responded when he said,

" My own experience of the grace, blessing and benefits of this great, special, and solemn ordinance, shall be an unanswerable argument to me against all heretics in the world." †

The delightful day ended, and soon we awoke to the fact that he was gone—gone to Virginia and the Carolinas. A little group of us sit in the graveyard of the Rehoboth plantation, as if mourning at the grave of

* Babes of that day : Somerset records.
† Extracts from *Answer to Keith.*

our Presbyterian hopes Yonder lies the dust of the brother of the judge, yonder the little babe Frances White, buried last year, and other sleepers are all around us. Here we sit—Peggy, the blue-eyed maid of Ulster; Mary, the rosy Scotch lassie; Margaret, the soft-toned singer of the Vincennes; Naomi, the young Virginia beauty—and we talk together of the planted vine, and of the frost which has fallen to nip it even in the bright Maryland springtime. Shall we who have come from so many lands sleep together in these Western graveyards, dust to dust, and no minister to offer a prayer at the bedside and at the burial ? The hope of our Presbyterian colonists seems to have been as frail as the little Frances lying beneath the hillock at our feet, dying within a year of her birth.

These thoughts are too gloomy. We go together and look at the vine, and we see that it has taken root deeply and shows no signs of blight. The label is still on it—" 1683." We know that there are offshoots from it at Snow Hill and on the Monokin and on the Wicomico.

After a while there came news from Mr. Makemie. He had gone down the great bay to Elizabeth River, and there preached to a mixed congregation of Dissenters, composed of Independents and Presbyterians, who lost their minister by death last year. Congregationalism had found an early home in Virginia, but it soon became one of storms Henry Jacob, who established the first Independent church in England, came over to Virginia in 1624 to preach to his coreligionists, and died there. Their numbers increased in Nansemond county and on Elizabeth River, until, in 1643, a petition for ministers was sent to Boston

signed by seventy-four names. Among the rest was
that of Captain Daniel Gookins, a man prominent in
Virginia, Maryland, and New England history. Three
ministers were sent, but they were discountenanced by
the government. The chaplain, Rev. Thomas Harrison, incited the opposition, and the three ministers
finally departed. Then came the Indian massacre in
April, 1644, and under that shock Harrison himself,
taking it as a judgment of God for sin, repented of his
bigotry, became a Nonconformist and preached to the
Independents in Nansemond and at Elizabeth River.
In 1648 he states that his church numbers one hundred and eighteen communicants, and that nearly a
thousand persons sympathize with their order of worship. But Governor Berkeley is aroused, secures an
act of Assembly prohibiting all worship except with
the use of the Prayer-book, and orders Harrison to
leave Virginia. The Puritans are pursued with rigor,
until they contract with Lord Baltimore for liberty of
conscience, and during these years (1648, 1649) mostly remove to Maryland.*

Remnants of these former churches Mr. Makemie
finds about Elizabeth River Their late minister was
from Ireland. They would have Mr. Makemie to stay,
but he perseveres in his purpose, and presses on to
North Carolina. Thence he embarks for the Southern province, but is caught in a storm and driven
back northward. God did not mean that he should
get so far away from us. The boisterous wind forced
the laboring bark far up along the Maryland beaches,
as if to remind him of those he had left behind. But
I will let him tell it in his own words·

* Neill's *Terra Mariæ*, p. 74, etc ; *Founders of Maryland*, p. 109, etc.

" REVEREND AND DEAR BROTHER   I wrote to you, though
unacquainted, by Mr. Lamb, from North Carolina, of my de-
signe for Ashley River, South Carolina, which I was so forward
in attempting that I engaged in a voyage and went to sea in the
month of May, but God in his providence saw fit I should not
see it at the time, for we were tosst upon the coast by contrary
winds, and to the North as far as Delaware Bay, so that, falling
short in our provisions, we were necessitated, after several essays
to the South, to Virginia, and, in the meanwhile, Colonel Anthony Lawson and other inhabitants of the parish of Lynnhaven,
in lower Norfolk county (who had a dissenting minister from
Ireland, until the Lord was pleased to remove him by death in
August last, among whom I preached before I went to the
South, in coming from Maryland, against their earnest impor-
tunity), coming so pertinently in the place of our landing for
water, prevailed with me to stay this season ; which the more
easily overcame me, considering the season of the year and the
little encouragement from Carolina, from the sure information I
have had.   But for the satisfaction of my friends in Ireland,
whom I design to be very cautious in inviting to any place in
America I have yet seen, I have sent one of our number to acquaint me further concerning the place.   I am here assured of
liberty and other encouragements, resolving to submit myself to
the sovereign providence of God, who has been pleased so unexpectedly to drive me back to this poor, desolate people, among
whom I design to continue till God in his providence determine
otherwise concerning me.

" I have presumed a second before I can hear how acceptable
my first has been   I hope this will prevent your writing to Ashley River, and determine your resolution to direct your letters to
Colonel Anthony Lawson, at the Eastern Branch of Elizabeth
River.   I expect if you have an opportunity of writing to Mr.
John Hart, you will acquaint him concerning me ; which, with
your prayers, will oblige him who is your dear and affectionate
brother in the Gospel of our Lord Jesus" (28).

So speaks the brave pioneer, and so speaks his
theology. To him there is no chance in the blowing
of the winds or the veering of the vessel. His love
is yet warm and considerate for his "friends" in Ireland,
but no less so for the "poor, desolate" Christians in

America. He wants still to be remembered by Mr. Hart of Derry, and he is stretching forth the hand of Christian affection to Increase Mather, the foremost man of New England.

And now, while we mourn and are disconsolate, and while Mr. Makemie shrinks from recommending to the ministry of Ulster that they shall face upon our destitute shores the hardships which he himself endures, the same sovereign God whom he serves has been preparing better things for us than the strongest faith had dreamed.

Shall I ever forget the hour? We had been spending the day in colonial social fashion at the house of Colonel Jenkins, on the farm just below the new Rehoboth town. The colonel and the attractive Mistress Mary are greatly in love with Mr. Makemie, and are still deploring his loss. For an hour we had been watching a merchant-vessel working her way up the curves of the river. We walked down to the shore, launched the little boat and went out to visit the trader—a common habit along these streams. They drop anchor opposite the town—now a legal place of import—and await our coming. Passing on board, we find ourselves among a number of immigrants and are examining some of the silks, Hollands, serges and broadcloths,* when I catch the names "Davis," "Wilson," "Trail." They are inquiring for the home of Colonel Stevens. The third name specially attracts my attention because of what I have recorded of the persecutions of Mr. William Trail in Ireland. Was this a relative of his?

I saw a man of noticeable presence, of over forty

* Alsop's *Character of the Province of Maryland*, p 68.

years of age— But I need not protract the recital. This was William Trail himself, the incarcerated clerk of the Presbytery of Laggan—the brave man who had stood before Ormond and the chancellor and the archbishop in the castle of Dublin—now sent of God to those who are sighing for the bread of life on our Eastern shore. The hero of our dreams is here— here to preach the gospel for which he has suffered bonds! And here, too, are these others, the Master sending us three of his heralds in the footsteps of our county's first evangelist (29). We escort them ashore and see them safely upon the Maryland soil. Widely flies the news with the wings of the wind, and again the Presbyterian heart is thrilled. Three ministers at Rehoboth next Sabbath !

That Sabbath was indeed an high day. Rouse's psalm arose :

> "I joy'd when to the house of God
> ' Go up,' they said to me ;
> Jerusalem, within thy gates
> our feet shall standing be."

Certainly it looks as if God means that our Church shall be firmly planted in the Western world, and that *just here* is to be the favored centre from which its doctrines are to radiate abroad.

That night I heard my father quoting the strict rules for ordination adopted by the Church in Ireland in 1672:

"After the intrant hath given distinct and positive answers to the questions usually proposed for showing his soundness in the faith and adhering to the truth professed in the Reformed Churches against Popery, Arminianism, Prelacy, Erastianism,

8

Independency, and whatever else is contrary to sound doctrine and the power of godliness."

I know of what my father was thinking. Mr. Trail had been ordained over the congregation at Lifford the very year those rules were adopted. God is ordering that the pure seed sown by Makemie shall be watered and cultured by safe hands—by one of the very men who had trained Makemie for the sacred office.

This year of momentous events went out with a marriage performed by our new minister. Mr. Davis has already officiated in a like ceremony since his arrival in the province.

Christmas has come and gone, and the colonists are still in the midst of the holidays, which they protract over New Year's. The big logs of oak and hickory are prepared for the large fireplaces; the nuts have been gathered and stored as carefully as the squirrels hoard them; the yellow pones are yellower than ever; the cider has been nicely boiled and kept untapped till now;* the hominy-mortar has been busy, and the largest pot is full, and hunters have been to the woods and made sure of the venison hams; and most of us are rejoicing in our new shoes and gowns.

During the cold season there is but little work. Even the servants are almost free. As said George Alsop eighteen years ago:

" In the Winter time, which lasteth three months, they do little or no work or imployment, save cutting of wood to make good fires to sit by ; unless their Ingenuity will prompt them to hunt the Deer or Bear or recreate themselves in Fowling, to slaughter Swans, Geese and Turkeys (which this country affords in a most plentifull manner) For every servant has a Gun, Powder and

* Boiled cider   Somerset records.

Shot allowed him, to sport him withall on all Holidayes and leasurable time, if he be capable of using it or be willing to learn."

During Christmas week this exemption from labor is enjoyed by all classes. On Friday the 26th of December, came the marriage—Mr. William Banes to Miss Anne Phesey. The cabin is full of guests, some sitting on beds, some on puncheons split from trees, some standing in the corners. The broad chimney, half across the end of the house, roars with the great Yule-logs. The cold blasts out-doors help to make the flames brisker and louder. Somerset has already begun the manufacture of woolen goods,* our county leading the continent. Here, to-night, we see these fabrics worn by the gay company and the bride and groom—the padded coats and short-clothes, the fanciful gowns and striped petticoats—for our weavers and cordwainers and the busy needles have been preparing for the wedding for many weeks.

The banns had been duly published at the court-house door, and soon the broad Scotch accents of Mr. Trail pronounced them husband and wife.

There is nothing in this new clime to stop the story of love, and hearts are wooed and won among the whisperings of the pine trees as sweetly as by the wells of Laban.

* *Provincial Records*, McMahon, p. 275.

CHAPTER VI.

A. D. 1685.

"The true Christian, in all states of life, whether in prosperity or adversity, in fulness or in want, in sickness or in health, in suffering or liberty, under reproaches or in good report, under enjoyment or want of religious privileges; is furnished with graces answerable, and exercises them suitably and agreeably—so as his whole life should shine with them as a light in a dark place."—MAKEMIE.

MR. TRAIL and his wife, Mistress Elinor, have been with us to make some purchases at one of our plantation-stores. Our guests are much amused at our currency. The new minister is a man of delightful humor—as was shown at his examination in Dublin Castle—and he sees the comical side of colonial life readily. He has heard the nauseous tobacco-plant called the meat, drink, clothing and money of the province,* and he enjoyed seeing us make our various purchases, some of which, unknown to him, were for his own cabin-home.

Let me preserve some of the items of our bill and the prices, paid in pounds of tobacco:

	Lbs.
4 ounces thread	20
6 doz. glass buttons	25
2 pair stockings	40
1 pair man's shoes	45
1 pair gloves	15

* British Empire in America, i. 343.

		Lbs
3 combs	. . . .	24
1 pair woman's shoes	. . . .	35
1 pair woman's shoes	. . . .	60
3 hats	. . . .	150
4 pair tongs	. . . .	24
16 yds. linen	. . . .	400
1 tin sass pan	. . . .	12
1 looking glass	. . . .	5
1 knife	. . . .	10
2 hanks thread	. . . .	16
Large ivory comb	. . . .	30
1 pound candle wick	. . . .	20
1½ yard broad ribbon	. . . .	30
1 ell broad linen	. . . .	30

"Yes, meat and drink indeed," said Mr. Trail as we paid for these further articles:

		Lbs
24 eggs	. . . .	6
1 bushel wheat	. . . .	30
1 large quarter mutton	. . . .	40
12 pounds salted beef	. . . .	12
1 turkey cock	. . . .	30
2 turkey hens	. . . .	14
1 gallon rum	. . . .	40 *

Taxes are assessed in tobacco; Colonel Stevens's salary is paid in tobacco; our planters around Rehoboth, Monokin and Snow Hill are raising subscriptions for Mr. Trail, Mr. Wilson and Mr. Davis in tobacco.

Mr. Trail tells us that early in the century Pope Urban VIII. fulminated the anathemas of the Church against the potent American weed, and that the present pope, Innocent XI., is doing the same. In Russia the noses of smokers have been cut off by law, and in Turkey, under Sultan Amuret, their heads. In his

---

* Actual bills from Somerset records of 1685, 1686 and 1687

Counterblast to Tobacco—one of the most sensible
things that ever emanated from a Stuart king—James
I. denounced its use as "a custom loathsome to the
eye, hateful to the nose, harmful to the brain, dangerous to the lungs, and, in the black stinking fumes
thereof, nearest resembling the horrible Stygian smoke
of the pit that is bottomless."

The conquering plant grows on, still gaining upon
the world, defying the authority of king and sultan
and czar and pope, and wielding over its enslaved subjects a power as despotic as theirs. To prevent the
culture of this plant from crowding out necessary
staples, our law compels every planter of tobacco to
till at least two acres of corn. This wise policy is
making our province the granary of New England.

We are rather glad when the planting-time has
come, the winter passed away; for, with all help of
Somerset woolens and furs, we cannot keep from
shivering sometimes in our unheated churches. Gathering early from our boats and horses at the nearest
houses, where the great fires are prepared on purpose,
we thaw snugly through and prepare to defy the winds
that howl over the forests and whistle around the log
meeting-houses for entrance. Here and there the im-
portunate blast comes in stinging. We young people
can only crowd closer together or nestle to the side of
our mothers

The staunch, hardy Presbyterian fathers sit the long
service through unmoved by the cold, unconscious of
discomfort, invulnerable. Some of these have worshiped in open moors or freezing glens, in rain and
storm, finding the rigors of the elements more merciful than the hatred of Sharp and Claverhouse. In

comparison, the severest blasts of Pocomoke, Monokin and Wicomico are mild and full of the love of God.

During these spring months there has come to us important news from across the sea, an earless, emaciated, impoverished exile bringing the tidings and the exemplification. In Galloway he has seen the bodies of the six men who were shot for no crime but prayer. He was not far away when a sick man was dragged from his bed and butchered at his own door in the presence of his family. Himself hunted down, refusing to take the hated oath, thrown into the crowded Bass, the barbarous shears of the executioner cutting his ears close to his head, life spared only on condition of banishment and slavery, —he has been driven to our shores and sits with us in our little church. How kindly our ministers grasp the hand of these persecuted countrymen! We are told that the brutal acts of the council last year were instigated and approved by proclamations from the Palace in London.*

In a day or two comes other news. On Sabbath, the 1st of February, while these horrors are at their height in the North, the profligate Charles is reveling in luxury and sin. Says an eye-witness:

"I can never forget the inexpressible luxury and profaneness, gaming and all dissoluteness, and as it were total forgetfulness of God (it being Sunday evening) which this day sinnight I was witness of; the King sitting and toying with his concubines, Portsmouth, Cleveland, Mazarine, etc., a French boy singing love songs in that glorious gallery; whilst about twenty of the

* See Wodrow, iv. 182, etc. The "Bass"—often mentioned in these days—was the state-prison of the Bass Rock, off the eastern coast of Scotland.

great courtiers and other dissolute persons were at basset round
a large table, a bank of at least two thousand in gold before
them, upon which two gentlemen who were with me made re-
flections with astonishment. Six days after, all was in the dust."[*]

Such were the Sabbaths in the palace while the
solemn old Presbyterian Sabbaths were made heret-
ical and treasonable. On Monday the king was taken
very ill, and on Friday, at noon, he passed to the
judgment-bar of God There are reports that he
was poisoned Much is said about a new and famous American remedy administered to him—the
noted "Jesuit's powder," which some physicians declare a medicine fit only for kings.[†] At length the
fact is established that this base monarch, who has
so long persecuted the Nonconformists in his three
kingdoms because of his pretended zeal for the Church
of England, was all the time a Papist at heart. In dying he refused to receive the sacrament from any but
the hands of a Romish priest.[‡]

Well may Mr. Makemie say of the schemes of
Popery:

" It deserves to be bewailed that in all their Jesuitical intrigues
and evil designs, they soon found too many Protestant tools un-
advisedly to concur with such sworn enemies of the Reformation."[§]

Mr. Trail has been telling us of the sufferings of his
father, one of the first Scotchmen to feel the ingratitude and treachery of Charles after the Restoration
The Rev. Robert Trail had opposed the schemes of
Cromwell, had been besieged in the castle of Edinburgh, had been wounded while defending the rights

---

* Evelyn's *Diary*, p. 467   † Quinine.   Evelyn's *Diary*, p 559
‡ Macaulay, i. 342   § Makemie's *Truths in a True Light*.

of Charles II., and had co-operated zealously with the Presbyterians of Scotland in bringing him back to the throne. In 1660, when the future course of Charles in forgetting all his pledges and his benefactors began to be foreshadowed, the father of our pastor committed the grievous offence of uniting in a respectful address to the king, reminding him of his promises and pleading for the rights of the Church. For this he and others were thrown into prison. From that prison his fellow-sufferer James Guthrie was never released until released by martyrdom. Then began that flow of blood not yet ceased.

In 1661, Robert Trail was brought before Parliament and made an eloquent defence, declaring what he had endured for the king, vindicating his loyalty, but asserting fearlessly the liberties of the country and of the Church. Our Mr. Trail, the eldest son of the accused, was then just twenty-one years old, a graduate of the university three years before, and himself looking forward to the dangerous office of the gospel ministry. Thus had he reached manhood, surrounded by the solicitudes of the Edinburgh parish for their pastor's safety and sharing the anxieties of mother and children for the life of husband and father.

Sent back to prison from that brave defence, about a fortnight after Mr. Guthrie had been led out to execution, the father wrote:

"We are waiting from day to day what men will do with us; we are expecting banishment at the best, but our sentence must proceed from the Lord; and whatsoever it be, it shall be good as from him, and whithersoever he shall send us, he will be with us and shall let us know that the earth is his and the fullness thereof."

He was liberated for a while, but sent away from his church in Edinburgh. Again, for expounding Scripture at family worship, he was arrested and banished from the kingdom at sixty years of age. Afterward he returned from Holland and laid his bones in his native land.*

Our minister has a younger brother, Robert, also a sufferer from the tyranny of the deceased king. Because of the obstacles in Scotland, William and Robert went to London for licensure in 1670. Eight years ago a tool of the government was paid a large reward for arresting the brother, charged with preaching at conventicles, and he was brought before the council. Standing firmly upon the rights of conscience, he was sent to the prison of the Bass. Thus have this godly family been pursued and wronged. All these things interest us here, showing of what stock has come our Eastern-Shore Presbyterianism.

And now the wicked king is gone to his reward! The victims of his cruelty are around us. In view of all that has come since, we think in sadness of the prayer of Mr. Robert Trail before Parliament twenty-four years ago:

" That he who is set over men may be just, ruling in the fear of God; that his reign may be long and prosperous and a blessing to these lands; that when he shall have fulfilled his days and laid by his earthly crown, he may receive a greater and better which fadeth not away but is eternal in the heavens."

With no mean pride the exiled son stood upon the banks of our little river and told of the staunch old champion of the Covenant. The king too had taken that Covenant. We felt the grandeur of character of

* See Wodrow, i., *passim.*

the man of God towering far above faithless royalty. Just from the burial of Charles II., one writes in England· "He is soon forgotten after all his vanity."*

Now another Stuart is on the throne Both Nonconformists and Conformists have reason to await the future with apprehension. There was no Bible at the coronation. For the first time in one hundred and twenty-seven years the rites of the Church of Rome have been publicly paraded at Westminster. James II. is a Papist undisguised. Yet the High Tories and Churchmen are playing the sycophant. The Papists in our province are said to be much elated. This will not lessen the feeling against them among the preponderating Protestant elements. It is said that the commercial Company of Maryland Merchants in London have obsequiously pledged themselves to pay the customs exacted by the illegal edict of the new king.†

In our own circle we have had a death and burial of some note. Mr. John White, a cousin and brother-in-law of Colonel Stevens, has passed away, and now lies in the graveyard near the residence of the deputy lieutenant. Mr. White was one of the original county judges appointed at the time of its organization. He was high sheriff when he died. Of course there was a great concourse at the funeral. The Maryland breezes sighed along the river-banks as if in sympathy with the widow and fatherless. My sister and I mingled our tears with the weeping daughters, Tabitha, Priscilla and Sarah. These burials are not so dreary as before the ministers came.‡

* Evelyn's *Diary*, February 14.   † Macaulay, i. 371, 374, etc.

‡ Date of death, place of burial, family, etc., of White, from the Somerset records.

We have heard from Mr. Makemie; he is still preaching at Elizabeth River. Our loss was their gain, and he knows that we now no longer need him. Poor and far from libraries, he is getting his supply of books from distant New England. These sometimes miscarry. He is corresponding with God's ministers, from South Carolina to Massachusetts. On the 22d of July he writes to Increase Mather:

" HONOURED SIR · Yours I received by Mr. Hallet with three books, and am not a little concerned that those sent to Ashley River were miscarried, for which I hope it will give no offence to declare my willingness to satisfy ; for there is no reason they should be lost to you, and far less that the gift should be [word illegible], for which I own myself your debtor. And assure yourself if you have any friend in Virginia, to find me ready to receive your commands. I have wrote to Mr. Wardrope, and beg you be pleased to order the safe conveyance thereof unto his hands. I have also wrote to Mr Thomas Barret, a minister who lived in South Carolina, who, when he wrote to me from Ashley River, was to take shipping for New England. So that I conclude that he is with you. But, if there be no such man in the country, let *me* letter be returned. I am yours in the Lord Jesus." *

So, in his far isolation, he stretches out his hands for books and for companionship with his brother-ministers ! The absence of all mail conveniences, and the irregularity of our coast trade, make such communication very uncertain and infrequent and deepen the feeling of loneliness. Here we have a miniature Presbytery within ourselves, and the ministers have pleasant days of mutual help and joy.

Mr. Davis is working on our river at a point which persists in growing into a town regardless of the act of Assembly locating it on Burrow's land, farther up

* Autograph letter, Massachusetts Historical Society.

the stream.* This settlement has been forming on the estate of Mr. Henry Bishop, on a sandy elevation near the Pocomoke, and the little village is taking the name of "Snow Hill." Mr. Bishop formerly lived in the Virginia counties, below, and is a man of large property, owning thousands of acres (twenty-three hundred) on Bocketenorton Bay, and many acres elsewhere in the county. Mr. Adam Spence—now twenty-three years of age and related to the persecuted Spences of Scotland—has his home there and is assisting in the development of the church. Mr. Makemie had not been slow in discovering fit locations for churches and eligible material out of which to construct God's spiritual temples (30).

Mr. Wilson is watching over our little flocks on the Monokin and the Wicomico. The Browns, the Erskines, the Galbraiths, the Fontaines, the Bostons and the Kings are earnest helpers in those regions. The offshoots from our Rehoboth vine are producing fruitful clusters all over the large county. They are glorious days when at communion seasons the ministers all meet and help one another in several days' service, and when the colonists come to the tables from bayside to seaboard. The ministers, then in their darkblue sacramental gowns and white bands, present to me a more solemn appearance than ever.

Mr. Trail is winning upon us all, passing among the people as a kind spiritual adviser, assuming no superior dignity, asserting no ecclesiastical prerogative. The cavil of the Quakers against all ordained preachers, as priests and tyrants, is utterly disconcerted by his genial ways. I heard him say to my father the other

* Provincial records.

day, while speaking of pastoral and Presbyterial usage :

"We forbear all words of power and authority. Whatever authority we may claim as ministers of the Gospel, we commonly waive that. And as Paul said to Philemon, ' Though I might be much bold in Christ to enjoin thee that which is convenient, yet for love's sake I rather beseech thee,' so we, whatever power we have as ministers to command, yet for prudence' sake we rather beseech." *

A letter from my friend William. I tremble as I read it; if intercepted in England, it would have been his death. He declares that the new king is the worst of the Stuarts—a cool, deliberate, cruel tyrant and a tool of Rome. From the beginning his pretended clemency to Protestants has been belied by the increased fury of the persecutions in Scotland—talking of toleration in England, but at that very time asking and obtaining from the servile Parliament in Edinburgh more horrible penal laws against the Covenanters. Says one of his victims,

"Now, Isabel, the hour is come that I told you would come when I first spoke to you of marriage."

The brains of the godly John Brown are blown out by Claverhouse in the presence of the poor wife, one child in her arms and another clinging to her knees. The maiden-martyr Margaret Wilson breathes out her heroic life in the tides of Blednock, brutally tantalized by the executioners with the death-struggles of the older Margaret, who had been placed farther out in order to intimidate the youthful martyr from her constancy.

"What do I see," she says, "but Christ in one of his members wrestling there?"

* Examination at Dublin Castle, Reid, II. 581.

Then she quotes from the eighth chapter of Romans until her triumphant voice is choked by the rising waves. "Many waters cannot quench love," is William's comment.

My friend goes on to tell of Argyle's insurrection in Scotland and that of Monmouth in England, of the utter failure of both, and of the king's making these a pretext for more relentless barbarities against our religion. North and south, the cry of death or of banishment to the plantations is in the air. The " Bloody Assizes," under Jeffreys, have had no parallel in history. From the judicial bench he cries,

" There is not one of these lying, sniveling, canting Presbyterians but, one way or another, had a hand in the rebellion Presbytery has all manner of villany in it. Show me a Presbyterian, and I'll show thee a lying knave "

With such words he adjudges Alice Lyle to be burned.

The king encourages all this. Corpses are dangling in chains at every cross-road. Hundreds have been transported and sold into slavery. The queen and her ladies of honor have become speculators in the infamous traffic, causing young girls to be thrown into prison in order to exact ransom-money from the parents.

While our rosy lass of Scotland and the blue-eyed maid of Ulster are talking with me of this lamentable news, the singer of the Vincennes joins the sad group with notes no less sad in her tones to-day. The iniquitous price for permission to marry the corrupt Madame Maintenon has been paid by Louis XIV. at last in the revocation of the Edict of Nantes. The fierce dragonnades are harrowing the homes of God's people in France The Huguenot churches are demolished, their ministers sent to the galleys, children wrested from their parents, whole districts pillaged, thousands slain. All who can do so, are flying to foreign countries.

When we think of Somersetshire, England, with her blackened quartered human bodies decorating the oaks in every village green, the hideous ornaments on every sign-post, the ghastly skulls on every church-spire, oh welcome the poverty, the coarse fare, the wild beasts, the half-naked savages, in our own county of Somerset!

I have not told it all. William writes:

"In February, I saw Mr. Baxter, now seventy years of age, brought before the wicked Jeffreys. Those white locks, that saintly face, ought to have moved a beast to veneration. All the decencies of a trial were utterly forgotten. Jeffreys browbeat the counsel for the defence and would not let them proceed. He denounced the prisoner in presence of the Tory jury The old man asked time to prepare his defence.

"'Not a minute, to save his life!' howled the infuriated judge. 'I can deal with saints as well as sinners. Yonder, out of the window, stands Oates on one side of the pillory , and if Baxter stood on the other, the two greatest rogues in the kingdom would stand together. This is an old rogue, a schismatical knave, a hypocritical villain. I know what you mean by bishops , rascals like yourself—Kidderminster bishops, factious sniveling Presbyterians!'

"As I listened to such words my blood boiled.

"By these measures Jeffreys obtained a verdict from a jury no better than himself, and condemned the grand old man to fine and imprisonment. This was in the first month of the reign of James II.—an index to all that has come since. I see my own Church endorsing this abominable tyranny at the hands of a Papist I too am now a Presbyterian If these scenes continue, I will say so openly and find a home in America."

CHAPTER VII.

A. D. 1686.

"I heartily wish you all Success and Prosperity in laying the Foundation for the Happiness of you and your Posterity."—MAKEMIE.

DURING the absence of Mr. Trail, who has been helping Mr. Davis at Snow Hill and Mr. Wilson on the Monokin, Mrs. Elinor has been staying with us; also my friend Naomi. We maidens have been sagely considering how unpleasant it must be to occupy the position of a minister's wife—how grand and solemn, and then so poor! We understand that Mr. Trail's annual salary at Lifford was only twenty-one pounds sterling; here it is paid in pounds of tobacco instead, and this of little value because of the heavy taxes and other restraints on trade.

Happening to remember certain words copied in my journal, I found them, and read as follows:

"Many are the relative duties of parents and children, husbands and wives, masters and servants. If the Christian religion were regarded by all ranks and stations, none in the world would be compared with them. Therefore it was not a vain nor groundless challenge one of the ancients made, when he challenged the world to show so good magistrates and subjects, husbands and wives, parents and children, masters and servants, as the Christian religion is able to produce."*

"So thought Mr. Makemie," I said; "and if Christianity can produce such models *anywhere*, it can do so in a minister's own household."

* New York sermon: Makemie.

Just then Mrs. Trail came in, plainly dressed and cheerful. Was not *she* too one of the founders of our American Church ?

I hear of a startling marvel connected with Mr. Trail, and long to ask Mrs Elinor about it, but have not the courage. It seems too sacred and unearthly. All such things are more awful in this deep Western wilderness, where the woods and streams and boundless regions, filled with wild animals and wilder Indians, are themselves one vast mystery. Sometimes, since we heard it, we young people almost feel an awe of Mr. Trail. And yet how genial and humorous he is, whether in Dublin Castle or on the banks of the Pocomoke !

Matchacoopah calls him "Atupquonihanque " ("the moon ") and Mrs. Trail " Poomolasuque " ("a star ").

" Then who is Mr. Makemie ?" we ask.

His answer is,

" Wawpancy-Keesequo " (" the daybreak ").

Shall I tell of a visit made by Naomi and myself this year, under the care of Colonel Stevens, to St. Mary's ? During the absence of the Proprietary in Europe, watching the efforts of Mr. Penn to infringe upon the Maryland charter, our friend Stevens spends much of his time at the capital across the Chesapeake Bay. For the rest of us Eastern Shoremen, secluded and obscure, such a visit is an event in our lives. Passing from the broad bay into the Potomac River, I was full of thoughts of the hour, forty-two years ago, when the Ark and Dove rounded into these waters and selected the place for our chief city. When our pinnace swept around St. George's Island into the St. Mary's River, two or three miles wide and bordered with green meadows, the forests rising back of them and the hills and cliffs interlacing up the stream, my enthusiasm was growing constantly. To prevent disappointment, Colonel Stevens read me a description of the town written by Lord Baltimore to the English Committee of Trade and Plantations eight years ago (1678):

"The principal town or place is called St. Marie's, where the generall assembly and provinciall court are kept, and whither all shipps trading there do in the first place resort. Butt it can hardly be called a town, it beeing in length by the water about five myles and in breadth upwards toward the land not above one myle; in all which space, excepting only my own house and buildings, wherein the said courts and publique offices are kept, there are not above thirty houses, and those at considerable distance from each other; and the buildings (as in other parts of the provynce) very mean and little, and generally after the manner of the meanest farme houses in England." *

But, however humble, it is to me the birthplace of the province and of the religious liberty we now enjoy —religious liberty for which we are indebted to none but God alone. Thank the great Head of the Church, a Protestant government could not confer upon a Catholic Proprietary the power to oppress Protestants, nor could he ask a Catholic Proprietary to force the Church of England upon his fellow-Dissenters. I think of this over and over.

On the lower horn of the crescent-shaped harbor stands the dwelling of the Proprietary, built of imported English brick, its main mansion two stories high, its right and left wings extending in various rooms and offices on each side. To the eye accustomed to plantation-life and lowly cabins, this brick

Report on Boundary-Line of Virginia and Maryland.

house, with its armorial bearings and floating pennon, appears quite lordly and imposing. Over upon the other horn of the crescent stands the State-House, built in the form of a cross, walls thick and heavy, surmounted by a spire. To me this was a grand building, costing twelve years ago (1674) four hundred and thirty thousand pounds of tobacco.*

Naomi and I were anxious to see the Lady Mary, the favorite of the young people and the patroness of our county. As soon as she heard from Colonel Stevens of our presence in St. Mary's, she sent a gracious message inviting us to the mansion. With trepidation we put on our best gowns, petticoats, bodices and scarfs, and venture toward those proud doors decorated with the escutcheon of the Baltimores. Naomi is beautiful, but, a simple peasant of the colony, what am I to do in the presence of nobility? A dignified servant in livery receives us and ushers us into the great room. I would feel less timid on my Chingoteague pony, dashing through the homes of bears and wolves on the Eastern Shore.

Another door opens, and the Lady Mary Somerset enters, plainly and chastely attired, an engaging smile on her home-like face, her hands kindly extended to each of us. The little woman dispels our fear in a moment.

"This is a daughter of Leah, and this of Rachel," said Colonel Stevens, referring to the book published by Mr Hammond and now lying upon the table; "they are close neighbors, and their hearts form a bond of amity between the two sister-colonies."

* McMahon, p 251.

"It is a pity," said her gentle Ladyship, "that Colonel Scarborough and my Uncle Philip had not run the divisional line a little farther southward and united such loving hearts in one province. But the two friends are equally welcome to our home."

Then the Lady Mary graciously asked many kind questions about the county which is to perpetuate her name. Were the colonists contented and happy? Was the county healthy? Were we ever homesick for England? Were the Indians friendly? Was the tobacco-crop promising? Was there much enthusiasm for the new king? Did the settlers up the coast toward Hoarkil prefer the Quaker's government or ours? Was there any bitterness against her Church? Had the young people many pleasures?

So good and kindly seemed the Lady Mary Somerset that I felt proud of the name. On that side of the bay I find far greater feeling against her Church than in our own county. The enthronement of a Papist, and his open parade of his religion, intensify the feeling. The deputy lieutenants are anxious and vigilant.

Colonel Stevens took us over to the State-House to see the two legislative bodies now in session—the Upper House, composed of the councilors of the Proprietary, appointed by himself; the Lower House, composed of twenty delegates, two elected by the people in each of the ten counties (31). We are told that these delegates are very tenacious of the rights of the people—that, while loyal to the Proprietary, they are ready to combat any apparent encroachment upon the popular franchises. How august they seem, to us maidens, these stern law-makers of the wilderness, here in this capital which but a little while ago was the Indian village of Yoacomaco! Are the members of the Parliament now sitting in England— Lord Halifax among the Peers or Edward Seymour of the Commons—more stately and proud than these?

Here are the artificial ringlets falling over the shoulders, the richly-embroidered coats of velvet, the enormous cuffs full of the great wristbands of lace, and the elegant hose reaching far above the knee. With these we see all the artificial courtesies of courts. Among this class is the imposing president of the Council, Mr. William Josephs, one of those nine deputies with whom the government has been left in commission, and of whom Colonel Stevens is one. Here, too, we see the rusty garments of the days of Cromwell, and the strong Puritan faces reminding me of the grand old man over on the Sinepuxent Neck. Here, too, are plain costumes and brusque manners of planters who can neither write nor read.

While this greatness and dignity is almost dazing the humble maidens from the Eastern Shore, we are aroused to new interest by hearing the law-makers talking of our own county. A new town is located on Mr. Arnold Elzey's land and the land adjacent at Oyster Neck, at the mouth of the Monokin. Then we find them talking about our own Pocomoke, and after various motions and readings the town located three years ago near the head of the river, on Mr. Morgan's land—commonly called " Burrow's "—is declared to be found by experience to be no ways fitting and convenient, and is, as they express it, " annulled and untowned " and transferred to Snow Hill, on the land formerly belonging to Mr. Henry Bishop, and left to his widow, Anne Bishop—the place where Mr. Davis is preaching. The law provides that all who have already built at Snow Hill shall have the lots upon the same terms as others in the government towns— an acre given free to any person who will build on it a house at least twenty feet square.* Shall not our church there also have an acre free of cost?

While they are multiplying these towns on paper, I recall Mr. Makemie's caution:

"Beware of overdoing at first, but make a beginning ; for by aiming to do all at once, you may do nothing at all."

We remain until the festival of St. Ignatius, on the 31st of July. The day brings great excitement and gladness to the Roman Catholics—their chapel adorned with evergreens and flowers, secular labor intermitted, the colonists in holiday dress, and processions moving to the first landing-place of the pilgrims and then back to the chapel. Priests lead the procession, and next follow reverently the Lady Mary and her retinue. Mass is celebrated, and the life and deeds and say- ings of Ignatius Loyola form the staple of the sermon.

Notwithstanding the high honors to their "tutelar guardian and patron saint," I see evident indications of anxiety on the faces of the worshipers. The so- licitude is very marked on the sweet, grave coun- tenance of the Lady Mary, for the news from Europe is of a character to deepen the hatred of the Protest- ants without bringing any assurance of royal favor

* Provincial records, 1686.

to the Baltimores. Among the Protestant spectators I hear mutterings of disapproval and prophecies that these scenes will not be always tolerated.

Colonel Stevens points to a man of sinister look, dark and determined, clerical in dress and manner, but with features bloated and pimpled by profligacy. His eyes are small and full of cunning, his voice is low and insinuating, his step is firm but stealthy. Wherever he passes he manages to leave a darker frown on the brow of the Protestants. This, I am told, is John Coode, a clergyman of the Church of England, but a man utterly devoid of moral character, five years ago under arrest for conspiracy against the Proprietary, and still nursing within his heart the bitterest resentment for that indignity. A cutlass hangs to his girdle.

Through the night the firing of cannons is heard in repeated salutes to the honor of the Jesuit saint, even till the morning dawn. Such is the annual custom, but Colonel Stevens thinks that its observance is growing dangerous to the peace of the province.*

Now home again, a traveled maiden, back to the quiet of the forests. As a present from the Lady Mary Somerset and a token of good-will to the county, I bring with me a stampt Persian silk petticoat broidered with lace, worn on a state occasion by Her Ladyship, and to be worn hereafter, she says, by a certain young maiden on the banks of the Pocomoke on her wedding-day.

A pleasant piece of news must be recorded here. Our minister has determined to make his home among us, and has purchased one hundred and

* Neill's *Founders of Maryland*, p. 104

thirty-three acres on the north side of our river, only a little over a mile below Rehoboth Town. It is part of the tract patented by Mark Manlove in 1665 and called "Son's Choice," afterwards divided, and this part called "Brother's Love." A son of the patentee, of the same name with his father, and now living in Pennsylvania, has sold it to Mr. Trail and signed the deed on the 8th of May (32), attested by Thomas Newbold, John Winder and James Dashiel. The plantation adjoins the Jenkins property, bringing our minister into pleasant neighborhood and convenient to the church he is to serve. The joy of the Presbyterians is great.

My return is in time to be at the house-raising. The colonists enjoy large gatherings for social pleasure. We maidens are there to cook and be complimented, the hungry workmen heartily praising our labors. It is exciting to see the logs go up so cheerily, the strong muscles gladly strained to their utmost tension, the calls and responses ringing loudly from the wielders of hand-spike and lever: "Ho-ye-ho! All together! Bravely ho!" The echoes sound abroad, as if a thousand Presbyterians were on their way to our help.

Mary, the rosy Scotch lassie, Peggy, the blue-eyed maid of Ulster, Margaret, the sweet-toned singer of the Vincennes, Naomi, our rare Virginia beauty, and my own English hands knead the large corn-cakes, pour out the cider, and bring the uncarved pigs to the perfection of brown roasting.

We collect the news from the Old World, each nationality inquiring anxiously for its own fatherland. James is proving himself a tyrant and a Papist open and undisguised, scourging his shoulders for his sins, but breaking the heart of Mary of Modena by his shameless profligacy, parading the mass publicly before all eyes, and parading his adultery just as publicly by making his mistress Countess of Dorchester; pretending to condemn the revocation of the Edict of Nantes in France, but silencing the refugee ministers, having Claude's history of the Huguenot persecutions burned by the hangman, and cheating the French sufferers out of the money contributed in England for their relief. Everywhere Papists are promoted to office and their priests permitted to inveigh against the Protestant faith, while Protestant ministers are forbidden to preach against the errors of Rome. The Jesuits, with Father Petre in the palace, are the king's honored advisers. The Tory churchmen are beginning to find that their doctrine of the divine right of kings may become double-edged.

Well might Mr. Trail say in Dublin Castle five years ago, " I do not believe that the king has power to set up what government he pleases in the Church."

Pursuing the Presbyterians of Scotland with unrelenting cruelty, the king has taken the Papists there under his especial favor, and is trying to secure laws in their behalf from the obsequious Episcopal Parliament. Some of the prelates basely give full consent to this on condition that the persecutions against the Presbyterians shall not be relaxed If there seems any abatement of these fiendish horrors, it is only because death and banishment have exhausted the supply of victims and many portions of the country have been made a solitude. In the absence of living victims, war is made upon the peace of the grave The great field-preacher Alexander Peden having died this year and been buried in the church of Auchinleck, his body was disentombed six weeks afterward by soldiers and buried ignominiously at the foot of the gallows in Cumnock. Mr. Peden was once a fellow-prisoner in the Bass with Mr. Robert Trail, brother of our minister.*

In Ireland, James is disarming the Protestants and leaving them at the mercy of the Celts, who are inflamed by both religious and race hatred. Clarendon is nominally lord lieutenant, while Tyrconnel, "the Lying Dick Talbot," one of the basest men in the empire, is virtually the chief authority in the island. Any day the half-barbarous Rapparees may assault the Presbyterians.†

Meanwhile, with implacable fury the bloody dragonnades are devastating the Protestant provinces of France. Pastors are banished or butchered, and the people, forbidden to emigrate, are subjected to all imaginable horrors in order to force them to abjure their religion. Children are wrested from their parents and immured in convents to be reared as Papists. Instigated by the French monarch, the Duke of Savoy is slaying the Piedmontese by hundreds.‡

These dark tidings make us more content with the hardships of the New World. It must be for some great purpose God is permitting the persecutor to drive so many of his best people over the deep. How blest are we to have these godly ministers preaching on our Shore! Of course there are frequent inquiries about Mr. Makemie and his work to the south of

---

* Wodrow, *in loco*.   † Macaulay and Reid, *passim*.
‡ Evelyn's *Diary* for 1686.

us. What is he doing? Where is he to-day? Is he making Presbyterians of his mixed congregations? Is he still on Elizabeth River, or in the Carolinas, or in Barbadoes?

News is afloat that Mr Penn has prevailed, and that our Proprietary has lost his possessions on the Delaware. King James seems to have taken the Quakers into especial favor. His love of despotism causes him to hate the old colonial charters, and that of Maryland had already been put in jeopardy by *quo warranto*. Probably Father Petre, the court Jesuit, has no great liking for the Baltimores because of their tolerance of Protestants. Out of these various influences has resulted the following decision against the claims of our Proprietary:

"For avoiding further difficulty, the tract of land lying between the river and bay of Delaware and the Eastern Sea on the one side, and Chesapeake Bay on the other, shall be divided into two equal parts by a line from the latitude of Cape Henlopen to the fortieth degree of Northern latitude "*

So passes away this part of Maryland's chartered possessions for ever. Colonel Stevens criticises Mr. Penn's earnest protestations of his purpose to be a good neighbor.

Thus, amid the hearty work of building at Mr. Trail's plantation of Brother's Love, we gather the news from Europe and America.

Among the colonists these "house-raisings" are occasions of rare pleasure. Our pastor was there with us—a man of weight in the Old World or the New. Mistress Elinor was with us, too, delighting the young maidens with her constant notice and commendations

* Neill's *Terra Mariæ*, p 170, McMahon, p 33

of their skill in the bread-baking. While she left us
a while to speak with the youthful Madam Mary Jenkins, our Huguenot singer paused to ask Naomi how
she would like to be a minister's wife. Naomi is very
attractive in the bloom of eighteen.

Some of us discuss the report which we hear about
Mr. Trail, and which seems to be confirmed. It is another mystery seemingly as impenetrable as that which
I encountered on the South Point of Sinepuxent. If
true, we shall feel that God is as near to our minister
as he was to Moses on Sinai or to Elijah on Carmel.

And now yonder stands Mr. Trail's forest-home
overlooking the waters of the Pocomoke and in close
neighborhood with the log temple at Rehoboth.
Humble as these buildings are, they are no less important in our eyes, and perhaps no less momentous
in final results, than the mansion of the Baltimores
and the State-House at St. Mary's.

CHAPTER VIII.

A. D. 1687.

"We are confident that a great part of our Teachings are Christian Experiences."—MAKEMIE.

NOW and then we have our great communion seasons—all the ministers present and the services protracted from Friday over Sabbath These eventful occasions seem almost like Presbyteries, or Meetings, as they are called in Ireland, when the three preachers confer with one another and with the ruling elders concerning the advancement of the gospel cause. To the exile the free messages of grace come as sweet balms. For Scotch, English, Irish and Huguenots the piney wilderness of Maryland is indeed a Bethel of privilege.

During one of these sacramental seasons at Rehoboth, Mr. Trail, Mr. Wilson and Mr. Davis spend Saturday night at my father's. The little Dove is loaded with preachers—far more honored, we think, than her namesake when she brought over her cargo of Jesuit priests The fragrance of the magnolia blooms charms us while the ministers tell of adventures for Christ and the Covenant along the loughs and streams of the Old World.

On Sabbath morning, when the robins and wrens and martins are waking the early echoes, I look from

my window and see Mr Trail pensively walking the
front yard.   Like the Psalmist, his devotions are evidently "preventing the dawning of the morning."

An awe comes over me, for again I think of the
strange rumor.   An irrepressible desire possesses me
to know the truth from his own lips.   I steal quietly
from bed, hurriedly bathe my face, put on my gown
and creep out to where he is standing.   At first he
does not see me, but he turns toward the river, notices
my presence and salutes me courteously.   He praises
the soft Maryland morning and thanks God for the
gift of such a day for our meeting.

I can keep in no longer, but tell him what I have
heard.

Then, with a solemnity such as I have never seen in
his mien before,* he speaks of how it used to startle
him at first—how it has come to be an expected
occurrence and no longer makes him unhappy.   Whenever there are important duties before him, three raps
on his chamber door are certain to awaken him at
about three o'clock in the morning. If, through
weariness or a disposition to indulge his drowsiness
a while longer, he disregards the reminders, there are
invariably three more at the head of his bed, which he
dare not disobey.   These mysterious calls never fail
on Sabbaths, and more particularly on communions.
No matter where he may be, the raps are always given
in time for him to prepare himself for the work of the
day (33).   This morning, while all were sleeping, deep
silence through the house and up and down the river,

* It must be remembered that this was an age of superstition, belief
in witchcraft, etc., even among the best people, both in America and
in Europe.

the warning had come, calling him to prayer and meditation.

I feel that we stand on holy ground. He speaks sweetly of God's care over his servants during these present years of danger. It does indeed seem that in her epochs of persecution and grievous suffering the communication between the Church and the heavens is closest, the manifestation of God's presence the most assured.

In the year 1634—troublous days in Ireland—Mr. Steward of Dunagor was standing by the grave of Josiah Welsh, and asked, "Who will be next?" No one answering, he said, "I know." He went immediately to his church and remained within two hours, taking leave of it, he said, and calling stones and timbers to witness that he had been faithful. Soon he was upon his deathbed, and there declared: "My hair stands to behold what I see coming on these lands. The dead bodies of many thousands who this day despise the glorious gospel shall lie on the earth as dung unburied Woe to thee, Dunagor! for the nettles and the long grass shall be in greater plenty in thee than ever were people to hear the word of God." These prophecies were fulfilled before his children died.*

To Mr. Alexander Peden, who died a year ago, singular predictions are also attributed, foretelling even the ravishing of his grave.†

Thus during her great tribulations the Church has been brought to realize the nearness of her sovereign Head in many and marvelous ways Here in the Western wilderness, along the Pocomoke no less than

* Reid, i 182.   † Wodrow, iv 396.

along the Foyle and the Ayre, we are reminded that
this messenger of the Most High is under his immediate guardianship, and that the sceptre of Omnipo-
tence is waving over the cradle of the infant American
Church.

That day the colonists flocked to the little river
sanctuary in great numbers, coming from all parts of
the county and from the country below.   Each season
brings new faces, driven from their home in Europe.
There, under the bright skies of Rehoboth, that day's
untrammeled, unmolested communion was glorious
indeed to the poor exiles.

Our friend the bachelor Scotchman, John Galbraith,
was there, of course, proud of our ministers and rejoicing in the freedom enjoyed by his banished countrymen.   We love him for his liberality in the support
of the gospel, his diligence in business apparently
inspired by a zeal to serve the Lord.   He is not too
far away to enjoy frequent hours of pleasant companionship with his fellow-Scotchman at Brother's Love.

I noticed Colonel Stevens, too, and thought how
manly he looked, and how elated at the Sabbath scene.
There he sat, lately home from St. Mary's, with his
honors upon him—a Protestant, but fully trusted by
the Catholic Proprietary and by all sects among the
colonists.   For over fifteen years, while George Fox
was here and before, his plantation has been a place of
assembling for worship, whether of the Quakers, Episcopalians or Presbyterians : room enough for all.   The
first to urge the sending out of a Calvinistic missionary
from Ulster, he has lived to see, during the seven years
following, four ministers of our faith officiating within
sight of his residence   When Mr. Makemie came, he

found the colonists already accustomed to meet on the judge's land for divine service, and here, of course, he began to preach and to organize. The results are seen to-day, and our deputy lieutenant is pleased. But in the midst of the delightful scene did he, on second and more searching look, appear worn and more pale than usual?

I would like to tell of a conversation I heard between Colonel Francis Jenkins and Sir Robert King about Mr. Makemie, but events are pressing me.

Not long that day did I forget the mysterious summons which prepared Mr. Trail for these duties; and whenever I looked over beyond the Jenkins plantation, it seemed to me that our minister's home at Brother's Love was lying very close along the verge of heaven, and that the valley of the Pocomoke is a favored spot in the eternal counsels. The flowering laurel was like great forests in bloom, and the blue of the skies was pure enough to overhang an Eden.

So there came, now and then, blessed days hallowing this obscure nook of the New World—days of privilege undreamed of in the lands of the despot.

This reminds me of something which I am disposed to transcribe into my journal from the incorruptible old bard Andrew Marvell, who died nine years ago. Here is his poem called " The Emigrants to the Bermudas "—which I preserve because the Church most like to Presbyterian of any other in this western hemisphere, until now, was organized there over forty years ago (1644):

" Where the remote Bermudas ride,
In th' ocean's bosom unespied,

From a small boat that row'd along,
The listening winds received their song:
' What should we do but sing His praise
That led us through the watery maze
Unto an isle so long unknown,
And yet far kinder than our own?
Where he the huge sea-monsters racks
That lift the deep upon their backs,
He lands us on a grassy stage,
Safe from the storms and prelates' rage;
He gave us this eternal spring
Which here enamels everything,
And sends the fowls to us in care
On daily visits through the air;
He hangs in shades the orange bright
Like golden lamps in a green night,
And does in the pomegranate close
Jewels more rich than Ormus shows;
He makes the figs our mouths to meet
And throws the melons at our feet.
But apples, plants of such a price
No tree could ever bear them twice,
With cedars chosen by his hand
From Lebanon, he stores the land,
And makes the hollow seas that roar
Proclaim the ambergris on shore.
He cast—of which we rather boast—
The gospel's pearl upon our coast,
And in these rocks for us did frame
A temple where to sound his name.
Oh, let our voice his praise exalt
Till it arrive at heaven's vault,
Which then, perhaps, rebounding, may
Echo beyond the Mexique bay.'
Thus sang they in the English boat
A holy and a cheerful note,
And all the way, to guide their chime,
With falling oars they kept the time."

So too a company of us sail and think and sing
during the early summer while floating among the

sand-islands where the sea-birds lay their eggs, and over to the long array of hills that fence the coast. The gentlemen are crossing Assateague Bay for salt, and the ladies are tourists for pleasure. Orange, pomegranate, figs and rocks alone are wanting to complete the poet's picture. More prized than all the rest is "the gospel's pearl upon our coast, safe from prelates' rage." The air is healthily laden with the balsams of the pine-woods, mingling with the salt odors of the seaweed and of the marsh-blossoms, blue and golden.

Far away to the northward I see the sharp point of Mr. Wale's plantation, and I again recall the venerable old man whose dignified bearing and mien of command remind my father of Cromwell's Ironsides. Ah me! what heroic, romantic histories lie back of these land-patents which environ our coast!

Dr. John Vigerous, our Rehoboth physician, Mr. John Franklin, Mr. Henry Hudson, Mr. Robert Peel and my brother John compose our escort. On my especial invitation, the sweet singer of the Vincennes accompanies us; for will not that voice delight my brother more than all sights and sounds of land and ocean? I have brought Marvell's poem, and soon a melody of Southern France times the English song very sweetly to the rippling of the waves.

Mr Henry Hudson is the provoking naturalist of our expedition, vexatiously addicted to the study of worms, beetles, crabs, stingrays and all creeping things. A vast unexplored continent, with sea and forest full of horrid monsters to frighten poor maidens with, is very attractive to him. The New World is for him a paradise of bugs!

During the day a little flotilla of canoes comes paddling down the bay, and on inquiry we find it to be our former acquaintance, Queen Weocomoconus, her son Knusonum and their body-guard, going on a visit to the emperor Toattam of Assateague.* They are attired in their gaudiest costumes and paints, and the queen in all the finery of her nation   At the suggestion of our chronic mischief-monger, we sail near their course; and then, to our dismay, this same Henry Hudson, assuming the most grotesque seriousness, arises and through Robin Interpreter makes formal proposals for the union of our tribes by a marriage between himself and the queen.   There suddenly grows no little excitement among the Indians, many words which we do not understand, and then they turn in disdain and hasten away.   It is hard to tell in what trouble this bug-hunter may some day involve us   The Nanticoke word for " queen " is *tattah-kesk*, for " king," *tatt-ak*.

While feasting on muscles and mamanoes upon the outer beach, unexpectedly the wind veers to the north-east, the sky is overcast, and we face a growing storm.   The bay, smooth and placid but an hour ago, is lashed into foam.   The mainland with its green forests shrinks away from us farther and farther, dim and hazy and afraid.   Not daring to risk our little ketch upon the angry bay, we awake to the fact that we are caught upon the beach for the night   The ocean looks like a maniac, and the black heavens seem sinking into the maniac's embrace.

The salt-boilers, living farther up the hills, welcome us to their rude cabins.   Before the grim night settles

* Mentioned in Somerset records, November 11, 1691

down utterly, I notice on the vast expanse of billows something laboring and tossing as if in a struggle for life. Mr. Franklin tells me it is a ship beaten by the tempest and hurrying perhaps to its doom. So Mr. Makemie had been driven up the coast three years ago.

During the terrific night I seem at intervals to hear screams, sighs, groans, calls for help; but the loud surf and the deafening winds swallow up all other sounds, and I curb my fancy and try to rest my jaded mind.

The slow morning dawns at length. The violence of the storm has somewhat abated, though the breakers are furious still. One of the beachmen runs with the alarm that a wreck is on shore, some of the sailors dead. There is hurrying toward the scene of the disaster—I hardly know how or who. The gentlemen are urging the women to remain under our rude shelter, but I only know that I did not heed them.

I am the first to notice an object beaten by the waves, partly floating, partly stranded, rising and falling in the surges. I see what it is—a human being, a corpse. I see the face, and I know no more.

When consciousness returns, I am in the cabin, Margaret holding my head, the other ladies around What does it all mean? Then I see Dr Vigerous attending upon another. Then I hear something like groans. Or is it the howling of the storm? for now I remember there has been a storm And soon it all comes back—the shore, the form, the face, the recognition, all!

I know what they are doing. I am myself again, and will not be stopped, and go to the side of the reviving young man. How glad I am that the doctor accompanied us!   The company knew not all, nor did I tell them then.   John knew, and Margaret learned from him ere long, and her soft Huguenot tones became softer.

The help had come in time, and the care and skill of Dr. Vigerous availed, I shall not protract the recital—the gradual recovery, the trip across the bay to the Chingoteague plantation of Mr. Robins, and then to our home.   The English youth had become more and more incensed against the oppressors of God's people; his generous heart leaned to the persecuted; his brave resentments brought him into new troubles, just as when he became my champion against the drunken cavaliers.   Finally, the same with us in faith and hope, he had started to the land of the free. Unknown to us, God had sent our company into the heart of that storm for his rescue.   It was William, the son of our old neighbor.

Before the year is done, news of sickness comes up the river.   In the latter days of August, we had heard of the making of a will by Colonel Stevens; Thomas Purnell, Philip Hammond and Henry Schofield were called over to the plantation for witnesses.   Then, "being in good health and memory, blessed be God! but considering the frailty of this life," he had arranged for the disposition of all property not already transferred to wife and children.   Among other bequests was the Cedar Hall plantation of five hundred acres to his cousin, Elizabeth White, widow of the sheriff, and to Edmund Howard and his son William Stevens Howard the plantation "where he now lives, being bounded by the river and branch through the Town to the Mill-dam, and from thence up the branch that parts the town and the plantation on which Richard Hill now lives as tenant to said Howard." In the will he speaks of his "dear and loving wife Elizabeth," and piously declares. "I commit my soul to God that gave it, hoping for its future happiness through the mercy of my Creator and merits of my Redeemer Jesus Christ."

A year of many important events is approaching its close. Tyrconnel, now lord lieutenant, is bringing all Ireland under Romish domination; only one sheriff a Protestant, and that by mistake—the sheriff of Mr. Makemie's county of Donegal. Our friends there are utterly at the mercy of their foes. In all his three kingdoms James has been trampling upon the laws. To divide the Protestant opposition to his illegal exercise of prerogative, he has been suspending the penal enactments against Dissenters and proclaiming liberty of conscience to all. It is well understood that these measures are prompted by no kindness to the Dissenters.

Whatever his motive, the churches of the Nonconformists are at length open and crowded with worshipers.* But no one knows what despotic act will come next. The old poet Edmund Waller has just died, eighty-two years of age, having said of James, "He will be left like a whale upon the strand."

I hear Mr. Trail and my father talking of the publication of a new book, called *The Principia*, by Mr. Isaac Newton, an astronomer. In it he claims that the heavenly bodies are all kept in their orbits by a wonderful mysterious force called "the attraction of gravitation." It is spoken of as a great discovery.

* Evelyn's *Diary*, p. 509

As December wears away, reports of severe illness come from the Rehoboth plantation. Great anxiety spreads along the river. The sick man has done more than any other for the development of our county, and, better still, has been the honored instrument in bringing the pure gospel to the Presbyterians of this poor land His son John is now eighteen years old; William, fifteen; James, eleven; and little Jane, seven. We think of these and the mother, and are sad The new country, with its rude society and struggle for life, is a hard place for widowhood and orphanhood.

Sunday, the 23d of December, comes and goes, and Colonel William Stevens is no more Christmas Day dawns on a sorrowing home. In order that notice may reach the many friends all over the county, the burial is deferred until Wednesday.

Wednesday comes, and the colonists begin to gather, arriving by road or river. Of course the county officials are there—the justices, the high sheriff, the coroner, the constables, the press-master, the wood-ranger, the burgesses. Among the county officers, ever since its organization, his has been a familiar form to them all. The rich are there, and the poor indentured servants Slaves group themselves in mourning, their black faces burned by African suns, their great white eyes running tears There, too, are Panquash and Annataughton of the Choptanks, King Daniel of the Pocomokes, Weegnonah of the Assateagues, Curremuccos and Tomehawk from the up-river town Askimmekonson, and our own Matchacoopah. Whether taking part in the impeachment of Major Trueman for his treacherous murder of the five Indian chiefs on the Western Shore, eleven years ago, or whether in the governor's Council at St. Mary's, or whether upon the bench in the Somerset court, the red men know that he has always been the friend of the children of the forest.

In the large assemblage are also the Episcopal clergyman, Mr. Hewett, and many Quakers. Never to my ear has the voice of Mr. Trail sounded more impressively. For three years he and the deceased have known each other well. As clerk of the Presbytery of Laggan, Mr. Trail had read the letter which seven years ago carried across the ocean our appeal for a Presbyterian ministry. The hand that wrote it is now cold in death; the hand that broke the seal is helping to bury him. Who could then have predicted that the clerk of that Presbytery would by this time have been owning a home within three miles of the home of the writer of that letter, and have been taking part at his funeral? God works marvelously.

A little way to the northward of his brick dwelling, by the graves of his brother Richard and his brother-in-law, Sheriff White, we laid the body of the pioneer. There he sleeps, near the waters of the ever-flowing river, awaiting the resurrection trump. On the records of the court over which he presided for more than a score of years they put the following memorial notice:

"Colonel William Stevens, Esq., one of his Lordship's Deputies for Maryland, died and was buried at his own plantation called Rehoboth, December 26th."

Said Matchacoopah in strange, weird wail,

"The straight *weensquaaquah*" ("cedar") of the Pocomoke has gone down before the *togh-poh*" ("frost") of the north wind."

CHAPTER IX.

A. D. 1688.

" Blessed be God for our seasonable and happy Revolution, that has in a great measure broke the deep projects of that Jesuitical Party; and by an Established Liberty to all Dissenting Protestants has bound the Hands of former Persecutors."—MAKEMIE.

MY friend William has become one of the strongest Presbyterians I ever saw. From the day when he resented the assault upon his playmate and declared, " I too will be a Puritan," he began to note the sycophancy of his Church toward the wicked Stuarts and her encouragement of the government in its persecutions of God's true people. Finally, her abject subserviency to the tyrant James and the parade of her doctrine of the divine right of kings broke the last tie of his heart to her communion, and he was one of the first to hasten to the reopened meeting-houses of the Nonconformists.

Soon finding that he was drawing upon himself and his parents the animosity of the rector, William decided to cast in his lot with those who sought religious liberty beyond the sea. It is pleasant to see him sit and enjoy the gospel in the little log church at Rehoboth. He loves Mr. Trail and compares him to Baxter, Manton, Howe, and other great Dissenters whom he has heard in England.

I believe that William is to be a thorough American.

He fears the wild beasts no more than he feared the drunken votaries of Prelacy whom he defied in defence of the Presbyterian girl. He and John and Matchacoopah have lately been upon a two days' wolf-hunt toward the head-waters of Pitts's Creek. They come home with a dozen wolves' tongues and ears for trophies. For each wolf killed they are entitled to two hundred pounds of tobacco from the county.*

Our two young men have taken advantage of the leisure season to attend the county court. William was astonished at the contrast between the technical forms in the old country and the common-sense proceedings in the new. Upon the bench he finds men of various trades, knowing nothing of law-books, and some of them unable to write or to read. The statutes of the colony are few and simple. The theory is to recognize the laws of the mother-country so far as applicable to our peculiar circumstances, but the practice is to decide each case upon its merits, regardless of precedents. My father thinks that justice is as often done as under the precise formalities of Europe.

The young men have been speaking of the attorney's oath administered to all who practice in our Somerset court, and just taken by James Sangster, Thomas Pool, Edward Jones, John Taylor, Edward Beauchamp and Josias Seward:

" You swear that you will do no falsehood nor consent for any to be done in this court ; and, if you know of any to be done, you shall give notice thereof to the Justices of this court that it may be [illegible] · you shall delay no man for lucre or malice ;

* Somerset records, 1688. So, also, all county incidents in this chapter.

you shall increase no fees but be contented with the fees of an attorney to be limited and appointed by this court; all such processes as you shall seal out of this court shall be sealed with the seal thereof, and further you shall use and demean yourself, in your office as an attorney in this court, according to your best skill and knowledge. So help you God."

The fee, as limited and appointed, is one hundred pounds of tobacco for each case. Mr. Sangster is made prosecuting attorney, and is to be paid said amount for each criminal he convicts—nothing, where he fails to convict.

For some reason which I could not understand, the company seemed greatly amused at the idea of a lawyer being bound up to truthfulness, or being pledged not to delay any case for lucre, or being sworn to be content with the lawful fee.

Mr. William Morris, who lives near Dividing Creek, was prosecuted and convicted on two counts—drunkenness and breach of the Sabbath—and was fined one hundred pounds of tobacco for each offence. I fear it is not the last time our neighbor will be guilty of such crimes.

Our Quaker friend William Day has been appointed justice, but, as he asks time to consider the oath, the matter is referred to the Council at the next provincial court. William Jones, another Quaker, constable elect, pleads conscience against taking the oath, and is excused from the office.

An order was made for repairing the pillory and stocks—a standing threat to malefactors. The high sheriff, Colonel Jenkins, was authorized to procure the legal scales and weights, of eight hundred pounds' capacity, for each of our seven towns.

Our young friend was much interested in the following lawful prices, copied while at court:

Indian corn, shelled, 18 pence, or 18 lbs tobacco, per bushel.
Wheat, 4 shillings, or 48 lbs. tobacco, per bushel.
Oats,   2   "   or 24 "   "   "   "
Barley, 6 pence,   or 6 "   "   "   "
Pease, 3 shil.,   or 36 "   "   "   "
Pork,   2 pence,   or 2   lbs tobacco, per pound.
Beef,   1½ "   or 1½ "   "   "   "
Bacon, 4   "   or 4   "   "   "   "

Mr. John Robins and his wife, Catherine, were prosecuted on a charge against the latter for calling the
wife of Samuel Collins a witch It was in evidence
that Mrs. Robins had declared that any live thing
bought of the said Mrs. Collins will not thrive, but
die. Defendants were fined two hundred pounds of
tobacco and bound over to keep the peace.

It is a serious matter to be accused of witchcraft
in these times. This very year all Boston is becoming
wild over the frightful contortions and convulsions of the
Godwin children under spells said to be put upon them
by an old hag named Glover. The frenzy is spreading
widely. I do hope that New England's furor may not
reach us. Perhaps the prompt action of our county
court may help to prevent such accusations. Sometimes I hardly know what to think When we reflect
that such great men as Lord Bacon, the famous Lawyer Coke, Bishop Hall, Mr. Baxter and Sir Matthew
Hale believed in such demoniacal possessions during
these troublous ages, it is not much wonder that
weaker minds should yield to the fearful panic. I
trust that the sound religious sense of Mr. Makemie, Mr. Trail, Mr. Davis and Mr. Wilson may keep
all these superstitions at a distance from our latitudes.

I feel greater interest in our young men's account of the scenes in court because my father has frequently spoken of Mr. Makemie himself as no mean lawyer.

News comes of terrific earthquakes in various parts of the world—in Lima, in Smyrna, in Italy and elsewhere—utterly demolishing whole cities. These physical convulsions are considered by many as omens of the wrath of Heaven against our earth—"forerunners," says John Evelyn, "of greater calamities. God Almighty preserve his Church, and all who put themselves under the shadow of his wings, till these things be overpast!"

Meanwhile, a greater earthquake overturns the Stuart's throne. In love with Popery, more in love with arbitrary prerogative, James II. has outraged the principles of the English constitution until the nation can bear no more. For a long while Prelacy continued to sustain the tyrant with its doctrine of passive obedience. During this very year bishops in Scotland, in an obsequious address to the throne, avowed that their allegiance was "an essential part of their religion," and they wished him "the hearts of his subjects and the necks of his enemies." So long as the despotic measures and cruel persecutions of James struck Dissenters alone, Prelacy was satisfied and cheered on the bloody work. In February the brave youthful Renwick died upon the scaffold—the last martyr for the Covenant, we trust. No protest against his murder was heard from prelatic lip or pen.

The king cares nothing for the Church of England only as it is a pliant tool for accomplishing ulterior

purposes. First, her clergy are commanded not to
preach against the Papacy. Then a full indulgence
and relief from all tests is offered to everybody. The
head of the Anglican Church and the Church herself
are at loggerheads, and both begin to bid unblushing-
ly for the favor of those whom both have persecuted
Each accuses these barbarities shamelessly upon the
other.* Baxter, Bunyan, Howe and a large majority
of their friends stand by the laws of their country,
although those laws are severe against themselves

The English clergy are commanded to read the
illegal Declaration of Indulgence from their pulpits;
many refuse, and seven bishops are committed to the
Tower. Nonconformist ministers visit them there
and offer their respect and sympathies. Letters come
to them from the Presbyterians of Scotland assuring
them of their support and confidence. The prelates
are brought to trial before a jury composed partly
of Dissenters, and are cleared. There are public rejoicings by all true-hearted Englishmen, irrespective
of denominational lines, and bonfires blaze everywhere.

In her strait Prelacy has been very zealous in court-
ing Nonconformity. Says Mr. Makemie:

"What condescensions and fair promises did they allow King
Charles II. to make, yea, and to take the coronation oath of
Scotland to maintain Presbyterian government there; and also
to give solemn protestations at Breda to Dissenters of England,
confirmed by a declaration for liberty to all tender consciences.
But soon after the Restoration, all was violated and soon forgot.
The next time they were under any fears, was at the discovery
of the grand Papist plot, and fresh pretences for moderation
were then published, but continued not long, ending in a sham

* See Macaulay, II , chapter vii

plot and a new persecution. And the next trouble the Church of England was in was when the seven Bishops were in the Tower, only for refusing to engage upon their honors to answer at the King's Bench to what should be objected against them ; and then in their petition to the late king, they professed a great deal of tenderness to Dissenters." *

We shall see how these professions will end.

James will not be warned by the rising indignation of an outraged nation. William of Orange sails for the deliverance of England, and lands at Torbay on the 5th of November—just one hundred years after the destruction of the Invincible Armada. Soon James is off the throne and flies to France. A Calvinistic Protestant grasps the sceptre.

In Scotland the Privy Council dissolves and disappears ; the persecution is over, the country is free. The prelatic curates are marched out of the places into which they had intruded only to harass and devastate. Now that revenge was easy, what magnanimity that no blood flowed, no fiercer blow was struck than that of snowballs ! Under the last two Stuarts eighteen thousand victims had suffered, eighteen hundred had been put to death. This was the work of willing ecclesiastical abettors. But for the long battling of bleeding Presbyterians, the three kingdoms would have been sunken into hopeless slavery.

While yet on his march from Torbay to London a deputation bringing congratulations reaches the Prince of Orange from the Presbyterians of Ulster. Soon bursts over the province the report of a threatened massacre of the disarmed Protestants by thoroughly organized Roman Catholics. The Presbyterian ministers urge the people to muster and arm. Rev. James

* *Truths in a True Light.*

Gordon of Clendermot persuades the citizens of Londonderry to close their gates against the advancing Papists.
Bishop Hopkins and his clergy earnestly oppose this
measure and inculcate non-resistance—the old story. A
body of bold young men, mostly Presbyterians, seize the
keys and lock the gates in the face of the approaching
" redshanks " While the loyal prelate is preaching
the duty of passive obedience to the Lord's anoint-
ed, one of the young Scotchmen cries out, "A good
sermon, My Lord—a very good sermon; but we
have not time to listen to it just now "

What will all this bring to us in these Western
wilds ?

On our return up the river from an excursion to
the log house at Brother's Love, where we had been
to learn from Mr. Trail the latest tidings from over the
ocean, we all stopped to see the new tomb lately
placed over the remains of our lamented friend.
Mary, the Scotch lassie, Peggy, the blue-eyed maid of
Ulster, Margaret, the Huguenot songstress, Naomi
Anderson, brother John, William and myself form
quite a group about the tomb. It is a large, broad,
thick slab of marble, resting upon a pedestal of brick,
beneath the shade of the trees. Having just heard
of the death of Mr. John Bunyan, the sure passage
of the good pilgrim through the gates of the Celestial City, we are all in a mood to think of death cheerfully.

Walking up from the river, we see some one sitting
upon the stone in the keen December air, and hear a
child's voice singing plaintively from old Rouse:

> " Such pity as a father hath
> unto his children dear,

Like pity shows the Lord to such
as worship him in fear."

As we drew near, little Jane recognized us through her tears.

"I was singing about papa," said the child.

On the heavy slab we read the following inscription:

Here lyeth the body of William
Stevens Esq , who departed this
Life the 23 of December 1687
Aged 57 years he was 22 years
Judge of this County Court one of
His Lordship's Councill and one of ye
Deputy Lieutenants of this
Province of Maryland.
Vivit Post Funera Virtus (34).

CHAPTER X.

A. D. 1689.

"That the God of all Grace would bless the World with a better Spirit is the prayer of, Sirs, your devoted Servant, in all Civility—
"Francis Makemie."

ALONG our rivers and swamps we are interested in remedies for the ague. I have just heard of one tried for seven years in England and recommended by Mr. John Evelyn as tested by himself:

"Bathing the legs to the knees in milk made as hot as can be borne, sitting also in a deep vessel full of the hot milk, covered with blankets, and drinking carduus posset; then going to bed and sweating." *

This reminds me of a physician's bill charged this year in our county, and which I preserve as illustrative of the times:

AUGUST 22.

1 visit	. 100 lbs. tob.
1 purgation & 2 decoctions	. 250 " "
1 vial cordial waters	. 400 " "
3 sweats	. 100 " "
2 potions laxative, with attendance	. 200 " "

SEPTEMBER 5.

Ferrying	. 30 lbs. tob.
Second visit	. 100 " "
6 laxatives in 6 days	. 300 " "
Sweating & oil & unguents	. 80 " "
1 stomack plaster, with attendance	. 50 " "

Carry forward 1610 lbs. tob.

* Evelyn's *Diary*.

164

SEPTEMBER 16.

Brought forward 1610 lbs. tob.

Ferrying . . . . 30 " "
Third visit . . . . 100 " "
1 cordial & spirits of salt . . . . 200 " "
1 diet drink, and this with attendance and syrup . 200 " "

SEPTEMBER 25.

Ferrying . . . . 30 lbs. tob.
1 purgation . . . . 100 " "
1 -decoction with ingredients . . . . 200 " "
Cordial medicines . . . . 100 " "
All time & attendance . . . . 800 " "

3370 lbs. tob.

The poor man died. The bill was disputed, suit brought and judgment obtained, George Layfield dissenting.

Naomi writes me that the Episcopal clergyman, Mr. Teackle, has just sued his vestry before the Accomack court for twenty thousand pounds of tobacco and recovered it, his salary being established by law at sixteen thousand pounds per annum. He has been officiating in the counties below us for thirty-three years —since 1656. He owns much land and a large library.* My correspondent also tells of the building of an Episcopal church at Assawaman two years ago (1687), not far eastward from her home. Naomi prophesies that the Presbyterians of Accomack will ere long have a preacher of their own, and then, in pure mischief, she drops the subject and leaves it a mystery.

In the exciting events now occurring in Europe, Mr. Trail is intensely interested At Rehoboth and the regions around he preaches to us the precious gospel

* Inventory of his books on Accomack records.

and continues to improve the grounds at Brother's Love, as if expecting to remain here always.   In June he presented a petition to our court to change the public road now running through lands which he is preparing for a cornfield.   But I sometimes fear that this " William Trail, Minister, settling a new plantation on Pocomoke," as the records describe him, may yet be persuaded back to his native heaths.

This year there are twelve hundred and sixty-six taxables in our county, and a levy is made for fifty thousand and fifty-one pounds of tobacco   The population of the province is estimated at twenty-five thousand.*

A petition presented by Mrs. Mabel Rounds that her fine be remitted on the grounds of insolvency in court is refused.   But, on account of her "reformation" and the prayer of her husband, the fine is remitted on condition that he put up "a substantial ducking-stool near the Court House where the old ducking-stool now stands," and keep it in repair for six years.   A wholesome warning to Mrs. Mabel, but rather hard on the poor husband.

James English is convicted of a double crime— shooting an unmarked hog "instead of nailing up its ears;" also a breach of the Sabbath, the shooting having been perpetrated on God's holy day.   He is fined and put under bond.

A gallon of rum is ordered, at the county's expense, by a sympathetic court, for the use of the grand jurors One of these jurors was also on the jury which would have a "sermon taught" in the county, seventeen years ago (1672).

* McMahon, p 273, Somerset records

A petition from a number of citizens is entertained in court:

"That acts passed by the last Assembly which seem to give encouragement for the making of English linen and woolen cloth may if possible be disannulled and made of none effect; otherwise it will not only endanger the peace and safety of this county but likewise hazard the ruin of many families, as also occasion many freemen to desert his Lordship's county."

Colonel Francis Jenkins stated that the Council told him "they would take no advantage of any of the inhabitants of this county in case they disannul it." Court so orders. Thus nullification is legalized in Somerset.

While Mr. Trail is peacefully engaged cultivating his cornfield, and while the jurisprudence of the county is pursuing its forms, startling events are occurring across the ocean and across the Chesapeake, and the county is soon to be His Lordship's no more.

The coronation of William and Mary has taken place in London. A Toleration Act has been passed, not accomplishing all that ought to be done, but relieving Dissenters of many burdens and enabling them to worship under protection of law. The king shows kindness to all Protestants and is anxious to secure greater harmony of faith and worship. But there is opposition. No small number of bishops and clergy have suddenly grown conscientious, and refuse to take the oath to the new king. Henceforth the Papists are not the only Jacobites.

William's hereditary hatred for France is gratified by the rising indignation of England against Louis XIV. Thousands of fugitive Huguenots—men of learning and worth—have helped to form and inten-

sify public feeling.   High dignitaries of the Anglican
Church, discussing the pouring out of the third vial
now thought to be going on, and the destruction of
Antichrist which is to follow, are assuming that the
Cevennes Christians and the Waldenses are the two
witnesses of the Apocalypse now being killed.   Of
martyrs so distinctively Presbyterian it is singular that
these dignitaries should admit that they "by all appearance from good history have kept the primitive
faith from the very Apostles' time until now." *

Tyrconnel has called the Papists of Ireland to arms,
and the country is desolated by thousands of Rapparees.   Exhausting the Southern country, these robbers
surge on toward Ulster.   Enniskillen and Londonderry
acknowledge William and Mary and nerve themselves
for a terrific struggle.

On the 12th of March, backed by France, James
lands at Kinsale.   He joins the Northern army, and
they reach St. Johnstown, five miles from Derry, in
April.   On the 18th the siege begins.   Lundy, the
traitorous Episcopal governor, tries to betray the
town into the hands of the enemy, but his purpose is
defeated by the gallant Adam Murry.   Although
Bishop Mossom for years prevented the erection of
a Presbyterian church within the walls, now, in the
time of need, there are fifteen of the defenders Presbyterians to one Episcopalian.

Through one hundred and five days the marvelous
contest continues.   There, in the North of the Emerald Isle, from the summit and sides of its hill overlooking the waters of the river Foyle, stands the
brave little city, the bulwark of civil and religious

* Evelyn's *Diary.*

liberty. Its beleaguered heroes fight and suffer and starve, while the fearless women serve out water and ammunition all through the furious struggle.

Famine and pestilence rage within the city. Horse-flesh and dogs and salted hides and rats are growing scarce as food. Prayers from starving, fever-stricken, yet unfaltering, men and women go up for strength and victory. On the 30th of July, English ships move up the Foyle, break the boom stretched across it by the enemy, and bring to the wharf ample supplies,* thus confounding the hopes of the followers of James II.

So ends one of the most momentous conflicts in the history of nations and of Christianity. From hearts like these our Presbyterianism came to this shore. Through those dreadful days of siege Mr. John Rowat, the successor of Mr. Trail at Lifford, with eight more of our ministers, was shut up amid all the horrors of the city. At St. Johnstown, where the enemy was encamped, and where James looked on and encouraged his Popish adherents, the Presbytery of Laggan used to meet until prohibited by its foes. There Mr. Makemie was received as a candidate for the ministry.

Six or eight miles away, Mr. Makemie's native hills have also been the scene of warfare and blood. The Isle of Inch, out in Lough Swilly, in sight of his father's house, was fortified and held by Protestant forces. At Ramullan, a little northward of our pioneer's home, Colonel Henry Hunter was attacked by greatly superior numbers under the Duke of Berwick. Defeated with the loss of two hundred men, the duke

* Reid, vol ii , and Witherow's *Enniskillen and Derry.*

retreated, inflicting many outrages on the Protestants of the neighborhood * The "Lough of Shadows" has been under darker shadows than the shadows of its mountains. The Isle of Inch, thoroughly garrisoned, supplies a place of refuge for many Protestants around its shores. Perhaps Anne Makemie, the beloved younger sister, found safety there during those dark days.

The same week with the battle of Newton Butler, when the heroic Enniskilleners gave the finishing-blow to their foes and hastened the rout of the retreating besiegers of Derry, the fiend Claverhouse, Earl of Dundee, falls at Killiekrankie in enfranchised Scotland. There expires the last hope of James II.—"the darling of Heaven," as he is called by his Episcopal friends.

To the authorities at Edinburgh comes the eloquent prayer of the scarred veterans of Scotland, urging that the throne be declared vacant and that measures be taken to secure the kingdom against such oppression for ever, pleading for these things—

"By the cry of the blood of our murdered brethren, by the sufferings of the banished free-born subjects of this realm, now groaning in servitude, having been sold into slavery in the English plantations of America; by the miseries that many thousands forfeited, disinherited, harassed and wasted houses have been reduced to; by all the sufferings of a faithful people for adhering to the ancient covenanted establishment of religion and liberty, and by all the arguments of justice, necessity and mercy, that could ever join together, to begin communication among men of wisdom, piety and virtue." †

Thus these noble men remember the exiles in the plantations of far America. How the hearts of our

* Reid, ii 384   † Wodrow, *passim.*

Browns, Erskines, Galbraiths, Wilsons, and hundreds of indentured servants, thrill under these burning words!

Among other declarations in their Claim of Right, the Scotch Estates respond:

"That Prelacy and the superiority of any office in the Church above Presbyters, is, and hath been, a great and insupportable grievance and trouble to the nation."

Now comes an explanation of Naomi's hint with regard to a Presbyterian minister in Accomack. It is Mr. Makemie, and he is living down on Matchatank Creek, a placid stream which enters the bay near the mouth of the Onancock, and which is sometimes called "The Little Onancock." The political excitement in Virginia probably hastened Mr. Makemie's removal to the more retired Eastern Shore.

Of late the Council of that province has been very abject in its declarations of loyalty to the Stuart, the colony smarting under the double despotism of James and of Governor Effingham. There went abroad frightful reports of plots by Papists and Indians. The people were aroused, and have been in arms. The Council has been prosecuting all who uttered a word in disapproval of the king's course. Colonel John Scarborough was brought to trial for saying that "His Majesty would wear out the Church of England." The parade of attachment to James and the attendant turmoil may well have loosened Mr Makemie from the Western Shore (35).

Meanwhile, the excitement in our own province bursts into revolution. The king's attempted aggrandizement of Popery, over the seas, had aroused the dread of our Protestant population. They knew that

James would not stop with fastening the papal yoke upon his European subjects (36). Nor could our Catholic colonists wholly conceal their gratification at the usurpation of James in his efforts to bring his Church back to power.

The base informer Titus Oates had included our Proprietary in his many perjuries, charging him with intrigues to uproot Protestantism from British soil. The fact was known that His Lordship preferred James to William, notwithstanding the part that James had taken in assisting William Penn to a large portion of his province, and notwithstanding the known truth that James was endeavoring to abrogate his charter-right to all the rest. Lord Baltimore seemed disposed to stand by the Catholic despot, though he would thereby ruin himself, and us too.*

Of course there were enough bad men to take the tide. While there have been good clergymen in America, yet the colonies have been afflicted with some of the worst in the English Church—men without good repute or support at home, whose only hope was in a new country where their lives were not known, and where there are no ecclesiastical superiors to call them to account. What is said by Hammond in his *Leah and Rachel* is still true.

"Many came, such as wore black coats and could babble in a pulpit, roar in a tavern, exact from their parishioners, and rather, by their dissoluteness, destroy than feed their flocks."

Said Colonel Berkeley of Virginia in 1671 :

" But of all other commodities, so of this, the worst are sent us, and we had few that we could boast of."

* Neill's *Terra Mariæ, passim*

These corrupt clergymen are the most intolerant of all toward Dissenters, and the most busy in stirring up strife.   One of these vicious men in holy orders—the notorious John Coode—has been prompt to seize the opportunity now afforded for agitation and revenge. Before in rebellion, but dealt with too leniently by the Proprietary, he has never forgiven His Lordship for defeating his plans and then pardoning him (37).

The deputy lieutenants have not been wise.   We feel that if Colonel Stevens, one of the nine, had been alive, the result might have been different.   Their president, William Joseph, weak and foolish in the hour of danger, has been contending for the divine right of legitimates as zealously as the Stuarts themselves. The Lower House of Assembly was called before the Upper to take the oath of allegiance to the Proprietary, contrary to the privileges of the burgesses and involving an unnecessary suspicion.   The electors would naturally resent this infringement upon the rights and honor of their representatives.   Another misstep was the arming of the province upon receiving the news of the invasion of England by the Prince of Orange, bearing the appearance of a purpose to take sides with the Papist tyrant against England's Protestant deliverer.

The deputies were at this juncture renewing treaties with certain Indian tribes, and rumors were sent abroad by the conspirators that this was done to enlist the savages in the Papist plot to fasten the yoke upon Maryland.   Steps were taken to suppress these rumors, blunder upon blunder thus hastening their speed and intensifying the damaging suspicions.

The other colonies were now proclaiming William

and Mary and putting themselves in line with the Protestant sentiment of Europe. We wait in vain for their recognition by the government at St. Mary's. Are not our authorities occupying the same position with the base Tyrconnel of Ireland? Had it only been known that our Proprietary, though at first loyal to James, had at last given in his adhesion to William and Mary and sent orders to America for their recognition, the results might have been different, but, unfortunately, the orders did not reach their destination in time. The deputies delayed. Delay at such an hour is ruin.

Our tranquil Eastern Shore has not wholly escaped the excitement. Many of us know not what to think. We admire our Proprietary and believe, if he had been in the province, he could have satisfied the people and poured oil upon the troubled waters. Those of us whose relatives are still bleeding under the cruelties inflicted in France and Ireland have reason to dread the Papists. But Catholic Baltimore is far better than Episcopal Coode.

Coode sees that his opportunity has come. In March it is reported that hostile demonstrations are made by the Indians on the Patuxent. Coode asks arms from the government for repelling the fabulous Indian invasion. With this bold leader falsehood and treachery are favorite weapons "If much dirt is thrown, some of it will stick," is his characteristic maxim. Arms are granted by the too credulous authorities—arms to be used against themselves.

In April is formed what is called "An Association in Arms for the Defence of the Protestant Religion and for Asserting the Rights of King William and Queen

Mary to the Province of Maryland and all the English Dominions." From the printing-press at St. Mary's— the first in Maryland, and one of the first in America —is issued a pamphlet justifying the movement, declaring the motives of the revolutionists and containing most serious charges against the administration of the Proprietary

Coode and his forces capture St. Mary's and besiege the Council at Matapony, on the Patuxent, the colonists still inflamed with falsehoods about the encroachments of the Indians. On the 1st of August, two days after the close of the siege at Londonderry, the garrison at Matapony are forced to surrender, and the government is in the hands of the Associators. His Lordship's power is prostrate, and by the terms of the surrender the Papists are henceforth excluded from all offices, civil and military, within the province. I tremble for Lady Mary Somerset amid all these distractions.

What is to be the result of this revolution? These men have no right to the government. Will the conduct of the usurpers be approved in England? What change will it bring to Dissenters? Warrants are issued by the revolutionists for the election of burgesses to a convention to meet in the latter part of August. Some of the counties observe the order, some refuse. The convention send to King William a favorable account of themselves and their purposes, and skillfully put the Maryland revolution upon the same footing with the revolution in England, for the establishment of his authority here.

One name among the Associators had influence in gaining the confidence of the Presbyterians—that of

Colonel Ninian Beall (38). He is a Scotchman, driven from home by the persecutions there, first settling in Barbadoes, then coming to Maryland and purchasing a tract of land between the Potomac and Patuxent, called "Upper Marlborough"—it was first named "New Scotland"—and to that point he has been inviting colonists from his native Fifeshire. To calm the fears of the people, early this year he made report to the Council that there were no grounds for suspecting the Papists of a plot. This was noble. In fact, his experience in Scotland would teach him to fear Prelacy as much as Popery. But, wisely preferring William to James, he is now among those who are anxious to guide the revolution to good results.

It is to be feared that Mr. Trail is losing some of his interest in the plantation of Brother's Love. Another plantation needing cultivators is upon his heart. Prelacy was abolished in Scotland by act of Parliament in July, but, out of the four hundred Presbyterian ministers ejected since the restoration of the Stuarts, only sixty remain alive to witness the final triumph of Presbytery. The wasted lands, the decimated churches, gaze on the vacancies and sigh for their banished sons.

In the midst of these stirring events and rapid changes, our native population increases. On the 29th of August, while the Convention is preparing its address to King William, another little native-born Marylander appears over on the Monokin and captures the heart and the name of Major Robert King. Mrs. Mary Jenkins is very proud of her royal brother.*

* Afterward the husband of Makemie's daughter.

Scotchmen will be Scotchmen.   The other day I heard Mary, our rosy lassie, singing to her old-bachelor friend John Galbraith a new song composed only a year or two ago and just sent her from her home over the deep,   While she sang I wondered if a pleasant memory stirred the exile's heart of some sweet face by some ingleside in dear Scotia.   Or has he made the Church the love of his life?   This is the brand-new ballad :

> " Maxwelton banks are bonnie,
>   Where early fa's the dew,
>   Where me and Annie Laurie
>   Made up the promise true—
>   Made up the promise true,
>   And ne'er forget will I ;
>   And for bonnie Annie Laurie
>   I'll lay down my head and die " (39).

12

CHAPTER XI.

A. D. 1690.

"We must purge away the spots and stains if we would appear beautiful in the eyes of our God."—MAKEMIE.

MR. MAKEMIE studies the capabilities of these shores from a business-man's standpoint. He says:

"I need not inform you what an excellent and desirable country you inhabit, not inferior to any Colonies in the English America; situate in a moderate 'Climate and Northern latitude, suitable and agreeable to European bodies; supplied with the spacious Bay of Chesapeake which runs thorow and divides first Virginia, next Maryland, running North and by East nearest, about eight leagues in breadth, capable of receiving vast fleets of ships without skillful pilots, not to be affrighted with dangerous rocks and dismal sands; a Bay in most respects not to be outdone by the universe, having so many large and spacious rivers branching on both sides; and each of these rivers richly supplied and subdivided into sundry smaller rivers, spreading themselves both on the North and South sides, to innumerable creeks and coves, admirably carved out and contrived by the Omnipotent hand of our Wise Creator for the advantage and conveniency of its inhabitants; so that I have oft, with no small admiration, compared the many rivers, creeks and rivulets of water in these colonies to veins in human bodies."

I am glad to know his high appreciation of the two sister-provinces. The attractions have been growing upon him since six years ago, when, after his first visit to Maryland, he wrote in reference to his friends in Ireland:

178

" I design to be very cautious in inviting them to any place in America I have yet seen."

Now he continues :

" Here we have a clear and serene air, a long and hot summer, a short and sharp winter, a free and fertile soil.   Here are vast quantities of timber for shipping, trade and architecture, our country being generally woody.   Here are in most places bricks to be made at every man's door for building; a soil suitable for producing anything agreeable for a Northern latitude and with as little labor and expense as any place in the world; spacious and flourishing orchards, replenished with fair and pleasant fruits; and will afford pleasant gardens by much less labor and expense than in Europe, furnished with whatever herbs, flowers and plants you are pleased to put into the ground.   Here are stocks of all sorts raised and maintained with little industry, and by better husbandry might be improved to a high degree. Here are all advantages imaginable for trade by water, conveniences for travel and transportation; commodious, easy and pleasant roads.   Here is a country capable of producing sundry staples, as hemp, flax, wool, silk, cotton, and wine too, and still overdo the tobacco trade." *

Mr. William Anderson of Accomack, and our sturdy Scotch friend John Galbraith, will not think less of Mr. Makemie because of his practical genius and public spirit.

Mr. Trail has left us, listening to the cry of Caledonia for her scattered sons.   Of the pastors driven to exile or death, only one in seven can be found for their destitute flocks.   These vacant fields are exceedingly anxious to secure those ministers who amid the late persecutions refused to bend the knee to Baal.   The pliant and wavering are not wanted.   Although our Mr. Trail could never, as he says, look upon blood without fainting, yet who is able to name a time when his moral courage has been unequal to the demands

* Makemie's *Plain and Friendly Perswasive.*

of the hour, whether in Dublin Castle, in the Lifford prison or in the American wilderness?

In February of this year Mr. Trail gave Mrs Elinor a power of attorney to convey his land as soon as a purchaser can be found, and not long afterward sailed for Europe * After what Scotland has done for us, it looks like ingratitude to resist his departure too strenuously; for the country of the mother-Church is now more poorly supplied with ministers than our own Lower Peninsula. But the wilderness will appear more lonely now that his voice shall be heard no longer at Rehoboth and his form be seen no more among the growing maize at Brother's Love.

Mr. Trail's going is an experiment as yet, for there are difficulties and dangers in Scotland, and King William has many troubles to face in all his kingdoms. Mrs. Elinor remains to look after the property and await the result of her husband's reception beyond the deep. The war with the French, with their cruisers abroad and the consequent boldness of pirates upon our coast, makes it hazardous for her to attempt the voyage. We shall have the pleasure of the presence among us of a minister's wife that much longer —an especially pleasant thought while Mr. Makemie persists in living a bachelor life.

The king has approved the act of the Associators in Maryland and entrusted the government of the province to them and the Conventions Under the representations so shrewdly used that our Maryland revolution was a counterpart of the English revolution, made in behalf of his interests and with a view to his assuming the royal control, it was not to be expected that

* Power of attorney on Somerset records.

he would condemn what they have done. Ours is now a Protestant government, the Catholics excluded from all participation in it; but whether the change will bring us good or evil remains to be seen.

This year, while Colonel Francis Jenkins, Mr. Makemie's friend, was on the judicial bench, he was treated with contempt by Mr. Walter Lowe of our county. Mr. Lowe ought to have known that these are perilous times for friends of the proscribed religion to provoke the hostility of the officers of the law. Even on the peaceful Eastern Shore, the smouldering enmity to Popery may be easily blown into a flame. With no little warmth, Colonel Jenkins declared that " he would not be affronted by any Irish Papist in the land." *

The Quakers, too, are in danger of being treated with less leniency than under the Proprietary. During the same week John Booch was fined for wearing his hat in the presence of the court.

By order of the Bench, the oath of allegiance and abhorrency was administered to our ferryman, John Moore, and to all officers, civil and military, in the county. Thus they swear that they *abhor* the doctrines and practices of the Romish Church—an oath devised in England for excluding all persons of that faith from civil office.

As a defence against all possible enemies, whether Indians, pirates, the French or imaginary dangers from the Papists, our county has its public arsenals —seventy-nine guns in all, distributed as follows: twelve at Edward Day's, six at Captain Winder's, fifteen at Colonel Brown's, ten at Mr. Weatherby's,

* Somerset records, 1690 So with other incidents.

twenty at Colonel Colburn's, six at Squire Layfield's, on the Rehoboth plantation, and ten on the seaside. So much for the safety and dignity of Somerset.

Says Matchacoopah,

"The loud-talking tomahawks of the white men command us all to be friends."

We hear of a Presbyterian minister over in the Upper Marlborough settlement preaching to the Fifeshire Scotchmen—the Rev. Nathaniel Taylor. Thus our Church is taking possession of both the Eastern and the Western frontier of Maryland— Presbyterianism of the pure type.*

A large colony of Huguenots, sent over to Virginia by King William, has settled on the south bank of James River, in Henrico county.† Our new Protestant king is proving himself a friend to the oppressed, and is endeavoring to secure entire toleration for all religions throughout his dominions. By supplying an asylum for the most valuable population and the best blood of France, he knows that he is indirectly striking at the vitals of his great rival.

Now news reaches us of our king's arrival in Ireland, and of his occupying, at Belfast, the house of Sir William Franklin. Sir William married the widow of the Earl of Donegal and has relatives in our own county. While the king was there, a deputation of Presbyterian ministers presented an address and were received with great favor. Soon afterward the royal bounty of twelve hundred pounds per annum was granted for the support of our ministry.

Mr Walker, with a delegation of Episcopal clergymen, also waited upon the king. This is the Walker

* Hodge, p 57.   † Campbell, p. 370

who was subordinate governor during the siege of
Derry, and who has since been arrogating to himself
and his prelatic friends all the credit of that heroic
defence, hurrying to England and publishing the one-
sided account which depreciated the services of the
Presbyterians and appropriated to himself stolen
honors. It is known that he was more than once
in favor of capitulation, and was seriously suspected
of treachery by the brave garrison. Some think that
William's shrewdness is beginning to understand him.*
This spring has been published Mackensie's narrative,
exposing Walker.

In trying to play its double game of loyalty to
both James and William, Prelacy has been badly puzzled. On the last Sabbath of June the bishops and
other clergy in Dublin prayed zealously for the success of James and the destruction of his foes; on the
next Sabbath they paraded their prayers just as earnestly for the triumph of William and the ruin of all
his enemies! So it has occurred, as has been said,
that "four times in one year they have been praying
backward and forward point-blank contradictory to
one another." The doctrine of the divine right of
kings has supplied a torturing dilemma for its adherents.

Meanwhile, between these two Sabbaths, the battle
of the Boyne has been fought, the army of the Irish
routed, the cause of James wrecked. By that little
river the contest for civil and religious liberty has
been waged and won. The Londoner, the Scot, the
English settler of Ulster, the Dutch Calvinist and the
French Huguenot have stood side by side for the

* Reid, ii. 402, etc.; Witherow's *Derry*, etc , chap. viii.

right.* James re-embarks and flees back to France. At the Boyne, Dr. Walker has been killed, and his body left stripped and naked on the field. "What brought *him* there?" was the abrupt question of William when the death of the officious clergyman was reported to him.†

In England the High Churchmen hate William for his tolerance of Dissenters, and would prefer the Heaven-ordained Popish king. The Tories in Parliament refuse to take the oath abjuring the tyrant James.

Next comes a sensation working its way over stream and through pine-forest from the Sinepuxent Shore. Not far from the wigwam of Queen Weocomoconus dwells the enemy to and one of the destroyers of an English throne. Often have I thought of the venerable man on the plantation of Geneser whose dignity and military bearing so much impressed me at the house of Mr. Wale. Well do I now remember his evident interest in European affairs, notwithstanding his studied disguise of that interest. From among the Middletons of Accomack, where they still live, the old gentleman had come up to Mr. Wale's, on the Pocomoke, about ten years ago. Until now not a word has been heard of his previous life. At length there is no longer any reason for keeping the secret. The Stuarts hopelessly off the throne, none remain to avenge the death of the "martyr-king." The revolution assured, Major-General Edward Whalley, the "Regicide," and the trusted friend and counselor of his cousin Oliver Cromwell, may now own his identity

---

* Knight, iv. 513.
† Witherow's *Derry and Enniskillen* p. 310.

and his great name.   The hero of many a fight, Nase-
by, Langport, Bridgeport, Sherborne Castle, Bristol,
Exeter, Oxford, Banbury Castle; one of the fifty-nine
judges who signed the death-warrant of Charles I.,
and who witnessed his execution; a fugitive for thirty
years with a price on his head; coming to New England with his son-in-law and fellow-regicide Goffe in
1666, and retiring from Boston to Cambridge, to New
Haven, to Milford, to Hadley, until, as they say in
Connecticut, one died and the other went off "to the
west toward Virginia,"—now for some time he has
been living obscurely among us, remembering in his
great old age the stirring deeds of his youth, but
breathing no word of reminiscence even to the melt-
ing foam along the shore.   Thus, with many others,
he has awaited the fall of the hated dynasty (40).

At last we hear of free meetings of the Presbyteries
in Ireland—a glorious change from the dark days when
a few outlawed ministers could stealthily assemble with
closed doors only!   We think of the secret session in
unrecorded privacy when our Makemie was ordained
to the holy ministry—a sin and a crime in the eyes of
prelates—and we thank God that Ulster at length is
free.

In Scotland, Presbyterianism is again the established
religion.   There, amid her hills and glens, had lived
and triumphed the brave principles—almost dead elsewhere—which have finally delivered the empire from
despotism.   The land of martyrs has her reward.   For
the first time in forty years the General Assembly has
now met, convening on the 16th of October and spending the first day in fasting and prayer.

Sitting as a member of this august Assembly, in

sight of the horrid Bass, where both his father and his brother were once imprisoned, is our own Mr. Trail. Sir James Stewart, who married Mr. Trail's sister, has property and influence at Borthwick, and on the 26th of July our minister was called to that church, and installed there on the 17th of September. In the scarcity of ministers so sorely felt in Scotland, happy is the parish that secures one whose record is so spotless. We feel it a privilege to send one of her sons back to the mother of martyred heroes.

In one of the most important and eventful Assemblies that ever sat on earth, with many and mighty problems facing them and awaiting solution, himself among the influences which are to mould the future of the great Church of Scotland, I wonder if Mr. Trail thinks now and then of the log house at Brother's Love and of his old friends in the valley of the Pocomoke?

While our late pastor is thus active in the cause of Presbyterianism across the ocean, Mr. Makemie is doing all he can to lay a sound basis of Calvinistic truth in America. Not only are his sermons sowing the seed up and down the coast, but from his home at Matchatank he has sent forth a Catechism of his own, full of the marrow of the gospel, for the indoctrination of the children of his people. Himself converted at fifteen years of age, this pioneer minister of our Church is zealously taking hold of the rising generation and trying to fortify their minds against the prevailing errors both of ignorance and of false doctrine. He well says :

" The advantage of an early instruction is witnessed by the experiences of many godly of all ages, where attended with the blessing of God and pursued with exhortation until they arrive at a riper age" (41).

It is pleasant to meet with this little volume of forty or fifty pages in the homes of the colonists along the bright shores of the Chesapeake, on the banks of its many tributaries, under the shades of the solemn forests, along the sunny seaside; these silent preachers impressing daily the great facts of Scripture from the first page, where the author begins, like the Bible itself, with the work of the omnipotent Creator, then on through his earnest exaltation of God's word as the only and sufficient rule of faith and practice, the mystery of the Trinity, the atonement of Christ, the office-work of the Spirit, the sanctity of the Sabbath, the duties to the ministry and of the ministry, the reverent use of the sacraments, the power of prayer. In this brief summary of doctrine and duty, Mr. Makemie claims that he has embodied "the judgement of all my brethren and particularly of those of the Westminster Assembly both in their Shorter and Larger Catechism." Brave and emphatic in his teachings, he thus fearlessly challenges the objector:

"In the Catechism many savory truths delivered, no sins indulged, most duties relating to our general and special callings enjoined, now how the receiving such a form of sound words containing positive Divinity should be prejudicial, let every one determine."

My honored father, watching all these movements with the eye of a philosopher, notices that the first literary publication of our Eastern Shore is a religious book, and for the children. While Mr. John Locke issues from the press this year in England his *Essay concerning the Human Understanding*, Mr. Makemie is wisely laboring to preoccupy the understanding of the young with divine truth as a mighty factor in advancing the Church of the future.

Colonel Jenkins has been speaking to us of the shores of the Chesapeake as the birthplace of American literature. The first American book was written by a man of action as well as of the pen, the chivalrous John Smith—*A True Relation of Virginia*, published in 1608, near the time and place of Mr. John Milton's birth. Virginia and Maryland one and the same then, we claim a share in the author's fame. So also in Percy's graphic description of the sufferings of the first colonists at Jamestown; in Strachey's magnificent portraiture of the shipwreck at the Bermudas, which inspired Shakespeare's *Tempest;* in the godly Whitaker's *Good News from Virginia*—his scholarly pictures of her needs, and his exhortation to come to her help with the gospel and to " remember that the plantation is God's and the reward your country's;" a share in Secretary Pory's sketches of travel—more especially because of his early visit to our own Lower Peninsula and account of it in 1620; and a share in the fame of the elegant translation of Ovid by George Sandys, who heeded in the wilderness the injunction addressed to him by the great poet Drayton :

> " Entice the Muses thither to repair;
> Entreat them gently; train them to that air;
> For they from hence may thither hap to fly."

The colonel spoke of young Maryland taking up the pen in the person of her Indian trader, Captain Fleet, in 1631 and 1632; then of the elegant Latin narrative of Father Andrew White at the time of the settlement (1634); then of the vigorous little book called *Leah and Rachel; or, The Two Fruitful Sisters, Virginia and Maryland,* published by John Hammond in 1656; next of George Alsop's book published ten years after, *A Character of the Province of Maryland,* roystering and verbose, but interesting—only the more so because written by an indentured servant who testifies that there were often intelligence and worth and happiness to be found among this class of our population.

"Thus," said Colonel Jenkins, " has American literature had her birth among the tributaries of the Chesapeake, and there uttered her first Western lispings. Why shall not her warblings or her thunderings be heard on this side of the bay and along our own Pocomoke ?"

Meanwhile, our busy apostle is pushing his tent-making energetically. He says:

"Have not the ministers of the reformed church of Scotland, these thirty years past, suffered persecution even unto death itself for preaching the Gospel under so much want that they have been necessitated to labor with their own hands and betake themselves for a time to merchandizing and yet never would dare to lay aside the preaching of the Gospel ? And it is 'not unknown how little ministers have had in maintenance in Maryland." *

On that shimmering arm of the bay, Matchatank, Mr. Makemie sees his sloop sailing away between the sand-islands and past the fishhawks' nests, bound for the broader waters with her cargo of wheat and pork, freighted for Barbadoes. Yonder flit the sea-birds again, as in other days among the shadows of Lough Swilly. He is a practical man of business, knows the

* *Answer to Keith.*

laws of trade and asserts his rights. Mr. William Finney sells him grain below the standard, and in November suit is brought and judgment obtained for "fifteen bushels of merchantable wheat to be delivered at the house of said Makemie at Matchatank." This same year he is assessed and pays for three tithables for the support of Mr. Teackle and the Episcopal church in Virginia. Laboring for his own bread, his people too poor to support him, our minister is compelled to contribute of his hard earnings for the maintenance of a Church which despises and oppresses his faith (42).

I have just learned the meaning of the playful badinage in Colonel Jenkins's manner while reading to Mr. Makemie the following extract from Alsop's wayward book :

"The women are extremely bashful at the first view, but after a continuance of time hath brought them acquainted, then they become discreetly familiar, and are much more talkative than men. All Complimental Courtships, dressed up in critical Rarities, are mere strangers to them; plain wit comes nearest their Genius; so that he that intends to court a Mary-Land Girle, must have something more than the Tautologies of a long-winded speech to carry on his design, or else he may (for aught I know) fall under the contempt of her frown and his own windy Oration."

But in this case she seems to be a Virginia "Girle;" for there are intimations abroad, flitting about as briskly as the pinions of the water-gulls, that the minister sails up Pocomoke Sound oftener than his merchandise or his pulpit requires; that on one of the streams below us is a sister whom our second Paul thinks he is entitled to lead about; that a daughter of Accomack is capturing the heart of the lonely son of Donegal.

CHAPTER XII.

A. D. 1691.

"It is the true character of a deceiver to possess others with prejudices against our principles, only by misrepresenting them, and fastening principles on us which we abhor."—MAKEMIE.

I HAVE not mentioned that my friend William has been clearing a little plantation for corn and tobacco. The new house, of cypress logs and shingles, presents an attractive appearance among the forest-trees, suggestive of some great happiness. Matchacoopah has been digging up the native honeysuckles and planting them all around the yard. Naomi has kept her secret, and I can keep mine.

"Weetah-tomps" ("the dove") "from the white man's land," says the Indian, "builds his nest in the flower-garden of Jaquokranogare and moans for a mate." *

Well do I remember the Sabbath at Rehoboth before Naomi became a bride. To us maidens never had Mr. Makemie looked so well or talked so beautifully. The pure cloudless azure bent very close while he said:

"We have not this world but Heaven for our city. Therefore if we would expect Heaven in the end, we must begin and in some measure live a life of Heaven upon earth; everything must tend Heavenward; daily preparing for Heaven, and so speaking or acting as if you were bound for Heaven; employed about Heavenly things, and elevated above the concerns of this

* "Jaquokranogare"—Iroquois name for Maryland.

lower world; only using the most desirable things thereof, as travelers to the New Jerusalem, as if we used them not; making sure of an interest in the Heavenly Canaan; making our acquaintance with the inhabitants of the Upper World, frequently conversing there by faith and contemplation, carrying on a constant trade and traffic with Heavenly prayer and supplication, having our hearts and souls soaring aloft and ardently breathing after our crown and kingdom, placing our affections on things above where our treasures are, yea, our chief ends, aims and endeavors tending and inclining that way." *

Notwithstanding the abounding wickedness abroad, while we listened that day our Western wilderness did not seem so far away from the celestial portals, after all. His figure of " carrying on a constant trade and traffic with Heaven " grew very naturally out of our pastor's commercial life.

As particular friends of the Andersons, we were bidden to the marriage. Peggy, the maid of Ulster, Mary, our rosy Scotch lassie, Margaret, the sweet singer of the Vincennes, and myself, helped to dress the bride and stood by her side. It was said that our smiles typified the benedictions of all classes of Presbyterian colonists upon the mating. Naomi, now in the full bloom of her twenty-second year, looked her loveliest, and Mr. Makemie, the handsome bridegroom, knew it, and would never be homesick any more for the green hills of Donegal—wedded henceforth for life and death to his holy mission in America.

Madam Mary Anderson's fingers were full of gold rings, and her figure was arrayed in a gown and petticoat of flowered silk whose cost we young ladies discovered to be over twelve pounds.† None but a Church-of-England clergyman or a justice of the

* New York sermon.
† Inventory of wardrobe: Accomack records

peace being authorized to perform the marriage ceremony in Virginia, Mr. Anderson could fill the latter
office very conveniently for the occasion.   I think
they are proud of their son-in-law.   Mr. Makemie
leaves his Matchatank plantation and will make his
future home near the Pocomoke, and nearer to us all.

Amid the general gladness, it amuses the guests to
hear Mr. Makemie's Scotch-Irish dialect pronouncing
our river "the Poccamok."*

The New World has rewarded her evangelist with a
helpmeet whose name is "Pleasantness" (43).

Our return up "the Poccamok" was cheered with
the odors of the marsh-grasses, fragrant as smell of
thyme-beds.   Passing the clearing of friend William,
our Huguenot songstress charmed us with one of the
sweetest canzos of the Troubadours.

While we still talk of our minister's young wife,
Mrs. Elinor Trail goes from our circles for ever to
rejoin her husband at Borthwick.   On the 25th of
April she succeeds in selling their plantation to Mr.
Archibald White.†   Their work here is done—God's
purposes are served.   The name "Brother's Love" will
perpetuate the fame of the good man and woman, and
Rehoboth must not forget them.

During the same month, Tuesday, April 2, Mr.
Makemie preached a funeral sermon in the Rehoboth church on the text, "The last enemy that shall
be destroyed is death."

On reaching the little town we noticed Mr. William
Morris, who lives near Dividing Creek, and who was
fined three years ago for drunkenness and breach of

* So spelled in his *Answer to Keith.*
† Deed on Somerset records.

13

the Sabbath, again intoxicated beyond self-control. His hardened ravings in such close contact with death were horrible to witness. But in this new land sin is brazen and defiant, and sinners will not think. Well does Mr. Makemie ask:

" Would men dare to live as they do ? would they not soon resolve and rectify their lives, if they did but duly contemplate that approaching change entailed on all mortals as a just debt due to the unchangeable appointment of Heaven ? Would the profane and dissolute neglect his just homage to his God, rebel against his Maker, fly in the face of Heaven, and abuse the rational creature, if he but considered how soon he may be dissolved and return to dust; which will put an end to the day of his salvation and dash the hope of the profane and the hypocrite and remove them beyond all possibility of repenting, believing, or praising God ? More especially if they were taking a view and prospect of that future account, that is to be given at the tribunal of God, of all our actions and deeds done in the body, and the eternal consequence of weal or woe which must follow that impartial judgment." *

Alas ! this direful appetite drives men wildly into the very face of death and judgment, and of all law, both human and divine.

Toward night the besotted man went over to the house of one of the justices of the peace, Mr. Edmund Howard, and thus put himself directly under the eye of one of the county officers. There, in the presence of Dr. John Vigerous and his daughter Anne, he continued to blurt out the most fearful oaths against Mr. Makemie and against death and against our blessed Saviour, reiterating his shocking blasphemies until after midnight (44).

Of course the wicked man was arrested and brought to trial. Here is the law under which he stands indicted:

* New York sermon.

"Whosoever blasphemes God, viz., to curse him or deny the Saviour Jesus Christ to be the Son of God, or shall deny the Trinity, or the godhead of any of the three persons thereof, or the Trinity or Unity of the godhead, or shall use or utter any reproachful speeches concerning the same or any of the three persons thereof, *shall suffer death.*"

During the progress of the trial, by the help of some unknown person, the guilty man escaped, and cannot be found. In November pay was asked of the court by Samuel Shewel for searching for him as far as Philadelphia, and for six days' fare at Assateague with the emperor Toattam and two days among the Indians at Assawaman. Such is the horror for this great crime, and such the zeal for its punishment.

Though Mr. Makemie cares nothing for the reproaches against himself, he is not indifferent to the enormity of such crimes, and advocates the execution of the laws. He says:

"Some offences are cognizable by officers and magistrates in the State as all are censurable by the ministry, and what *they* cannot do by the Word, the magistrate is to do by the sword. For magistracy is an ordinance of God and they are invested with his own name—'I have said ye are gods;' and they are appointed not to be a terror to good works but to evil, Rom. xiii. 3. That the magistrate may do his duty, penal laws against vice and immorality must be made, and no Christian state can be safe without them. Would beastly drunkenness be so common, swearing and cursing so ordinary a dialect, whoredom so impudent, profanation of the Lord's day so visible and frequent, if our rulers and magistrates everywhere were spirited with zeal for putting our penal laws in execution against scandalous offences? Would to God such as are in authority and vested with the sword of justice were exercising it boldly and faithfully against sin and all immoralities in life, and that impartially according to their oaths of office." *

I must mention a Quaker sensation this year—the

* New York sermon.

greatest since their famous founder went blazing like a meteor through our colony twenty years ago.   Just as we hear of the death of George Fox in England, and of William Penn's venturing out of his hiding-place to attend the burial of the great Mystic in Bunhill Fields,* there comes another inspired apostle through our county from Mr Penn's province, attended by a retinue of supporters and denouncing all who will not accept the tenet of Quaker infallibility.   A man of far more learning than his predecessor, and evidently far less honest, a partisan presumptuous and aggressive, some of his sect believe that the mantle of George Fox has fallen upon this George Keith. Among these strange people there are many excellent Christians, but it is a pity that they are not satisfied with the enjoyment of their own views without indulging in such bitter denunciations of others.   Advocates of non-resistance and of peace in the state, the most of their leaders have been anything but friends of peace in the kingdom of Christ.

This present champion of the Inner Light is a native of Aberdeen, Scotland, and was educated at its university—a classmate of Gilbert Burnet, the present Bishop of Salisbury.   Keith was originally a Presbyterian, but turned Quaker, and has been prolific of books in advocacy of Quaker principles.   On coming to America he settled at Monmouth, New Jersey, and was afterward made surveyor-general of that province.   Four years ago he ran the boundary-line between East and West Jersey.   In 1689 he took charge of the Friends' public school in Philadelphia.†

* Macaulay, iv. 19.

† Anderson's *History of the Colonial Church*, iii. 222, etc.

Mr. Makemie says in reply to the charge of preaching for money :

"I know not what evasion can be found for Keith's hundred pounds per annum settled on him by the Government in Pennsylvania, exacted of a mixed people, who neither hear him nor enjoy any benefit or advantage from his school-keeping." *

Exposing this expedient of the Quakers to support their preacher by public tax, our minister declares :

"This is their only shift and back-door they would fly out at."

In the midst of Keith's present crusade against all but Quakers, a report reaches us that he is not upon good terms with a large element of his own sect at home—that the Friends in Pennsylvania are not internally altogether friendly.

Mr. Makemie has told us of Keith's "malicious, uncharitable book against New England ministers." Now his chief assaults are upon our pastor and his Catechism. With so much wickedness around us, it is sad that the learning and ability of this man could not be expended in a better way than in attacking God's people, but our minister tells us that "Keith's trade has been to foment contention and stir up strife in the churches of Christ." The sacred beliefs once loved by him are now the most hated, for, according to Mr. Makemie, "Keith's invidious malice is most commonly set against the Reformed Chuch of Scotland, verifying the ancient and common saying, *Omnis apostata sua sectæosor.*"

At the house of Squire Layfield, the learned Quaker wrote out and left a review of the Catechism of Mr.

---

* Makemie's *Answer to Keith.* So other quotations following.

Makemie. This popular compendium of precious truth he is very anxious to uproot from its strong hold in our families. Growing bolder down in Accomack, and unwilling to leave so able a standard-bearer undemolished behind him, he and his admirers press the war to Mr. Makemie's very doors. Soon follows a great flourish of trumpets proclaiming the utter rout of our minister, boasting of a challenge to discussion given and weakly declined, Presbyterianism discomfited, Quakerism triumphant! Such reports have been diligently circulated everywhere, from Houlston's Creek to the Wicomico. From Mr. Makemie himself we have since had a full account of the matter:

"I had a visit from Keith at my house in Virginia, which though promised and intimated by his harbinger to be on Friday, was not performed until Saturday in the afternoon; and by the uncertainty of his coming, was prevented of having any of my friends present, though some dropped in occasionally. At which time we had several charges and questions concerning several things which were too tedious to rehearse. But I wish they had been recorded then to prevent many misrepresentations spread abroad by that party. And though there was no real debate, and he oft told me he came not to dispute with me, yet soon after they boasted of a victory. Yet after more discourse, he impudently charged me as a false teacher, and challenged me to a public debate before the multitude; which I scorned with a sharp retorsion, and that for the following reasons:

"First, Their principles were unknown, because never unanimously agreed upon nor fairly published to the world; therefore not to be disputed with in words. Second, We would dispute before an ignorant and illiterate multitude who would be most incompetent judges. Third, Because he would run into learning and I must follow, and so what should be delivered would not tend to their edification but fall to the ground and be lost.

"But afterward I gave him a challenge to oppose my Catechism or principles in writing, and he should have an answer to every particular. Keith gave not the least intimation of the paper left behind him, though he dropped an expression which I understood not then, That he would write no more than he had done. This I took for declining my challenge.

"Now I leave it to all to determine whose challenge or overture was fairest. For, First, What either of us should deliver should be on record and we could not fly from it. Second, If the hearing a verbal debate in angry words should edify, much more a written debate frequently read over. Third, Many might be judges of a written debate who had no opportunity of hearing it disputed publicly."

In this face-to-face encounter on the banks of the "Poccamok" there was unquestionably some sharp work done between the son of the University of Aberdeen and the son of the University of Glasgow —this North-Scotland Mystic and this North-Ireland Calvinist. We know that our minister did not spare the pretensions of their preachers, male and female, to "an immediate, extraordinary and Apostolic call, of which," he says, "Keith in a vain manner has boasted and affirmed at my house." Unflinchingly Mr. Makemie pressed the charge published in his Catechism— that Quakers are enemies to the Sabbath—and he sustained the charge by mention of names and places; but he says:

"Notwithstanding all reasons given to Keith and others, they seem still to be dissatisfied, but it is for the most part the temper of such as wrangle and oppose all reasoning. I am the more confirmed in that which I charged him with at my house, That most of his writings are quibbling controversies and his debates a disputing about words, little to the edification of souls."

After the visit to Mr. Makemie, Keith went to Snow Hill and there made flagrant misrepresentations of the conversation to Mr. Samuel Davis. Our minister has since declared.

"I must greatly suspect what Keith told me at my house as another lie and calumny, That Mr John Cotton of Hampton, in New England, acknowledged in a public dispute that he derived his ordination from the Pope. And the rather because he abused me, upon his return, to Mr. Davis, affirming the same thing of me, That I owned our mission and ordination from the Pope of Rome. I am confident his own conscience could not but witness the contrary to his face. For I not only abhorred, disclaimed and denied it, but positively and plainly affirmed our mission was from Jesus Christ and warranted from the Scriptures."

Such has been the first theological tilt in the birth-place of American Presbyterianism. This is not the end. Mr. Makemie has secured from Squire Layfield Keith's manuscript strictures upon the Catechism, and is preparing a reply for publication. He is a man of peace, but now they have aroused him; and my father's opinion is that the Quaker aggressors will be severely handled. Our minister says:

"This debate was first set on foot by themselves and, by promoting it, gave occasion for laying open both their principles and their practices more in these corners of the world than they have yet been."

I have heard Mr. Makemie summing up certain of the defects of this Quaker sect as follows:

"They cannot be looked upon as a church; having not unanimously and fairly or faithfully published all their opinions and principles, which is the cause many espouse they know not what. They have not in any of their writings declared their church order, constitution, government nor discipline. They have no orderly way of admission for teaching-officers, but as many men and women as say the Spirit of the Lord is upon them, must be received though they can give no convincing proof but to those already deluded to their way. From which they want [are without] the pure and powerful preaching of the Gospel and all administration of the sacraments, which they ridicule rather than own. They hold or maintain a common Christ in all, even in the reprobate in whom the Spirit of God, says

Christ, is not; and a sufficient saving light and grace in all, even the children of darkness; denying original and damnable guilt in any infants even in their natural state; railing against singing of Psalms; denying the resurrection of the same body; many of them scoffing at the imputed righteousness of Christ for our justification and salvation, maintaining an absolute perfection for many years in this life by a Popish possibility of keeping all God's commands, of which neither they nor Papist could ever in any age produce one known instance."

This demand for an example of sinless perfection is a severe test for the dogma.

With our sweet-voiced Huguenot, I have been talking about the deliverance from persecution just effected for the Waldenses by the treaty between the Duke of Savoy and our Protestant king.* To the same brave heart she looks hopefully for the relief of her friends from continued barbarities in Southern France. Margaret has lately been up to the shop of Mr. John Dorman, at Snow Hill, and from his stock—of ironware and drygoods, hoes, axes, stirrup-leathers, linens, stuffs, silks, serges, hats, haberdashery ware and hoods †—she has purchased herself a very nice silk gown and petticoat. I am a little suspicious.

The war in Ireland is over. At Aghrim, Mackay the Puritan and Ruvigny the Huguenot have met the army under Saint Ruth—"the hangman," as he is called by the oppressed in France—and the hangman is killed and his forces are routed. Limerick falls, and Tyrconnel, the viceroy of James, dies drinking and jesting, struck with apoplexy. The Presbyterians of Ulster are worshiping without molestation. Their Synod meets and shows its characteristic zeal for securing an educated ministry.

* Knight, iv 530.
† Dorman's stock this year. Somerset records.

In Scotland the prelates and Jacobites are thoroughly united and doing what they can to obstruct our Church. Because they cannot tyrannize as heretofore over their late victims, they are raising a loud cry of persecution. In England the non-juring High Churchmen have been detected in inviting an invasion from France.

All this does not increase our desire for the establishment of the Church of England in Maryland. Its adherents are in the majority, and are determined not to rest content without state support. Rev. Mr. Yeo's cry of fifteen years ago and Rev. Mr. Coode's long-delayed ambition have an echo in the hearts and on the lips of many impatient partisans. Not very pleasantly do some of us remember that this year again Mr. Makemie is taxed three tithables for the support of Mr. Teackle and that grasping church in Virginia.

Sir Lionel Copley has been appointed royal governor, and will reach our province some time next year. Thus we have passed directly under the administration of the Crown. Our county lawyer, Mr. Peter Dent, has become attorney-general of Maryland —an honor to the Somerset bar.

We are glad that the English government orders that the act of outlawry against our rightful Proprietary be removed, and that his lawful revenues, withheld by the Convention, be henceforth duly paid him; but he is to have no civil authority in the province.

My friend William has just dropped a tear to the memory of the great Baxter. During this last month of the year, "the Kidderminster bishop," as Jeffreys called him, has loosed from earth and gone peacefully home—yea, to "the saint's everlasting rest." This year has Mr. John Flavel also ascended to his reward. On the shelves of our minister's growing library I find several of the sweet books of this good man.

And now the year is approaching its close with an anxiety in our hearts lest another may pass from our earth who would leave as great a vacancy here as Baxter and Flavel left in England. I have not mentioned the tedious affliction which has fallen upon our own Makemie. What is to be the result? Our "moderate climate and Northern latitude, suitable and agreeable to European bodies, the same with the Mediterranean," as he has heartily described it,—is it to undermine his health and drive him from us, after all? I am glad that God and Virginia have given him Naomi to brighten these months of suffering.

From Mr. Makemie's library I take down a volume of the sainted Flavel and read:

"It is a certain truth that all the results and issues of Providence are profitable and beneficial to the saints."

Our pastor is not ignorant of the sustaining power of religion. He who faced unshrinkingly the darkening clouds of persecution which overhung the years of his consecration to the ministry, from 1680 to 1682, knows what it is to trust and be strong. I have heard him speak very beautifully of "the experiences of thousands of the godly, of ravishings of soul, and ineffable joy and comfort from praising God " (45).

Meanwhile, the great Manager has been making provision in his own way for our afflicted Makemie and his fellow-laborers. While the sunshine of August was beaming upon the sparkling waters of the Annamessex and keeping in tune the trill of the red-winged blackbirds in the marshes, our bachelor Scotch merchant passed from earth to be seen in his accustomed place in the Rehoboth and Monokin churches no more for ever. God had taught him to love his servants. I will preserve the will, for the incorrigible Henry Hudson questions whether there is more of pork or piety in the document:

" In the name of God Amen. The twelfth day of August in the year of our Lord God one thousand six hundred and ninety and one. I John Galbraith, of Somerset county and Province of Maryland, merchant, being sick in body but of good and perfect memory, thanks be to Almighty God, and calling to remembrance the uncertain estate of this transitory life, and that all flesh must yield unto death when it shall please God to call ; do make, constitute, ordain and declare this my last will and testament, in manner and form following, revoking and annulling by these presents all and every testament and testaments heretofore by me made and declared either by word or writing, and this to be taken only for my last will and testament and none other.

" And first, being penitent and sorry from my very heart for my sins past, most humbly desiring forgiveness of the same, I give and commit my soul to the Almighty God my Saviour and Redeemer, in whom and by the merits of Jesus Christ I trust and believe assuredly to be saved and have full remission and forgiveness of all my sins, and that my soul with my body at the day of resurrection shall rise again with joy and through the merits of Christ's death and passion and inherit the kingdom of Heaven prepared for his elect and chosen ; and my body to the earth, to be buried decently at the discretion of my executor hereafter named."

Thus the sturdy old believers of this generation aim to put on record their calm faith in the face of death, their clear views of God's plan of salvation and the soundness of their theology. Whoever should read over the wills made during these years in Somerset county would have no small knowledge of divinity. He proceeds :

"And now for settling my temporal estate and such goods and debts as it hath pleased God far above my deserts to bestow upon me, I do order, give and dispose of the same in manner and form following; that is to say, first, I will that all those debts and duties I owe in right or conscience to any person or persons whatsoever, shall be well and truly contented and paid or ordained to be paid within convenient time after my decease by my executor hereafter named.

"I give and bequeath unto Mr. Samuel Davis, minister at Snow Hill, in the county and province aforesaid, five thousand pounds of pork convenient within twelve months after my decease to be delivered unto the said Samuel Davis or his order.

"I give and bequeath unto Mr. Francis Makemie, minister of the Gospel at Rehoboth Town, within the said county and province, five thousand pounds of pork convenient to him or his order within twelve months next after my decease.

"I give and bequeath unto Mr. Thomas Wilson, minister of the Gospel at Monokin, in the county and province aforesaid, five thousand pounds of pork, to him or his order within twelve months after my decease.

"I give and bequeath all the rest of my goods, chattels, debts, house, land, and all other things belonging to me in any manner of way whatsoever, as well elsewhere as in this aforesaid province, both at home and now abroad, unto my trusty and well-beloved friend Major Robert King of Monokin in the county and province aforesaid, and to his heirs and assigns. And I, the said John Galbraith, do by these presents constitute, ordain and appoint my well-beloved friend Major Robert King aforesaid my whole and sole executor and administrator, duly and truly to execute and perform this my last will and testament.

"In confirmation and full assurance of the truth above written that this is my last will and testament, I the said John Galbraith have hereunto set my hand and fixed my seal at Annamessex the day and year first above written " (46).

Pretending not to know that pork is a merchantable legal tender, our mischievous Henry rejoices that for once the ministers' smoke-houses and pewter platters will be well filled. The names of Makemie, Trail, Davis and Wilson now adorn our county records.

This eventful year goes out with the hearts of Eastern-Shore Presbyterians very anxious about the health of their pastor.   Says Matchacoopah:

"While the good man is *hunt-oi-mip* and *wee-sa-way-u*" ("sick and yellow") "Pocomoke looks *oas-kay-u, tah-ki-u* and *dah-qua-an-u*" ("black, cold and sorrowful").

CHAPTER XIII.

A. D. 1692.

"You must not imagine to build a righteous Superstructure upon a rotten and sinful foundation."—MAKEMIE.

BROTHER JOHN, the mighty hunter, is rejoicing in the invention of the flintlock, just now coming into use in place of the old wheel-locks. The one sent him from England, and missing fire no more than half the time, signalizes for him this year of grace. He has lately been with Matchacoopah up to the beaver-dams, on the road toward the old Buckingham plantation of Colonel Stevens, and has come home rich in spoils. The Indian says,

"The little stone spit its fire, and Nataque" (the beaver) "was so astonished he fell down and died."

On their way back, around by the town of Askimmekonson, John bought a fan made of the feathers of the heron, the marsh-hen and the red-bird, and has hurried with it over to the house of our Huguenot maiden. His haste in delivering the fan is remarkable, when we remember that it is cold wintertime.

In February, Mr. Makemie becomes the owner of four hundred and fifty acres more of land, under the Virginia law which gives fifty acres for every new settler brought into the province. The certificate is granted by the Accomack court under rights of the following nine : Francis Makemie, his nephew William Boggs, Mr. Allen, Eliza Clayton, Matthew Spicer, Ruth Smith, negroes Major and Mary, and an Indian named " Peter " (47). We are glad to see our pastor attaching himself more closely to the soil. This year he pays for four tithables to the support of the Established Church Can it be entirely comfortable for Mr Teackle and Mr Monroe to live upon the scant salary and business labors of the Presbyterian minister? Mr John Monroe is now rector of the parishes of Hungar's and Nuswuddux, in Northampton, lately united and called " Hungar's." *

Reports are reaching us of the witchcraft excitement in New England—Salem wildly bewildered. When they tell us of these distressing troubles in the house of the Rev. Mr. Parris, and of Mr Cotton Mather's faith in these things, what are we to think? But I fear that Maryland is becoming almost as sadly bewitched with the desire to establish Episcopacy.

During the spring our new governor arrives. On the 9th of April he appears before the Convention in St. Mary's, shows his commission and dissolves the body, which was called by the Associators and which has been legislating for two years. Copley issues a proclamation to all the counties to elect burgesses to an Assembly to be convened at early date. The Somerset court directs the constables to notify all qualified freeholders to meet at the court-house on the 28th of April to cast their votes. This symbol of the rights of freemen is greatly prized by the colonists—a prerogative which has been theirs from the first settle-

* Bishop Meade's *Old Churches*, 1. 258

ment; of which they were very jealous under the Proprietary, and which they expect to keep inviolate under the royal government. The qualification for both a burgess and an elector is the fee-simple of fifty acres of land or the ownership of forty pounds sterling of personal property. But many are too poor to vote.

Quakers and Episcopalians are very active in the canvass. An impression is abroad that there is much at stake religiously. This is a strong Quaker county, and the rest of the Protestant vote is divided.

The important Thursday comes, and the narrow roads are lined with electors coming from all parts of the county to the one appointed place for voting. You see upon the riders the conscious dignity of the franchise. The crowd increases, until the court-house grounds are thronged with noisy talkers.

The county is entitled to four burgesses, and the contest is sharp. It is needless to say that the " hot waters " flow, and that there is no little indignation against the four-pence-per-gallon tax upon the importation of this popular luxury. On the bench is an imposing array to superintend the important ballot, Francis Jenkins presiding, sustained by his father-in-law, Robert King, John Winder, James Dashiel, James Round, Samuel Hopkins, Thomas Jones, John King and George Layfield. All the majesty of the law is required to maintain order among the excited colonists. Finally, the result of the poll is declared, and rounds of huzzahs ascend over the success of the Rev. John Hewett, Captain William Whittington, Mr. Thomas Evernden and Mr. John Goddin.

Mr. Hewett has been preaching in the county over twelve years. Of course the Episcopalians are jubi-

14

lant at his success and cannot disguise their chief motive in the election. The Quakers are no less elated at the triumph of Evernden and Goddin. Evernden is a prominent man among them, and is now married to the widow of George Johnson, one of our first judges, and "the Proteus of heresy," as Colonel Scarborough called him.

The Assembly met in May, and soon some of us in Somerset are having a good laugh. Hewett, Evernden and Goddin are disqualified and cannot take their seats —the first because of a law excluding ministers, and the other two because of their refusal to take the oath. Our Captain Whittington alone sits as burgess.*

Governer Copley in his opening message shows a just appreciation of the rights of all parties and urges moderation. None can reasonably object to his wise words :

" The making of wholesome laws, and laying aside all heats and animosities that have happened amongst you of late, will go far towards laying the foundation of lasting peace and happiness to yourselves and your posterity. And this, I know, will be very acceptable to their Majesties, who are eminent examples of Christian and peaceable tempers. "

But the Church of England has the ascendency of numbers in the Assembly, and there is to be no moderation. After an address to their Majesties, the very next act is what they call "An Act for the Service of Almighty God and the Establishment of the Protestant Religion." Correctly interpreted, this means "An Act for the Service of Prelacy and its Enthronement upon the Neck of all other Systems." We now become Dissenters from the State-Church of Maryland The

* For election and other facts, Somerset records.

counties are to be laid out into parishes, and a tax of forty pounds of tobacco per poll for every taxable is to be collected by the sheriff. This is to be used in building its churches and paying its clergy.* The poor in our struggling churches, unable to support our own ministers comfortably, must contribute of their hard earnings to strengthen the Church which drove them from Europe.

The news from over the sea is not of a character to reconcile us to the change. The bishops in Ulster are beginning to obstruct the king's tolerant policy toward the Presbyterians, though they there number fifty to one Episcopalian. In Scotland, too, certain disagreement between the General Assembly and the king has supplied Prelacy an opportunity to show what it would do if again in the ascendency. While England is suffering great scarcity from bad crops, is bled by the rise and reign of stock-jobbing, and is dispirited by the French victories at Namur and at Steinkirk, a plot is discovered for the assassination of King William by the emissaries of James. All this hatred is encouraged by the High-Church party. And now, while the whole empire murmurs at heavy taxation, new taxes are to be levied upon *us* to pamper this ungracious Church. Margaret tells us of its bad treatment, at this very time, of the Huguenots in Carolina—denied the rights of subjects, their estates liable to forfeiture, their marriages pronounced void and their children bastardized. These things do not lessen our solicitude at the sudden aggrandizement of Episcopacy among us. Meanwhile, the terrific earthquake in Jamaica, the frightful shocks in Europe, the unusual

* Bishop Hawks's *Maryland*, p. 71.

activity of all her great volcanoes, fill the mind with apprehension of some vast calamity.*

The work goes on. In our county, commissioners from the various hundreds have been appointed to lay out the parishes, and on the report of this commission four parishes have been constituted, as follows (48):— Monokin and Mony Hundreds into one parish, called "Somerset;" Pocomoke and Annamessex into one, called "Coventry;" Wicomico and Nanticoke into one, called "Stepney;" Bogatenorton and Matapony into one, called "Snow Hill." This report was made and approved on the 22d of November before their Majesties' justices of the peace. A meeting of freeholders is ordered on the 27th of December for electing six vestrymen for each parish, according to law, the freeholders of Monokin and Mony to meet at Somerset Town; of Pocomoke and Annamessex, at Pocomoke church; of Wicomico and Nanticoke, at the house of the Rev. John Hewett; of Bogatenorton and Matapony, at Snow Hill. For the elated Episcopalians it will be a delightful addition to the festivities of the Christmas holidays.

It looks strange to see Colonel Brown, Colonel Jenkins and other Presbyterians, as county officials, assisting in carrying into effect the law for the establishment of the Church of England, but there are not a few who think it will be better than to be at the mercy of Popery, accepting the former as the lesser of two evils. Lord Baltimore himself was tolerant and gracious to all, but in this he never satisfied his own

* Reid, ii 415, 419; Hetherington, p. 308; Macaulay and Knight, *in loco;* Anderson's *Colonial Church,* ii. 465; Evelyn's *Diary,* pp. 551, 709

Church, and evidently provoked thereby the enmity of the Jesuit advisers of James   No one can tell how soon the peace policy might have been changed into one of bloody persecution.   Though we must pay this forty-pounds tax to an adverse system for protection, there are those who think we shall be safer under the pacific influence of William and the reign of law than we were before.

With others there is bitter opposition and great excitement; they still bear the scars inflicted by Episcopacy in the old country. Some think that the levy cannot be enforced; the resolute Quakers will resist it with all their might. I have obtained, and I put upon record, the tax-assessments per poll for four years: 1689, 58 lbs tobacco; 1690, 88 lbs.; 1691, 31 lbs ; 1692, 176 lbs * This is a heavy increase.

Loathing Popery with all his soul, Mr. Makemie has but little more respect for the High-Church party among the Prelatists. He admires King William and feels kindly toward moderate Episcopalians like Burnet and Tillotson. While thanking God for the seasonable revolution and the degree of liberty secured to Dissenters in the British Isles, he thus expresses his mind freely of another class still rampant across the sea ·

"I wish the persecuting spirit and inclination were gone too, and that many unawares were not promoting and encouraging again the old malice and grand designs of the common enemy by their tongues, in railing, reproaching, and decrying a great part of the purest Reformation, under the discriminating names of Presbyterian, Puritan, Fanatic, Calvinist, and what not? How many are simply led away by a hot, violent party and suffer themselves to be imposed upon, who know not the mat-

* Somerset records.

ters of our lesser differences and say nothing of intolerable Popery and the most dangerous heretics, but all their industrious venom is spewed out and leveled against their Protestant brethren of the same Reformation." *

Mr. Makemie pillories that class in the Anglican Church who hate the present king for his kindness to Dissenters, and who would gladly restore the Popish James to secure new barbarities against the Presbyterians.

We are rejoicing that our minister has at last recovered from his long affliction Do not the water-lilies at Rehoboth wear happier faces than ever? Says Matchacoopah,

"The waters of Pocomoke sing and dance and laugh" (*nuck-und-oh* and *zdoh-cumb* and *wi-aih-e-mit-a-ha*).

How full of laughter that last Indian word!

Mr. Makemie's first strength is used for copying out for publication his *Answer* to Keith's attack on his Catechism. This he completes at Rehoboth on the 26th of July—the first book ever born along our little river. Literature and Presbyterianism are making joint claim that *there is room for both* on the Eastern Shore. The author's confidence in the truth appears in these words :

"They boasted of a victory, which if they find after a diligent perusal and impartial consideration of these sheets, let them improve and post if they will." †

After long laboring to the southward of us, in Virginia and Carolina and Barbadoes, our zealous missionary keeps his eye on the country farther north. Corresponding with the New England divines, he has

* *Truths in a True Light.*   † *Answer to Keith.*

never lost sight of the vast regions lying between them and him. Philadelphia is growing rapidly, and his natural forecast sees in that central town a strong strategic point for the future advancement of our Church. Accordingly, he determines this year upon another apostolic journey, "having," he says, "in August, 1692, satisfied my longing desire in visiting Pensilvania." True Presbyterianism was stretching forth its hand toward the scattered brethren in East Jersey and Long Island, where, at Freehold, Shrewsbury, Jamaica, Hempstead and Newtown, there are seeds of our pure faith, but with the worship and discipline still modified by the original mixture of Independency from New England.

Mr. Makemie finds that, though so exacting in their conventionalities, Quakers are not everywhere the same. He says:

"I no sooner arrived in that government but I perceived a remarkable difference between the gestures and behavior of Quakers there and all others I have been acquainted with elsewhere; males and females using that masculine way of bowing the body."

In another place he criticises the Catechism of George Fox, which, while omitting such weighty matters as the doctrine of the Trinity, the Ten Commandments and the Lord's Prayer, "fills up a great part," he says, "with stuff wherein there is no religion, far less can they be called fundamentals; as salutations by words and gestures, covering and uncovering the head, condemning preaching in steeple-houses and churches." If a religious sect is going to revolutionize our social manners, he would have it done in a more decent way:

"Seeing they decry the civil salutations of the kingdom and people among whom they live, what warrant can they produce for their singular, ugly and bad-natured salutation—their males and females taking one another by the hands or waists, continuing a considerable space, wringing them hard and looking steadfastly in each other's face, without one word speaking?"

Thus God permits the paradox of a body of religionists claiming to be so spiritual as to abjure the divine sacraments and all the externals of worship, yet making it a part of their religion to insist upon these uncouth social forms, set up by human authority only, and bound on the conscience.

Our minister finds Quakerism in its American stronghold very unhappy—rent into two fierce factions led by the lieutenant-governor, Loyd, and our late acquaintance George Keith. At the time the latter made his descent upon our county and was proclaiming Quaker infallibility to the very doors of Mr. Makemie, dissensions were raging in their own ranks and loud denunciations were being hurled from each at the other.

Before presenting Mr. Makemie's account of the disturbances in Mr. Penn's city of brotherly love, I want to transcribe the words of another Quaker champion, written this very year, affording a suggestive commentary upon what is to follow. Their celebrated disputer, Thomas Story, thus delivers himself:

"I sat quiet and inward a little and the truth arose as a standard against it, and the opposing darkness vanished and truth reigned in me alone, and then I began to speak concerning the many divisions in the pretended Christian world, happening upon the pouring forth of the seventh vial by the angel of God mentioned in the book of the Revelation of John. That the pretended Christian Church with all her various false notions, opinions and doctrines, is that Babylon. That her three great divisions are the Papacy, the Prelacy and the Presbytery, with their several sub-divisions and confusions; who being departed from the Spirit of Christ the Prince of Peace into the spirit of envy and persecution, were now and from the time of that vial warring and destroying each other."

First or last God humbles self-righteousness. Mr. Makemie returns Keith's visit, is at his house in Philadelphia, hears his side of the controversy, and is also among the other party and hears theirs. He says:

"This breach is risen to such a height that the railings, revilings, bitter and uncharitable accusations they were wont to vomit maliciously against all the Reformed Churches, are now justly turned against one another; for Loyd and his party fly out against Keith, calling him 'a reviler of the brethren,' 'brat of Babylon,' 'accuser of the brethren,' 'one that always endeavoreth to keep down the power of the truth,' 'drawing from the gift of God,' calling him also 'Pope,' 'Primate of Pennsylvania,' 'Father Confessor;' accusing him of 'envy, extreme passion, a turbulent and unsubdued spirit.' It deserves observation that in their Epistle to their Brethren and their Commendation, what high, lofty and proud titles, scarce applicable to men, they gave George Keith; as, that 'he walked in the counsel of God,' 'was lovely in that day,' when 'the beauty of the Lord was upon him and his comeliness covered him;' and immediately with the same breath they throw him down and look upon him as 'fallen from the high places of Israel,' as a 'man slain in his high places,' and so they fix hard names upon him as formerly; who pays them home again in the same coin, and calls Loyd and his party, which are some thousands, 'fools,' 'ignorant heathens,' 'silly souls,' 'liars,' 'heretics,' 'rotten ranters,' 'Muggletonians,' etc."

Mr. Makemie's native humor crops out in his comment:

"If we were inclinable to give them names, we have no room, for they have done it to our hands themselves. And I must confess they are better able than we, for they are better acquainted with one another and privy to their errors, heresies and other hidden works of darkness, which they have hitherto been ashamed to publish to the world.   And yet it is admirable to think where these men find such a stock of confidence as to wipe their mouths and say they have not railed all this while, but all they have said on both sides is in the uprightness of their hearts and all these names given are truth.   I shall leave them so, disproving neither."

Again our minister tells us:

"Thomas Loyd in a public meeting affirmed no man could differ with George Keith but he was in danger of the life of his soul by him, and farther that he had been a more vexatious adversary to Friends than Hicks or Scanderet or the greatest enemies.   George Keith affirmed that 'no such damnable heresies and doctrines of devils were tolerated in any Protestant Society as among Quakers at Philadelphia.'"

These are very diverse sentiments to be entertained by people equally under the guidance of the Inner Light.   Keith has already published two books in the controversy—*The Plea of the Innocent* and *The Reasons and Causes of the Separation.*

Mr. Makemie read and listened, and with his usual thoroughness has gone to the bottom of these differences.   He says:

"I shall give a relation from their own writings, and also from their own testimonies, and the open and public discourses of both parties I conversed with at Philadelphia."

My father thinks that this episode in the early religious history of our neighboring colony is of sufficient importance to go upon my journal—especially because it is a description by an eye-witness who is exploring the way for the establishment of our Church in that city as an antidote to all these errors.   Mr. Makemie tells us:

"The occasion of all this clamor and heat is given by Keith to be an accusation of Keith by W Stockdale, an ancient Quaker teacher, for preaching two Christs, because he preached faith in

Christ within them and faith in Christ without. Keith having dealt privately with the said Stockdale but unsuccessfully, laid his complaint before twelve of their ministry in a meeting at Mr. Ewer's house, who rather defended and excused Stockdale than condemned him. Whereby ten of these able Doctors, two only dissenting, became as guilty of ignorance and errors as Stockdale himself. And next the Yearly Meeting at Philadelphia, and so at length six several meetings, had this matter in debate under their determination ; who gave so slender a determination at last that they all appeared rather at a stand and demur about it, and Keith justly accuses them of partiality, ignorance and unbelief."

Says our authority caustically :

"All may perceive from the Unchristian labyrinth in which these men have involved themselves about so weighty and so plain a fundamental, how great strangers they are to the true knowledge of the Gospel mystery of Christ Jesus; that of six several meetings of their greatest Dons, they are in confusion about the Christ to be believed in for salvation, and understand not Christ as he is revealed in the Scriptures, God-man suffering and dying for us Whence it is evident what Christ the generality of Quakers have been believing in, which is clear from the prayer of Thomas Fitz-Walter at a meeting, saying, 'O God that died in us and laid down thy life in us and took it again,' etc., which George Keith justly called blasphemy. Arthur Cook accused George Keith for saying that Christ's body, that was crucified and buried, is gone into Heaven and was and is in Heaven, even the very same body; which Cook and others called a novelty imposed upon his ancient brethren. John Simcock asked Keith, Did Christ's bones arise ? Thomas Loyd did object against Keith's imposing unscriptural faith on his brethren , further, that faith in Christ without us, as he died for our sins and rose again, was not necessary to salvation ; and further, that Christ within did all I leave it to others to determine what sort of Christians Quakers must be , and also what we must judge of their sufficient and saving and divine light, of which they have been boasting universally and magnifying themselves above all others in the world."

Nor was this all. The need for an orthodox Christain ministry in that town is great indeed Mr. Makemie proceeds :

"Many other most dangerous positions were urged and disputed among them. Many of them denied the day of judgment and any resurrection but what they have already attained. John Willsford said, Christ was a Mediator for no drunkards and wicked persons but for his own disciples. Many of them denied God's presence in all his creatures, arguing most ignorantly and blasphemously, If God be in herbs and grasses, then who tramples on them tramples on God. This occasioned a new dispute, whether God be present in lice, some denying they were any part of his creation. Another preaches that Christ cureth men's souls perfectly at once and makes them free of all sin; and when we are perfect, we are kings and are not to beg or pray to God for ourselves. Another said he did not believe to be saved by that which died at Jerusalem."

Condemning both, Mr. Makemie evidently considers his old Accomack opponent nearer right than the other faction. But the influence of those in authority and that of the illiterate ministry carry the majority with them, and our informant tells us that on the 22d of last December their monthly meeting passed judgment against Keith. Commissioners sent all the way from England failed to harmonize the discord.

I cannot follow the labyrinth of controversy all the way through. Libels, prosecutions and imprisonments follow. Says our minister:

"This makes a great noise both in city and country, that Quakers begin to imprison and persecute one another, proving what they would do to others if they had power, opportunity and provocation. They make use of the same plea as all other persecutors do, even the disturbance of the peace and subversion of the government. But this salve will not cure the sore."

Mr. Makemie thus completes the history of these anomalous distractions:

"Great things were expected from the Yearly Meeting at Burlington, which was to be within a few days. Though little expectation of a friendly accommodation, for George Keith kept out of town lest he should by a prison be prevented to attend that meeting. But Keith came off there with flying colors For the other party, being summoned again and again to appear, declined it. Whether they disowned the authority of that meeting, or suspected the badness of their cause which they had reason to do, or feared George Keith's party to be too strong, they can best answer for themselves, but that meeting justified George Keith and condemned Loyd and his party, discharging them to preach or pray in public meeting till they had condemned their former judgment by a public writing. How this order was slighted is too palpable to be denied.

" But while the Meeting at Burlington clears Keith, the Yearly Meeting at Maryland condemns him and justifies the other party. Whereby that *infallible discerning spirit* Quakers boast of and say is in every true Quaker, is overthrown, for great Meetings of their greatest Dons can be mistaken and make contrary and contradictory orders. I am informed the division has reached London. One party who were against Keith bought up all his pamphlets to prevent the spreading of the difference; another party orders a new impression of all his books relating to that controversy. This I had lately from one of themselves."

Our minister amuses himself with several of the ludicrous aspects of this unfriendliness of the Friends. He says :

"George Keith is blamed for calling Stockdale and a whole meeting ignorant heathens But, says Keith, if there is light sufficient to salvation in all men without the man Christ, then an honest heathen is a true Christian. Hence every man may learn that honest heathens are good Quakers, or Quakers are good heathens."

We can imagine the smile upon Mr. Makemie's face when he dryly remarks :

" Whoever would have more of this nature, even the spiritual war among Quakers, chiefly promoted by the carnal weapon of the tongue, I recommend them to Philadelphia."

While Mr. Makemie is exploring the regions to the north, we hear of an addition to our ministerial force on the Chesapeake. Mr. Makemie's former flock on

Elizabeth River has another bachelor preacher from the North of Ireland. Mr Josias Mackie comes from the little town on the Foyle where the Presbytery of Laggan formerly held its most frequent meetings, and where Mr. Makemie was received under its care, when he says, "I gave requiring satisfaction to godly, learned and judicious discerning men of a work of grace and conversion wrought on my heart." The son of Patrick Mackie of St. Johnstown has breathed from boyhood the bracing atmosphere of the Covenant and associated with the heroes who were immortalized in the defence of Derry. Three years ago James sat down in the little town to await the surrender of the Protestant garrison, but waited in vain. His avowed purpose to Romanize America has failed, and from his very camp comes over another laborer to advance the Protestant cause. On the 22d of June, Mr. Mackie takes the oath before Justices Thomas Butt and James Wilson and formally qualifies to preach at three points —a house at Mr. Thomas Ivy's in Eastern Branch, a house belonging to Mr. Richard Philpot in Tanner's Creek Precincts, and at a house belonging to Mr. John Roberts in the Western Branch. In the neighborhood of the preaching-place on the Eastern Branch are the house and lot owned by Mr. Makemie.

This is probably the first case of the recognition in Virginia of the Act of Toleration passed in the first year of William and Mary By taking the oath of allegiance and subscribing the declaration against Popery, also the Thirty-Nine Articles of the Church of England, except those having reference to the government and power of that Church, Dissenters are relieved from attendance upon the parish church and permitted to worship in their own, provided they have their places of worship legally recorded and keep them unlocked, unbarred and unbolted. This is a scant measure of justice,* a standing reflection upon the loyalty and doctrinal soundness of Nonconformists ; but even this poor boon has been won through the persistent influence of William against the factious opposition of the High Churchmen of England. It is a singular fact that our Calvinistic ministry can conscientiously subscribe to all the doctrinal Articles of the Church of England, which hundreds of their own Arminian clergy cannot do without perjury.

Thursday, October 27, under proclamation of our court, was observed as a day of thanksgiving to God for prospering the armies of King William It had more especial reference to the great naval victory of La Hogue over the French fleet on the 19th of May, when the threatened invasion of England was utterly defeated. Somerset was not behind the British Isles in the spirit of loyalty and enthusiasm, in the firing of guns and the waving of flags and the flow of rich autumn cider.

But some of us are even more thankful for the divine favor in the gift of five genuine Presbyterian preachers for the regions around the tributaries of the Chesapeake—Josias Mackie, Nathaniel Taylor, Samuel Davis, Thomas Wilson and Francis Makemie, who is the foremost of them all. No other region in America can show such a galaxy in this year of grace 1692. Nor do we forget, amid our gratitude, the minister of Lifford, Brother's Love and Borthwick—Mr. William Trail—and his five years' work at Rehoboth.

* Hallam's *Constitutional History*, p. 586.

CHAPTER XIV.

A. D. 1693.

"The Church of Israel in Egypt and in all their other Captivities were Dissenters. The three worthies in Daniel were Dissenters in Babylon; and Daniel under Darius was a Dissenter. Our Saviour, all his Disciples and Apostles, with their Christian followers, were Dissenters, until Constantine's Reign. It were hard and uncharitable to condemn *all these* as Traytors and Schismatics!"—MAKEMIE.

I MUST mention a noted Pocomoke wedding— the forerunner of others no less interesting, perhaps. For some while it had been noticed that one of our justices was riding often toward the old Stevens plantation—the original Rehoboth. The sensation has culminated in the marriage of Squire Layfield to Mrs. Elizabeth, the widow of Colonel William Stevens. Such a wedding causes considerable stir in colony-life.

This year the names of George Layfield and Elizabeth "his now wife, relict and executrix of Colonel William Stevens deceased," have been jointly signed upon a deed conveying the plantation of Carmel, in the north end of Sinepuxent, to John Johnson, "for fifteen thousand pounds of good fat merchantable pork." Widows with plantations do not remain widows long in the provinces.

The "cyder" used at the wedding can be bought this season at eight pounds of tobacco per gallon. I think of other weddings to be, and do not wonder that

224

the name "Mary-Land" should run into the suggestive pronunciation "Merry-Land." This is all very
well, but let not Mr. Makemie's version of the name
of our river prevail—"Poccamok"! Martha thinks
my laugh at his accent shows very little reverence.

From Mr. Makemie's sloop we have lately made the
following purchases:

1 barrel molasses	600 lbs. tobacco.
2 Banburry stock locks	120 " "
2 match coals	240 " "
1 peck salt	25 " "

I hope the profits from this trip will be sufficient
to pay his tax upon the three tithables assessed against
him this year for the support of Episcopacy in Virginia (49).

I learn that a deed has been made on the 21st of
this February by Robert Hutchinson to "Francis Makemie, Gent.," of three hundred and fifty acres of land
"bounded north-westward on part of Matchatank
Creek, beginning at the head of said creek, and
from thence running down the south-west side unto
the land that was formerly belonging to James Price,
and now to the said Makemie." Virginia acknowledges Mr. Makemie to be *a gentleman*, though not
disposed to admit that he is a minister of Christ. He
now owns all the south bank of the sunny Matchatank,
while his father-in-law owns the thousand acres stretching between its northern shore and the Onancock.

I am reminded of a present just made by the wealthy
Mr. Anderson to one of his neighbors. When spon-
sors are selected for the children of Episcopalians, it is
the custom to recognize the honor by some valuable

15

gift. The following paper, formally signed, has been
put upon record in Accomack this year by William
Anderson, Gent.:

"For an affection which I have and bear unto my God-
daughter Anne, daughter of Thomas Welburne, Gent., I have
given, granted and delivered and by these presents do give,
grant and deliver unto Arcadia Welburne, mother of the said
Anne Welburne, one black heifer about three years old, together
with her increase, which said heifer and all her increase are now
running at Chingoteague."

I do not suppose that "my God-daughter" is the
owner of a very large heifer. The first cattle brought
to this continent were landed at Jamestown in 1608,
and others in 1610 and 1611. To kill any of these or
their increase was felony and death. Thus protected,
they had grown in 1639 to about thirty thousand in
Virginia. Small and poor from the beginning, they
have been badly fed and tended ever since. So also
with the cattle brought over by the Swedes on the
Delaware From these two sources have sprung the
"native cattle" along our coast. Not the best from
the old country originally, and almost utterly neglected
since, they are lean, ugly brutes, hunting their living in
the woods and on the marshes, or, like Annie Welburne's heifer, running wild on the beaches.

Must I own that the children of the people have
known almost as little culture ?

As a matter of moment in the history of the times,
we must notice the charter for a college in Virginia
signed by their Majesties on the 8th of February. For
some while Mr. Commissary Blair had been pressing
this enterprise, until finally the Assembly seconded
his efforts and sent him to Europe to solicit the requi-

site authority and aid.   His energy and perseverance have won deserved success

Mr. Blair is a Scotchman by birth, a graduate of the University of Edinburgh.   Presbyterially ordained, he was admitted into episcopal orders by the Bishop of Edinburgh without further ordination.   In 1685, while Mr. Makemie was preaching at Elizabeth River, Mr. Blair came as a missionary to Henrico county, and in 1689 was appointed commissary by the Bishop of London.   On landing in Virginia, his Scotch soul was grieved to find no schools nor school-teachers, the youth growing up in ignorance, and, worse still, a sentiment prevailing against education on the ground that " it would take our planters off from their mechanical employments and make them grow too knowing to be obedient and submissive."   Said Governor Berkley in 1670 :

" I thank God there are no free schools, nor printing, and I hope we shall not have these hundred years , for learning has brought disobedience into the world and printing has divulged them and libels against the best governments.   God save us from both."

The following extract from the statutes of the young college gives a fair picture of the present state of learning in both Virginia and Maryland :

" Some few, and very few indeed, of the richer sort sent their children to England to be educated, and there, after many dangers from the seas and enemies and unusual distempers occasioned by the change of country and climate, they were often taken off by small-pox and other diseases.   It was no wonder if this occasioned a great defect of understanding and all sorts of literature, and that it was followed with a new generation of men far short of their forefathers ; which, if they had the good fortune, though at a very indifferent rate, to read and write, had no further commerce with the muses or learned sciences, but spent their life ignobly with the hoe and spade and other employments of an uncultivated and unpolished country."

Mr Makemie deprecates this state of things no less earnestly than does Mr. Blair, especially in its religious aspects. In his preface to his Catechism he had spoken of his sympathy for multitudes in the province who were without proper instruction and in darkness. Keith thus taunts him with it:

" Whereas he mentions his compassion over the tender souls in an American desert ready to perish for want of a vision, in his epistle to the reader, his Catechism can nothing help them in that respect, for not one word in all his Catechism directeth people where to find the true vision of God in any measure, but on the contrary, according to his and his brethren's false faith, all true vision and revelation and all divine inspiration is ceased since the Apostle's days, both among teachers and people, and God committed his counsel wholly to writing. All the people in Virginia both English and Scots whom he seemeth to reflect upon for their ignorance, have the Holy Scriptures without, and the holy teachings and illuminations of God and Christ within, to teach them what is needful to their salvation, if they will hearken thereunto, far better than the Catechism of Francis Makemie."

This sophistical appeal of a university graduate to the prejudices of the uncultured meets a deserved rebuke. Our pastor replies both as to the general illiteracy and with a deserved thrust back at the Quakers:

" Though he constructs my compassion over the tender souls in an American desert to be a reflection against the Scots and English in Virginia, I am satisfied it has not been so received by them for whom it was intended, neither judged so by the Spirit of God who, much after the same manner, pities and compassionates the ignorance of his own people by the prophet Hosea—' My people are destroyed for lack of knowledge.' I am persuaded that Quakers should not have had so great success in drawing aside silly souls from the truths and ways of God if it were not for the abounding ignorance of Virginia and other dark corners of the world. And none deserves more to be pitied for their ignorance than Quakers, and of the most fundamental truths, notwithstanding of their high pretences to the Spirit and Light within. As John Drummond, a reputed and received Quaker, a reader of Keith's books, who lately at my house at Poccamok, before Keith and several other witnesses, published his gross ignorance of that fundamental article—That none could be saved without faith in Jesus Christ. From which I understand since that he had oft reproached me, drawing his own ignorant conclusions from thence. If Quakers are ignorant *thereof*, what can they pretend to know?"

Among the families all around us we have examples of the deplorable want of education. This very year a legal document has been recorded in Accomack court under the signatures of Mr. William Anderson and his rich wife, the latter, notwithstanding all her silks and laces, being compelled to sign *her mark* This is the case also with the sons of Colonel Stevens and with their mother.* It is noticeable that prominent families in county or State soon lose their political prestige—station and influence passing from their illiterate offspring into the hands of educated men newly arriving from Europe.

The college has been named, for their Majesties, "William and Mary." The plan for the building has been supplied by our great contemporary architect Sir Christopher Wren It is the second American college, Harvard having been founded as a "schoole or colledge" in 1636. The support is partly provided for by a duty of a penny per pound on all tobacco exported to the other colonies from both Virginia and

* The testimony of Accomack and Somerset records, and in many other instances For other facts, in reference to college, etc., see Campbell's *Virginia*, Neill's *Colonial Clergy*, Anderson's *Colonial Church* and Makemie's *Answer to Keith.*

Maryland.   For once the nauseous staple is applied to a good use.

The energetic Scotch commissary is the first president of the youthful institution.   Of course it is wholly under the control and auspices of the Episcopalians:

"That the church of Virginia may be furnished with a seminary of the ministers of the Gospel, and that the youth may be piously educated in good letters and manners, and that the Christian faith may be propagated among the western Indians, to the glory of Almighty God."

Governor Copley is proving himself considerate and kind to all sects, practicing carefully the moderation which he recommended to his first Assembly.   The opposition to the tax for building Episcopal churches and supporting their clergymen has been so firm as to make the law almost a dead letter.   The Quakers especially, forming the majority of the Dissenters, are determined and unyielding.   A large part of the preaching of Fox and his followers has been in denunciation of steeple-houses and salaried clergymen, and this "forty-per-poll law," as it is called, falls upon them more heavily than upon any others.

The conciliatory spirit of the governor is seen in his appointment to office of one of our Somerset citizens not of the Established Church, and to the very office responsible for the collection of this tax.   On the 9th of August, Mr. Ephraim Wilson, a Presbyterian, and of the Ulster Wilsons, had his commission as sheriff, over the signature of the governor, recorded in court. Such acts seem to be a guarantee of peace.

The Assembly, recognizing the obstacles to the enforcement of the unpopular law, has partly yielded, ordering that the tax in counties which did not levy last year shall not be levied this year, but that it shall be doubled to eighty pounds in 1694. It is felt that it will not do to press an indignant people too far.

Among our Episcopal neighbors we find, as might be expected, two classes of men—some who are opposed to all concessions, hungry after the tithes and impatient for the enforcement of the obnoxious edict; but there are others who are excellent Christians, regretting the turmoil this law has occasioned and anxious that justice may be done to all. This difference of spirit is a reflection of that now exhibited by the High-Church and Low-Church parties in England. I remember Mr. Makemie's words:

"All who study histories of the Protestant Reformation may be assured that the Reformed Church of England consisted all along of two sorts of men. First, many sober, moderate, sound and tender men, who never were for persecution of Protestants and would willingly have parted with many unscriptural ceremonies for the churches' peace and gaining Dissenters And the seed and root of these have been from the original of the Reformation and abounded in the reigns of Queen Elizabeth and King James I., and were Anti-Arminian and faithful to the first doctrine and Protestant Articles of the church of England and continued the prevailing party until the reign of Charles I.

"There was also another hot and violent party who were ready to brand the sober and serious of their own church as Puritans, Precisians and Fanatics, betrayed their own Articles, embraced Arminianism, and grew more zealous for rights and ceremonies than for the essentials and substantials of religion; crying up uniformity and conformity more than true Christianity; acting supra-canon and, instead of coming farther from Rome by a further Reformation, which our first Reformers designed and the moderate party desired, they both in doctrine, practice and ceremonies made several advances toward Rome; as Dr. Du Moulin, sometimes history-professor of Oxford, relates in his *Short History* thereof, which advances gave Popes and Papists no small hopes of England's return to Rome.

"This party was rampant in Laud's time, who had a party of monstrous tools who published Arminian and downright Popish doctrines, and tyrannical and enslaving maxims of state, and were so countenanced and protected by the King and some of the Court that they carried all before them, and it was no small crime for any to speak against the Romish innovations and intolerable usurpations both in Church and State, as in the cruel, unchristian and illegal punishments inflicted on some of their own communion, until their designs were seasonably opposed and checked by such of their church who were sincere and uncorrupted, when backed by Lords and Commons assembled in Parliament in the year 1640 complaining in bold speeches of those that went after the Popish way.

"Though Laud had justly meted to him what he measured out to others, and though many suffered almost twenty years abdication from the pulpit during the Civil Wars, yet it is to be feared the seed and spawn of this faction has been growing since in the church and so prevailing a party as were able to obstruct that union, accommodation and comprehension designed between the Church of England and Dissenters, first by a commission from our most gracious King and Queen, and next by a convocation who had but very small regard to their Majesties' supremacy in Ecclesiastics, and who so vigorously opposed what they had so lately addressed their Majesties for."

Mr. Makemie here speaks of King William's strenuous efforts four years ago to secure entire toleration for all Protestants, their admission to civil office, and such alterations in the Liturgy and Canons as would satisfy the consciences of Nonconformists and open the way for union with them. The High-Church party hated William the more for these efforts. My father notes the fact that whenever our monarchs have been inclined to harass and persecute Dissenters, these adherents of Prelacy have been always zealous in preaching the divine right of kings and the absolute supremacy of these heads of the Church; but whenever our rulers have inclined to leniency and toleration, these extreme Prelatists are first to discard the doc-

trine of the divine right of kings and oppose all supremacy which favors the Nonconformists.   While
now in Britain they are setting themselves violently
against the conciliatory policy of the king, here in
Maryland, where William encourages the establishment of their Church, they are demonstratively
loyal.

Our county is highly favored in having one among
us who understands so thoroughly the weaknesses of
both Quakerism and Episcopacy, and who is competent to guard our people from the loose no-Churchism
of the one, and the pretentious, exclusive High-
Churchism of the other.   It is a privilege to sit with
him and Naomi under the shade-trees of our flowing
river and hear him vindicate the claims of our Church
to be the soundest part of the Reformation   A branch
of the transplanted vine hangs over us with fragrant
clusters.   He says:

"In Scotland they were the first Reformers of that kingdom
from Popery, though originally by mean and inconsiderable men
and in opposition to a strong Court party, and not only without
but against the authority of the state ; which demonstrated the
more of the hand of Divine Providence therein.   And notwithstanding all their strugglings with Popery and Prelacy, which in
the late reigns have been imposed upon them, contrary to laws,
oaths and repeated establishments of that kingdom, yet they
went a greater length in reformation than their neighbors in
England, who upon prudential considerations retained some
ceremonies lest it should.be dangerous to reform all at once as
Scotland did.

"As to the Presbyterians of England, they were from the beginning a part of the English reformation ; for the best histories
inform us that those who chiefly had the first management of the
reformation were divided into two classes, much-what equal in
number and quality of interest.   Some of them, as Bishop
Hooper, Coverdale, John Fox, John Rogers and Peter Martyr,
appeared vigorously for an absolute and thorough reformation

according to the model Calvin had given of it, and so it would have been a Presbyterian reformation. But others, as Cranmer, Ridley, Cox and others, were peremptorily of the judgment that a reformation *in all parts at first* would be of dangerous consequence, and at once to reform all would be to reform none at all. And though the judgment of the latter prevailed, yet all approved of the former as best; though some approved not the juncture as seasonable until the people who were all Papists were better instructed and disposed to receive the impressions of this entire and perfect reformation.

"Therefore they were left not without hopes of a further reformation from their posterity and successors, which we were assured of by a sentence in the Preface to old Common Prayer Books, left out of the new. It was for that time agreed on that, for the better gaining of Papists, some ceremonies and a great part of the Roman service were to be kept. Thus both parties concurred and united, in hopes of a further reformation, until the bloody Marian persecution, under which some of both classes fell and died, others became refugees abroad. Upon their return, instead of a further reformation, uniformity acts were promoted and passed in the first of Elizabeth. Yet, during the lives of some good Bishops and for several years, no subscription nor use of all the Common Prayer nor an exact observance of the ceremonies was urged, until Whitgift ascended the chair, whose zeal for ceremonies was boldly impugned by learned Cartwright.

"And now subscription and conformity was required under penalty of suspension and deprivation. Harder things were soon contrived and imposed, to the casting out of many able and godly ministers, followed by multitudes of people. And these, being cast out and kept out to this day, are Nonconformists and Dissenters and the most considerable part Presbyterians. Those of Ireland are partly from England, partly from Scotland, who since the conquest joined with others in settling that kingdom.

"As to the Protestant foreign countries, they are either Calvinists or Lutherans. But all the Calvinist churches, as lately of France, Geneva, Holland, Piedmont, and many other places of High and Low Germany, are Presbyterians By all computation Presbyterians and Calvinists, with such as are in full communion with them, are the *greater* part and, from the judgment of our first Reformers, are the *better* part of the Reformation." *

The Presbyterians of Maryland make no factious

* *Truths in a True Light.*

opposition to the Establishment.*   We shall feel it heavily, but it is a matter of course in this age that those in the majority will have State and Church united.   Others are taxed for the support of our Church in Scotland, Mr Trail now living upon the tithes at Borthwick.   In Ireland they have the *regium donum.*   Our county has been exempted from the payment of the "forty pounds per poll" for last year and this, but finally it will come.†   Mr. Makemie pays his assessments uncomplainingly for the support of Mr. Teackle, only asking that to himself may be conceded the privilege of preaching without compulsory support.   He says proudly:

"Whatever others have done, I dare affirm I never bargained with any people about a maintenance; and have oft refused money when freely offered; and never enjoyed any maintenance but what was most freely offered   I deny not to the magistrate a power of determining maintenances when necessity requires it; though I could wish it were voluntary offerings." ‡

As Mr. Makemie moves in the midst of many difficulties, sensible and well poised, I think of Matchacoopah's description: "God's *matt-ah-ki-ween*" ("warrior"), "whom no blast of the north-easter can drive from the rock."

Shall the contact of these sons of the forest with such men ever lead to civilization?   They have more settled towns in our county than the whites, and continue to be fully protected by our courts   The other day, from one of their villages, called "Tondetank," up in the Wicomico country, several of their "great-

* Bishop Hawks's *Maryland,* p 78.
† Order of Assembly postponing on Somerset records.
‡ *Answer to Keith*

men Indians " appeared before our bench of judges and charged Thomas Camplin with being accessory to the death of Dr. James. So come these savages of the wilds into the halls of justice on behalf of law and order.

Thus our obscure county touches on the one side the problems of the Indian's destiny, and on another the great problems now pending in civilized Europe. On the 8th of June one of the little trading-vessels from our waters, the brigantine Stephen and Mary White, owned by Stephen Horsey and commanded by William Round, was attacked and captured by the French near the island of Ache.* This is one of the little ripples from the great war raging in Europe between William, the champion of Protestantism, and Louis XIV., the arch-persecutor. This year, for the support of the war, begins in England a public debt of which, says my father, no one can foresee the end.

Our first royal governor has not remained with us long. His course pacific and fair to all, he had made many friends, refusing to force the Church Establishment suddenly and harshly upon an unwilling people. There was sincere mourning when we heard that Sir Lionel Copley was no more. The lieutenant-governor being absent in Europe, Sir Edmund Andros of Virginia must be the acting governor until Nicholson arrive. The reputation of neither is very attractive.

* So sworn in court next year : Somerset records.

CHAPTER XV.

A. D. 1694.

"Neither did ever any of them produce one instance of this absolute perfection."—MAKEMIE.

MY friend William has been consulting me about furnishing his "little wigwam among the pines," as he calls it. It was so absurd, his asking *me*, that I took down Captain John Smith's *History* and read his list of "such necessaries as either private families or single persons shall have cause to provide to go to Virginia." The list begins with a man's apparel, then victual for a year, arms, tools, and "household implements for a family of six persons," the latter as follows :

	sh.	d
1 iron pot	7	0
1 kettle	6	0
1 large frying pan	2	6
1 gridiron	1	6
2 skillets	5	0
1 spit	2	0
Platters, dishes & spoons, of wood	4	0

William had often smiled during my reading of the long list. Then he said saucily,

"But all that is for a family of six, and I am thinking of only two. Nor did your chivalrous knight say anything of the gown and petticoat and veil."

Whatever it may be in the Maryland air that brings

237

the sudden color to maidens' faces, I am determined to keep my secret. He said something about a favor he had to ask of Mr. Makemie, and of the sweetly-blooming honeysuckles which Matchacoopah planted; but I hasten to colony and county matters.

The Assembly has just passed a wholesome law prohibiting the carrying of the murderous "fire-waters" to Indian towns and cabins. Another law has been enacted, not so wise and paternal, made specially for the Indians in our own part of the province, forbidding the *striking of fish* in Dorchester and Somerset counties. This is the red man's favorite method of securing a large part of his food, and it is very selfish to exclude the original owners from Maryland's abundant supplies of the finny tribe. They have friends to resent the wrong, and justice will yet be done them. Peter, Mr. Makemie's Indian tenant, *strikes* all he pleases on his side of the divisional line, and pities the Pocomokes.

We are to have a new temple of justice. In March it is ordered by the court that a tract of land not exceeding two hundred acres be purchased near Dividing Creek, and a house there be built on the following plan : It is to be fifty feet long by twenty feet wide, overjetted, the gable-ends of brick, with a chimney above and below, and with brick underpinning.* Colonel Francis Jenkins and Captain William Whittington are appointed commissioners to buy the land and superintend the construction. On the road running north from Rehoboth and Pocomoke Ferry, passing over the horse-bridges of Dividing Creek and Nasiongo, and thence

* Somerset records   Very old frame houses with ends of brick are still seen in the county.

up to "the great bridge" at Snow Hill, there is a little elevation of land, affording an eligible site for the building. There the imposing structure is to stand. It is a point accessible from all parts of the large county (50).

Notwithstanding the excitement about the Church Establishment and the determined opposition of the Quakers, they are still employed in public trusts on our side of the bay. At this same March court, John Goddin and George Truitt, the latter one of their most prominent men near Snow Hill, at whose house all their traveling preachers are entertained, made favorable report as commissioners upon the repairing of "the great bridge at Snow Hill." Henry Hudson says they are credited with *sufficiency of light within* to inspect one of the most important works in the county.

We notice that on the 1st of November a petition was presented to their court by the Quakers of Accomack that the house of Thomas Fookes at Onancock be recorded as their place of worship, accompanied with the statement that their meeting-house at Muddy Creek has lately been burnt. This is the first application on the Eastern Shore for the benefits of the Toleration Act. I have not learned whether the petition has been granted or not. The burnt meeting-house was not far from the plantation of Mr. Anderson. Mr. Anderson and Mr. Fookes are closely related (51), and both own property at the county town. To this point their traveling preachers all direct their course.

While speaking of the courts, I may mention an application made to our justices on the 14th of August by Mr. Anderson for an order for the payment of two notes due Mr. Makemie through his commercial transactions along our river. In the absence of our minister, pushing his tent-making and missionary journeys from Maryland to Barbadoes, or possibly at this time superintending the publication of his book in Boston, his father-in-law appears with power of attorney for collection of the debt. Both notes are under date of March 4, 1693, one signed by James Maynard, witnessed by Henry Scholfield and John Dryden (spelled "Dreden"), for twelve hundred pounds of tobacco, to be delivered "at some convenient landing appointed by act of Assembly on Pocomoke River." The other, signed by the same, is for thirty bushels of corn, which is to be delivered "at the mill at Rehoboth." * Judgment is confessed and payment ordered. The primitive mill, with its importance to us colonists, its pretty pond white with lilies, does not know that it will be indebted to Mr. Makemie's speculations in corn for its second mention in history, Colonel Stevens's will being the first.

In July we hear of the arrival of the new governor, Sir Francis Nicholson. He has already served as governor in New York and Virginia, and is said to be the champion of arbitrary power both in Church and in State. Nevertheless, he is affable and courteous to the people, ambitious of popularity and flattery—at once a courtier and a demagogue. He comes to our colony parading his zeal for Prelacy, and yet his morals are known to be very loose. In Virginia he caught the popular breeze by instituting games and offering prizes for shooting, running, riding and wrestling; here he spreads his sails on the watchword of Church Establishment.

* Somerset records. The mill is still in operation—a legacy of the fathers of two centuries ago.

Soon six clergymen follow him from abroad, more than doubling the number in the province. Sneers the Quaker Dickinson of England,

"They had heard that the government had laid a tax of forty pounds of tobacco on each inhabitant for the advancement of the priests' wages."

The outlook is not very cheering. True, prompted by the pious governor, the Assembly passes another law in place of the former abortive enactment, but the wily Papists and the stubborn Quakers have compacted their opposition, and the effort is again palsied. A report is circulated that the province is about to be restored to Lord Baltimore. In face of the rejoicings inspired by this rumor, the Episcopal clergy and their followers are disheartened.* It is interesting to watch the alliance existing between the Romish party and the Quakers. Mr. Makemie says:

"Rome and all that party sufficiently know, there are none so opposite to, nor so faithful and zealous against them as Dissenting Protestants were; no, not Quakers themselves, who would not have been so great at the English Court in the late reign if they had."

Mr. Makemie loves to banter them upon their marvelous loyalty to a Popish tyrant; so he taunts the Philadelphia authorities about the proclamation against George Keith:

"It is observable that in their proclamation there is not any mention of their Majesties' names, but of the *late king twice. Verbum sat sapienti !*"

Even when the obnoxious tax is collected, but little money is secured from it. There are many grades of

---

* Bishop Hawks, p. 78, etc. For character of Nicholson, see the same writer; also Campbell's *Virginia* and McMahon's *Maryland.*

tobacco, and Dissenters select the forty pounds from the worst. And—tell it not in Gath!—Episcopalians have not been slow to learn the trick. Finally, it turns out that the law has been so unskillfully drawn that it meets the royal dissent. Thus the hungry Church, impatiently waiting and alternating between hope and disappointment, seems to look rather to tobacco than to divine grace for help.

Says a writer of their own:

"Now and then an itinerant preacher came over, of very loose morals and scandalous behavior, so that, what with such men's ill examples, the Roman priests' cunning, and the Quakers' bigotry, religion was in a manner turned out of doors." *

Of course the writer means religion of prelatic type. Thinking only of the Western Shore, he knows nothing of the spiritual worship of almighty God by the Presbyterians of Somerset, their people law-abiding citizens and their ministers men of character unimpeached. Says a letter to the Bishop of London, mourning the misfortunes of Prelacy:

"There was a sort of wandering pretenders to preaching that came from New England and other places; which deluded not only the Protestant Dissenters from our Church, but many of the Churchmen themselves, by their extemporary prayers and preachments." †

Another difficulty is pressing sorely. The general failure in crops, and the deadly disease raging among the cattle and hogs of the province, make the infliction of a Church establishment only the heavier. The colonists are having a harder time to live than at any period since we came to America. Our ministers share these hardships. We know not where it will end. In a

* *British Empire in America*, i. 333.   † Hawks, p 77.

new country, where the majority of the people are poor enough already, and where our isolated condition makes the case desperate when home-supplies fail, a future of increasing destitution is frightful to contemplate.* This dark pressure of growing scarcity seems not to be considered for a moment by the governor and his ecclesiastical friends. We love at such a time as this to see the approaching sails of Mr. Makemie's sloop.

While pressed upon the one side by Ritualism and on the other by extreme Anti-Ritualism, we have been reading Mr. Makemie's new book, just issued from Boston. Its blows for righteousness and orthodoxy are well directed and vigorous. The extravagances and inconsistencies of Maryland Quakerism have needed a brave exposure and an unvarnished record for future days. Says my father,

"Presbyterianism, slow to strike, has never been known to cry for quarter when conflict for the truth is forced. Here, on our lower Eastern Shore, this first war of doctrines has been invited and provoked by an aggressive sect, and the future years must prove which is to go down in the struggle " (52)

Of this book (*Answer to George Keith's Label*) and its author, the strong men of New England, Increase Mather, James Allen, Samuel Willard, John Baily and Cotton Mather, speak thus in no mean praise:

"When the foundations are stricken at and those articles on which our hopes for eternal life are built be undermined, it is time to arm in defence of them. The following discourses will be found both seasonable and profitable; in which the venom and sophistry of a grand apostate and one of the most unwea-

* For condition during 1694 and 1695, see McSherry's *Maryland*, p 103.

ried supporters of that tottering fabric of Enthusiasm, are detected, and the perverse spirit which God hath sown among them, in suffering them to lay open each other's follies, is discovered by the reverend and judicious author. We do therefore commend him and these labors of his, to the blessing of God ; who alone can recover the fallen, settle the wavering, and confirm such as stand, and make the faithful endeavors of this his servant become instrumental to these desired ends."

Mr. Makemie is impatient of all *shams* I use the new word which came into vogue under the second Charles. All forms of self-righteousness are very repulsive to our minister's honest nature. He easily detects and mercilessly exposes the boasted attainments of these perfectionists. He says :

" I cannot but admire the instability of many who are so easily and soon drawn to embrace and espouse that persuasion and way of those called Quakers ; and that because of an outward and seeming sanctity, made of those things that are not peculiar to Quakers only , of not swearing, drinking and ranting. Thousands of professors exceed them in a shining holiness and Christian universal piety. The most of their religion is composed of negatives, for many of them are as void of the positive part of religion, as worshiping God in the public, private and secret duties of religion, as many moral heathens. If we take a view of their principles, they are not only repugnant to truth, contrary to God's word and the public received doctrine of the churches of Christ for many centuries past, but also dangerous and damnable."

These are the days of vehement diction between controversialists, and Mr. Makemie goes on to maul the Quaker images with sledge-hammers double-handed. In youth he remembers the thunderbolts of the mighty Mr. John Milton, who died only the year before Mr. Makemie's matriculation at the university. Since then he has grown familiar with the works of the puissant Puritan logicians who have never shrunk from calling heresy and sin by their right names wherever found.

In his book he publishes the manuscript left by Keith at Squire Layfield's, and then answers, point by point, the strictures of the Pennsylvania crusader. Keith has prefaced his paper as follows:

" Kind friend George Layfield, my dear love in the Lord Jesus, Christ saluteth thee, with earnest supplication and prayer to God for thee, that God who hath begun his good work in thee, may perfect it until the day of Christ, and that the precious seed that God hath sown in thy heart may grow not only to be the greatest of herbs but a great tree, bringing forth fruit to God's everlasting praise and to thy soul's everlasting comfort and happiness."

Our reviewer says:

" I waive that complimenting and flattering preamble they have ever condemned in others, and withal am glad to hear they have any charity for any of a different opinion from them."

He then proceeds to answer every criticism, general and specific, against the Catechism, restating and defending the great Calvinistic doctrines and Presbyterian landmarks, and dealing vigorous strokes at Quaker errors and follies whenever they come in his way. In all points of theology, the sacraments or Church government, he proves himself a polemic of the staunchest Scotch type.

As to the charge of omitting " many necessary truths and doctrines," he says :

" That there are omissions, willful and designed omissions, I shall never deny, for after it was first composed, I did compendize and abbreviate it, oftener than once, to suit it to the capacities of such for whom it was prepared, even young ones, to whom Quakers have had little regard hitherto as to their religious instruction in religious fundamentals. It is no strange thing to find them quarreling our succinct way of composing our principles for young ones, because they are opposite to so early edification. Which practice is very inconsistent with Scripture precepts and precedents of training a child when young."

After replying to other general charges, he vindicates his Catechism on the doctrines of the Spirit's office-work, the creation, the sufficiency of the Scriptures as a rule of faith and practice, the insufficiency of the light of nature, the Trinity, the offices of Christ, the extent of the atonement, the perseverance of the saints, the Sabbath, the gospel ministry, baptism and the Lord's Supper. On all these subjects the heresies of his opponents are mercilessly exposed. This is followed by his illustrative picture of their dissensions and mutual accusations in Philadelphia :

" This is our comfort, we shall not be judged in the last day by Quakers, who must, as well as their neighbors, give an account of their rash and uncharitable judgings to a Most Righteous Judge "

This published defence secures new and increasing influence to the Catechism among the colonists, and attracts attention and confidence to the man who has demonstrated his ability to vindicate the truth he preaches. While his antagonists on both sides are absorbed with the question of Establishment or non-Establishment, Mr Makemie goes on steadily, by living voice and effective pen, with his work of planting a pure faith on this Western continent.

While scarcity and want are prevailing around us, we hear of failure of crops and frightful ravages of the small-pox in England. Our king has suffered great reverses in the war, and the nation is clouded with despondency. Marlborough has conveyed information to James which has lost the country another victory, and the Jacobites are busy everywhere.* Still, His Majesty remains firm, trusting in God, and wields the allies at his will.

Fanaticism flourishes. In Buckinghamshire, England, a preacher proclaims that the Saviour has told him that "he has now come down, and will appear publicly at Pentecost and gather all the saints, Jews and Gentiles, and lead them to Jerusalem and begin the millennium." Thousands are living in daily expectancy. Says John Evelyn:

"This brings to mind what I lately happened to find in Alstedius, that the thousand years should begin this very year 1694. It is in my *Encyclopedia Biblica*—my copy of the book printed near sixty years ago." †

My father says it is remarkable how frequently such human supplements to prophecy are repeated and disappointed along the history of the Church.

Before the stern devotion of Scotch subjects to their traditional principles, His Majesty has thought best to bend from his Erastianism. A political "oath of allegiance and assurance" being made the condition of ministers sitting in ecclesiastical courts, they positively refused, and collision with the civil authorities was imminent. For the independency of Christ's kingdom and crown they had battled too long to betray them now into the hands of even a Calvinistic Cæsar. The king yields, and the heroes of the Covenant hold their Assembly under God's sceptre alone.

In some of the northern counties of Scotland, under the encouragement of Jacobite abettors and in violent defiance of law, the Prelatists have been driving out the Presbyterian incumbents and obtruding themselves

* Knight, iv. 582–591,   † Evelyn's *Diary*, p. 557

upon their parishes.* It is hard for these old tyrants to learn that their days of mastery in Scotland are over.

In Ireland an ecclesiastical commission from the Crown has been trying to purge the prelatic Church from its scandals. An archbishop has been deposed for utter neglect of duty and on other charges. A bishop has been deprived of his sees "for selling of livings and preferments, and many other crimes committed by him in the exercise of his episcopal jurisdiction." A dean has been deprived "for the crime of adultery and incontinence of life." The Prebendary of Kilroot was convicted "of intemperance, incontinence of life and neglect of his cures." The commissioners say:

"If we would give way to the passions and animosities of the clergy here, who are not sparing in their informations against their brethren, I believe we might deprive, or at least suspend, one half of them" †

Such are the men who would drive Presbyterianism out of Ulster, and such, perhaps, will be those who are lusting for the forty-per-poll law in Maryland.

The Christmas holidays have brought sadness to the palace at Kensington. Small-pox has entered the doors of royalty, seizing upon as noble a queen as ever graced the English throne. On the 28th of December, Queen Mary died, leaving the king broken-hearted and desolate. In that stern, impassive bosom, here was the one tender spot. In tears, prostrated, he declares that during the whole course of their marriage he has never known one fault in her. When told her danger, "she thanked God she had always carried

---

* Hetherington
† Report of commission, Reid, II. 439-441.

this in mind, that nothing was to be left to the last hour."

In his castigation of those perfectionists who have claimed the privilege of assaulting all churches without receiving the merited exposure, Mr. Makemie asks:

"Why are Quakers so hot and zealous for King James, a Popish and abdicated Prince, and never were so for any other Protestant king, though King William and Queen Mary have been kinder than any other by giving liberty established by law?"

While the good queen has been dying in England, our little capital at St. Mary's has received her death-blow. Unless some future city spring up along the Chesapeake to preserve the name and the fame of the Baltimores, it seems that everything that is specially the work of their hands is doomed. The site of Yoacomaco, where they first landed and planted the cross, must yield its honors to a point of land at the mouth of the Severn, made a town on paper in 1683, and called "the Town at Proctor's."

Ignatius Loyola, the patron saint, has not been able to protect his honors from blight nor his votaries from ridicule. Has not the power of Popish rule passed from the province for ever?

CHAPTER XVI.

A. D. 1695.

"Latitudinarian opinions are commonly attended with an answerable practice."—MAKEMIE.

THE great scarcity continues and increases. Often we sit at our tables with nothing but maize before us, and not much of that. During last year and this, twenty-five thousand four hundred and twenty-nine cattle and sixty-two thousand three hundred and seventy-five hogs have died in the province, leaving the poor still poorer.* Of course these hard times tell upon Mr. Wilson and Mr. Davis.

It is fortunate that the seashore and the bayshore and these scores of rivers, are near with Nature's supplies. Said the adventurous Smith years ago:

"We found in places that abundance of fish, lying so thick with their heads above the water as for want of nets (our barge driving amongst them) we attempted to catch them with a frying pan; but we found it a bad instrument to catch fish with. Neither better fish, more plenty, nor more variety for small fish, had any of us ever seen in any place so swimming in the water, but they are not to be caught with frying pans."

These fish are a godsend now.

The colonists have become so disheartened of late that they have been deserting the province. The population was thinning to such an extent that the Assembly has been compelled to issue an order,

* McSherry's *Maryland*, p 103

which has been read at our Somerset court, against persons leaving and going to the southward.*

Amid the pressure of want and despondency, the " Crown requisitions " for help in defending New York against the Canadian French and their Indian allies, come upon us. It is claimed that Albany is a frontier of Maryland and Virginia! We are assessed one hundred and thirty-three pounds sterling—enough to bankrupt the province. New York, being asked to send a commissioner to witness our distressed condition, answers that such a commission would be too expensive for her resources—that the last one cost the government nineteen pounds! Reply is returned that the expense of nineteen pounds was extravagant, and that the aforesaid messenger " kept drunkening up and down and of very ill and rude behavior during his stay, and that it was no wonder for him to bring them in such an account of expenses, considering the character his brother Vander Brugh, at New Castle, bears." †

Here we catch a glimpse of the diplomacy and the poverty of the early American governments. The poverty of our struggling Somerset churches may be inferred

On the 28th of February the Assembly held its first session in the new capital and called it "Annapolis," in honor of the sister of our late gracious queen. It may be wise to secure the favorable notice of one who will probably succeed to the throne. The Assembly has been prudent enough to repeal former Establishment acts and let the province breathe a while. The blight of these acts, combined with the

* Somerset records of 1695.   † McMahon, p 265, note.

threatenings of famine, is injuring the colony sadly.
But the agitation goes on.

In Philadelphia a church has just been built by the
Episcopalians, and they have a clergyman by the name
of Clayton.   Hitherto there has been no regular worship but by the Quakers and the Swedes.   The latter
are now without a pastor.   Mr. Makemie is the first
Presbyterian minister ever in the place   He keeps his
eye upon it, and will be able hereafter to receive information more promptly from the Quaker city.   Letters sent across the Chesapeake will strike a post-route
established this year, the first in America, and running
from Newton's Point, on the Wicomico of the Western
Shore, to Allen's mill, to Benedict Leonard's Town,
over the Patuxent to George Lingan's, to Larkin's, to
Annapolis, over to Kent, to Williamstadt, to Daniel
Toaf's, to Adam Peterson's, on to New Castle, and
thence to Philadelphia,   The postman must travel the
route eight times a year for an annual salary of fifty
pounds.*

Mr. Makemie's neighbor, William Teackle, died in
January, after a life on the Peninsula of thirty-nine
years.   Three   daughters—Margaret,   Elizabeth   and
Catherine—and a two-year-old son named John, survive him   He leaves extensive possessions in land
and a fine library.† He has had both friends, and
enemies, and felt no hesitation in collecting his tithes
by law. We cannot forget that our own minister
helped to pay these tithes. Six days before his departure to other climes, the clergyman closed his will with
the prayer, "And now, Lord Jesus, come quickly and

* McMahon, p 266.

† Accomack records. full inventory of books

let me receive thy gracious call, in thine own good time, to thy servant." A solemn, beautiful prayer, and not from the Prayer-Book.

The Virginia clergy are clamoring for increase of salary. The House of Burgesses has just returned to their petition the following answer:

[The clergy] "have considerable perquisites by marriages, burials and glebes, generally of the best lands, not less in most places than four or five hundred acres, and in some places not less than twice that quantity; which glebes are well provided with houses, orchards, fences and pastures, to that degree that most if not all the ministers of this country are in as good a condition in point of livelihood as a gentleman that is well seated and hath twelve or fourteen servants."

The burgesses declare that they

"are assured by their observation and certain knowledge that, when the ministers have proved frugal men, they have still raised their fortunes, from which it cannot but be necessarily concluded that the greatest part of the clergy are well content with their present provision, and that all informations made to the contrary have proceeded from none but such as are too avariciously inclined." *

Such is the testimony of the burgesses, themselves Episcopalians. Rev. John Monro, rector of Hungar's parish, a brother-in-law of Commissary Blair, and living not far below Mr. Makemie's Matchatank plantation, is one of these petitioners thus rebuked. Such facts do not stimulate our enthusiasm for an Establishment.

My father has taken me with him up to the new court-house at Dividing Creek, an imposing structure among the neighboring cabins. After crossing the river we stopped by the plantation of Squire James Round, one mile above the ferry, and Mrs. Mary

* Anderson's *Colonial Church*, ii. 388, etc.

Round went up with us, sitting her pillion gracefully.
This family are neighbors of ours, the plantation Good
Success having been patented in 1686, the year Mr.
Trail bought the plantation of Brother's Love.   When
we came in sight of the noble court-house building,
standing upon its hill of light-colored soil, with its
staunch brick gables and overjetted roof, its broad
front of fifty feet facing the road, unenclosed as yet,
the forest-trees casting their primeval shades about it,
and the background of the swamps of creek and river
shutting it around with their peculiar gloom, we
reined up our steeds for a while, awed in the presence of this enthronement of law in the heart of our
American wilds.

Soon the dignified array of justices take their seats
—James Round, John Bozman, Matthew Scarborough,
George Layfield, Thomas Newbold, Samuel Hopkins,
Thomas Jones, Edmund Howard, Arnold Elzey, and,
presiding over them, Mr. Makemie's warm friend Colonel
Francis Jenkins. The original bench of commissioners
of the peace appointed by Lord Baltimore nineteen years
ago are all gone. As one of the presiding judges of the
original array could neither read nor write, so it is with
a number of these; but they are none the less conscious
of representing in their persons the majesty of the law
and the fortunes of a new empire. Some wear the
broadcloth of Europe, some the product of the looms
of Somerset; but, whatever the garb, the pride of
high public trust is upon these sturdy colonists, and
their mien is stately   I could see that Mrs. Round
regarded her husband with great complacency.

Among the constables, no less conscious than the
justices of official importance, stands Mr. Thomas

Purnell of Bogatenorton Hundred. I never see a colonist from the seaside without thinking of the grand old major-general of Cromwell's Ironsides living up there amid the plaudits of the loud-voiced surf. After the court has been called and order commanded by Sheriff Ephraim Wilson, and after all the formalities of the opening have been observed, royalty itself appears as petitioner, and with far more probability of justice than King William at the hands of the Tory High Churchmen of his English Parliament. Daniel, king of the Pocomokes, with his retinue of attendants, comes to the bar and states his complaint —that the white man John Parker of Matapony is trespassing and building upon the land of this American monarch.

The Indian is asking his rights at the hands of a court that has never failed to mete out justice to his race. The question of boundaries is referred to eight commissioners, four of them selected by King Daniel and from his own friends of the forest—Assateague Weegnonah, Nuswuddux Dick, Pocomoke Thomas and Morumsco James. The white and the red commissioners visit the land together, each one of equal authority with the other. Mr. Parker, a relative of Mr. Anderson and a friend of Mr. Makemie,* is a man of wealth and position. The report is made in favor of the king of the Pocomokes, and the trespasser must retire from the Indian's domain.

I was proud of my county that day, and again denied to William Penn the exclusive and special credit for protection of the rights of the aborigines. Our little Lady Mary Somerset has no reason to be

---

* One of the witnesses to Makemie's will.

ashamed for giving her name to the county. Says Matchacoopah :

"The strong *mah-squallen*" ("hawk") "has guarded the nest of the *kuh-hos*" ("the crow") "in the pine-tops."

We listen to an order authorizing the building by Walter Taylor of a pasture-fence around the court-house land, two hundred and sixty panels, with posts and four rails; also for building on this land a prison fifteen feet by twelve, that the Pocomoke as well as the Thames may have its Tower of London; also for the construction of a bridge over the head of St. Martin's River. Under the same high sanction, Edward Stevens is recognized as ferryman of Pocomoke at the reduced salary of five hundred pounds of tobacco; a few years since, it was three thousand. In such years as this, public officers must share the hardships attending the scarcity. We hear of the law just made across the bay at the new capital, and now to be enforced, against the frequent assembling of negroes. Perhaps our burgesses have been frightened by the reported conspiracy of negroes against their masters on the island of Barbadoes two years ago.

While our heroic king is gaining the victory over his great rival at Namur, while the English Parliament wallows in the corruptions of bribery, while Presbyterian Scotland leads the world in her purpose to establish a school in every parish, while Dean Swift succeeds the deposed prebendary of Kilroot, while the Presbytery of Laggan is memorializing the king for the benefits of toleration to those Presbyterians whose early zeal turned the scale for his cause, and while their petitions and rights are opposed with jeers and taunts by Bishop Pullen (Mr. Makemie's old neighbor at Ramelton),—here, on our retired Eastern Shore, the officers of the law are sitting in the dignity of a primitive jurisprudence, managing the interests of our large county, and superintending its varieties of nationalities and of races.

On returning home that evening, we find Mr. Makemie's sloop at the shore, and are not long in inspecting the following packages from his store · *

2¼ yds. broadcloth, 120 lbs. per yd . . . . . 267 lbs tob.	
6 dozen hair buttons, 10 lbs. per doz . . . . . 60 " "	
3 yds Scotch cloth, 26 lbs. per yd . . . . . . 78 " "	
6 yds. lawn, 24 lbs. per yd. . . . . 144 " "	
Tobacco box . . . . 24 ' "	
Wooden-handled knife . . . . 6 " "	

The broadcloth is for John, and I am more and more suspicious. Yesterday he was over toward the Monokin; and when the twilight began to make everything look thoughtful under the Maryland haze, I noticed that he sat a long time by the silent river's edge humming a soft Troubadour air. John certainly has a right to be a little sentimental, but he is not the less soundly practical. You see that he succeeded in getting a reduction of three pounds of tobacco on the total of the broadcloth figures.

There is around us a sad disposition to depreciate sound doctrine, and to think that it matters little what we believe if we are only sincere. Therefore I listened the more attentively to Mr. Makemie that night :

"A great impediment to regular and right living is latitude, or looseness, in principle and opinion, which has always a powerful

* Somerset records, 1695; connection with the sloop imaginary.

17

influence upon words and actions For the understanding commonly dictates to the will and the will sways the words and actions of life Some from error in judgment call good evil and evil good and such must go astray in acting. Many suppose, if they take up with some things of virtue and Christianity, they shall no way be culpable if they omit and neglect many things though weightier than those that are done. Others have loose notions of real religion and true piety and imagine and say there is no need of that severity and strictness in walk which some Precisians do cry up and practice; and hence indulge themselves in omissions and commissions daily which causeth irregularities in life Some place religion in such things as have nothing of true virtue in them and are more strict in these than in the weighter matters of the law Others deny the Divine authority and Gospel institution of the sealing ordinances annexed to the covenant of grace; therefore not only live in the neglect of them but deny and ridicule them, Some in opinion deny any moral precept in the fourth commandment, therefore profane the Lord's Day at an unchristian rate." *

This led to some conversation about the open profanation of God's holy day by the Quakers. Mr. Makemie said:

" The charge that highly offended many of that gang, is concerning a question in my Catechism concerning the Sabbath. In the answer I affirm, Quakers and profane persons are enemies to the Sabbath All the Quakers I ever conversed with in Europe or America declared this as their undoubted judgment that all days were alike under the Gospel and none of perpetual observation as a day of rest; and, further, that they were as free to work or labor in their several callings and trades on the first day of the week as any other. I am able to give several instances. I am lately informed of several servants of Quakers, otherwise educated, who have made complaint to magistrates of their masters' causing them to follow their daily labor. A witness yet alive can declare, being on a Sabbath at Thomas Evernden's house, he perceived no manner of worship with his family but great diligence in despatching one of his servants with necessaries for building a sloop. I have met one of them with a gun in the woods on the Sabbath while we were going to the public worship of God. As many as know Quakers in England, Scotland and

* New York sermon.

Ireland cannot be ignorant how, neither from obedience to God or man, could they be persuaded to observe the first day of the week but would keep open their shops and follow their several callings, for which they were often drawn to prison and their goods carried away. This was not done in a corner but manifest and known to all." *

Whatever may be the occasional virtues of the Quakers, it is very natural that Mr. Makemie and those of us who have been trained in reverence of God's holy day should be shocked at the contempt put upon it by these people.

The next morning our Pioneer, dropping good seed by the way, sails on up toward Snow Hill to trade at its wharf and to preach for Mr. Davis on Sabbath. Our clouds of mosquitoes cannot deter him from his work. We remember the contemptuous answer of Governor Bradford of the Plymouth colony to those complaining of this annoyance: "They are too delicate and unfit to begin new plantations and colonies that cannot endure the biting of a mosquito. We would wish such to keep at home till at least they be mosquito-proof." Mr. Makemie has been bitten by many a mosquito.

Thomas Story, another champion of the Quakers, who not long ago left Episcopacy for the other extreme, thus ventilates his estimate of Mr. Makemie's old opponent, writing of a man in England who approached him this year on the subject of the schism:

"Advancing toward me he began to discourse about George Keith, saying that we had missed our way in contending with him as we did; for he being a man of learning and knowledge, might have been very serviceable to our Society in helping us over some mistakes we labor under. I replied that we were not

* *Answer to Keith.*

under mistake about the Christian faith or religion or any part of it, and did not want instruction from George Keith or any other like unto him, we being taught of the Lord." *

It is amusing to see two violently antagonistic parties making the same arrogant pretensions to divine guidance and infallibility. Mr. Makemie's exposure of this is giving a heavy blow along our shores to the extravagant self-righteousness of both.

John and William and Martha and I have been trying to sing from the *Bay Psalm-Book* just obtained from a New England trading-ketch. It was first published in 1640—the first book issued from the American press. Ours is the ninth edition, issued this year, with the air and bass—the first music published on the continent. Here are the glorious tunes regarded by many as almost inspired and a sin for any other to be substituted—"Oxford," "York," "Litchfield," "Windsor," "St. David's," "Martyrs"—and directions are given for setting the tunes so as to avoid "squeaking above or grumbling below." So we did our best upon the fifty-first psalm, trying first or last all the tunes:

> " Create in mee clean heart at last,
>   God; a right spirit in mee new make.
> Nor from thy presence quite mee cast,
>   thy holy spright not from mee take
> Mee thy salvation's joy restore,
>   and stay mee with thy spirit free
> I will trangressors teach thy lore,
>   and sinners shall be turned to thee."

Henry Hudson, as he rowed up to the bank, heard our efforts and charged us with both "squeaking above and grumbling below."

* Story's *Works*

CHAPTER XVII.

A. D. 1696.

"The heart and spirit of man is so stirring and active a thing that it is never at quiet or rest but always employed about either good or evil."—MAKEMIE.

THE winter through which we have passed has been one of the hardest in the history of the colony. Deprived of our native supplies of beef and pork, we have had little with which to purchase anything from abroad. An opossum or a raccoon or a bear from the woods has brought timely relief to many, and for these the poor Indians have been constant competitors. The Assembly has relented and repealed the law against striking fish in Dorchester and Somerset, and the red men have brought much of this food to our doors.

What could we have done through these dark days without the gospel? There was gloom along our many streams and gloom along the seaboard; the clam-shoals and the oyster-banks and the fishing-coves have been our chief dependence. The very cry of the fish-hawks seemed to tantalize with rivalry and need. Through it all, at Snow Hill, at Monokin, at Rehoboth, the voices of Samuel Davis, Thomas Wilson and Francis Makemie have been heard telling of the faithfulness of the covenant-keeping God and proclaiming the privileges of the saints in Christ. We saw our ministers sharing with us the hard times.

Two heavy blows to her prosperity have fallen upon Maryland—these afflictive years of threatened famine and this attempted change from perfect toleration to religious tithing and persecution. Immigration has been checked and our own population alienated.

In the midst of troubles like these, it is cheering to sit in our primitive Rehoboth temple and listen to the minister dwelling upon the blessed old gospel themes. For a while we would be rapt away into oblivion of all the sorrows of earth. Shall I ever forget the tones of Mr. Makemie's voice while the words "glory" and "glorious" rang, and rang again, through the inspiring climax?

" This consists in two steps ; one is at the dissolution of soul and body by death, when the souls of the renewed and righteous, in whom the seed of saving light and grace have been sown, which has appeared with some suitable fruit and improvement in a day and season of grace, shall lay aside their earthly veil and clay tabernacle for a time, and shall ascend into the world of spirits above, into the kingdom of our heavenly Father, there to be glorified or translated into his likeness by beholding his glory ; and so shall be fit to dwell and converse with the spirits of the just made perfect ; and shall be with Christ in unspeakable and inconceivable glory where nothing shall enter that defileth, and where no stain or spot of pollution shall cleave to any soul , but a perfect rectitude and conformity of soul to the image of God, shall shine in its full meridian, made possessor of that glorious peace where are many glorious mansions prepared by our glorified Redeemer ; where there are a glorious company of sinless and pure angels and purified spirits made perfect ; and a glorious and unchangeable state of rest and reward for ever, without sin, suffering or temptation And all this while their bodies are paying their debt to the dust and passing through corruption, as it were performing their last sleep, only in order to a more joyful awakening and resurrection unto an endless life in the last day.

"But the final perfection and absolute consummation of this promised salvation, shall be after the resurrection, when, after the final appearance of the Lord Jesus to the last Judgment and reunion of soul and body, they shall be solemnly adjudged and openly declared to be what they were, living and dying, the blessed and redeemed of the Lord Jesus, and shall be invited with a, 'Come ye blessed of my Father,' and ushered in and put into an eternal and uninterrupted possession of an uncorruptible crown and heavenly kingdom wherein both body and soul shall be cloathed for ever with incorruptible glory that fadeth not away." *

Notwithstanding the privations everywhere endured, the votaries of Church establishment are pressing their aims unflinchingly. Our governor has urged the collection of tithes in some of the counties, and has effected the erection of churches in St. Mary's, Calvert, Charles, Cecil and Talbot. If his zeal for a pure Christianity were equal to his zeal for the Church, we would be more patient under these exactions. This year all former laws have been repealed and another enacted, in which, among other provisions, they want a bishop on a large salary, to sit in the Upper House as one of our rulers. They have blundered again, and we are confident that the new law must fail in getting the assent of the home government. The Episcopal legislators are so eager that they forget to observe the simplest legal formalities. In this case I am told that they have included in the enactment several important matters not named in the title, thus vitiating the whole. The Quakers and the Catholics are awake for the detection of such irregularities, and have their agents on the alert at home.

* New York sermon.

For we all still speak of the fatherland as *home*.

In Virginia they have just advanced the salary of their clergy to sixteen thousand pounds of tobacco in addition to their glebes. Thus the opposition of legislators eventually yields to the pertinacity of these demands. Of course our own preacher must pay his proportion of the increased tax. On the records of Accomack for this year appears the minute that Mr. Makemie brings a negro slave Jack into court, "desiring ye court's inspection of his age that he might be accordingly duly entered in the list of tithables; whom the court accordingly judged at eleven years of age." Thus the law-abiding Presbyterian divine makes no factious opposition to "the powers that be."

Meanwhile, one of the best Church-of-England clergymen thus writes to the Bishop of London:

"Your clergy in these parts are of very ill example. No discipline nor canons of the church are observed. Several ministers have caused such high scandals of late and have raised such prejudices amongst the people against the clergy that hardly can they be persuaded to take a clergyman into their parish. I must tell you I find abundance of good people who are willing to serve God but they want good ministers, ministers that be very pious and not wedded to this world as the best of them are. The clergy is composed for the most part of Scotchmen, people indeed so basely educated, or little acquainted with the executing of their charge and duty, that their lives and conversation are fitter to make heathens than Christians."

So testifies the Rev. Nicholas Moreau, telling tales out of school.*

Since the domination of Prelacy has passed away from Scotland, many of the former rectors and curates —late spies and informers against the persecuted Presbyterians—have been prompt to conform, subscribe the

* Bishop Meade's *Old Churches*, etc., i. 384.

Confession of Faith and creep under the wing of a Church which they hate, while others look abroad for their bread; so that the facts support Mr. Moreau in thinking that it is not greatly to the credit of any Episcopal clergyman to hail from Scotland during the last few years. We notice that a number have lately come over to Virginia with Scotch names.*

This same year, in Ireland, Bishop King is opposing the admission of Presbyterians to office with the unanswerable argument that if this be done many of the present adherents of Prelacy can be retained neither by reason nor by Scripture, and declares that "most people value their interest more than their religion." This is a low estimate to be put upon his own flock by a bigoted prelate.

In the midst of these discouraging aspects of the Establishment question, we are glad to hear of the appointment by the Bishop of London of a really good and devoted man to the office of commissary of Maryland. Dr. Thomas Bray is said to be an able clergyman, of irreproachable character, now forty-five years of age, full of zeal and of sterling piety. We shall sincerely rejoice if this leading ecclesiastic of our province is to be one whose influence shall be for Christ and for the restraint of an unworthy ministry. He has waited upon the princess Anne and asked her acceptance of the respect intended in giving her name to our State capital. She acknowledges the honor very graciously by offering a donation to purchase books for a library at Annapolis.

John Coode, the leader of the Associators, has been plotting against the government again. Elected to the

* Neill's *Virginia Colonial Clergy.*

Assembly, he was prevented taking his seat there on the ground of his being "in holy orders." His holy orders have their comment in the fact that he has been publicly asserting that religion is a trick, reviling the apostles, denying the divinity of Christianity and alleging that all the morals worth having are contained in Cicero's *Offices*. He has been indicted by the grand jury of St. Mary's for atheism and blasphemy, and has fled to Virginia. This is the man who was a revolutionist in the name of the Church! Nor would all this have been likely to disgrace a churchman in the estimation of our governor had not Coode declared he had overthrown one government and would pull down another.*

There is a growing zeal for free schools among our rulers. The former law passed during Nicholson's administration having proved inefficient, another is now passed looking to the establishment of a school in every county. An academy called "King William's School" is placed, under this act, at Annapolis, and another prospectively on the Eastern Shore at Oxford. For carrying all this into effect a corporation has been formed and the Rev. John Hewett of our county appointed one of the body. Says Mr. Makemie, whose notice no public interest escapes:

"The smallest and meanest of schools cannot be maintained without a competent number of scholars, which has been our great discouragement in Virginia and Maryland, where the number to be entertained together are too few to maintain any Master or Mistress, who are necessitated to shift from place to place until they cannot live at all by that calling So that in many remote corners many families never had opportunities of schools and therefore remain without all knowledge of letters." †

* McMahon and McSherry, *in loco*   † Makemie's *Perswasive*

The hardships of the last two years have done some good in giving a new impulse to our home manufactures Somerset has led the province in this industry, in both linen and woolen goods. We have visited the looms of Lawrence Benston and Malachi Glass and bought some of their cloths. Were it not for the selfish hostility of the English government to any competition in her colonies, why should not these streams be bordered by thousands of looms, and Somerset become as famous as Somersetshire, England, for her "reds" and "whites" and "azures" and "blues"? (53).

Those who welcomed us to the continent on our first landing, sixteen years ago, are rapidly passing away. Early this spring Mrs. Elizabeth Layfield— formerly Mrs. William Stevens—dies, and is buried by the side of her first husband. The graveyard is fast filling up For the dead as well as for the living —"Rehoboth"—there is room!

News comes to us of great scarcity in Scotland, financial panics in England and new plots for the assassination of the king. The loss of his faithful queen makes his lofty elevation an enthronement of loneliness, and now, under the constant harassments of his reign and the base ingratitude of those whom he came to deliver, it is said that the marvelous fortitude of William has almost failed him, and that he is talking of relinquishing the crown and retiring to the Indies.* Anon his spirit reacts. he is the brave hero of old; and the attempt at assassination is likely to establish him more firmly in the hearts of his people.

While thinking of the troubles of royalty in Eng-

* Knight's *History*, v 34, etc

land, some of us start upon a trip to a royal palace on our own shore. Matchacoopah has long been inviting us to the town up the river. Henry Hudson forms one of the party of exploration, and Margaret and Mary and Peggy and myself are in constant dread of his hideous discoveries. The rich autumn foliage looks like a forest on fire, blazing down into the depths of the reflecting waters. Like dying Christians, the birds are singing their sweetest notes before taking flight for winterless climes The herons gaze at us unaffrighted, and the stately cranes stand along the edge of the almost tropical river, dignified and contemplative

"Straight-faced Presbyterians at prayer," says the wicked Henry Hudson.

"*Ana-sup!*" whispers Matchacoopah. His quick eye has discovered a raccoon hunting frogs among the tuckahoes, and his practical arrow transfixes him. Now he sees a large fish in the waveless waters, and *ik-ke-hek* (the spear-head) strikes, and the game is his "The white man's bad law has died as *kosh-kik-ene-suc*" ("the perch") "dies," says the Indian, in triumph.

Now a little settlement of colonists is seen on the right as we ascend—a hill of sand almost as white as snow; scattered log cabins, many of the old forest-trees still standing; garden-patches of ripened maize and potatoes; narrow, crooked paths running through the settlement from cabin to cabin; two or three larger buildings used for both stores and dwellings; a shed warehouse for tobacco near the river, a more imposing edifice of cypress logs and shingles standing back among the trees upon the hill. This is the Presbyterian meeting-house in which Mr. Davis has preached for so many years.   It is a plain building about thirty feet long, but venerable as a sanctuary of the great God from which the gospel light beams gloriously forth upon the wilderness.   This is the dry, elevated point where the town insisted upon locating itself instead of obeying the act of Assembly which would have sent it farther up the river, to "Morgan's land commonly called Burrow's."

At the shore are a dozen or twenty Indian periauguas, their tawny owners up at the licensed stores trading furs and game for the white man's tempting wares.   By the law passed four years ago, no one is permitted to traffic with the savages without license. Here float the fleets of commerce from the city of the aborigines on beyond.

A gentleman dressed in the woolen cloth of our county's manufacture is walking one of the paths through this village of primitive cabins.   As he comes nearer we hail him respectfully—for is he not God's servant?—and ask him to become one of our company.   We feel greatly honored at his prompt acceptance of the invitation and at his pleasing recognition of the representative voyagers of England, Scotland, Ireland and France.   Henry Hudson gives him the title of "chaplain of the grand armada of allied nations."

Passing under the great Pocomoke bridge, we see workmen repairing "the causeway in the mesh opposite the Snow Hill landing," as ordered by the court this year.*

Ascending the stream, that continues to narrow and widen, between low islands and groves of trees which grow out of the waters, we come ere long in sight of

* Somerset records

a town upon our left considerably larger than the one we had passed. Out through the pine-forests the wigwams straggle away irregularly, built of poles and covered with bark and surrounding a larger cabin in the centre. Numbers of men sit near the wigwam doors silently smoking. In the maize-patches the women are at work gathering and bringing in the yellow ears. This is Askimmekonson, the chief seat of the Indians along the Pocomoke, the capital of their *tatt-ak*, or king.

Off to one side we see the burial-place of the tribe, the cemetery of the royal city. For the Indian too must die, and in the years to come the dust of the sons of the forest and that of the sons of Europe will mingle, the old graveyards of the one becoming the new graveyards of the other. In the grave the Indian corpse is placed in a sitting posture, buried with its favorite weapons or trinkets, and covered only with the bark of trees. It is not pleasant to go near these places of the dead.

Besides this, there is a house, which they call *mantokump*, in which they keep the bones and the embalmed bodies of some of their dead; that for their chiefs and great men is called *quioccason*. The art of embalming is said to be a specialty of the Nanticokes. For these bodies they have great reverence, and the *quioccason* is to the Indians a nobler house than the palace. Our irrepressible Hudson was almost overborne by his curiosity to invade this citadel of the dead, and would gladly have carried off some of the hideous contents.

Certain favorites of the royal wigwam come to the shore and lead us to the presence of majesty, King

Wynicaco. Matchacoopah acts as interpreter. The old chief welcomes us with dignified courtesy and has us seated around him in the oblong çabin. Special attention is paid to our minister as the wizard-man of our tribe. The pipe is brought, and it passes from the monarch's mouth to his, and then around the circle until it has touched the lips of all. It is fortunate to have Mr. Davis with us, for through our interpreter he succeeds in bringing out information which I have been very anxious to secure about the history of our Somerset Indians. In Captain Smith's explorations I knew that the river Nanticoke, from which they now take their name, was called "Cuskarawaock," and that he mentions along its banks their four towns of Saripanagh, Nanse, Aroeck and Nantaquack. The latter is suggestive of their true name. This was in 1608.

The old king inquired for George Fox, whose strange utterances he remembers, and he seemed impressed when we told him that the great "Quakel" had passed away five years ago. In answer to inquiries by Mr Davis, the monarch of Askimmekonson spoke as follows (54):

"We are the grandchildren of the Lenni Lenapes. Our grandfather now lives to the north When Mannitt, the Great Spirit, was sending our fathers from the far west toward the coast, he asked, 'Who will hunt the wild beasts in the mountains and dark forests? Who will love the rivers and bays, and spear *wammap'*" ("the fish") "'and trap *nataque'*" ("the beaver")? "And our fathers answered, '*We* will set the traps along the streams; *we* will take *wammap* from the waves; our children shall swim in the waters. Let others hunt over the mountains and plunge into

the miles of gloomy forests where Mann-ann-tote'"
(the devil) "'goes up and down.' And Mann-itt"
(the Good Spirit) "said, 'It is well.'

"Then came our fathers to the land of streams and
bays. Mann-itt called us 'Nentego.' Our grandfather,
the Lenapes, called us 'Unechtgo.' The Iroquois
called us 'Sganiateratichrohne' All these mean *the
tide-water people*. Because across the Nassiango, the
Aracoco, the Pocosin, and hundreds of other streams,
we cut down the trees and fix our traps upon them,
therefore the Mohicans call us the 'Otayachgo' and
the Delawares call us the 'Tayachquans,' meaning that
we make a dry passage over rivers. And now *wammap*"
("the fish") " comes swimming to our wigwams. *Nataque*" (" the beaver") " smells our traps. *Kaw-scheh*"
("the oyster") "and *moon-nin-nack*" (" the mannose")
do not run from our canoes. The land of a thousand
streams and talking waves is dear to the Indian's heart.

"We love our dead. When we pull down our wigwams and go, they go with us. We cannot leave them
to pine in a land of strangers. The touch of rude
hands upon their graves would break their hearts.
Tsee-ep" ("their ghosts") "would moan through the
woods uncomforted.

"We have a poison that is dreadful. Mann-itt
showed it to us for our safety. It sweeps whole settlements into death. It strikes as the lightning strikes
pah-scanemintz" (" the beech tree") "and *wee-seeke-
mintz*" (" the oak tree") " of the forests. The enemy
trembles and falls.

"We have wise men and wizards who tell us what
Mann-itt wishes. They bewitch those whom they
hate. They destroy an army by puffing their breath

at them. They bring the north-easter or make it cease to blow Their power is great

"Our poisons and wizards are not for the palefaces. They have been good and kind They will not let their bad men steal our land. We punish bad Indians who kill their hogs. We will enjoy together the thousand streams and talking waves."

Matchacoopah goes near King Wynicaco, as if to ask a boon, and seems to secure the quest. Then he takes my brother and myself and leads us to the door of another wigwam, entering, while we remain at the door. A mat wrought of corn-husks and cat-tails is lying before the fire. Matchacoopah goes and sits upon one end of it, laying down a string of beads, which I had given, and two otter-skins There he sits without speaking a word Now we see a light-colored, dark-eyed maiden come from another part of the cabin in silence and hand him a wooden platter of hominy. While he quietly eats it, she modestly turns her face another way, and sits down near him on the other end of the mat.

The parents of the maiden and ourselves have looked on without speaking This means approval, and the brief marriage ceremony is ended and our friend and the bright-eyed maiden are henceforth one. We turn our prows down the Pocomoke, bearing away upon its bosom as bride the belle of Askimmekonson.

Mr. Davis has lately heard from Mr. Josias Mackie of Elizabeth River, and tells us that he is living comfortably upon his hundred and fifty acres of land near the Back Bay. In addition to his former three places of preaching, he has just had a fourth place recorded

18

—the house of Mr John Dickson, in Southern Branch.*

While putting the Snow Hill minister ashore, we stop a while at the store of Mr Spence and make the following purchases (the last six articles are a present from our gentlemen to the bride): †

1 quire paper	15	lbs. tobacco.
12 lbs. 6-penny nails	70	"
1 m. pins	20	"
1 pair gloves	18	"
2 pair of girls' stockings	20	"
1 sifter	30	"
Needles and thimble	6	"
1 pair steel tongs	6	"
1 match coal	120	"

Mr. Makemie regrets the inconvenience in trade occasioned by our want of a better currency. He says:

"Carolina, Barbadoes, Pennsylvania, New York and New England carry from us the little scattered coin we have among us, but, which is the worst of all, they prey upon that little money we have in England by purchasing bills of exchange. Our pay at present is very bad and uncertain, being in parcels of tobacco and scattered abroad for sundry years before it amounts to a sum." ‡

If the colonists generally were as enterprising and public-spirited as our minister, many of the disadvantages of our colonial condition might soon be obviated.

I must not forget to inform Mr Makemie of the late visit of Mr. Davis to the Presbyterians at Hoarkil (Lewes), and of what he tells us of the building this year of the first Episcopal church in New York. Our preachers still keep watch to the northward.

* Sprague's *Annals*.
† Bill from Somerset records, 1696.
‡ Makemie's *Perswasive*.

CHAPTER XVIII.

A. D. 1697.

"The universal scope of the Word of God is to direct, instruct, promote and accomplish this thing; not only to assume a name, to fill our heads with fruitless notions and empty speculations, or gain a religious reputation—but, *a godly life* "—MAKEMIE.

MAJOR KING was over from the Monokin, Mr. Venable from up on the Wicomico, Mr Spence from Snow Hill, and Mr. Ambrose White from the banks of St. Martin's River. They had been attending court at Dividing Creek, and rode over to spend the night with us. Our cattle and hogs nearly all dead, we feed our guests upon yellow pone and timely captures from water and woods. John is always ready to issue at the muzzle of his new flint-lock gun that writ with the Latin name mentioned by the indentured servant George Alsop:

"Fowls of all sorts and varieties dwell at their several times and seasons here in Mary-Land. The Turkey, the Woodcock, the Pheasant, the Partrich, the Pigeon and others; especially the Turkey, whom I have seen in whole hundreds in flight in the Woods of Mary-Land, being an extraordinary fat Fowl whose flesh is very pleasant and sweet. These fowls that I have named are intayled from generation to generation to the Woods. The Swans, the Geese and Ducks, with other Water-Fowl, derogate in this point of settled residence; for they arrive in millionous multitudes in Mary-Land about the middle of September and take their winged farewell about the middle of March. But while they do remain and beleaguer the borders of the shoar with their winged Dragoons, several of them are summoned by a Writ of *fieri facias* to answer their presumptuous contempt upon a Spit."

I was greatly interested in seeing the strong Presbyterians of the American wilds turn so easily from the common details of colonial life to the deepest questions of theology.

First they discuss the current news—a fine imposed for riding or leading any horse into our new court-house, an order that Mr. William Fassett be joined overseer of the roads for Seny Puxone (Sinepuxent) with Mr. John Freeman, the appointment of Mr. John Powell as constable for Bogatenorton Hundred; a permit granted to Mr. Edward Jones to keep an ordinary, or place of entertainment, with food and the fire-waters, on the court-house grounds; a law made by the Assembly for quieting differences between Indians and whites in private controversies; the report of Samuel Hopkins, John Franklin and William Round, commissioners for dividing Bogatenorton Hundred:

"Divisional line to begin at the mouth of John Franklin's Creek and up the said Creek and branch to Golden Quarter bridge and from thence still up the said branch known and called by the name of the Tanfatts on the north side of Mr. Wales' plantation at Coy's Folly, and from thence to extend to the branches of Pocomoke river upon a north-east line."

The new division is to be called "Baltimore Hundred." Notwithstanding the displacement of the Proprietary, our part of the province thus honors him.

Our guests speak of the falling off in colonial prosperity under the royal government, the population rather declining than increasing. They tell of the late dismissal from office of Mr. Cheseldine, another of the chief Associators, because of negligence. So the leaders in this religious revolution fall one after another.

Now I hear them talking of the humiliation of Arthur Whitehead, in Accomack, in being compelled by judicial order to confess in open court a base slander against Tully Robinson, one of Mr. Makemie's Virginia friends. The way of the trangressor is hard indeed when he falls into the hands of colonial justices. Our guests also discuss the accusation just brought against our province by the Virginia clergyman, Hugh Jones :

"They are, generally speaking, crafty, knavish, litigious, dissemblers, and debauched. A gentleman (I mean one of the Cambro-Briton temper) is *rara avis in terris*. As to the people's disposition in matters of religion, they will follow none out of the path of interest and they heartily embrace none but such as will fill the barn and the basket. Most sects are here professed, but in general they are practical atheists." *

"The reverend author did not associate with the Dissenters," said Mr. Venable, smiling.

Our friends speak of the frightful mortality prevailing in Charles county—the worst ever known in the province. The Romish priests have been too attentive to the sufferers to suit the few inefficient Episcopal clergy, and it has been brought to the notice of the Assembly. The pliant Assembly have requested the governor to restrain the priests from these offices of mercy, by proclamation. These parties are more zealous in protecting their Church from rivalry

* Campbell's *Virginia*, p. 357.

than in protecting the colonists from pestilence and death.*

Mr. White has heard that Mr. Vesey, the first Episcopal minister in New York, preached for the first time in Trinity Church on the 6th of February. A graduate of Harvard and sent by Increase Mather to confirm the minds of the Congregationalists who had removed thither from New England, he has been brought over by the governor, and will, of course, become a violent High Churchman.†

The conversation crosses the ocean to the excitement caused in London by the attendance of the lord mayor in the trappings of his office upon the services in a meeting-house of the Dissenters. One would think, from the clamor made, that he was guilty of high treason. The grievances of Presbyterians increase in Ireland, the prosperity of our Church arousing the hostility of the prelates more and more. Attempts are made to prevent the sending of children to any except Episcopal teachers, to prohibit all marriages except by the prelatic clergy, and even to forbid the burial of the dead without the reading of the prescribed service by Episcopal lips.

Again we are back upon the Pocomoke. and they speak of the order of the justices that the Rev. John Hewett, the Rev. Samuel Davis and the Rev. James Brechin attend court and give a list of all persons whom they have married by publication or license. Thus a record of marriages of first settlers is begun, to which they are adding births and deaths—a matter of no little interest in the days to come, if our lower

---

* McSherry and McMahon, *in loco.*

† Gillett's *History of the Presbyterian Church*, p. 136.

Eastern Shore is ever to have a history. Mr. Makemie lives in Virginia, and Mr. Wilson has passed away; so that there are but three ministers in the county (55).

Our guests talk of the continued efforts for the Establishment. The zealous governor has been gathering information about the churches for the use of the ecclesiastical authorities in England, and has instructed the counties to send him statistics. Our sheriff is said to have reported as follows:

"Here are neither Popish priests, Lay Brothers, nor any chapels. As to Quakers and other Dissenters, to the first none as I know particular; and the others hath a house in Snow Hill, one on the road going up along the seaside, and one at Monokin, about thirty feet long, plain country buildings all of them" (56).

These statistics are gathered very loosely, and not often under the official signatures of the sheriffs. Even the number of Church-of-England ministers in the colony has been variously stated at from three to sixteen.

When I heard the conversation again, these colonists were in the very depths of doctrinal themes, deploring the laxness of thought and sentiment around us, and avowing their own staunch Trinitarian faith. My father takes down his copy of Mr. Makemie's last publication and reads the reply to Keith's criticism on the statement of the Catechism, page third, that there are three Persons in the Godhead. Keith had written:

"This is not Scripture language, to say Three Persons The mystery of the Three, to wit, the Father, the Son and the Holy Ghost who are one God, is great and glorious and ought to be reverently conceived and expressed in Scripture words which the Holy Ghost hath taught, but not in words of man's wisdom."

Mr. Makemie's acquaintance with Church history is a valuable help in detecting the reproductions of hoary heresies among modern sects. My father reads as follows:

"I incline not to rip up the gross errors of ancient heretics concerning this doctrine, as of Apollinarius, Arius, Rhosianus, Nestorius, Sabellius and others; and am not a little concerned that Quakers, pretending to so great and so good things, should join hand in hand with such, whose subtilties have been long since cunningly silenced and exploded. As when Solomon Acles of Barbadoes asserted this doctrine to be a Presbyterian fiction. Waving that uncharitableness Keith was notoriously guilty of concerning me and others, I conceive he only contends about words by calling Three Persons in the Godhead not Scripture language but words of man's wisdom, as all our doctrines and writings are commonly calumniated.

"All such are censured in the words of holy Calvin, that eminent man of God, Lib. 1. Cap. 13. 'What hinders,' saith he, 'but we may in more plain words express such things as are mysterious to ordinary capacities where there are necessary grounds urging thereunto?' 'Such,' saith he, 'as quarrel this, must be reputed to be grieved at the light of the truth; because he quarrels this, that the truth is made so easy and plain to be discerned.' And the reason given by this author why the churches of Christ are necessitated to use such novelty of words, if they be so called, is when the truth is to be defended against wranglers who deride it with quibbles. So the old Fathers, being troubled with false doctrines, were necessitated to express themselves in exquisite plainness lest they should leave any crooked by-ways to the wicked, to whom the doubtful constructions of words were hiding-places of errors."

Said Mr. White:

"Mr. Makemie and holy Calvin, as he calls him, see the advantage, in times like these, of clear formularies of doctrine—recognized symbols and creeds based upon the Bible and so lucidly defined that there can be no mistake or subterfuge. These are a powerful safeguard in formative periods of society and of the

Church, and are always intensely hated by the enemies of the truth."

My father read on:

" All that Keith would seem to allege is that it is not Scripture language; whereby he would seem to favor the great fundamental principle most of his brethren have been blasphemously barking against these thirty or forty years, and devoutly to say for himself, There are Three in one. If this great and fundamental truth would be made plain to the edification of the Church of God, to which it is so highly necessary that God can neither be known, believed in or called aright without it, then some denomination must be ascribed and given differing from one another in incommunicable properties. For they must either be three somethings or three nothings. The latter being rejected, if three somethings, they must be either three Gods, three essences, three parts of the same essence, or three qualities, or three names, or three manners or ways of subsisting. To assert to Three Gods were insufferable blasphemy. Though Josiah Coal is guilty of as great blasphemy in a letter to George Fox, which, as it came from a Quaker, was also approved of by Penn himself in his answer to Mr. John Faldo, a minister I lately saw in London."

Said Mr. Spence:

"Our Proprietary was unable to protect his charter against the claims of Mr. Penn: we have no fear that Mr. Makemie will be as easily dislodged from his strongholds of faith by Mr. Penn's loose theology."

My father continued to read the close argument showing that the term "three" cannot apply to three essences, or three parts of the same essence, or three qualities or accidents, or three names. He proceeds:

" So that it must be three distinct manners, methods or ways of subsisting, and is termed in the Schools, *Ens,* or *Modus Entis.* And according to the unanimous opinion of our Reforming and Reformed Divines, a Person in the Godhead is whole God, not absolutely or simply considered, but by way of some personal properties or a manner of being or distinct subsistence having the whole Godhead in it.   Usher and Calvin call a Divine Person a subsistence in the Divine nature, which having relation to others is distinguishable from them with incommunicable properties ; so that, though the Father, Son and Holy Ghost be really and essentially the same in essence or being, yet they have something differing from one another.   For if the Word, John i. 1, had been simply and absolutely God without anything peculiar to itself, it had been improper and amiss to have said it was not only God but with God.   To which doctrine Tertullian agrees, saying there is in God a certain disposition or distribution which changeth nothing of the unity of the essence.   I need not heap up the manifold testimonies both of Old and New Testament, asserting Three in One and One in Three; and if any quarrel the word ' person,' they shall find this plain Scripture, Hebrews i. 3, speaking of Christ the Second Person of the Trinity, saith, he ' is the brightness of his glory, and the express image of his person.' "

"Our minister is strong in doctrine," said Major King.   "He feeds us on substantial food."

I must own that my mind had sometimes failed to follow the writer, but it was not so with these sturdy colonists.   There are those among us who are ready to grapple with the gospel's deeper truths, and who can appreciate the triumphs of sound doctrine.   In these minds Mr. Makemie is building.

When my father laid down the book, our friend from St. Martin's said:

"Our pioneer is no less practical in his teaching. With him creed and conduct go together.   He thinks of the physical system as well as the mind.   I have heard him say:

" ' In respect to our bodies, the advantages of holy living are very conspicuous ; for is it not by breaking God's Rule of Life we owe all our intemperance and riotous excess, we owe our diseases, pains, aches, decay of strength, and all other that befall our bodies here ? when by regular living we should prevent many calamities that befall our mortal bodies even in this life and ofttimes would prolong our days and not be guilty of a lingering and gradual suicide which many debauched persons really have had a hand in. And I have with concern observed, since I came to America in 1683, most of the untimely deaths that have happened within the compass of my knowledge, were occasioned by excessive irregularities, of Sabbath-breaking, drunkenness &c.' " *

"It is a grand thing," said Mr. Venable, "to have in these days a brave, pure ministry whose lives, as well as whose lips, are faithful in their rebukes of sin."

The evil effects of the prevalent intemperance, lamented by Mr. Makemie, have had an illustration this year in the person of one of Major King's fellow-justices. Since Squire Layfield became a widower, there have been rumors of his interest in a niece of Colonel Stevens, whose widow he first married. Priscilla White and her sisters, Tabitha and Sarah, were favorites of the lieutenant deputy, and in his will their uncle left them a thousand pounds of tobacco apiece to buy a service of silver plate. Now both Priscilla's silver and herself are to adorn the table of the squire. On the 15th of October the climax came. The Rev. James Brechin and our Snow Hill minister were at the house of Mr. Layfield, with a considerable company besides. Jamaica rum had flowed too freely, and the host himself, according to the testimony of Mr. Brechin, had been "overtaken in drink." I will let Mr. Brechin describe the anomalous wedding in his own words:

"Esq Layfield said, 'Here are two ministers; why cannot I be married?' Mr. Davis' reply was that he was going to the new country, to wit, to Jersey, and if Esq. Layfield would accompany him to Hoarkil (Lewes) he would marry them. But Mr. Dennis, master of a vessel, who is a Quaker, said to Mr.

* New York sermon.

Davis, ' If you will give the Esquire, I will give Mrs. Priscilla.'
So they joined their hands—I desiring them to be cautious and
considerate in their proceedings. Esq Layfield said, ' I take Priscilla White to be my lawful wife in the presence of God and this
company and will be loving and faithful to you.' And she said
she took him to be her lawful husband Mr. Davis said either,
' Whom God join,' or ' I join,' ' let no man put asunder.' Mr.
Davis said ' Amen.' John Starret said, ' Cursed be him that
puts them asunder.' I said according to my judgment this marriage was authentic and would stand by virtue of law, a Quaker
having said the ceremony and being confirmed by Mr. Davis
saying, Amen, and all the rest did affirm that it was lawful.
Esq. Layfield did demand a certificate to testify his being thus
married Mr Stanfield did write a certificate declaring them to
be lawfully married. I said it was convenient that they relate
the particular occurrences. They desired me to write it. I wrote
the several instances that George Layfield Esq. said that he took
Priscilla White to be his lawful wife in the presence of God &c.;
and Mrs. Priscilla White in like manner; and that Mr. Dennis
passed the ceremony and that they all declared them lawfully
married Unto which they all subscribed and they desiring me
to subscribe, I wrote these words, ' I do witness the above.' All
this I attest, without aggravating any one's doings or saying, and
not estimating what I myself said " (57).

This wedding has caused no little excitement. Many
declare it illegal, and there is talk of prosecution. I
am sorry that Mr. Davis was there or had anything
to do with it. Were I in Priscilla's place, I should
be miserable.

Meanwhile, there were two other souls who were determined that no such legal cloud should overshadow
their mating. "The little wigwam in the pines" is all
in order, the honeysuckles are expecting to bloom in
the spring, and my friend William is in a hurry. He
has been to Dividing Creek and searched the records
for precedents. On the first page after the organization of the county in 1666 he found a penalty imposed
because of bonds of matrimony not published by set-

ting up the names at the court-house door according to Act of Assembly.   Two months afterward, November 27, he found a record of "bonds of matrimony published between Cornelius Ward and Margaret Frankling both of Annamessex."   He traced farther, and learned that these two were married by Henry Boston, Justice, in January of the following year. Therefore there must be the setting up of names at the court-house door and a legal ceremony afterward. He knew that Mr. Trail and Mr. Davis had married couples thirteen years ago, and that these marriages were recognized as no less valid than those by the county judges.   It was very embarrassing to think of our names nailed up there together at Dividing Creek, the most public place in the county.

When the November days grew dreamy and the air was full of poetry, hastening the time a little because our minister was soon to start upon another mission to the West Indies, we stood together before Mr. Makemie and followed his solemn words with our solemn vows.   While all Britain was rejoicing in the establishment of peace by the Treaty of Ryswick, and poor James and his Jacobites, the Quakers and High Churchmen and Papists, were mourning over the acknowledgment by France of King William's title to the English throne, here, upon the banks of our gladsome river, there was rejoicing in two happier hearts in the settlement of my own King William and his loving queen in the little wigwam in the pines.

Says our friend Matchacoopah,

"Wee-tah-tomps" ("the dove") "of England has cooed to his nest the Water-Lily of the Pocomoke."

Mr. Makemie's parting benediction lingered about

our doors while his sloop spread her wings and flew
away to the southward.   The winter finds him in the
land of everlasting summer.   Naomi must spend the
Christmas holidays alone, but she is growing used to
these frequent absences of her husband.   He is in the
Barbadoes, the island of which Columbus wrote two
hundred years ago so enthusiastically to his sover-
eigns :

"It seems to me as if I could never quit a spot so delightful;
as if a thousand tongues would fail to describe it; as if the
spell-bound hand would refuse to write."

Early in this century the ubiquitous Captain Smith
gives the following account of the island:

"The first planters brought hither by Captain Henry Powell
were forty English, with seven or eight negroes.   Then he went
to Disacaba in the maine where he got thirty Indians, men, women
and children, of the Arawacas, enemies both to the Carabes and
the Spaniards.   The Isle is most like a triangle, each side forty
or fifty miles square."

The description that follows of its fertility and luxurious fruits and vegetation is as characteristic of the
first American author as of Barbadoes itself.

Since Smith wrote, the island has seen many changes,
rising rapidly to wealth, and then used by Cromwell
as a place of banishment for the adherents of the
Stuarts.   The Church of England has always been
established by law, and the stocks put up by the
wardens in every churchyard are very suggestive.
The vestries and clergy are often at loggerheads, the
latter frequently having a hard time of it.   One of the
latter, the Rev. Mr. Godwyn, formerly of Virginia,
speaks of "the arbitrary talons of vestries, made up
for the most part of sordid plebeians, the very dregs

of the English nation, with whom to be truly conscientious is the very hight of madness and folly." Fines
and penalties being their chief gospel incentives, of
course there is but a low ebb of piety among them.
Some good has been done by the Quakers, Fox,
Edmundson and others, visiting the island and preaching zealously to the negroes. During the latter years
no little trouble has arisen from conspiracies among
the slaves. There has always been much wickedness
in beautiful Barbadoes.*

In August,·1678, Captain Archibald Johnson applied
to the Presbytery of Laggan for a Presbyterian minister for Barbadoes. Mr. Makemie was at this time a
student in the University of Glasgow. But the request remained upon the hearts of the Presbytery,
and was finally to bear fruit. As bold a navigator
as Columbus, as knightly an explorer as Smith, our
Christian pioneer soon sought out the hungering
Presbyterians there and broke to them the bread of
life. He found our Church utterly misrepresented
and our principles misunderstood, and he has been
at every visit telling the truth in faithfulness. While
preaching there, it is like standing in the gate of
the continent, for hundreds and thousands of the
traders and emigrants from Europe touch by that
colony on their way to the main. Defending his
own faith bravely, he pleads for moderation and charity between the Protestant churches. This Christmas,
to those in ecclesiastical authority he is saying:

" Let me humbly and earnestly, with all submission, address
the Conformable clergy in this island, to instruct their people
that they and we profess the same Christian and Protestant re-

* For account of Barbadoes, see Anderson's *Colonial Church.*

ligion, only with some alterations in external ceremonies and circumstances; that we may unite in affection and strength against the common enemy of our Reformation and concur in the great work of the Gospel for the manifestation of God's glory and the conviction, conversion and salvation of souls in this island, instructing such as are ignorant in the principal and great things of religion, promoting virtue and true holiness, and reproving all atheism, irreligion and profanity, sealing and confirming all by an universal copy, pattern and example of a holy and ministerial life and conversation."

These are noble words—a handsome challenge. Thus he holds out his hands to the Church of England and proffers hearty co-operation in advancing all that is best in religion.   In addressing the municipal officers he is no less faithful and brave :

"I have often done it, and I continue to pray for the zealous concurrence of the secular power and civil magistrates, to whom the sword of justice is committed for the terror of evil doers and praise of them that do well, that for promoting visible reformation in this island from the evils that have long exposed us to the heavy judgments of a Righteous God, they *would first reform their own lives* and impartially execute those good laws, according to their oaths, against all blaspheming, cursing, swearing, Sabbath-breaking, all profanity, impiety and irreligion, that our land may be exalted by righteousness and sin may no longer be our reproach."

Thus, on the 28th of December, sitting, perhaps, under a palmetto at the capital-town of Jamestown, or at Bridgetown, or at the Spring, or at the Thickets, or at Pumpkin Hill, or perhaps enjoying the soft sea-breeze beneath a cedar on the Hacklestone Cliff, looking out over the district called "Scotland," which borders the coast, or feasting his eyes upon the lovely tropical valley which lies just in front,—there he signs his name to a strong defence of Presbyterian polity and doctrine, and sends it forth to the world under the name *Truths in a True Light* (58).

CHAPTER XIX.

A. D. 1698.

"You have not tasted of the saving fruits of Christ's Death and Redemption if the holy effects and blessings thereof are not visible in your Lives and Practice."—MAKEMIE.

IT was during one of those soft, grateful February weeks that sometimes come to our Eastern Shore with prophecies of spring and summer-time, the airs of the tropics breathing over into the temperate zone, when Maryland puts away her thin covering of ice and thinks of flowers. With the young housekeepers, the pleasure is increased by the presence of our minister and his Naomi. She has brought me from her husband's store a new plush saddle, a present from her father. I shall go to Rehoboth in state to-morrow upon my Chingoteague pony.

The preparation of that dinner was an event in the history of our "little wigwam in the pines"—our *villa ad pinum*, as the learned would say. My mother is no longer in superintendence, and I am left to my own resources, but the pig—a product of a new importation —browned nicely, the musk-rat was young and tender, the apple-dumplings softened daintily, the pone mellowed lusciously, and the boiled cider was in its prime. Naomi came into my plain kitchen and helped to brighten the pewter dishes, and praised all she saw. Mr. Makemie commended the dinner above all the luxuries he had seen in Barbadoes, and I think that my William was prouder than his great namesake in the palace at Kensington.

It delights me to see my husband admiring our minister so enthusiastically I feared lest, won to Christ by the godly Baxter, he might never love another preacher so well. Mr. Makemie tells of his defence of our Church polity and doctrines against the misrepresentations made by the Episcopalians in the Southern isle. William always enjoys these accounts of the minister's missionary expeditions. Mr. Makemie shows great interest in both the religious and the temporal prosperity of my husband. Himself successful in business affairs, whether as a merchant, a marine trader or a trader in land, his testimony with regard to the value of Christianity in these practical matters comes with greater weight. Seeing us just beginning life together, and entering heartily into all our hopes, he spoke to us words, as we sat that night around the fireplace of blazing pine-knots, that I well remember :

"God, the Eternal and only wise Lawgiver, has framed a Law every way quadrate and suited to advance our secular interest. If all the wits in the world had been combined in one counsel to consult and carve out a rule of obedience, leveled directly to promote our advantage, they could not have fallen upon a more advantageous rule of obedience than what God has prescribed to us. In keeping the Divine precepts there is great reward ; godliness being profitable unto all things, having the promise of the life that now is, and that which is to come."

I expected that Mr. Makemie, according to his wont, would enter into the particulars of his theme, and we were very attentive while he continued:

"How expensive a darling sin and vice has proved to many

families and particular persons who have been brought by irregular and riotous living to want and poverty! And that by sundry ways and means. First, By neglecting our affairs, our lawful concerns must suffer. Second, Irregular living consumes that time we should spend about better things. Third, It justly draws the indignation of heaven upon all our concerns and ofttimes creates a moth in our estates; all which a religious life might effectually prevent. Fourth, It would highly conduce to the preserving and maintaining the credit of our reputation and good name; for it is justly sin and disobedience which blasts our names and stains our reputations and sticks so close that it oft reaches to posterity, who are infamous from the disorderly and scandalous lives of vicious ancestors." *

While Mr. Makemie was speaking, I was wondering what would be the honor or dishonor two hundred years hence of the families planted around us. Whose children would continue to rise to worth and position, borne forward by the character and the prayers of godly forefathers? Whose would degenerate and descend, blighted by the inherited iniquity of to-day?

While God's faithful servants are thus proclaiming the will of the Lord in the pulpit and from house to house, our Assembly is still tinkering upon the Establishment. Another act is passed, empowering vestrymen to assess and collect taxes for repairing and finishing churches. The adherents of Prelacy volunteer no contributions to complete these buildings, but deliberately await the execution of compulsory measures to wring the means out of the hands of others. Now they are trying to enforce a law unquestionably invalid.

My husband, remembering the sufferings of Mr. Baxter and others, and believing that there are those among us who would treat Mr. Davis and Mr. Make-

* New York sermon.

mie just as cruelly if they had the power, becomes very indignant sometimes, and I have been afraid that he may express himself to Mr Hewett in a way that would not be pleasant. There are others of us, too, who feel that the very names of Charles and James Stuart ought to be repulsive to all lovers of freedom and of purity, and we have but little patience with either the High Churchism or the Quakerism that would put the wicked dynasty back upon the throne. Therefore, too, we regret to learn of the marriage, in January, of Benedict Leonard, heir of Lord Baltimore, to the granddaughter of the infamous Barbara Palmer, Duchess of Cleveland, the favorite of Charles II. The royal blood in the veins of the bride is vicious blood, and we want nothing upon Maryland soil which will give respectability to the baseness of that court When we think of such a Lady-Proprietress leading colonial society, we cannot very sincerely mourn the displacement of the Baltimores.*

In our own social world there has been no little agitation over the marriage mentioned last year Squire Layfield, prominent before, has come into a less enviable prominence through that unfortunate step. To those of us who revere the memory of Judge Stevens, it is sad to witness the distress brought upon those he loved, and in the house of an associate on the bench who married both his widow and his niece. Can we recognize the family any longer?

The Quakers defend the family, for their Captain Dennis took part in the ceremony and pronounced it valid. Some of the Presbyterians also stand by

*She went in the ways of her grandparents, and was divorced in 1710 See Neill's *Terra Mariæ*, p 232

the Layfields because Mr. Davis had a part in the wedding, although he was doubtful of the legality of the marriage and preferred that they accompany him to another province. There are those that denounce as well as those that defend.

The law is relentless. At the court-house at Dividing Creek, where he has often sat as judge himself, Squire Layfield and Priscilla are compelled to appear for trial. There is great excitement. A week's northeaster could not cause wilder confusion among the pines when they bend and creak and groan before its fury. A judge of the county is himself to be judged! The hill and the pasture are filled with horses of the gentry. The higher classes are intensely moved. I think of the honored grave of Stevens, and I wish that Priscilla's husband had not been "overtaken in drink." Not Indians alone suffer from the poison of the fire-waters.

The verdict is rendered: "Guilty!" Upon each of them is imposed a fine of twenty shillings sterling, or four hundred pounds of tobacco. Again the tempest rages about the hill and up and down the Pocomoke and out over the Somerset fields. I fervently thanked God for the untarnished honor resting over the love and happiness of our little wigwam in the pines.

If the people would profit by Mr. Makemie's faithful instructions, there would be but little need of court-houses. No Quaker can say that this picture of true Christianity is not practical:

"We must lay aside the disorders and irregularities of our lives. The profane curser and swearer must lay aside his horrid oaths and impious imprecations. The beastly and sensual drunkard must abstain from his intemperate cups and companions. The backbiter must forsake his railings and defamation. The liar must learn to speak truth to his neighbor. The thief and purloiner must grow honest. The profaner of the Day of the Lord must learn to spend it more religiously. And the profligate scoffer at the creatures of God, the people and followers of God, the way and worship and religion of God, must lay aside this base abuse of their tongues. These evils and many more— as pride, covetousness, carnality and worldliness—must be purged out of our lives."[*]

In the customs of the people around us, there is much in high and low to justify these plain reproofs of sin. It is a great blessing to have a minister brave enough to expose both errors in doctrine and errors in morals.

This year the Synod of Ireland has enacted the rule of the Church of Scotland that no young man be licensed to preach the gospel unless " he subscribes the Confession of Faith in all the articles thereof."[†]

Our Assembly has just made an appropriation for building houses of entertainment for poor impotent folk at the Cool Springs, in St. Mary's county. These "fountains of healing waters," as they are called, are held in high repute, and the people resort thither from all parts of the province to enjoy their famous virtues. To extend the benefits to the diseased poor as well as to the rich is regarded as a notable charity[‡] In the staunch orthodox ministrations of Mr. Makemie, we feel that Somerset possesses a fountain of healing waters for "impotent folk" of far greater efficacy than all the springs of St Mary's.

Another Quaker apostle is heard in our county this

[*] New York sermon   [†] Reid, ii. 495.
[‡] Colonial records, 1698.

season, proclaiming the gospel of the Inner Light. Thomas Chalkley sails over from the Western Shore with Thomas Evernden—perhaps in the very sloop by which the owner had profaned the Sabbath in building, and which desecration Mr. Makemie had severely rebuked. Crowds follow this evangelist from point to point over the county—from the western borders to George Truitt's, beyond Snow Hill. He seems much interested in the Indian town up the river.*

While this new enthusiast visits our county, but is careful not to follow the steps of George Keith to the house of Mr. Makemie, a Presbyterian minister settles in Philadelphia. Rev. Benjamin Woodbridge, Congregational, of New England, had preceded him a while this year, but soon returned North. A Baptist preacher named Watts has also been officiating for some while in the Barbadoes Store in that town, with a congregation of nine of his own faith and a few other Dissenters, English and Welsh and Huguenots. Some of these are Independents, and some are Presbyterians.

This store stands at the corner of Second and Chestnut streets, belongs to the Barbadoes Commercial Company, and was used by Keith and his party as their place of worship during Mr. Makemie's visit to Philadelphia six years ago.

The Episcopal clergyman Clayton has tried in vain to win the Baptist minister and his heterogeneous flock over to the Church of England.

This summer we are glad to hear that a young preacher—Mr. Jedediah Andrews—has come to Philadelphia from New England. Our pioneer has long

_____
* Chalkley's journal p. 29, etc

known the advantages of a station for our Church there.

Mr. Andrews is a native American twenty-six years old, having been born at Hingham, Massachusetts, in 1674, while Mr. Makemie was preparing for the university. Mr. Andrews graduated at Harvard College, near Boston, three years ago. Among our little constellation of ministers in this part of the continent, he is the first that has been born and educated on this side of the ocean. Propositions for some kind of a union have been made to him by the Baptists, and correspondence to this end has been begun this fall with him and six of his friends—John Green, David Giffing, John Van Lear, Samuel Richards, Herbert Corry and Daniel Green. The attempt seems to fail, and the Baptists charge the failure upon Mr. Andrews. This looks as if the young man were disposed to stand firmly and bravely for the truth as represented by himself and his few supporters. Acquaintance with Mr. Makemie will not fail to confirm his orthodoxy.*

We must note a change of governors at Annapolis —Nicholson transferred to Virginia, and Blackiston appointed his successor. Nicholson's zeal for the Church is having its comment in the accusations by Clarke and Sly of sad licentiousness in his past history. These charges have kept his violent temper in a ferment and provoked most vindictive efforts to crush his accusers. Coode too has been a constant thorn in the side of this patron of the Church and kept him long at bay.† Nor have the zealous Episcopal governor and the zealous Commissary Bray

* Hodge, p. 69 , Gillett, p 20; Webster, p 312
† McMahon, p 263

been able to prosecute their Establishment schemes in harmony.* Vain, passionate, of questionable morals, the persistence with which he has pushed forward the aggrandizement of Prelacy has covered a multitude of sins in the esteem of many and drawn upon him the fulsome flatteries of the Assembly to the end.

Of our capital an eye-witness writes :

" There are several places for towns, but hitherto they are only titular ones, except Annapolis where the Governor resides. Col. Nicholson has done his endeavor to make a town of that place. There are about forty dwelling-houses in it; seven or eight of which can afford a good lodging and accommodations for strangers. There are also a State-house and a free-school, built of brick, which make a great show among a parcel of wooden houses. And the foundation of a church is laid, the only brick church in Maryland. They have two market days in a week, and, had Gov. Nicholson continued there a few months longer, he had brought it to perfection." †

There rests that brick foundation, waiting upon bad laws and good tobacco-crops.

The Assembly has just shown greater justice by the following enactment in behalf of the native tribes of the Eastern Shore :

" It being most just that the Indians, the ancient inhabitants of this province, should have a convenient dwelling place in this their native country, free from the encroachments and oppression of the English ; more especially the Nanticoke Indians in Dorchester county, who, for these many years, have lived in peace and concord with the English and in all matters in obedience to the government of this province ; Be it enacted that all the land lying and being in Dorchester county and on the North side of the Nanticoke river, butted and bounded as follows [description, containing about fifty square miles], shall be confirmed and assured and, by virtue of this act, is confirmed and assured

* Meade's *Old Churches*, etc , p 158

† *British Empire in America*, i. 333

unto Panquash and Annotoughquan and the people under their
government or charge and their heirs and successors for ever."

Says Matchacoopah,

"When *seequino*" ("the spring"), "*mashaquapanu*"
("the summer"), "*weesawpanu*" ("the autumn") and
poopponu" ("the winter") "shall have come for *muttah-
tashakipana nuquotacukquomai*" ("a thousand years"),
"will the white man's law still say *for ever?*"

Alas! the red man and the white alike have learned
the desolations of Time. The lofty and the lowly
must fade and pass away. The *quioccason* house
and the marble tomb both crumble into dust.

The home of wealth which we loved so well to visit,
down on the little creek in Accomack, standing there
in sight of the sparkling strand, has been under the
shadow of the great destroyer. With the early falling of the leaf, our friend William Anderson passed
away, and Naomi and Comfort are orphans. There
are no public graveyards, and they laid him to rest on
his favorite plantation. Among the large concourse
who stood around his bier that day, we saw his relatives the Parkers, the Hopes, the Scotts, the Barons,
the Fookses, and his valued friend Mr. Edmund Custis. Standing nearer still, in deeper grief, are the
home-group—the widow, and Mr. and Mrs. Makemie,
and Mr. and Mrs. Taylor with their three daughters,
Elizabeth, Naomi and Comfort.

Mr. Makemie, who has so often spoken words of
comfort to the bereaved, is now himself numbered
with the mourners. He and the deceased were
warmly attached. Closely associated in business and
for some time occupying the same house, no one
understood and admired the character of our pioneer

more than did Mr. Anderson. His habit has been to call our minister "Son Makemie," and so he is termed in the will.

As far back as the 23d of July, already weak in body, the long and careful will was made.* "My soul," he says, "I commend to my Creator, trusting, through ye merits of my blessed Lord and Saviour Jesus Christ, to enjoy eternal life."

We were naturally desirous to hear the bequests, and, as expected, they show plainly that his heart was to the last inclining to Naomi and her husband. She was his first-born, and she and "Son Makemie" are the chosen and favorite representatives of the Anderson name and honor.

To the widow Mary Anderson he gives a life-right in the Occocomson plantation, over on the seaside, near Wallops, if she continue single and will live thereon. At death, or one year after marriage, the land reverts to any second son of Comfort Taylor, if such there be; if none such be born, it is to be divided among the three daughters. If she will not remove from the Pocomoke plantation, she is to have the old room and her own room, with the chambers and the cellar belonging to it; also the use, in common with the Makemies, of the horse-mill, the well, the copper, still and oven; also of certain pastures and orchards and one-third of "the keeping-apples." If she marries, nothing is left her except a life-title to the land where Gabriel Waters lives. In confining his principal bequests to her widowhood, Mr. Anderson knows that no one would marry so old a woman except for her property. He himself became

* Probated October 4.

possessed of a large part of his property by marrying the widow of another man.

To his daughter Comfort Taylor there had already been a deed of gift of lands at Sikes's Island, and he now gives other lands adjacent. Her children are to hold the reversion of the rest of his lands should the Makemies die without issue.

To his nephew and godson Anderson Parker he gives the four hundred acres at Pungoteague; in remainder to Thomas Parker; in remainder to Matthew Parker. To his nephew William, son of George and Temperance Hope, he gives two hundred and fifty acres at the forked neck at the head of Pitts's Creek, being one-half of the tract called " Fooks's Choice." Thus he endows those who are to help in perpetuating his name. There are legacies to his four sisters, Mrs. Barons, Mrs. Temperance Hope, Mrs. Nock and Mrs. Comfort Scott.

Mr. Anderson seems to have had consideration for widows. " It is my will and desire," he says, " that all widows, Widow Lucas only excepted, who are directly indebted to me, be wholly discharged from said debts "

To appraise and divide the estate and serve as referees in case of differences, he appoints Mr. Edmund Custis, giving him his horse Captain Sorrel and three pounds to buy himself a beaver; Edward Moore, giving him his silver-headed cane and five pounds; the testators' brother, George Hope, giving him his plush saddle and best bridle and five pounds; and Thomas Perry, giving him his horse Murry, a good bridle and saddle and the choice from his wardrobe of a complete suit of apparel, including vest, coat, breeches, shirt, hat and stockings.

Mr. Anderson shows his appreciation of the culture so difficult to secure in these provinces by leaving fifty pounds for the education of his three granddaughters.

The bulk of the property goes to the Makemies; and, while it is expressly required that all devises made to the Taylors are to be held by his daughter Comfort independently and beyond the control of her husband, Mr. Elias Taylor giving bond to this effect, there is no such slighting of "Son Makemie."

Naomi is to have whatever she may claim as hers in the house and on the premises without let or delay; also the negro slaves Dollar, Hannah the elder, Darkish and young Sarah, and a third of the other personal property remaining after all debts are paid. To Mr. Makemie he gives the money loaned him, together with the sloop and its furniture; also the three lots at Onancock, all in his own right. To him and wife he gives the thousand acres bordering on the Matchatank, opposite our minister's own lands. But—the most valued of all the estate—to them he bequeaths his home-plantation, of nine hundred and fifty acres, on the Pocomoke Strand. Here, on its western border, he had lived for thirty years; here his children had grown to womanhood and married; here his ashes were to mingle with the Virginia soil (59); here "Son Makemie" had wooed the first-born; and here for some time the two families had lived as one. The owner had been known as "William Anderson of Pocomoke;" here would be the graves of his descendants. The anxiety shown in his will that his lands shall not pass out of his family culminates upon his favorite plantation "at Pocomoke."

There is in men a strong desire to identify their names and their memories with landed estates, and thus to hand them down together to an endless posterity. With no son of his own to perpetuate the name, and with Comfort Taylor's little boy gone to the grave, Mr. Anderson provides that Occocomson shall revert to a possible second grandson. In default of such male heir, it goes to the granddaughters, each authorized to sell her part to the other, but not outside of the Anderson blood. The same care is taken to keep other lands in the line of descent. But the chief interest centres upon the Pocomoke plantation.

If Naomi becomes the mother of more than one child, "the most worthy of blood" is to have Pocomoke, the next to have Matchatank. If she die childless, his present three granddaughters are to have Pocomoke as coheirs,

"giving them liberty to sell each of the parts of the value to each other, the price of the whole being valued by any three or four honest neighbors who may be made choice of for that purpose, to prevent either inconvenience in living so near each other or other differences that may happen by unequaling in the value; but not any one to have any power or authority to sell, lease, let, or by any ways or means to dispose of any part thereof out of the family that hath proceeded or may proceed from my loins."

How anxious he is that his homestead shall continue in good condition, just as he leaves it!

"Said Makemies and the survivor of them, if my daughter Naomi have no issue, shall keep the Dwelling House in repair, and whatever other useful houses worth preserving thereon; likewise orchards; neither remove or dispose of the horse-mill, still and copper, but them to remain and pass with the freehold to my heirs aforesaid."

To his executors, Mr. and Mrs. Makemie, he entrusts his funeral and grave:

"My body I submit to fall, hoping itt may have a Decent Christian Burrial at direction of my Executors hereafter named."

The dying man does all he can to preserve his home and place of sepulture from the neglect and vandalism of strangers "for ever."

So lived and passed away William Anderson of Pocomoke; and Mr. Makemie is the heir of many broad acres and the guardian of his tomb.

Czar Peter of the Russias has been traveling and studying upon the continent of Europe, and working with his own hands in the shipyards. We hear that this year he is in England, pursuing his plans for the elevation of his rude countrymen, occupying the house of John Evelyn, and disgusting the owner by leaving it as filthy as if a savage had dwelt there.* But the Czar means the uplifting of his people. The University of Oxford gives the half savage the honorary degree of D. C. L., and the world is likely to confer a higher title still.

Along by these tributaries of the Chesapeake, in obscurity and untitled, is there not a prince in Israel laboring just as earnestly and effectually for the elevation of the people and the planting of a spiritual kingdom, nobler and grander?

* Evelyn's *Diary*, p. 571.

CHAPTER XX.

A. D. 1699.

"Let us value unity in doctrine and the greater and more weighty matters, preferring it before an exact and accurate uniformity in every punctilio of circumstance and ceremony; which no nation hath hitherto attained, the Church of England not excepted."—MAKEMIE.

UNDER the fanatical claim of divine inspiration by the Inner Light, the pretensions of the Quakers to infallibility have been just as positive and presumptuous as those of Rome. And yet they themselves have greatly changed, and have differed among themselves! I transcribe two or three questions addressed to them five years ago by Mr. Makemie:

"What is the reason Quakers are so far metamorphosed or changed both in judgment or practice at this day from what they once were at their first rise in Europe? What is the reason Quakers, that look upon themselves as the only pure church in the world, have never yet adventured to publish a form of sound words according to the Apostle's language, containing a confession of their faith and principles unanimously agreed upon among themselves, as all other churches in the world have done? Wherefore did they write and bark so much against all witnessing to truth and conviction of falsehood in Judicatories by an oath as sinful and unlawful under the Gospel; and now in Pennsylvania and Maryland seem only to quarrel the manner and way of swearing on the book according to the English form and are willing to swear now in Judicatories with lifted-up hands, which many look upon to be more solemn than the former? Whether two men differing in a fundamental truth, absolutely necessary to salvation, can be guided by the same infallible Spirit?"

304

These were included among " several mixed Queries
to be resolved by Quakers for the justification of themselves and satisfaction of others." Instead of answering them, the great Quaker champion to whom they
were first addressed has himself changed front and
deserted to the Episcopalians. Born a Presbyterian,
George Keith left the safe middle-ground between
Ritualism and anti-Ritualism and went over to the
extreme wing in the rejection of all forms and sacraments. Now the pendulum oscillates, and he is just
as violent for uniformity and sacramentarianism.

This year, through the influence of Dr. Bray, the
Maryland commissary, there has been organized in
England "The Society for Promoting Christian Knowledge," intended to assist in supporting missionaries and
in supplying libraries for the poorer clergy both at
home and abroad. The first book chosen by this
society for circulation is a Catechism, lately published
by Keith, containing an enthusiastic exposition of the
teachings of the Anglican Church. A metamorphosis
indeed! He left America in 1694, and on his arrival
in London found himself there condemned by the
Yearly Meeting of the Friends—no longer *friends*, as
Mr. Makemie intimates. After a while he gravitated
toward Prelacy, and finally became as zealous in its
defence as once he was zealous against it.* Such is
human nature, notwithstanding all its former pretensions to the miraculous apostolic call and mission.
Once he thus taunted Mr. Makemie.

" Nor doth he in the least declare that he receiveth any one of
these things, delivered by him in his said Catechism, from any
inward opening or discovery of God's Spirit in his heart. With-

*Anderson's *Colonial Church*, iii. 369.

20

out breach of charity I can freely say he is a great stranger to the inward dealings and workings of God's Holy Spirit in the hearts of his people."

What now becomes of the paraded "Inner Light," and of "the call immediate, extraordinary and apostolic, of which," said Mr. Makemie, "Keith in a vain manner publicly and privately has boasted, and affirmed the same at my house"? We remember our pastor saying five years ago, "Farewell, then, immediate mission!"

We have always felt that the growing influence of our pioneer was sure, first or last, to bring upon him the dislike and the jealousy of the Established Church in Virginia. In her Eastern-Shore counties there has always been less intolerance than beyond the bay. The Presbyterians were but a handful, the Scotch and the Irish preferring to settle in our own county, where there was less danger of molestation. Our minister has always had strong personal friends among the Accomack Episcopalians. Such men as Andrew Hamilton, John Watts, Robert Pitts, John Parker, Tully Robinson, and the many relatives of his father-in-law, have been a strong defence against bigotry. His principal preaching-places being in Maryland, there has been less to expose him to the ire of Virginia extremists. In Accomack he has gone on quietly, a valuable citizen, paying his tithes, preaching in no defiant manner, and holding all religious services in his own houses. The Toleration Act, in force for ten years in England, has never been put upon the Virginia statute-book. Here and there, as in the case of Mr. Mackie at Elizabeth River and of the Quakers at the house of Thomas Fookes at Onancock, Dissenters' meeting-houses have been recorded; but the law has never been formally recognized by the Provincial Assembly, and there are those in Accomack who have not forgotten it.

Mr. Makemie's eloquence and popular gifts have been attracting too much attention to please certain parties. His influence widens along the coast—known at Elizabeth River and holding property there; also at Urbana, under the very shadow of Rosegill, the mansion of the Wormleys, where live the proud family in English state, and where the wine sparkles, the dance goes round, the fox-hounds bay, the racehorse neighs, and the great Church overlooks old Middlesex as if in assured proprietorship * Coming now into possession of large landed estates at home, no one can tell to what height the influence of this dangerous Dissenter may tower He holds the certificate of qualification in Barbadoes, according to English law, having taken the requisite oath under the Toleration Act, but they care nothing for the doctrinal purity of this law-abiding man while he remains a Nonconformist. There are those in whose eyes this is a crime. Well does Mr. Makemie retort:

"What uniformity is between your Cathedral and Parochial worship? between such churches as have organs and those that want them? between such as sing or chant the service and such as do not? between such as read the whole service and others that mince it and read only a part? between those that begin with a free prayer and such as do not? And in the same congregations, what uniformity is between such as use responses and such as do not? between such as bow to the East or the altar and such as do not? between such as bow the knee and those that bow only the head at the name or word Jesus? What uniformity between such as sing Psalms and most that do not? I find many of the sons

* Bishop Meade's *Old Churches*, i. 369.

of the Church break uniformity and canons as well as their neighbors. What Uniformity Act or Common Prayer allows any to begin with a prayer of their own, *as the greatest and best have done*, though others call it a Geneva trick? What Uniformity Act enjoins organs and singing boys? And where is bowing to the East and altar, with all other Church honors, commanded? What warrants the use of the public form for private baptism? Why is the burial service read over any Dissenters, that are all excommunicated by your canons?"*

Only last year one of their own clergymen bore testimony: "No discipline nor canons of the Church are observed." And yet they would compel other churches to obey what they themselves disregard!

Now comes the news that our minister has been arrested and carried across the bay to Williamsburg. There is indignation in all the regions round about Rehoboth. Once before has Virginia struck at Somerset, and now she strikes more severely than when Scarborough and his forty horsemen made their fierce irruption upon the Monokin. What will they do with our pioneer? Shall the owner of the sunny Matchatank lands and the Pocomoke homestead be outlawed and banished as the Quakers have been before? This outrage cannot make the thought of a Maryland Church Establishment more attractive.

Soon follow the tidings of the brave defence, the conciliatory but firm plea for religious liberty according to the will of God and the magnanimity of King William. The governor and the Council are carried away by the eloquence of the advocate. Mr. Makemie is released, and before the spring closes, on the 15th of April, the Toleration Act is officially recognized as the law of Virginia (60). Our pastor returns

* *Truths in a True Light.*

in triumph, the Matchatank and the Pocomoke sparkling welcomes as he comes.

During the year Mr. Makemie places beyond dispute his legal right to preach in his adopted province.
On the 15th of October the following statement is put
upon the court records of Accomack:

" Whereas Mr. Francis Makemie made application by petition
to this Court that, being ready to fulfill what the law enjoynes to
Dissenters, that he might be qualified according to Law, and
prayed that his own dwelling-house at Pocomoke, also his own
house at Onancock, next to Captain Jonathan Livesley's, might
be the places recorded for Meeting, and having taken the oaths
enjoyned by Act of Parliament instead of the oaths of allegiance
and supremacy, and subscribed the test, as likewise that he did
in compliance with what the Law enjoynes, produce Certificate
from Barbadoes of his qualifications there, did declare in open
Court of the said county and owned the Articles of Religion
mentioned in the statute made in the 13th year of Queen Elizabeth, except the 34th, 35th and 36th, and those words for the
20th Article, viz.,—' The Church hath power to decide rites and
ceremonies, and authority in controversies of faith;' which the
Court have ordered to be registered and recorded; and that the
Clerk of the Court give certificate thereof to the said Makemie,
according as the Law enjoynes" (61).

Our own Assembly at Annapolis is still busy legislating about vestrymen, assessments, and building and
repairing churches. They pause for a while to pass
an act of gratitude to a Presbyterian elder, Colonel
Ninian Beall, for his brave services upon "all incur-
sions and disturbances of the neighboring Indians,"
voting him seventy-five pounds sterling to be paid for
three serviceable negroes for himself, wife and children.* This is the man who testified that there was
no foundation in the charges upon which the Associators based the revolution. His integrity and his pub-

* Neill's *Terra Mariæ*, p. 193.

lic service now bring him deserved honor, while the active revolutionary partisans Coode and Cheseldyn are in disgrace. Another act is passed to restrain the importation of Irish Papists, aping the spirit of the Parliament of England in the atrocious laws of imprisonment and confiscation which they have been passing against the Catholics and their children across the water. There being a scare along the coast and in the Chesapeake about the buccaneers, a law is passed for the punishment of pirates. But, more dreadful to our laborious statesmen than Popish or pirate scare, they see standing yonder in Annapolis the foundation of that Episcopal Church neglected and incomplete; the godly Assembly fines the builder, Edward Dorsey, for breach of contract, and passes an order to bargain with other workmen for finishing the job. This ambitious abortion of a church is the type of many half-built structures throughout the colony.

On Thursday, July 13, about four or five o'clock in the afternoon, while one of Maryland's heavy thunder-clouds is overhanging the little town, a bolt leaps forth and strikes the State-House, killing one of the burgesses and setting the building on fire.* In a few minutes the Capitol is a wreck. Ere the year ends, a shock no less sudden and violent strikes the friends of the Establishment, and, to exaggerate the chagrin, the thunderbolt is hurled through the hands of a Quaker.

The Council of State in England has annulled the law for the Maryland Church Establishment on a technicality, and the Episcopalians are astounded

* *Annals of Annapolis.*

and bewildered. The mortification is deepened by the order being sent over in charge of an agent of Mr. Penn, one of the proscribed and jubilant sect.* This looks like a deliberate insult to Prelacy. The Quakers and the Papists do not try to conceal their exultation.

Suffering defeat after defeat, the Ottoman empire, which lately threatened Europe, has finally been crippled and humbled, and has just now been stripped of territory and greatness by the treaty of Carlovits. The pashas of the sultan in these surrendered provinces can feel but little worse to-day than do the rectors and the missionaries of the Episcopal Church in Maryland, left again without legal status and without state support.

The Assembly must try its hand at Erastian statesmanship once more, assisted by a strong helper. In the same ship which brought over the ill-omened Quaker came also the zealous Commissary Bray—Ritualism and Mysticism in a race for the New World. If the one little craft could carry the two so widely diverse without sinking, surely our great Maryland should be able to bear us all without shipwreck. Rehoboth—"there is room."

What complaints and sighs and pleas of grievous wrong and indignation on the part of these Churchmen at their ill-treatment because they have again been delayed from preying upon us all for the completion of their churches!† One would suppose them to be innocent victims of the grossest injustice, a sadly persecuted people.

Mr. Makemie loses none of his interest in Barba-

* Bishop Hawks's *Maryland.* † *Ibid.*, p. 89

does. The sloop which visits the island for its tropical products carries the gospel too. I have just been reading his *Truths in a True Light*, the pastoral addressed two years ago to those people, but not published until this year (58). In this little volume, after showing the folly of Protestants fighting one another, after drawing a broad line of distinction between the Laudian High-Church party and the truly evangelical Low Churchmen, after proving that the Church of England has fallen short of the purpose of her earlier Reformers and is in fact but half reformed, and that, in the British Isles and upon the Continent, the most thoroughly reformed are found among the Presbyterians,—he states his purpose as follows in defence of the latter:

"That you may more fully and distinctly know them and not suffer yourselves for the future to be imposed upon, I shall, as one of the meanest of them, show what at this day they believe and do; or wherein they agree and are the same with the established church of England, and, next, what they dissent from and neither will nor dare do without sin; and all this only for your information, without the least design or intention of raising any new debate or beginning any new controversy on those differences sufficiently controverted by many hands on both sides."

These are timely subjects in our own latitudes as well as in Barbadoes. A thorough acquaintance with the history of the Reformation and with the earlier and later phases of doctrine and polity, and an intelligence that keeps him fully abreast of the questions of the day in Europe and America, prepare Mr. Makemie, as shown in this pastoral, to meet all the demands of his responsible work and to guide his people successfully. In an extended postscript to the main discussion he says:

"Among the misrepresentations of the principles and practices of the Presbyterians in this Island, I cannot forbear taking notice of one, because it strikes very deep into the vitals of religion ; 'tis that the doctrine of Election and Reprobation as taught by the rigid Presbyterians of the Kirk of Scotland, is contrary to the Word of God and a great discouragement to piety."

After placing himself emphatically upon the Scottish platform and reminding his readers that our Shorter Catechism is still learned and taught by many in the Church of England, and after stating the scriptural doctrine in the words of our Standards, he proceeds to show from the Thirty-nine Articles of the Church of England, the Lambeth Articles, the Articles of Ireland, the votes of the Anglican delegates to the Synod of Dort, the prayers of the Prayer-Book, the authorized Homilies and the testimony of Primate Usher and others that the Episcopal Church holds the doctrine in just as staunch and rigid a form as our own. Then, with a touch of his native Irish humor, he says :

"I am very unwilling to engage in a further controversy about this doctrine so fully handled and sufficiently vindicated already, lest I should engage some of your Island in a most unnatural war against their own Mother Church. And should it not be a paradox to Barbadoes to hear of a Presbyterian taking up the cudgels in defence of a fundamental established doctrine against a son, member and minister of the English Church ?"

While Mr. Makemie is leading in these great interests of God's kingdom, he is also proving his ability as a man of affairs, and exhibiting his legal knowledge in the management of his own enlarged possessions and in the settlement of the extensive estate of his father-in-law. In June he is forced, as executor, to bring suit in the Accomack court against the estate of Samuel Hudson, and in August against John Miskell. In these cases he enters the name of no counsel, but appears as his own lawyer.

We hear of many Huguenots coming to Virginia this year and settling on the James River, led by their pastor, Claude Philippe de Richebourg. There they are planning for the manufacture of cloth, and for making claret wine from the wild Virginia grape. While a furious High-Church Tory Commons have disbanded the chivalrous Huguenot soldiery in the British Isles and are trying to drive their good friend the king to desperation, these noble French refugees are welcomed and valued in our two colonies. Here that generous blood and our own are to go on mingling down the centuries.

On the 31st of December, adopting a favorite custom of Scotland—that of marrying on the last day of the year—my brother John, never having recovered from that first Troubadour canzo, stands side by side with the sweet singer of the Vincennes, and they are made one by the published banns and by the voice of our Scotch-Irish minister. Such is the blending of national customs and of nations in one marriage and in the American future.

What a century it has been, the century now closing! What a tumultuous sea of human passions! Above the loud surges we hear the voice of the pledged Covenants of Scotland and the holy songs of Marot in France; and the very billows that raged the wildest have lifted God's true Church and thrown it upon these Western shores. In the words of Sir William Temple, who has just passed away—the man who brought about the marriage of William of Orange and the princess Mary, and who is called the polisher of English prose—"passions are perhaps the stings without which, it is said, no honey is made." It may be that much pure honey may yet be gathered from the dead carcass of the seventeenth century. On its tomb I here inscribe the words of Makemie:*

"CHRIST IS THE SOLE KING, HEAD AND LAWGIVER OF HIS CHURCH."

* *Answer to Keith.*

CHAPTER XXI.

A. D. 1700.

" I hope these things will engage you to be more favorable and charitable to Dissenters until you more rationally weigh and consider the grounds and reasons of their dissent."—MAKEMIE.

HIS name is Francis—the tiny Pocomoke boy born in the little "wigwam in the pines"— Francis Makemie Winston. Dr. Vigerous pronounces him a noble American specimen, worthy of his namesake. My father prophesies that it is but the beginning of many similar echoes of the name far beyond the century now opening (62).

This same year there have been born two other little boys—one in England, by the name of James Thomson, and another in Wales, by the name of John Dyer. A precocious boy twelve years old by the name of Alexander Pope is scribbling verses and begging to be introduced at Will's Coffee-House that he may see the famous poet Dryden, who dies at sixty-nine before the year ends. Another little fellow of twelve is named John Gay. In Scotland there is a juvenile Allen Ramsey fourteen years old, and in England a certain Edward Young of nineteen, and a Thomas Parnell of just twenty-one. In the fatherland there are also some sprightly young men—an Isaac Watts of twenty-six, and a William Congreve and a Joseph Addis n, b h of twenty-eight. Also Jonathan Swift

of thirty-three, Matthew Prior of thirty-four, and
Daniel Defoe, Richard Bently and Matthew Henry
—all of thirty-eight. In France there is a Fénelon
of forty-nine, and in England a Mr. John Locke of
sixty-eight, feeble and fading.

Over all these as little boys, mothers have dreamed
their dreams of love and hope as another mother by
the Pocomoke now dreams and sings over the cradle
of our own baby Francis, their contemporary. Is not
the young century itself born to holy aims and grand
achievements?

In the log church at Rehoboth, now beginning to
look old and straitened, we stand, William and I and
the child, and Mr. Makemie tells how we received the
ordinance—not from Rome, as the Quakers charge,
but from Jesus Christ; and he speaks earnestly of
the evils arising from unfaithful training:

"The lot of many and the bane of thousands, who were born
and nurtured in families where no godly or religious instruction
is enjoyed, no true religion is practiced or performed, neither
are any imitable or desirable patterns presented for imitation.
How many are there among such as call and repute themselves
Christian families where many are born and propagated to succeed them in their estates and bear their names, but few educated to honor and glorify God and trained up to walk when young
in the way they should go? And when neglected or corrupted
in their first education and tender years, it is a hard matter to
rectify them during the following course of their lives." *

While he urged upon us the duty and the privilege
of leading our offspring early to Christ, I could not
help thinking of the minister's own conversion in boyhood, and of the useful life which has grown out of it.
The boy-Christian of Lough Swilly is now the Paul
of the Chesapeake, and the water which fell from his

* New York sermon.

fingers upon the brow of the child seemed only the more significant for the recollection of that youthful conversion in the country of the Laggan.

After service, Mr. Bray—our elder, not the commissary—Mr. Fenton, Mr. Whittington and Colonel Jenkins were kind enough to gather about us and compliment the young Marylander. Madam Mary Jenkins held him while I was mounting the pony, and left a nice baptismal present in my hands. When the bundle was opened, I found a little dress embroidered with her own needle, and a bright new copy of Mr. Makemie's Catechism.

I saw the two Rehoboth lots owned by our pastor, on one of which there begins to be some talk of erecting a new Presbyterian church. A little flock still, we bravely think of enlargement. When this is done it will be by the free suffrages and the voluntary contributions of our own people, not by forced exactions upon the tobacco-crops. Most of the prelatic churches now standing in the province were built under enactments admittedly illegal. "Unlawful conventicles" has been a phrase frequently upon the lips of certain parties, but it is well to remember that there is another side to that story.

Mr. Makemie's old opponent, George Keith, having at last completed his somersault, has been admitted to holy orders in the Anglican Church. Preceding this step, he publishes his *Reasons for renouncing Quakerism and entering into Communion with the Church of England.* When deserting the Presbyterians for the Quakers, his chief zeal was against the former; now his heaviest assaults will probably be waged against his late associates.

Shall we see George Keith receiving the pecuniary support which he has bitterly stigmatized, assailing the Catechism for saying that "people are to maintain their ministers," and reproaching its author because "he doth not inform the people that all true ministers of Christ, as they have freely received, so they freely give, without desiring or bargaining for any settled maintenance nor exacting it by force as Presbyterian ministers commonly do"?

As heretofore, our pastor declines to contract for any fixed salary. He manages his secular affairs with success, and is carefully administering upon the Anderson estate. Notwithstanding his large business, he has seldom been engaged in litigation for himself, but as executor he is frequently forced into court On the 15th of March he brings suit in Accomack, another on the 2d of April, and three more on the 4th of June. The next day he files a power of attorney for transaction of business on behalf of Joseph Pickman of Cork, Ireland, mariner, who calls him his "trusty and well-beloved friend" and affixes the title of "Clerk," the term for clergyman. His reputation is established as a man of affairs as well as a servant of God.

In Virginia they have been celebrating the first commencement at William and Mary's College. It was a great event, talked of far and wide. Planters gathered from all the country around, and sloops went to Williamsburg with visitors from Maryland, New York and Massachusetts. Fifty-eight years before, the latter colony had celebrated a similar event at Harvard. At Williamsburg the astonished red men of the forest assembled to witness the exercises of the graduates. With so many of the youth growing up in ignorance, the whole Chesapeake seems moved under this novel sensation—the rocking of the cradle of literature and science.

With my little boy in my arms, I have been thinking, mother-like, of that commencement, and of other commencements in the days to come. Why shall not little Francis be a scholar and a preacher like his namesake? Of Presbyterians, Mr. Makemie testifies:

"They are highly for School education and learning and Academical accomplishments; for fitting and preparing men in an ordinary way for ministerial offices in the Church; not excluding but including particular gifts and qualifications and a call from God to that great work." *

The Virginians are having a lively time with their governor, the friend of arbitrary power in Church and in State. We watch his course with interest because of his great zeal for the Establishment while here, and because our pastor still lives under his government. Nicholson and Commissary Blair are at open rupture, the vestries taking part with the one and the clergy with the other. Next come the absurdity and the madness of a wild love-affair. One of the nine daughters of Lewis Burwell unfortunately wins the heart of our chivalric knight, and he demands her hand in fine style, aping royal pomp. She declines, as fair maidens have right to do, and he rages, declaring to her that he will slay her father and brothers unless she accedes to his suit. He tells the commissary that if she marry any one else he will cut the throat of the bridegroom, of the officer who issues the license, and of the officiating minister.

* *Truths in a True Light.* For college commencement, see Campbell's *Virginia*, p. 361.

The Rev. Mr Fowace visits Miss Burwell, and the governor denounces him and pulls off the clergyman's hat with insults Thus among these high officials of the Virginia Establishment the tragedy—or comedy—goes on,* causing as great excitement in that province as the second visit of William Penn is causing among the Quakers in Pennsylvania.

Maryland too has her excitements signalizing the opening of the century. Were it not for the presence of the zealous commissary, the dispirited Episcopalians would seem disposed at times to relinquish all hope of the Establishment Some of them are very willing to let the law default in order to escape the tax upon their own tobacco.† Dr. Bray perseveres. Notwithstanding instructions given to colonial governors that when a law has been reversed or rejected by the king in council no bill of the same nature shall be passed again, the commissary goes energetically to work, visiting through the province, calling conferences of the clergy and pleading with the governor, to secure another enactment. When the Assembly meets, he preaches and lobbies, until a law concocted by the united talents of himself and the attorney-general is passed with enthusiasm.

Coming over to America with loud praises sounded before him for conscientiousness and sanctity, Dr. Bray has now become privy to a wrong which must for ever meet the execration of all good men. It must be remembered that repeated failures in the past had caused great care and precision in the wording of this enactment. At my father's suggestion I preserve part of it:

* Bishop Meade's *Old Churches*, ii. 291.
† Bishop Hawks's *Maryland*, p. 99, etc

21

"The Book of Common Prayer and administration of the Sacraments, with the rites and ceremonies of the Church according to the use of the Church of England, the Psalter and Psalms of David and morning and evening prayer therein contained, shall be solemnly read and by all and every minister or reader in every church, *or other place of public worship,* within this province"

Of course nothing else would be needed to force their Liturgy into our churches at Rehoboth, Monokin, Snow Hill and Rockawalkin, and those who drew the law cannot be ignorant of the fact.*

Jubilant in their success, the visitation held at Annapolis in May by Dr. Bray and seventeen of his clergy, sent delegations conveying their hearty thanks to the governor and to the speaker of the House. On one of these delegations was Mr. Trotter, rector of the parishes of Somerset and Stepney. These men of God cannot repress their great gratitude for being clothed with authority to appropriate to their own use the meeting-houses of Dissenters! Among those sitting with them and voting heartily for this ebullition of gratitude is a Rev. Mr. T—— (full name not published), whom the commissary, before adjournment, charges with polygamy, and whose only defence is that he lived in adultery with the former reputed wife ! †

Dr. Bray reminds him, as an aggravation of his offence,

"This scandal is given at a juncture when our Church here is weakest and our friends seem to be

---

* Bishop Hawks tries to believe that it did not mean what it said. Anderson (*History of the Colonial Church,* ii. 413) puts unqualified condemnation upon the law.

† Hawks's *Maryland,* Appendix: " The Acts of Dr. Bray's Visitation, Held at Annapolis in Mary-Land, May 23, 24, 25, Anno 1700."

fewest and our enemies the strongest. And what more popular argument could they use than 'You see what sort of persons the forty pounds per poll goes to maintain'?"

Of course! Credit should be given the commissary for doing his best to enforce discipline among his clergy, and to prevent any more of these corrupt men from coming over. He speaks of another, now gone to Virginia, who "had lately so wofully behaved himself." Dr. Bray well says,

"I am apt to suspect those as not great enemies to a vicious life themselves that of all men can be favorable to an immoral priest."

Honoring the commissary for many good traits and deeds, we only regret that his zeal in pressing his one great purpose has now led him to an utter disregard of the rights of other Christians. His anxious clergy hurry him back to England to look after the iniquitous law and prevent its miscarriage. But there it fails, the attorney-general condemning the objectionable clause as utterly subversive of the Toleration Act, and of every principle of justice. To the impatient and hungry beneficiaries around us this is another sad defeat. After the passage of the enactment, for which they were so grateful, Dr. Bray had said,

"We should look back upon the deliverance this infant Church has so lately received as having been, in human appearance, totally stifled and extinguished till the re-establishment it has received within a few days by a new law."

Now, as that new law is annulled, the Church is "stifled and extinguished" again! Rectors' faces are longer than the faces of Puritans! No one seems to dream of the Church living and growing by its own labors and upon its own merits.

We have often trembled along the coast at the frightful stories of the buccaneers. Three years ago Carthagena was captured by them with immense booty. Since the Peace of Ryswick they have been less in number, but pirates still infest the ocean, and it is not children only who shudder as we hear of their robberies. Mr. Makemie's sloop, with many others, runs the gauntlet upon every voyage. We are often solicitous for our preacher's safety. The pirate Captain Kidd has looked over the Sinepuxent beach, and has passed within the capes of the Delaware. This year a pirate has captured several vessels in Lynnhaven Bay, almost in sight of Mr. Josiah Mackie's plantation, giving terrific fright to the people along-shore. A man-of-war arriving opportunely, an action took place on the 29th of April, and the pirate surrendered within the capes of the Chesapeake.* This is coming very near us. Sailors tell of being chased, and tales of blood and pillage have often scared away our sleep.

In the defeat of this year's law of Establishment, we escape ecclesiastical piracy no less cruel and wrongful than that which has hovered around our coast. While talking of this attempt to obtrude their ritual into our churches, William takes down Mr. Makemie's Barbadoes pastoral and reads as follows:

"We dare not receive nor comply with stinted and imposed forms or liturgies of worship, because not commanded nor warranted by the Word of God, nor known in the purest and original centuries of the Gospel churches; but composed without

* Campbell's *Virginia*, p. 361.

Divine commission, and required merely by men in the degenerate and latter ages of the Gospel

"Such ministers as have received of God and have given sufficient proof to many of their praying gifts and abilities, dare not ordinarily and in their ordinary administrations, tie themselves to and only use these prescribed book forms, lest they should be guilty of not using and improving but hiding and burying their gifts and talent, and so incur the character of unlawful servants.

"We dare not read as a part of public worship the Apocrypha Books which are enjoyned and read; seeing they are acknowledged by all not to be Canonical Scripture, and owned by many and in many things false and fabulous; especially while we have the Scripture by us, that perfect rule of faith and manners.

"We cannot nor dare not allow in public worship, which should be for the edification of all, that inarticulate and unintelligible way and noise of the people; all, or most, confusedly speak together, one man's voice drowning the accent of another, which seems to be so far from order that it appears confusion, as service in an unknown tongue. Hickeringill tells us he suffers no such babbling in his church at All-Saints in Colchester as is made by alternate responses.

"We cannot allow women to speak in the church, as many of yours in your whole services talk more in a day than some Quaker women, condemned by most for that practice."

Our pioneer accepts absolutely Paul's commanded silence of the women in public worship. Think of Naomi Makemie preaching in one of our pulpits! Her husband said to Keith,

"God has laid down all the qualifications of ministers of the gospel, which Quakers can never find in all their teachers, *especially of the feminine sex.*"

After the above scriptural *hit* at our proud Episcopal ladies, he continues:

"We dare not add to the sacrament of Baptism an any sign of the cross that perishes with the using, more than spittle, oil and salt; nor allow the spiritual signification imposed by men and explained in the 30th Canon, seeing Baptism signifies all that and more. And you own in the form for private Baptism that it is valid and sufficient without it   And, further, it is abused at this day to idolatry in Romish churches.

" We cannot, we dare not in Baptism exclude the parents from engaging and promising in behalf of their own children, and take in other sureties whom none expect to perform what they promise and undertake; which indeed is impossible for any to perform, especially when more ignorant and more irreligious sureties are called in than the excluded parents; as Papists, ignorant and profane persons, strangers, and sometimes young children; which we apprehend to be a willful promoting of known perfidiousness and a downright mockery of God.

" We dare not assent to the damning sentence of Athanasius' Creed, which many of the elder sons of your church wished never had been in Common Prayer We dare not say, Every person baptized is immediately regenerated; for so all baptized would be saved.

" In the Burial of the Dead we dare not call every one, whether we know them or not, our dear sister or brother, and, as a part of public worship, say, ' We have a sure and certain hope of their resurrection to eternal life, ' and to make no difference between the wicked and the godly, a Protestant and a Papist, an atheist once baptized and a serious Christian, allowing them the same charity and character, seems an encouragement to ungodliness and a discouragement to holiness.

" Though we are for visiting, instructing, convincing, admonishing, praying for, and comforting the sick, according as we find their state and condition various and different, yet we apprehend the burial service to be symbolizing with Rome and no part of God's public worship or any commanded part of a minister's work. And, though it is said it has no relation to the dead at all but only for the edification of the living, why was it denied to the living at the funeral of the Rev Mr. Henry Vaughn ? Why is it denied to the living at the funeral of unbaptized and excommunicated persons ? Why is it read ofttimes when the people are gone except two that remain to cover the corpse ? Why do the deceased persons pay for it ? And lately there was a poor man to whom it was denied, being unbaptized. Actions with vulgar people are more demonstrative than words. And what edification does that afford to the living that is read to the entry of the church-yard, of which few or none hear one word ? and why is it not all either read in the desk or at the grave ?"

My father thinks that this extract will be valuable in

days to come as casting illustrative light upon the customs of the time and upon the attitude of opposing
parties, especially in view of the Obtrusion Act passed
at Annapolis this year. Of one thing, however, we may
be sure—that the Book of Common Prayer will never
be enthroned in our Rehoboth pulpit.

CHAPTER XXII.

A. D. 1701.

"We do not maintain a perseverance depending on the will of man, but on the gracious covenant, the everlasting purpose of God, the unchangeableness of his love, and efficaciousness of Christ's death."—MAKEMIE.

MATCHACOOPAH and his friend Assateague Weegnonah have been to see us, bringing gifts to the little Francis Makemie Winstone. The presents are strings of *roenoke* and *peake*, the two kinds of coin used by the Indians and supplied largely for commerce by the Chingoteague, Assateague and Assawaman tribes. The *roenoke* is made from cockle-shells wrought into small pieces like beads with holes drilled through them. It is of darker color and less valuable than the *peake*. The latter is a longer cylinder, also perforated, and made of the finer conchshells, carefully polished.* They both have exact values, reckoned sometimes by bulk-measure, but more frequently by the yard after being strung. *Wampum*—the name for both kinds of money—means "shells." These money-beads are often made into belts and other ornaments.

I find that Thomas Cornwallis, one of the most prominent of the founders of Maryland, was licensed by our Council, in 1637, to trade with the Indians for

* Bozman, ii 77, 590.

roenoke or *peake,* this new American currency being thus officially recognized as a legal tender. In the inventory of Clayborne's property seized by Lord Baltimore's government at Palmer's Island in 1639 is this item: "Six yards of *peake* and one and a half of *roenoke.*" In 1614, when the sister of Pocohontas was asked in marriage for one of the colonists, her father answered that he "had sold her a few days before to a great Werowance for two bushels of *roenoke,*" so that it was a legal tender in the matrimonial market as well as in commercial circles.

The wigwams along the seaside are mints for the manufacture of this coin. Our little boy may now wear as an ornament that for which his reverend namesake has often trafficked, paying for the furs of the Indians in money by the yard, while they paid for his molasses in money by the quart.

Says Matchacoopah,

"*Wahocki-a-wauntet* (man-child) is *waap-pay-u* and *whuis-kai-u* (white and new). He is *wee-eet* and *wee-e-eet* (good and pretty)."

"Good" and "pretty" are very nearly the same in the Nanticoke dialect. "Pretty is that pretty does," as we say.

My husband leads Weegnonah to tell of the time when the white traders first entered the Assateague and Sinepuxent bays:

"*Pipseeque* (a bird) brought tales across from the big sea on the west. My *now-oze* (father) told of days before I was born. Where Pocomoke is lost in the large waters, the Indians had seen long ago a great floating wigwam. With the wings of the *quahaw-quunt* (wild-goose) it flew nearer. Faces like

quono (snow) were in it. They asked for water, and
drank and carried it away. From the Nanticokes
other birds came with stories. The Nanticokes were
warlike, and shot their arrows at the floating wigwam.
Then *awah-shuck* and *ton-que-ah* (thunder and lightning) burst from the terrible sea-wigwam. The frightened Nanticokes dare not fight. They knew it was
cuip-shee-in-quo (foolish). They made signs of *e-wee-
ni-tu* (peace). They wanted no *mat-ah-ki-ween* (war).
Then the pale-faced gods gave them beads and
bells, and glasses in which the Indians could see
themselves."

We saw that Weegnonah was giving the traditions
surviving among his people of the explorations of
Captain Smith along the shores of the Chesapeake
nearly a century ago. He continued:

"So the fathers had told us. It seemed like the
song of *ah-mitton-qua* (the mocking-bird), which had
flown away. It was a day in the Shad Moon (March).
Weegnonah was old enough to chase the butter-
flies. Canoes had come from the sand-hills of *mauk-
nippint* (the big pond), bringing conchs to make the
peake. But, lo! far toward the island of the Chingoteagues, something else moves upon the waters. It is
a mighty sea-gull. No; it is the palace of some great
toatum. No; it is the house of Mann-itt The white
lemuckquickse (hills) seem to shrink away The voice
of *mauk-nip-pint* is troubled. On the wings of *ayewash*
(the wind) it draws nearer.

"Some recall the tradition of the Pocomoke and
Nanticoke, and say it is the pale-faced gods. Some
say it is Matt-ann-tote (the devil). They call the
wizard. When he blows, our enemies fall and die.

He says these strangers are *matsepootquat* (bad)
—that they are witches. He will drive them out
of the beautiful bay. Our chief promises *roenoke*
and *peake*. The wizard comes to the shore dressed
in bearskins. He has long claws; his eyes are like
flame. He is dreadful. He blows at them the breath
of death They do not sink!

"The wizard runs for his poisons. He flings them
at the great winged *youck-huck* (house). It will
not stop. Then he throws his poisoned spear (*ne-
poikeehek*), and at the signal the Indians raise the
frightful whoop and throw theirs. Then there came
a burst of fire and smoke (*sunt* and *niponquōtai*).
It thundered, and *ahkee* (the earth) shook beneath
us.

"The wizard falls down in terror. He crawls away
to *pamp-tuck-koik* (the woods). He says that the
witchcraft of the palefaces is too strong for the witchcraft of the Nentegoes (the tide-water people). He
declares it is Matt-ann-tote (the devil).

"We know better now. These were your own people. It was the first boat of the white man. Where
Indian canoes had been paddled many ages, it went
up and down the waters, flying upon the wings
of *ayewash* (the wind). Assateague and Sinepuxent loved the deep keels. We traded our peltry.
They brought us beads and red cloth and the fire-
waters. Assateagues and white men were friends.
Tobacco grows for both. We drink from the same
calabash. We smoke the white pipe (the pipe of
peace, *eweenitu*).

"Once *match-kat-quot* (a cloud) appeared. In the
moon of Roasting-Ears (August) palefaces from the

land of the Accomacks wanted war. The black wampum-belt, the red hatchet painted on it, was sent from chief to chief along the seaside and over beyond the Pocomoke. The *tatt-ak* (king) of the bad whites was angry, and came with horses and guns."

Weegnonah was evidently speaking of the expedition of Edmund Scarborough against the Assateagues in 1659 * He proceeded:

"After a while the cloud went down The Quaekels" ("Quakers") "came into our land. The bad white chief and his friends had driven them here They loved peace. But at one time he put on his war-paint and swam the Pocomoke, and followed them to the Monokin. He hated the Quaekels. Once we thought of killing all the whites while in a quarrel and divided. But the Quaekels were kind to the Indian. Then the great father across the bay said the bad white chief must stay beyond the marked trees. The smell of the smoke from the white pipe is *wee-ing¹un* (sweet)."

The dashing Virginia cavalier, Edmund Scarborough, had left his memory deeply impressed upon the minds of both Indians and Quakers in the lower Maryland peninsula

A relative of this Scarborough, Edmund Custis, a man of wealth and a warm friend of Mr. Makemie, died early this year. The first Virginia Custis, an innkeeper of Rotterdam, had married the daughter of Scarborough, and from the latter Mr. Makemie's friend had inherited the Christian name. Mr Anderson spoke of Edmund Custis as his own "worthy

* *Report on Boundary of Virginia and Maryland*, p. 22

friend," gave him his favorite saddle-horse and appointed him to an important position in the settlement of his estate. This had already brought him and our minister into intimate business relations, and had afforded him opportunity to test Mr. Makemie's qualifications as a financier.

On the 4th of February—the Frog Moon, as Weegnonah would call it, because on some of its warm days the "Virginia bells" first begin to ring—the will of Mr. Custis was recorded in court, Mr. and Mrs. Makemie its executors. The trust is greater because there are minor children to be cared for and educated. The choice of a Presbyterian minister to this important trust in Virginia in these days of proscription is a high testimonial to his integrity, business tact and sterling worth.

To Mr. Makemie he bequeaths his sloop Tabitha, with her boat and appurtenances—the sloop named for his daughter, Tabitha Custis, not quite seventeen years old. A few more wills like those of Anderson and Custis will entitle our minister to the title "Admiral of the Chesapeake." When the North-Ireland boy was launching his bark-navies upon the waters of Lough Swilly, did he dream that he would some day be freighting his sloops with tobacco and furs in the fabulous American wilds?

There is another bequest—not very clerical—and Colonel Jenkins is joking our pastor about it. And yet during his long horseback rides through the lonely forests, a man of means subject to attack by bad Indians and worse white men, or when chased upon the deep by pirates, the gift may not be inopportune. The War of the Succession will increase the number of marauders along the coast, and, it may be, will endanger the pleasant home and store near Pocomoke Strand. Interested for the personal safety of his friend and not doubting his courage, the dying man leaves him " my new large pair of pistolls."

" Put it down, of course," said my father, speaking of my journal. " Yes, put it down: it will help to picture the times."

To Mrs. Makemie he gives his own saddle-horse, Button; also ten pounds sterling, to buy a ring and a scarf. Button may well be proud of his new rider thus adorned.

The will contains a provision which is likely to make the duties of the executors not wholly pleasant, and, according to certain prophets, our admiral will earn his sloop. There is another Tabitha in the case —Tabitha Hill, the grandmother of the Custis children. To please the old lady, it is provided that the executors shall consult her in all they do. She will probably interpret this to mean that her judgment must be final in every difficulty.

On the fifth of the same Frog Moon a suit instituted by Mr. Charles Scarborough against Mr. Makemie is dismissed for default, the plaintiff not appearing, finding, perhaps, that he had no case.

In the same court, record is made of the public spirit of our busy minister. In this new country there is a great scarcity of mill-facilities, and the colonists must carry their grain long distances or depend upon horse-mills, hand-mills or hominy-mortars. The horse-mill, which Mr. Anderson's will would keep permanently upon the Pocomoke plantation, supplies the convenience of Mr. Makemie and his neighbors, but his enterprise reaches out to the growing settlements east and south-east of him. The Rehoboth mill stands alone in a broad belt from the bayside to the seaside, and has already done long and faithful service.

In 1667 the Virginia Assembly, possessed with zeal for internal improvements, passed an act granting certain privileges to any who would construct water-mills. For some while Mr. Makemie has had his eye upon one of the watercourses near which he passes while riding over to Mrs. Anderson's Occocomson plantation. This year he purchases an acre of land from Mr. Thomas Stockly, "beginning on the southernmost side of the Upper Church bridge, upon the brow of the branch next the Creek, and running up the hill along the main road." This " church " is the Assawaman Episcopal church, built in 1687—the year of Colonel Stevens's death. In the recorded conveyance our minister binds himself "to build at the said Church, alias Taylor's Bridge, one grist-mill, also a fulling-mill;" with the privilege to cut from Mr. Stockly's land any small timber for ever, except board timber and some white oak, and Mr. Stockly and his heirs " shall be hopper-free as long as said mill shall grind."

On the 5th of August, Mr. Makemie makes application to the Accomack court, asking encouragement in the construction of the mill according to act of Assembly. They take it under consideration Surely the authorities will not fail to reward the energy of one of their most enterprising citizens!

On the same day begin the troubles from the old grandmother. With no marked reverence for Presby-

terian preachers in general, Madam Tabitha evidently
intends valiant fight against Mr. Makemie in particular.   He is mismanaging the business, doing the
heirs injustice, "wasting" the Custis estate! She refuses her consent to what he attempts, delays the
settlement, and then lays the blame on him.   Undoubtedly she means to make him pay dearly for the
sloop which bears the name of herself and her granddaughter.   She comes boldly into court and charges
him with malfeasance.   Does she expect to worry and
drive him out of the executorship, forgetting the *per-
fervidum ingenium Scotorum?*   Her charges can be
met by having inspectors to examine into all this pretended "wasting," and the court appoints them.

Our Somerset court has just ordered the building
of a prison at Rehoboth, the prison erected at Dividing Creek six years ago proving insufficient.   Henry
Hudson suggests that the new gaol be located near
the church for clerical accommodation, prophesying
that the Episcopalians in Somerset and Madam Tabitha Hill in Accomack will soon make it a necessity.

The two churches, Episcopalian and Presbyterian,
the mill, the prison and the adjacent farms of prominent citizens are causing the little Rehoboth village
to be a centre of considerable note.   The preaching
of the sound doctrines of grace renders it more illustrious still.   Staunch Calvinism well suits a region of
many trials, temptations and hardships.   Scattered
Presbyterians, coming from the midst of enemies
beyond the sea, and living here in poverty and amid
growing opposition, are strengthened in their lot by
strong meat from their strong teacher:

"Such as deny the perseverance of the saints must be ignorant of what Christ has done for the confirmation of the gracious state of believers.   First, His redeeming them from all the demands of Divine Justice with his precious blood.   Second, Redeeming them from the power of Satan.   Third, From the dominion of sin.   Fourth, He is gone to prepare a place for them. Fifth, He makes intercession in Heaven for them.   Sixth, He promises his Spirit to abide in them, to complete his begun work in them and establish them ; all which is abundantly confirmed from Scripture."

Thus he would guard the Christian heroes of the New World from any relaxing distrust of God's faithfulness and power :

"The final and total fall and apostacy of regenerate saints is inconsistent with the nature of grace ; which is an incorruptible seed that cannot be totally extinguished where'er it is planted of God.   And further, it much weakens the faith of the saints, their hope and confidence in God's preservation of them from falling, which the experience and confidence of the Apostle Paul testifies they firmly believe, Rom viii 35–39, and that in their deepest trials and afflictions.   Finally, it robs the regenerated children of God of their spiritual joy and holy consolation in the Holy Ghost, by filling them with perpetual fears, anxiety and doubts about their state.   It destroys the promise of God's establishing and confirming Spirit and leaves the Catholic Church of God, which the gates of hell cannot prevail against, upon a most ticklish foundation." *

Mr. Makemie intends to place our American Presbyterianism upon no such "ticklish" basis.   The bone and sinew and nerve of no solid, enduring Church grows out of a gospel of falling and lapsing.

We are glad to see our Rehoboth elder, Mr. Pierce Bray, with a home of his own   He has just bought a tract of land of Mr. John Walton and become a

* *Answer to Keith.*

freeholder on the great continent.* May the elder-
ship, the voice of the people in ecclesiastical government—that scriptural bulwark against priestly tyranny—become firmly rooted to the American soil!
The arbitrary authority of a titled hierarchy Mr.
Makemie finds nowhere in the New Testament.
He says:

"Another thing wherein we dissent is concerning the government of the church by Archbishops, Bishops, Chancellors, Com-
missaries, Deans, Deans and Chapters, Arch-deacons, etc.; as
not having foundations in the Scriptures, nor in the government
of the Gospel Churches, nor agreeable to the government of the
first centuries after our Saviour. And though we are for Scripture bishops, both name and office, and wish with Dr. Wild in
his poetic flight, 'Where there is one, there were ten,' neither
would refuse the government of the first two or three hundred
years after our Savior; yet there are several things in which we
dissent, and which many of yours dislike, in English or Diocesan Bishops or Prelacy; as—

" 1. Creating and erecting new offices and officers besides what
Christ gave to and instituted in his Church, the names whereof
are not so much as known or mentioned in the Scriptures

" 2. Promoting pre-eminence, and destroying that ministerial
parity our Saviour commanded and industriously maintained in
his days, forbidding all mastery and dominion over each other.

" 3. Their assuming high and lordly titles and temporal dignities and civil places, being advanced above most peers and statesmen. This was offensive to good old Latimer, who in a sermon
advised King Edward VI. to unlord all the Lordly Bishops and
remove them from all their temporal offices and employments
that they might follow their spiritual plough-tail.

" 4. Their frequenting the Court, attending the Council Table,
and sitting in Parliaments, to the utter neglect of their charge
and work, being above preaching, praying and administering of
sacraments and church government too Therefore a non-preach-
ing Bishop called a preaching Bishop a preaching coxcomb. And
what prejudice would it be to the State, but what a great advan-

* First mention found on Somerset records. He sat in Presbytery in
1710

tage to the Church, if the Government saw it meet to revive again that old vote of a Church of England parliament recorded in Baker's *Chronicles*, That no Bishop should have any vote in parliament, nor any Judicial power in the Star Chamber, nor bear any sway in temporal affairs, and that no clergyman should be in commission of the peace.

" 5. Their grasping at a larger charge over many great congregations of a vast diocess, whereby an Episcopal charge and care can no more be performed or discharged in the sight of God—as over the diocess of London and all English plantations, while so much time is spent at Court and in secular affairs—than the Italian Bishop can be Metropolitan of the Christian World " *

The population of Maryland at this time is said to be twenty-five thousand; of Virginia, forty thousand; and of Pennsylvania, twenty thousand.† In our province there has been little increase in numbers or prosperity since the Baltimores were displaced and the agitations against religious liberty superseded the previous toleration ‡ Church-of-England parishes and their tobacco churches are the monuments of Maryland's decline.

Mr. Penn is still in America, and, on the eve of returning to Europe, has just issued a new form of government. His colony is thereby again placed squarely on the side of full religious freedom, it being provided:

" None shall be in any case molested or prejudiced because of his or their conscientious persuasion or practice, nor be compelled to frequent or maintain any religious worship, place or ministry contrary to his or her mind, or to do or suffer any other act or thing contrary to their religious persuasion."

Yet this very year, in the face of these emphatic guarantees of perfect toleration to all, the High Churchmen of that province deliberately refuse to

---

* *Truths in a True Light.* † Campbell's *Virginia*, p 362.
‡ McMahon, p. 273.

sign a paper exculpating Penn from the false charge of persecution.* To place all churches upon an equal footing and give them a fair field upon which to prosper or die according to their own merits is a crime against Prelacy! They shamelessly decline to perform this act of common justice to one who is protecting them!

This same spirit is giving great trouble to our friends in Ireland. When Londonderry and Inniskillen are remembered, well may the Synod say:

"We cannot think our late active zeal for the preservation of this kingdom can be forgotten by those who found our assistance so heartily granted and useful."

These patriots are ruthlessly pursued by the bishops' courts, which harass with litigation our ministers who solemnize marriages, declare those thus married adulterers and try to bastardize the children. The petition of Synod cleverly reminds these oppressors that numbers of their own clergy and laity are descended from marriages solemnized by Dissenters. The king disapproves of such high-handed injustice, but his hands are tied by the Tory High Churchmen.†

We think of all this while we hear of Commissary Bray working indefatigably in England to fix the Establishment upon Maryland. He adopts the shrewd expedient to have the law drafted by the English authorities, then enacted in the province and sent back to London for confirmation. This will probably succeed, but at the expense of a valued principle of colonial liberty.

The zealous efforts of the commissary have succeed-

* Watson's _Annals of Philadelphia._   † Reid, ii. 483, etc.

ed in effecting an organization called " The Society for the Propagation of the Gospel in Foreign Parts " The design is a worthy one, if they will only send a better class of missionaries than have fallen to our lot heretofore. To the north of us there are not half a dozen Episcopal clergymen; only one in all Pennsylvania. Of the material to select from at home, Bishop Burnet himself says :

" I have observed the clergy in all places throughout which I have traveled; Papists, Lutherans, Calvinists, and Dissenters; but of them all our clergy are much the most remiss in private, and the least severe in their lives." *

In September, James, the abdicated king, dies in France. His son is at once recognized by Louis as king of England. No less promptly, I suppose, will the Tory High Churchmen transfer to the young Stuart their ardent affection for that dynasty. This act of Louis will hasten the war for which William has been preparing since the death of the King of Spain. A reaction has already taken place in England against the factious Parliament, and the people will sustain their great leader. The grand alliance with the nations of the Continent, brought about by his wonderful diplomacy, will serve him in good stead. Weak in body, frail and fading, he stands nobly forward as the champion of Protestantism.

We again change governors, the administration devolving upon Colonel Edward Loyd, president of the Council. Because of ill-health, Blackiston resigns and goes to England. He is a man of integrity and honor, and carries with him the love and the confidence of the people. He is to act as agent and

* Burnet's *Own Times*, vi. 183

friend of the province in counteracting the influences set on foot by our former governor, the lovesick Nicholson, to induce the English government to establish arbitrary power in America.

In reply to inquiries from the home authorities as to the condition of the colony, our Council accuses Pennsylvania of being a harbor for fugitive seamen and debtors and runaway servants, and of being resorted to in late years by pirates. These sea-robbers still infest our coasts and bays. Captain Kidd—whose name has been a terror, and whose treasure is said to be buried along the seaboard—has just been hung in chains in England.

In the midst of all these varied events, Mr. Makemie, Mr. Davis, Mr. Mackie, Mr. Nathaniel Taylor, Mr. John Wilson and Mr. Jedediah Andrews stand in their lot and preach the blessed gospel (63). The latter has this year been ordained in Philadelphia— the "Grove of the Long Pines," or *Kuequenakee* (koo-ek-wen-aw-kee), of the Indians. There the little flock gather around their young pastor and wonder if they will ever be stronger.

Some time during these passing years Mrs. Elinor Trail, after an eventful life, has gone to the rest above. She was the first brave woman that trod our county's soil as the wife of a Presbyterian minister. This year, on the 8th of July, Mr. Trail marries again, taking to his home, in Borthwick, Jean Murray, the widow of David Moncrieff of Boghall. We think of the plantation of Brother's Love, and of her who used to sit close to the first pulpit in the little log church at Rehoboth.

CHAPTER XXIII.

A. D. 1702.

"In favor of some Dissenters I shall only lay down one saying from 'Hale of Schism', 'All pious assemblies in times of persecution and corruption are the only lawful congregations; and the public assemblies, though according to form of law, are indeed nothing but riots and conventicles, if stained with corruption and superstition.'"—MAKEMIE

OF this year the Shad Moon has been the most eventful month. On March 16 the law of Establishment has been enacted by the Assembly; and, inasmuch as it originated in England and had the approval of the authorities in advance, it will meet their final sanction. After just ten years' blundering and attempted enforcement of illegal enactments, Prelacy now is happy. No doubt it is better for Dissenters that its authors were driven to England to formulate the statute, for it came back with the Toleration Act safely embodied in it, and with permission to Quakers to affirm instead of taking oath For this they have been pleading since 1674 The law is more favorable to us all than any that could have been obtained from the Maryland clergy.

As William works his tobacco-field he brushes off the great green tobacco-worms, calls them "Maryland parsons," and dispenses a more rigid discipline than any yet secured by the efforts of the commissary. The sheriff henceforth will collect the products of the sweat of my husband's brow and apply them to the support of the rector of Coventry Parish. If the churches and churchyards need repair, and the forty pounds per poll and the fines and forfeitures arising under this act prove insufficient for the purpose, another tax of ten pounds per poll may be assessed.*

After paying these taxes, the Dissenters are permitted, in great condescension, to worship undisturbed, provided they have their meeting-houses registered at the county court and keep them " unlocked, unbarred and unbolted." Our ministers are required to take the oath of allegiance and to subscribe the doctrinal articles of the Church of England. In these articles there is nothing objectionable, and our ministers can far more conscientiously accept them than can their own Arminian clergy. But these very provisions which secure our protection are an intentional badge of inferiority, a reflection upon our loyalty, an implied suspicion of danger to Church and State from locked conventicles. This, too, while the Presbyterians have been far more true than the Anglican Church to our noble king!

My father says that an important principle of colonial freedom has been betrayed. Heretofore the province has stood very firmly upon its right to originate its own laws, maintaining this right against both the Proprietary and the English authorities. Now, for the sake of loaves and fishes, these ecclesiastical plotters have sold out one of the strongest safeguards of our civil liberties. The English authorities, on the alert for opportunities to infringe upon the rights of the Plantations, planning the destruction of the charters,

* Hawks's *Maryland,* p 113.

and encouraged in their encroachment by Nicholson and others, must have laughed in their sleeves when solicited to go beyond their former veto-power and to dictate in advance the law. Tobacco has supplanted patriotism.

King William was never to sign the Act of Maryland Establishment. While the nation, no longer under lead of the Tory High Churchmen, were backing their monarch enthusiastically and were voting men and money for avenging the indignity offered by Louis in the recognition of the pretended Prince of Wales as king of England, our royal William, cheered and happy, was riding at Hampton Court on the 21st of February, when his horse stumbled at a mole-hill, and the rider fell to the ground, fracturing his collar-bone. The little mole had overthrown the hero whom all the armies of France and the plots of the non-jurors had failed to dethrone. On Sunday, the 8th of March, the great champion of toleration died.

Friends of arbitrary power in Church and State in England are toasting William's horse for throwing him, and are drinking to the health of "the little gentleman in velvet" which caused his fall.*

The princess Anne, sister of Mary, is now queen. She is in sympathy with the Church Tories. Dissenters have but little hope of favor at her hands. The Parliament tries to demean the memory of William, declaring, "We promise ourselves that in your reign we shall see the Church perfectly restored to its due rights and privileges." What right and what privilege had been taken away except that of persecution?

A laughable joke has just been played upon the ex-

* Knight's *England*, v. 107.

tremists. An eloquent pamphlet appears, advocating
the most atrocious measures against the Nonconformists. The High Churchmen fall into the trap and ap-
plaud Now it transpires that *The Shortest Way with
the Dissenters* is a shrewd literary hoax written by the
Dissenter De Foe, full of the keenest irony against
the ultra-party themselves. They are furious.

The Scottish Parliament notice the undisguised exultation of the Jacobites and reiterate their determined
adhesion to Presbyterianism. In Ireland the enemies
of our Church are elated into new aggressions. Persecutions for marriages grow more virulent. Bishop
King of Derry testifies of the Presbyterians:

"Nothing could show more clearly the interest they thought
themselves to have in his late Majesty's favor than the dejection
that appears amongst them at present." *

This is the prelate who denounced the closing of
the gates of Derry against King James as arrant rebellion, and was so ready afterward to court the notice
of William and to seek to prejudice his mind against
the brave Presbyterians.

Notwithstanding all these things, Ulster flourishes
spiritually. The number of congregations constantly
increases. New Presbyteries and Synods are forming.
The Presbytery of Laggan has become the Synod of
Laggan. More ministers are badly needed, but the
Church in no degree lowers her standard of orthodoxy
or of culture. The candidate must subscribe the Confession of Faith in every article. The Synod has just
decided to enter no one on trials until he has studied
divinity four years after completing his literary course.
These are the people that trained and indoctrinated

* Reid, ii. 489, etc.

our own pioneer. Mr Makemie believes in the exercise of great care in admitting men to the pulpit.
In his *Answer to Keith* he thus speaks approvingly
of the usage of our Church :

"They firmly believe and strenuously hold a fixed and standing ministry to be always in the church to the end of the world ;
and churches to be furnished with all officers warranted in the
Scriptures duly qualified and orderly set apart according to the
Word of God. After a long and most strict examination and
trial, some are allowed first to preach only as probationers or
expectants for a proof of their preaching gifts and praying abilities and of a holy conversation ; and when called to the pastoral
charge, submitting to a second examination, they are orderly set
apart, or ordained, to the whole work of the ministry, according
to the Apostle's phrase, by the imposition of the hands of the
Presbytery."

England and her allies have formally declared war
against France. The Duke of Marlborough, Queen
Anne's favorite, takes command on the Continent.
Again we may expect the ravages of privateers and
pirates along our coast

Meanwhile, Madam Tabitha Hill prosecutes her
declaration of war against Mr Makemie with a persistence unexcelled by that of the great Marlborough
himself. She finally wins an apparent victory. On
the 4th of March, while our king was upon his dying-
bed, the executors of the Custis estate are non-suited
in a case against John Stanton on the ground that they
had not first asked the old lady's advice, according to
the letter of the will She is willing for the estate to
suffer loss if she may thereby worry and defeat the
Presbyterian preacher and his wife. On the 8th of
April she herself brings suit against him, but fails to
appear, lets it go by default and pays the cost. In
the same court Mr. Makemie gains a suit against

William Jarman. The month before, a suit against the executors was dismissed This litigation is not for himself, but officially, as executor My father says that all this experience in court may be preparing our minister for new conflicts for religious freedom before judicial authorities in the days to come.*

In October, jointly with Mr. Henry Jenkins, Mr. Makemie patents one hundred and fifty acres of land on Watts's Island, planting his possessions at the gate of Pocomoke Sound Yonder, to the west, the island dimly rises in sight of his Accomack home. Over to the other side of him, he goes on building his mill at Assawaman, and thinks of the old water-mill near Ramelton around which his boyhood's steps used to play.

Amid the bitter struggle of the Episcopal commissary Blair with the Episcopal governor Nicholson in Virginia, the former finds time this year to write:

"There is a sort like Presbyterians here which is upheld by some idle fellows that have left their lawful employment and preach and baptize without orders." †

If the distressed commissary means the Presbyterians about Elizabeth River and in Accomack, and intends to apply the term "idle fellows" to Mr. Mackie and Mr Makemie, certainly there was never a worse misnomer. The former works his plantation of one hundred and fifty acres near the Back Bay, superintends his store, takes care of his "valuable stock of horses at the seaside," studies his "scholastic books of learned languages, as Latin, Greek, Hebrew,"‡ and preaches regularly at four registered places of public

* For above facts see Accomack records.   † Webster, p 89.
‡ Mackie's will; Sprague's *Annals.*

worship; while Mr. Makemie, one of the most industrious men in the province, successfully manages his own large property, settles the estates of others, conducts works of public improvement, writes books and proclaims the gospel everywhere. If the crime of these consecrated men be that no prelate's hands have ever rested upon their heads and they are therefore "without orders," the commissary ought to remember that his own clergy are now pressing—very inconveniently—the terrible charge of a want of episcopal ordination in his own case.

But it need do us no harm to know what our enemies think of us. Talbot, a missionary for the Society for the Propagation of the Gospel in Foreign Parts, is just writing from Philadelphia:

"The Presbyterians here come a great way to lay hands on one another; but after all I think they had as good stay at home for all the good they do. In Philadelphia one pretends to be a Presbyterian and has a congregation to which he preaches."[*]

Talbot and George Keith are now traveling through the colonies, zealous propagandists—the latter as violent for Prelacy as formerly for Quakerism. The fiercest assaults of this proselyte are directed against his late *friends*, forcing himself upon their meetings, interrupting their worship and denouncing their principles to their face. On Long Island, by false charges, he secures the arrest and imprisonment of the Quaker preacher Samuel Bownas. The influence of governor and of judge is exerted in vain to obtain from the grand jury an indictment against Bownas. In his schemes Keith finds a worthy accomplice in the profligate governor.[†]

[*] Gillett, i. 20.   [†] Bownas's *Journal, in loco.*

Lord Cornbury is a cousin of Queen Anne, and a grandson of the famous Earl of Clarendon, the unreliable historian and apologist of Stuart and Laudian tyranny. Openly immoral, bankrupt in property and reputation in England, flying from his creditors across the sea, made governor of New York and New Jersey, this outlawed spendthrift seems ambitious to prove himself the patron of the Churchmen, and they are glad to use him. Of meaner character and meaner abilities than our own Nicholson, he is a fit tool in the hands of the advocates of civil and ecclesiastical despotism Until of late there has been toleration in New Jersey and New York; but, under instructions from the queen, Episcopacy has just been established by Cornbury in the former, and he is determined to override the law and to force the yoke of subjection upon the necks of the Reformed Dutch and other Dissenters in the latter province And this notwithstanding the fact that his fellow-religionists are in a pitiable minority!

At Jamaica, Long Island, a church composed of Congregationalists and Presbyterians has been in existence for about thirty years. They came from New England mostly, and brought with them the spirit of firm and conscientious dissent. Their ministers nearly all Congregationalists, the influence of Independency predominated. In many of these churches to the northward, under a necessary compromise, the two systems of Independency and Presbyterianism so shade into each other that it is hard to say where the one ends or the other begins Any compromise is an adoption of the laxer system. The Dentons and others have always preferred Presbyterianism, and two years ago the Jamaica church called Mr. Hubbard, a classmate of Mr. Andrews, and voted that he should be ordained "in the Presbyterian way." Henceforth we may hope for the church to come more fully into accord with our own (64).

Our friends in Jamaica own a stone church worth six hundred pounds, and a parsonage and glebe worth fifteen hundred. Without any pretence of moral right to the property, the Episcopalians intrude and seize the church amid scenes most disgraceful. The governor encourages the outrage and prosecutes the real owners for resisting the trespass. Worse still, flying from the deadly malady now raging in New York, he takes refuge in Jamaica, and, finding the parsonage the most commodious dwelling there, he presumes to ask Mr. Hubbard to vacate it for his accommodation. The minister generously submits to the inconvenience. Now follows the base treachery. When returning to New York, Cornbury deliberately defrauds the man that befriends him, and hands over parsonage and glebe to the Church-party and their clergyman Bartow.

A despicable character named Cardale—the sheriff —is the willing tool of Church and State in executing these iniquitous measures against Bownas and Hubbard. If the "Venerable Society" countenances such crimes and permits its missionaries to be parties to them, it must redound to its lasting shame.*

Will the heroic Keith, whose strictures upon Mr. Makemie's Catechism sneered at "Prelate, Priest and Presbyter of the Pope's making," venture another visit to our minister at Pocomoke? Bold in challeng-

* McDonald's *Jamaica Church, passim.*

ing, he has never answered our pastor's rejoinder. Now himself a priest in the regular succession, though near enough to us to look across the bay from his daughter's home at Kekoutan (Hampton), he does not seem anxious to encounter Mr. Makemie again.

My husband's peach trees, now coming into fragrance and fruitage, remind me of Mr. Makemie's estimate of our country:

" Here are spacious and flourishing orchards, replenished with fair and pleasant fruit, and will afford pleasant gardens by much less labor and expense than in Europe, furnished with whatever herbs, flowers and plants you are pleased to put into the ground."

Our minister, interested in every step of improvement, shall have our first ripe peach.

My father has been talking of perhaps the earliest historical mention of peaches in America. In an account of a visit to the James River in 1633, the Dutch captain De Vries speaks thus of the home of Minifie, who had come to America ten years before:

"Arrived at Littletown where Minifie lives. He has a garden of two acres full of primroses, apple, pear and cherry trees, the various fruits of England, with different kinds of sweet-smelling herbs, rosemary, sage, marjoram, thyme Around the house were planted peach trees, which were hardly in bloom." *

As far back as the year of our county's organization, thirty-seven years ago, a Mr. Barnabe made provision in his will for planting an orchard of two hundred fruit trees on his estate.† Nature's own wild crops of strawberries, whortleberries and grapes are fragrant with suggestions of horticulture.

* Neill's *Founders of Maryland.*   † Somerset records.

Amid the sweet flowers and fruits of the lower Eastern Shore, my Huguenot sister-in-law sings of Languedoc, but sings in sadness. In the Vincennes an arch-priest—Du Chailu—has been guilty of the most brutal enormities, torturing prisoners, flogging and mutilating children, killing young girls. The mountaineers, enraged by these atrocities, have risen in insurrection, killed the fiendish priest and demolished his castle. Cavalier, a brave young hero, has marshaled these bold Camisards, determined to conquer or die, and the stories of their heroism stir the currents of Huguenot blood over here. Our Margaret has just been thrilling the Maryland air with one of the songs of her people.

With the Toleration Act just legalized in Maryland, it seems a great wrong that the Catholics should be excepted from its benefits,—that the Baltimores, who ruled with such equal kindness to us all, must see their own religion alone proscribed. But when we remember these long-continued barbarities in France and the rage of the Papists against the Protestants in Ireland while lately in power, it is no wonder that our authorities are legislating against the importation of Irish Catholics and refuse to tolerate that faith which is still perpetrating its cruelties across the ocean. While we would persecute nobody, we fully indorse Mr. Makemie's statement of the dislike of Presbyterians for that apostate Church:

"They abhor, renounce, and abjure Popery, Idolatry, Superstition and Heresy, with every error they are convinced and persuaded is contrary to the Word of God; universally believing the Popes of Rome to be the grand Antichrist." *

* *Truths in a True Light.*

23

I must not forget to record, for our pastor's sake, the legal marriage-fee of five shillings just established by act of Assembly.

William Bozman has been commissioned as our county ranger by Governor Blakiston, to take up "and convert to the Ranger's own proper use" all wild horses, neat cattle and hogs wherever found. But there is another county ranger, who cares for no commission from Annapolis, passing at will from neighborhood to neighborhood and interfering recklessly with affairs civil and ecclesiastical. He comes with cadaverous mien from swamps and frog-ponds, and leaves his yellow brand upon the faces of judge and jury, and even upon the fresh complexion of Pastor Makemie. This wild ranger is one of the worst persecutors of the times, the ruthless Eastern Shore ague and fever—whose fame is already making its way into verse:

> " With Cockerouse* as I was sitting,
> I felt a Fever Intermitting,
> A fiery Pulse beat in my Veins,
> From Cold I felt resembling Pains:
> This horrid seasoning I remember
> Lasted from March to cold December;
> Nor would it then its Quarters shift
> Until by Cardus turn'd adrift.
> And had my Doctress wanted skill,
> Or Kitchen-Physic at her will,
> My Father's Son had lost his Lands,
> And never seen the Goodwin Sands
> But thanks to Fortune and a Nurse
> Whose care depended on my Purse,
> I saw myself in good condition
> Without the help of a Physician.
> At length the shivering ill relieved,
> Which long my Head and Heart had grieved." †

* A person of quality.　† *Sot-Weed Factor*, published 1708.

CHAPTER XXIV.

A. D. 1703.

"A Church without Discipline & Censure is like a Kingdom without Rule & Government."—MAKEMIE.

IN sight of our churches is constantly beheld the clearing of new lands—trees cut down, stumps on fire, roots digged out and piled for burning. Among these growing plantations, Mr. Makemie's similitude is well understood:

"As the husbandman must hew down and grub up his field ere he can sow and reap the fruit of his labor, so must the sinner lay the axe of repentance to the root of his old sins if he would bring forth the fruits of righteousness in his life. Hosea x. 12— 'Sow to yourselves in righteousness and reap in mercy.' And how shall this be done? 'Plough up your fallow ground.' Would you lead righteous or religious lives, you must return and fall foul of your old sins and spare them not; but repent and turn from them. How necessary this pungent and heart-piercing repentance is to eternal life and salvation we are oft told. Luke xiii. 5.—'Except ye repent, ye shall all likewise perish.'"*

On this text he had preached in Ireland when twenty-one years younger. The voice, as the voice of the Forerunner, is still crying in the wilderness.

After service, Mr. Makemie and my friend Naomi came home with us to the "little wigwam in the pines." Both of us mothers now, how we love to

* New York sermon.

see her little Elizabeth and my own Francis playing together! (65). Francis shares with his playmate the store of hickory-nuts, chestnuts, walnuts and beech-nuts brought him by Daniel, King of the Poco-mokes.

The "American desert" has bestowed upon Mr. Ma-kemie this home-treasure, little Betty, in return for his life's devotion to its material and spiritual cultivation. While living for the good of the children of thousands yet to be, God has finally given him a darling of his own to cheer his latter days as nothing else could do. It is very pleasant to hear these playmates exchanging quotations from her father's Catechism. From page ten sweet Betty recites as follows:

" Christ revealeth the will of God to us by his Word and Spirit."

My son replies from page eleven:

" The Holy Spirit worketh faith in us and uniteth us to Christ."

After a while she says from page twelve:

" Effectual calling is a powerful call of God whereby he calls and draws sinners out of sin into grace."

He answers from page sixteen:

" Justification, adoption and sanctification once had, can never be wanted."

She repeats from page thirty:

" The godly cannot keep God's commands perfectly."

He responds from page forty-one:

" The Holy Spirit teaches us to pray aright and acceptably to God." *

* Extracts from Catechism, found in Keith's strictures and Makemie's *Answer*.

Well does our pastor say in his reply to Keith:

"The advantage of an early instruction is witnessed by the experiences of many godly in all ages, where attended with the blessing of God and pursued with exhortation until they arrive at a riper age."

Again we think of the "experience" of the boy-convert on the hills of Donegal.

Of his Catechism, Mr. Makemie says:

"After it was first composed, I did compendize and abbreviate it, oftener than once, to suit it to the capacities of such for whom it was prepared, even young ones."

In those days he little knew that it was finally to be tested in a household of his own, by his own "young ones"—the best test of all good preaching.

We have been laughing at Naomi about the conduct of clergymen's wives down in Virginia. Rev. Mr. Collier, now rector of Hungar's Parish, is married to a widow who had previously assaulted somebody in church, and who has lately been presented to court for cursing and swearing.*

"Put it down in your journal," says my father, "as a comment upon American tithes and glebes."

Our busy pastor is beginning to talk of a visit to Europe for the purpose of awakening an interest there in our needy fields and securing more ministers. Mr. Davis is living at Lewes, leaving this entire broad county dependent upon Mr. Makemie. Who is to take his place when he departs or dies?

Missionaries of the "Venerable Society" are still arriving. Talbot and Keith are making their journeys from New Hampshire to Currituck, bold and aggress-

* Bishop Meade's *Old Churches*, i. 258.

ive everywhere. The latter passes up and down our Western Shore, but pays no more visits to the "Poccamok." Quakers are his favorite game.

"I have baptized several persons," says Talbot, "whom Mr. Keith has brought over from Quakerism."

With his old fellow-Broadbrims, there is war all along the lines.

Keith speaks of the courtesy of the New England Independents, meeting them at the commencement at Cambridge, preaching frequently in their churches and seeming to interpret their courtesy as indicative of leanings to his Church. From Philadelphia he writes :

" They have here a Presbyterian meeting and a minister, one called Andrews ; but they are not like to increase here."

The future will test the prophecy.

Keith is flattering profligate Lord Cornbury. He preaches before him at Burlington, compliments him, and finds the godless governor as enthusiastic for Episcopacy as himself.* A delegation of Churchmen from Philadelphia wait upon Cornbury, laud his zeal and express the amiable hope that his good cousin the queen may be induced to extend over them the ægis of his beneficent government. They say that they are longing "to enjoy the same blessings others do under his authority"! He comes to Philadelphia and encourages these demonstrations. William Penn is so disgusted with the turbulent spirits that he begs the Lords of Trade to buy him out or let him buy out "the hot Church-party." †

* Keith's *Journal.*
† Anderson's *Colonial Church ;* Webster, Gillett and Bishop Hawks, *in loco*

The desire expressed by Philadelphia Churchmen to enjoy the same blessings which others do under Cornbury's authority is illustrated by his persistent ill-treatment of our people and their minister at Jamaica. Thanking Bartow for his riotous intrusion into our church, he pursues Mr. Hubbard with every harassing device whenever the latter attempts to recover legal possession of the property wrung so wickedly out of his hands. Do these Pennsylvania petitioners desire to see the same course pursued toward Mr. Hubbard's classmate, Andrews? The disgraceful immoralities of the flattered Cornbury throw a lurid light over these proceedings.

I wish all this were otherwise. In that Church are many noble men and women, and their Articles of Religion are pure and Scriptural. Says Mr. Makemie:

"We agree in all points of faith and Divine ordinances or parts of worship, with the Established Church of England, and are the likest to them of any Protestants, differing only in ceremonies, government and discipline. We are Protestant brethren and in unity with them in the great and substantial points of Christian and Protestant religion; and therefore not to be treated as many ignorantly do. Of all Protestants that differ with them, we differ in the least and smallest matters "*

It is deplorable when bad men gain the ascendency in Church and State and give their evil tempers the name of Christian zeal. There is an especial absurdity in being unchurched by the drunken and the licentious. This year an immoral clergyman, driven from Virginia by Commissary Blair because of baseness of character, secures one of the best parishes in Maryland, and comes into possession of one of the largest parochial libraries sent over by Dr. Bray. The pre-

* *Truths in a True Light*

cautions taken by the commissary in the Visitation held by him at Annapolis in the year 1700 have never been enforced, and the irregularities are growing worse.*

Says the Episcopal missionary Talbot:

"We want a great many good ministers here in America, but we had better have none at all than such scandalous beasts as some make themselves, not only the worst of ministers but of men." †

Dr. Bray will not return to America. We are sorry; for though privy to one great wrong in trying by his law of 1700 to foist his ceremonials upon the churches of Dissenters, yet he had many noble traits and earnestly desired the purifying of his Church. His endeavors have fixed the Establishment upon us, and we have a right to demand that he will labor to correct its scandals. For cleansing the Augean stable, which he found too heavy a task for himself, he seeks the appointment of another commissary. In our own county we have a monument of Bray's zeal for parochial libraries—Snow Hill Parish, ten volumes; Somerset Parish, twenty, Coventry, twenty-five; and Stepney, sixty.‡ Was the gift to the latter larger because of its being named for the great Stepney Parish of London?

In the face of the prevalent corruptions in clerical ranks, we are very proud of the unsullied fame of our Makemie. Not one calumny taints his good name. This is the more remarkable when we think of his wide activities as a business-man as well as a minister, bringing him into contact with so many clashing in-

* Bishop Hawks's *Maryland*, p 121.   † Gillett, i. 22
‡ Neill's *Founders of Maryland*, p 173

terests. Even the vigilant Madam Tabitha Hill can find no flaw in him.

Such a minister can stand in the pulpit unabashed and plead against the laxness of the times with open brow:

"As kings and princes have their laws for government in their several dominions, and a power lodged in the hands of particular persons specially qualified for executing such laws, so our Lord Jesus has prescribed spiritual laws and constituted a suitable government and spiritual rule in his Church, intrusted to particular persons, to be duly executed upon offenders; and this discipline is to be employed about such as are within, and not without, the visible churches. This government or discipline is specially distinct from the secular power and is called the power of the keys of the Kingdom of Heaven.

"This spiritual rule and government is appointed by our Lord Jesus, not only for reclaiming irregular and offending brethren, but for deterring others from the like offenses, and also for purging out that corrupt and sinful leaven that, if not taken away, will defile the whole lump Such proceedings with delinquents are not to punish their bodies or mulct their estates, but for afflicting the conscience of offenders by censure and conviction, according to the nature or dement and circumstances of their crimes. Where this watching, admonishing, and censuring and suspending power of discipline is impartially and jealously exercised, it prevents a multitude of irregularities which would scandalize Christian Societies." *

Thus, with Bible in hand, our pioneer plants the principle of a pure discipline in the same furrows where he is planting the American Presbyterian Church.

In February there comes a tardy report from the Accomack court—asked eighteen months ago—setting apart to Mr. Makemie, according to act of the Virginia Assembly of 1667, an acre of ground for the water-mill at Assawaman, a sister to the mill at

* New York sermon.

Rehoboth and to the old mill at Ramelton. This achievement of his enterprise will be of permanent benefit to all that region.* John and William Laws have just deeded to our pastor two hundred acres of land on the southern branch of Forked Neck. Thus the founder of our church roots himself more firmly to the Virginia soil.

Our pastor is preparing for his European trip. On the 1st of August he executes and puts upon record a power of attorney to his wife, Naomi and her cousin John Parker, for the management of both his own property and the Custis estate. It would be strange if there were not a longing now and then in this warm heart for a sight of the familiar scenes and the loved faces over the sea. Who can tell how often during his journeyings of the last twenty years our Paul has yearned "toward his brethren, his kinsmen according to the flesh"?

Had our minister embarked according to expectation, he might have encountered at sea that terrific tempest which in November sweeps the British Isles with consternation and strews their shores with wrecks. "Not to be paralleled," says Evelyn, "with anything happening in our age." To foreign courts Marlborough speaks of the storm as a grievous national calamity.†

But Mr. Makemie would have found a storm scarcely less violent raging in the political and ecclesiastical world. The nations of Europe are marshaling for war. In the Cevennes young Cavalier and his heroic Camisards are winning immortal renown—sharp thorns in

* The Assawaman and Rehoboth mills are still running (1884).

† Knight, v. 126. So with allusions following.

the side of the arch-persecutor of France at such a time.   In Scotland there is strong feeling against the English government.   Queen Anne is becoming more unpopular with the Presbyterians.   While their General Assembly has been asserting its privileges and reminding the queen that the Reformation from Popery was effected by Presbyters, that Prelacy has always been an intolerable grievance, and that Presbyterianism henceforth must rule, the Assembly has been suddenly dissolved in the name of Her Majesty.   The prelatic party recklessly show their delight, parade the former rancor, try to avoid the oath of allegiance and begin again the game of intrusion into our churches. Scotch spirit is aroused.   Parliament takes up the matter, passes an act in defence of Presbyterianism in the very words for which the Assembly was dissolved, and proceeds to guard more strenuously the independence of kingdom and Church against outside dictation.   This is an eloquent hint to the queen and her advisers.*

In his native kingdom our pastor would have met the increasing encroachments of Prelacy.   Bishop King—now made Archbishop of Dublin—will have greater power for evil.   This man, who pronounced the patriotic defence of Londonderry rank rebellion, advocated passive obedience and warmly welcomed James to Dublin, now has the effrontery to charge the Presbyterians with Jacobitism ! †

There has been even greater excitement in England. On the question of Occasional Conformity, upon which they were beaten before, the High Churchmen are again wild.   While the country moves forward into

---

* Hetherington, *in loco*.   † Reid, ii. 498, etc

a tremendous war, these factionists rend and tear the nation in the rear. Of the outrageous turmoil Jonathan Swift writes in caustic humor:

> "It was so universal that I observed the dogs in the streets much more contumelious and quarrelsome than usual; and the very night before the Bill went up, a committee of Whig and Tory cats had a very warm and loud debate upon the roof of our house. But why should we wonder at that, when the very ladies are split asunder into High Church and Low, and out of zeal for religion have hardly time to say their prayers?"

If during these hot conflicts our minister had gone down into Lincolnshire, to the rectory of Epworth, he would have found upon the bosom of Samuel and Susanna Wesley a great-grandson of one of the ejected ministers of 1662; and the name of the new-born babe is John Wesley.

But Mr. Makemie will not this year encounter the storms of Europe nor listen to the quarrels of Dean Swift's dogs and cats. Before he can start, his mother-in-law begins to decline, and before winter the old lady has parted from all her finery and is no more. She was not Naomi's own mother, but came into the family when Naomi was only ten years old. Mr. Anderson had requested "Son Makemie" and Naomi to be "kind and assisting" to the aged widow, and in her feebleness of mind and body their kindness was needed.

In her nuncupative will, proved in court in November, Mrs. Anderson bequeaths all her wearing-apparel and other property to be divided between Betty Makemie and Betty Taylor, the two young cousins Her own blood-kin are passed over for the sake of her husband's grandchildren About this there has been much talk.   In her inventory made in December we find ten gold rings, gold buckles, silver clasps, amber necklaces, nine hoods, nine headdresses, six caps and six night-caps; eleven gowns, some of them of very rich silk and costly; twenty-two petticoats, a number of these of expensive silk and lace; twenty-seven forehead cloths, six waistcoats, eighteen aprons, eight pairs of ruffles, besides bodices, scarfs, stomachers, gloves, pinners, stockings, handkerchiefs and a parcel of paint   The two Bettys will be well clad for some time to come   They do not need the paint!

This brings Mr. Makemie an increase of legal business.   On the 8th of December he petitions for an appraisement of Mrs Anderson's property, and also of that of Mr. Custis   No possibility is to be left by which the Argus-eyes of Madam Tabitha can find him tripping   On the 17th he and Elias Taylor petition for administration on Mrs Anderson's estate

Mrs Anderson sleeps by the side of her husband in the family burying-ground, near the homestead, not far from the little serpentine creek which half a mile away flows into Pocomoke Sound.   This same year Priscilla Layfield becomes a widow and another justice of our court is interred near Colonel Stevens on the Rehoboth plantation   These ought to be famous graveyards in the far-away days to come. Speaking of the time when all these tombs must open again, Mr. Makemie says:

" It will not be inquired, What faith you professed; What persuasion and opinion you were of; To what Society did you belong? But, What have you done? What lives have you led? Were they ordered aright according to God's will?" *

* New York sermon.

CHAPTER XXV.

A. D. 1704.

"From many Years' Experience in America, and particularly in Virginia and Maryland."—MAKEMIE.

ON crossing the ferry you will notice that all the roads converging thither are indicated by three notches, at equal distances from one another, upon the trees along the highway. Turning toward the court-house at Dividing Creek, you will find the trees on both sides of the road marked with two notches near together and another notch at a wider interval. Roads to parish churches are marked by a slip on the sides of the trees, near the ground. All this is prescribed by provincial statute. No municipal law points the worshiper to Presbyterian churches, but the divine law is clear enough, and we find our way without help from Annapolis.*

The Legislature has also established our legal rate of interest at six per cent. With tobacco and pork for currency, we must calculate our interest upon the sotweed and swines' flesh. Mr. Makemie, urging to other forms of enterprise, writes:

"We are, both in ourselves and by increasing the number of our servants and slaves, so growing a people, that our planting, or tobacco-trade, of Virginia and Maryland is overdone, and all Markets cannot consume the quantity; so that tobacco-trade

* Enactments of Assembly of 1704 So, too, the following

seems to be ruined both as to the planter, purchaser, adventurer and factor   Therefore an absolute necessity for falling off the excessive part of tobacco-making and falling upon something else.   Our present war is such a bar to trade , and if we should enjoy a Peace, we know not how soon we may have another war more injurious " *

The legal toll at the mills is set at one-sixth for Indian corn and one-eighth for wheat.   So runs the hopper at Rehoboth.   Again our minister protests against the bad management by which both the coin and the wheat are carried off:

" Our neighbors drain from us the marrow of our estates , for Carolina, Barbadoes, Pennsylvania, New York and New England carry from us the little scattered coin we have among us   They buy up our old iron, brass, copper, pewter, hides and tallow, which we often want and might use ourselves.   They carry away our wheat and return it again to us in bread and flour, and make us pay for transporting, grinding, bolting and baking.   But, which is worst of all, they prey upon that little money we have in England by purchasing bills of exchange." †

On Irish servants the toll is higher than on corn or wheat, being one pound sterling per poll on every Papist immigrant.   The Assembly increases its rigor against the Catholics.   A fine of fifty pounds and imprisonment for six months have been imposed upon any

" Popish Bishop, Priest or Jesuit who shall baptize any child or children other than such who have Popish parents ; or shall say mass, or exercise the functions of a Popish Bishop or Priest within this province ; or shall endeavor to persuade any of her Majesty's liege people of this province to embrace and be reconciled to the Church of Rome."

After being once convicted, if any Popish bishop, priest or Jesuit shall say mass or exercise any function

* *Plain and Friendly Perswasive.*   † *Ibid.*

of a priest within the province, or if any persons professing to be of that Church shall keep school or take
upon themselves the education, government or boarding
of youth at any place in the province, all such shall, on
conviction, be sent to England to endure the penalties
there in force against that Church. Worse still, if any
child of Popish parents claims to be a Protestant, the
law compels the parents to make separate provision
for the support of the child.* Although this is but
a mild return for the persecutions of Rome, it does
not seem to me right. My father says boldly:

" It is an odious law. It puts a stain upon Maryland. Where
Popery tolerated Prelacy, Prelacy persecutes Popery. It is impossible to conceive of a statute more iniquitous than one that
offers a premium for the disobedience and hypocrisy of an un-
filial child." †

The injustice of the laws against the Papists is
somewhat mitigated by permission given the priests
to officiate in private families of their own communion.
They are taking advantage of this provision by building little chapels as additions to private dwellings.

This year the State-House burns down—not much
matter if the zeal of the Assembly is to be chiefly expended in pampering the Establishment and oppressing those who are out of its pale. It seems to be a
year of fires. At Williamsburg the College of William
and Mary, where the Virginia Assembly has been holding its sessions, has also been burnt.

As my father's accountant, let me record some of
the prices now paid in the line of family expenses:
Beef, one halfpenny per pound; making a coat, three

* Bacon's *Laws of Maryland 1704*, ch xcv.
† Hawks's *Maryland*, p 126.

shillings six pence; fifteen gallons of cider at one-half bushel of Indian meal per gallon. At the little wigwam in the pines, as in most of the families, we use cider instead of coffee and tea. This reminds me of the hero of the *Sot-Weed Factor:*

> " Presently amongst the rest
> He placed his unknown English Guest,
> Who found them drinking for a whet
> A Cask of Syder on the Fret,
> Till Supper came upon the Table,
> On which I fed whilst I was able
> So after hearty Entertainment
> Of Drink and Victuals without Payment;
> For Planters' Tables, you must know,
> Are free for all that come or go;
> While Pone and Milk, with Mush well-stored,
> In Wooden Dishes graced the board;
> With Hominy and Syder-pap *
> (Which scarce a hungry dog would lap)
> Well-stuffed with Fat from Bacon fried,
> Or with Mollossus dulcified "

Now comes along Mr. Makemie's sloop Tabitha, and we sell our pork at two pence per pound, our corn at twenty pence per bushel, our wheat at fifty pence; and we lay in a supply of sugar—a great luxury—at nine pence per pound.†

This being Saturday, and the Tabitha being on her down-trip, William, I and the little Francis are taken on board with the promise of hearing a Virginia sermon to-morrow. Every sermon is precious now, for Mr. Makemie is soon to depart upon his Transatlantic trip. On the 30th of May he executed a power of

* Food made of small hominy and cider.

† Prices from Somerset records—without mention of Makemie, however.

24

attorney to his wife and Andrew Hamilton and James
Kemp for the management of all his business, including that of the Custis estate and the care of the Custis children. "Being bound in a designed voyage for
Europe," says the recorded document. The cry for
laborers is loud around us, and, notwithstanding his
disappointment last year, his purpose remains un-
changed.

Beating down the placid Pocomoke sails the Tabitha, her wings filled with the breezes of June. Sparkling, dashing, cheerily saluting, the quick kingfisher
plies his vocation along our way, while the hovering
fish-hawk wages his warfare against the finny tribe.
The Jenkinses wave their handkerchiefs to their minister's sloop as she passes, and the Whites—to whom
Colonel Stevens gave his Cedar Hall plantation—hail
us presently from the other side. As we leave the shell-
banks of the natives upon the right and wind out to
the sound, the canoes of the Maryland Indians, headed by Morumsco James, and the canoes of the Accomack tribe, headed by Matahocka, are taking oysters
to the right and the left (66). These rival claimants
are the probable forerunners of other contestants in
the future.

The Tabitha turns away from the open sea into the
mouth of Houlston's Creek, seeming to know the way
home. To the right stands the two-storied house
covered with cypress shingles. In the green yard
which stretches down to the shore, his brown hair
made golden by the rays of the setting sun, sits our
pastor thinking of his Sabbath sermon and watching
the play of his two little girls upon the grass at his
feet. The second pet, Baby Anne, is but a wee one,

named for the pioneer's favorite sister, whom he is expecting soon to see in the home at Ramelton. Betty, the older, very dignified in her silk dress inherited from the wardrobe of Madam Anderson, is anxious to teach the baby an answer from page twelve of her father's Catechism—

"God in turning or calling sinners unto himself, does convince them of sin and misery, enlighten their minds with the knowledge of Christ, renews their will"

—but the teacher herself breaks down and has to begin it all again. The wide ocean will soon be rolling between the father and his little daughters.

Mr. Makemie welcomes us in his own hospitable way, and seems delighted with the cargo of Presbyterian guests which the Tabitha has brought him. We are ushered into the hall-chamber.* It has its old comfortable look—kept very nearly as left by Mr. Anderson, who was anxious that this should remain the memorial family mansion. There are the old olive chest of drawers and the two cabinets, also a chest and trunk and a small iron hearth with a pair of brass andirons, a pair of firedogs and one brass shovel and tongs; seven chairs, a bed nicely furnished, and a matting in front of it. Otherwise the floor is uncarpeted, according to our custom. In the proper receptacles are seventeen pieces of earthenware, eleven pairs of sheets, over three dozen napkins, six damask towels and ten tablecloths, damask, diaper and huckaback. Naomi gave me a look into these abundant supplies. The two windows are curtained. Over the table hangs a looking-glass; in another place are two statuettes, and

* Names of rooms and their furniture taken from inventory in the Accomack records.

on the wall is a picture of King William and Queen Mary. Through their royal influence alone is our minister able under sanctions of law to preach on his land and in his own dwelling-house. I see no portraits of the Stuarts

Soon Naomi invites us out to supper. In this dining-room are three oval tables, one of them quite large, also a square one. There are thirteen cane chairs, a couch and a chest of drawers. In sight are a punch-bowl, a syllabub-pot, a crewet, two teapots, a case of agate knives and spoons, two tea-servers, a dozen cups and a case of bottles; also, on the wall, a looking-glass, three small pictures and four maps Here, too, are a watch and a fiddle with its case. Standing about the table are Indian Peter and the negro slaves Old Dollar and Young Hannah. One of these plies the brush to keep the flies and the mosquitoes away. At the appointed time another slave—Vulcan—comes from his fires of hickory, and brings the oysters roasted in their shells. We feast also upon West India dainties—contributions from Barbadoes to the larder of our Presbyterian missionary, merchant and navigator.

After supper we sit cozily in what is known as " Mrs. Makemie's room " until the hour of retiring. Here are another olive chest of drawers, two sealskin trunks, a cupboard and a bed furnished and curtained. On the windows are green curtains, and on the floor are two rugs, one green, the other speckled. For some time green has been the prevailing color in the fashions of the day This room is the sacred inner enclosure of the preacher's home. Here he plans his work for America, and here he rests from his long absences. Wife and little ones gathered about him, he devises the eternal elevation of the wives and children of a future empire How plain the family-room!

In these Scotch-Irish families the Sabbath seems to begin before Saturday is done. To-night we all feel that the holy day is at hand. Religious themes are the subject of conversation, mind and heart turned toward God. In the moonlight a mocking-bird is singing in the trees, full of the coming dawn. I am glad to hear William asking Mr. Makemie about the difference between the Quaker doctrines of perfection and the presence of Christ within his people, and the true Scripture doctrine He answers:

"All of us firmly believe that unless the Spirit of Christ be in us we are none of his, and Christ is in us except we be reprobate, and he dwells in us believers. But from Paul's words it is by faith—Ephes. iii 17, as I declared and that fully from the text, Col. i. 27, Christ in you the hope of glory. It is no contradiction to affirm and believe that God hath called sinners out of sin unto grace, yet at the same time to feel and assert that all have remaining sin in them ; for it is no hard matter to distinguish betwixt sinners being under the power, dominion and slavery or drudgery of sin, and a sinner's having some relicts and remainders of sin and corruption in them, whereby even in believers there is a constant and spiritual warfare raised in the believing soul. Whereas formerly the strong man kept the house, the Apostle gives us this distinction—Sin shall not have dominion over you, you are not under law but under grace And the same Apostle, even after conversion, complains of his own sinfully-wretched corruption and at the same time triumphs in the victory, for in the next breath he cries, Thanks be to God who has given us the victory. If sin in some measure be not cotemporary with saving grace or conversion, what must become of Quakers' universal, sufficient and saving grace ? And all the multitudes of them I have ever seen must according to their own opinion be void of conversion, grace, and justification, for sin has been easily discernible in all; neither did ever any of them produce one instance of this absolute perfection." *

* Answer to Keith.

William remarked with a smile,

"This is the crucial test for perfectionists of every age."

We learn that Mr. Makemie's old Quaker opponent —now the redoubtable prelatic champion—is just going back to Europe. For three years Keith has been the sturdiest and most successful advocate Episcopacy has ever had in America, doing more to plant the Church of England to the north of us than any other man. If while yet a Quaker enthusiast he had the "immediate, extraordinary and apostolic call," which he boasted in this very house, and if at that time he had attained to perfection, what is the present type of call and perfection, now that he is sixty-six years old and in another apostolic succession?

After worship, with the usual catechising, we retire to the guest-chamber. Here are two beds, neatly furnished with bolsters, pillows, a linen bedspread and a suit of linen curtains. There are also a pair of brass dogs and a pair of brass andirons. On the wall hangs a looking-glass. There are no carpets anywhere, but all is snug and tidy.

I may as well speak now of the rest of the house. Besides that which has already been described, there is also what is called the "green chamber," with furnished bed and a looking-glass. They have, too, a garret with two beds—one quite old—a trunk, eleven horn-hafted knives, a mat, fifty feet of glass, whole and broken, a jug and a lantern, eleven shoe-lasts, a small case of shoemakers' tools, and twenty hogsheads of tobacco.

Running back of the house is a large shed-room, among whose varied contents I noted the following: a small physic-case, a box of surgeons' instruments, an old warming-pan, two chafing-dishes, four brass candlesticks, three guns, a bed all furnished, one bellmetal mortar, four bolting-cloths, two gauging-rods, a scimeter, an old barbers' case with three razors, a little looking-glass and basin, a brass sundial, two burning-glasses and a tinder-box, a half-hour glass, a ship's compass, pewter dishes and plates, spinningwheels and a loom and weavers' gears, and many more articles which I lack space to mention.

Near by is the store, the largest for many miles, with its ample supplies of groceries and hardware and a few drygoods.

Nor must I forget the library of eight hundred and ninety-six volumes—English, Latin, Greek and Hebrew, theological, miscellaneous and law-books—all in good condition, besides a lot of old volumes with broken backs or in paper binding. This is a great change since 1685, when as a lonely wanderer in Maryland, Virginia and the Carolinas he had to borrow books from Increase Mather, all the way from Boston, which were frequently lost in the transmission.

Since 1699 this house has been recorded as a licensed place of public worship under the Toleration Act of the king and the queen whose portraits look down from the wall in the hall-chamber upon the assembled congregation. Hither come the Taylors, Hamiltons, Littletons, Brittinghams, Parkers, Fookses, Custises, Poulsons, Middletons, Hopes, Sanfords, Jollies, Kemps, Robinsons, Barrets, Boggses, Wises, Corbins, and others of Mr. Makemie's friends and neighbors; for this brave Dissenter has many warm friends even in the Established Church.

Seated apart, with white eyes and sable faces, is another portion of the audience, men and women and children, waiting to hear the gospel from the lips of their honored master—Dollar, Scipio, Vulcan, Frank, Toby, Harry, Jack the Cripple, Sambo, Dick, Sandy, Old Jack, Old Nan, Young Nan, Tobia, Betty, Guy, Johnny, Mollie, Minger, Robert, Rose, Peggy, Kate, Anne, Old Hannah, Young Hannah, Dorcas, Sarah, George, Adam, Sue, Robin and Benoni.* These thirty-three slaves, with others from adjoining plantations, form an interesting congregation to be trained for the heavenly Master. Nor are faces of the aborigines wanting to remind us in whose land we are worshiping the God of the whole earth.

It is sad to think of the unfortunate illustrations of Christianity afforded the red and the black races by its professed adherents. Mr. Makemie well says:

" How natural it is for apostate man to follow the multitude to do evil! 'Evil communications corrupt good manners.' Was it not from repeated evil examples that Joseph learned to swear by the life of Pharaoh? It is a hard thing to lead righteous lives in the midst of multiplied and repeated evil precedents, as it is to touch pitch and not be defiled therewith, or to put coals into our bosoms and not be burnt therewith. Lot found it no easy matter to maintain his righteousness in the midst of an unrighteous Sodom. Therefore when rulers and magistrates give evil example, who by their office and power should be a terror only to evil doers, it is no wonder to see people trace their evil steps. When such as the leaders and guides of souls go astray, well may the flock wander. When parents and masters cast daily an evil copy, must it not affect or rather infect their children and servants?" †

In the evening we see Elizabeth, with Baby Anne in

* These names are from the inventory on the Accomack records.
† New York sermon.

her arms, teaching their father's Catechism to the little dark Tobies, Robins, Adams, Peggies, Rosies and Amies. Slavery was introduced into Virginia eighty-five years ago, a Dutch man-of-war selling twenty negroes to the settlers at Jamestown in 1619. Now there are about sixteen thousand in the colony. The first in Maryland was brought over by Father White, the Jesuit, in 1635—a mulatto named Francisco. They now number four thousand four hundred and seventy-five. Few hesitate to buy these pagans. Even William Penn is a slaveholder.

We return home, and our pastor is seen at Rehoboth no more. Mr. Samuel Davis, at Lewes, where he has gone into business, and Mr. John Wilson, at New Castle, where he has preached many years, are the only Presbyterian ministers left on the Peninsula. Mr. Andrews and his small flock in Philadelphia have begun to build a little church on Market street, between Second and Third. Lord Cornbury is still trying to force Episcopacy upon the Dissenters of Long Island. The Rev. John Thomas, just transferred thither from Philadelphia, writes:

" The country is exceedingly attached to a Dissenting ministry, and were it not for His Excellency my Lord Cornbury's most favorable countenance to us, we might expect the severest entertainment here. I have scarcely a man in the parish real and steady to the interest and promotion of the church any further than they aim at the favor or dread the displeasure of his Lordship. The people are all stiff Dissenters ; not above three church-people in the whole parish [Hempstead]. If it had not been for the countenance and support of Lord Cornbury and his government, it would have been impossible to have settled a church on the island."*

Thus the fugitive debtor and debauchee is lauded as

* Webster, p. 87.

the patron of Prelacy, and still endeavors to thrust it down the throats of an unwilling people.

In our own county the Rev. Alexander Adams has just taken charge of Stepney Parish.* We are not very pleasantly impressed.

The spring brought us a new governor in the person of John Seymour, who seems not so much disposed as were some of his predecessors to make the Episcopal Church the pet of the government. Before Mr. Seymour left England, Dr. Bray, late commissary, attempted to obtain possession of him, introducing a Rev. Archdeacon Hewetson of Ireland, and seeking to secure for the latter, as commissary, the additional office of the judgeship in testamentary cases with a salary of three thousand pounds. A handsome endowment indeed of wealth and dignity! The governor, positively refused, and Dr. Bray talks bitterly of rude treatment to himself and to the disappointed archdeacon.† So the pampered Church is ever grasping.

Failing in his modest demand upon the new governor, Dr. Bray writes to the speaker of our Assembly, urging that the Legislature set apart one of the best parishes for a suffragan, to be appointed by the Bishop of London, and asking that they build a house on it and stock the glebe with twenty cattle, twenty hogs and ten negroes! To make the ecclesiastic as independent in his palace as possible, he would put this high dignitary over on our Eastern Shore with the broad bay flowing between him and the governor. Seymour declares that he will have no commissary in

* Neill's *Terra Mariæ*, p. 190.
† Bishop Hawks, p. 124; Neill's *Founders of Maryland*, p. 174.

the province.   By this time he has seen enough of the character of the Maryland clergy to put him wholly out of patience with them.   Their morals grow worse and worse, the efforts made by Dr Bray in the Visitation of the year 1700 having proved utterly abortive, and that failure having apparently instigated to more brazen corruptions.   "A Maryland parson" is becoming a term of humiliating reproach—a synonym for extreme insolence and immorality.*

My twelve-year-old friend of 1680, now thirty-six, is getting to be quite a business-woman   Acting under power of attorney given by her husband, Naomi has already had one case in court, being sued on the 4th of December by John Custis for twenty-three pounds three shillings ninepence.   Mrs Makemie and Mr. James Kemp confess judgment, and will recover the amount from John Haskins, by whom the debt is really owed.

We think of Mr. Makemie tossing upon the Atlantic's billows.   The dangers on the sea from privateers and from pirates are many and constant   Kidd is in his grave, but the war-ships and the prisons of France are scarce less terrible.   Occasionally we receive a copy of the Boston *News Letter*, the pioneer newspaper of America, first issued on the 24th of April this year.†   Martha laughs at me for expecting to get any news of Mr. Makemie from the two double-columned pages in this twelve-by-eight-inch journal.

* The author would hesitate to assert these things were it not for such authorities as Bishop Meade and Dr. Hawks of the Episcopal Church.

† Edited by John Campbell—a Scotchman, of course; printed by B. Green; and sold by Nicholas Boom at his shop "near the old meeting-house."

But our pastor has escaped the perils of the deep, and is again upon his native shores. Eventful years have passed since last he trod the turf of the Green Isle. Most of the ministers he once knew in the Presbytery of Laggan are dead or in Scotland. Many of his friends fell at the Break of Killileagh and at Londonderry. Of his immediate family and his boyhood's companions, not a few suffered from the ravages of the Duke of Berwick around Ramullan.

But the hills of Donegal are the same, and the vales of the Laggan, and the shadowy waters of Lough Swilly, and the playgrounds of his youth near Ramelton. Brothers John and Robert and sister Anne are yet alive to welcome him back and tell of many incidents that have occurred since he sailed away to Maryland. He can take on his knees his little nephews—both called Francis for his sake—and speak to wondering ears of the howls of the American wolf and the whoop of the equally savage Indian.

It is not strange that Mr. Makemie should seek out the survivers of the Presbytery which ordained him in solemn secrecy. They will be glad to hear of the labors of the young missionary—not so young now—whom more than a score of years ago they sent forth to the unsolved problems of the mysterious continent. How he will enjoy the long communion seasons, beginning as early as seven o'clock in the morning and running through seven or ten tables until late in the afternoon! * They will not seem long to him.

Our pastor becomes an eye-witness of the base ingratitude of Prelacy and the government toward the Presbyterianism which stood in the breach against the

* Reid, ii 496. Also for facts following.

Stuart and Popery and secured the kingdom to William and to Protestantism. At Lifford he may see the public excommunication by ecclesiastical courts of members of our Church who have been married by our own ministers, and who refuse to confess themselves guilty of adultery. He beholds the operation of the infamous sacramental test, imposed this year to drive Dissenters from all offices of public trust and emolument, no one being permitted to hold any position, civil or military, under appointment of the sovereign, without taking within three months the consecrated bread and wine kneeling at the chancel in some parish church. In the historic city of Londonderry, illustrious with their valor, ten out of twelve aldermen and fourteen out of twenty-four burgesses are ignominiously turned out of their places.

As successors to these ousted officers, and all over Ulster, Mr. Makemie sees promoted to honor those whom De Foe well describes as "men of little estates, youths, newcomers and clergymen, having nothing to recommend them to the dignity of magistrates but their going to church."

If some indignation stirs our minister's bosom, it need be no marvel, when he remembers the stories of Presbyterian prowess that came to him over the sea during the Revolution days.

But the woodbine of Donegal still blooms about his way, the waves of Lough Swilly still sparkle on toward the ocean, and beyond the great Atlantic are Naomi and the children and the church which he has planted and for whose prosperity he prays. We can imagine his zeal to discover fit helpers for the vast Western work, his efforts to arouse new missionary spirit in the Presbyteries, his endeavors to enlist the young ministry to the call of America and of God.

The Dissenters of London are in better condition to aid, and to them also he applies. He finds the nation fired with Marlborough's unparalleled campaign upon the Danube, and with the magnificent victory of Blenheim on the 13th of August. On the 7th of September comes the enthusiastic thanksgiving, with bonfires and great rejoicings and Te Deums in the churches. In Spain, Gibraltar is taken by the English, though they know not yet the full value of the capture. If Mr. Makemie's patriotism is thrilled by these grand events, his contempt must be no less moved by the poorly-disguised regrets of the Jacobite High Churchmen at the success of British arms over Louis. In the very midst of the national joy, these factionists continue their agitations against Occasional Conformity and try to tack on their favorite measure to a money-bill necessary for the prosecution of the war. The country is becoming disgusted with "the Tackers," as they are called, and the great duke reaches home in time to vote against their miserable schemes.*

While these noisy events occupy the public mind, Science gains her own quiet victories in the retired study of her industrious votary. In the bookstores, and published this year, our observant pastor will notice a new book of no little fame—*The Optics* of Mr. Isaac Newton.

Meanwhile, Mr. Makemie never loses sight of the mission which has taken him to Europe, for in its prosecution he knows that he works for a nobler cause than that which enlists the diplomacy and the generalship of Marlborough or the genius of Newton.

* Knight, vol v , *in loco.*

CHAPTER XXVI.

A. D. 1705.

"Tyed up from exeicising their Ministry without License."—
MAKEMIE.

I OVERHEAR Matchacoopah giving our little Francis Makemie a lesson in the natural history of Maryland in the language of the Nanticokes.

"What is the word for 'bird'?" asks the child.

"*Pipseeque*," answers the Indian.

"'Eagle'?"

"*Ah-whap-pawn-top.*"

"'Hawk'?"

"*Mah-squallen.*"

"'Owl'?"

"*Quoo-waant.*"

"'Turkey'?"

"*Pah-quun.*"

"'Wild goose'?"

"*Qua-haw-quunt.*"

The child notices how frequently the cry of the birds is imitated in the names given them in the Nanticoke dialect. The lesson proceeds:

"'Raven'?"

"*Uek-quack.*"

"'Crow'?"

"*Kuh-hos.*"

"'Duck'?"

383

" *Quah-quamps.*'
" ' Blackbird ' ? "
" *Husquinook.*"
" ' Crane ' ? "
"*Ah-seeque.*"
" ' Dove ' ? "
"*Wee-tah-tomps.*"
" ' Pigeon ' ? "
" *Not-si-mini-suk.*"
" ' Pheasant ' ? "
" *Uh-quas-capitz.*"
" ' Partridge ' ? "
" *Kittycawndipqua.*"
" ' Buzzard ' ? "
" *Moh-waas.*"
" ' Mocking-bird ' ? "
" *Ahmittonqha.*"
" ' Red-bird ' ? "
" *Pish-quip-eeps.*"
" What is your word for ' tree ' ? "
" *Pelnieque,*" replies the teacher.
" ' Pine ' ? "
" *Quaat.*"
" ' Cedar ' ? "
" *Weens-qua-a-quah.*"
" ' Poplar ' ? "
" *Wee-saa-quak.*"
" ' Ash ' ? "
" *Paw-kawque.*"
" ' Beech ' ? "
" *Pah-scan-e-mintz.*"
" ' Maple ' ? "
"*Waw-see-ke-me.*"

"Oak'?"
" *Wee-seek-e-mintz.*"
"'Chestnut'?"
" *Eh-qua-mintz.*"
"'Hickory'?"
"*Psee-cun.*"
"'Walnut'?"
"*Ah-sin-n-mintz.*"
"'Locust'?"
" *Kla-one-nahq.*"
"'Mulberry'?"
" *Whee-in-quack.*"
"A vine?"
" *Mal-law-co-min-i-mintz.*"
" What is the word for ' hill'?"
" *Lemuck-quickse.*"
"'Valley'?'
" *Qualliquaukimuck.*"
"'River'?"
" *Pamptuckqua.*"
"'Creek'?"
" *Pamptuckquaskque.*"
"A spring?"
" *Moo-nip-pque.*"
"'Pond'?"
" *Nippip.*"
"The sea?"
" *Mauk-nippint.*"

The last name seems to remind the Indian of one far beyond the great waters, and he interprets the feelings of us all:

" Lonely looks the wigwam in the pines. Lonely is the house of Mann-itt at Rehoboth, The good talker

25

of the palefaces has gone over *mauk-nippint*, and Pocomoke is in *dah-qua-a-nee* (sorrow)."

Matchacoopah speaks the truth We prepare to build the new church on Mr. Makemie's lots, but the time of his absence seems long. Will he succeed in securing other preachers? or, when he shall wear out and die, must the Presbyterian ·cause die with him? We are taxed to support the Rev George Trotter of Somerset Parish, Rev. Robert Keith of Coventry, and Rev. Alexander Adams of Stepney; but they do not give us the gospel for which our soul thirsts. I think that the latter two clergymen will prove specimen " Maryland parsons " and do all they can to obstruct the work of our church.

From *Truths in a True Light* I have just been reading Mr. Makemie's strictures upon defects of administration in the Anglican Church. He says :

"We dissent from the Discipline and Censures of the Church of England , and, though they are without all church-discipline and censure in every plantation of America, yet, even as it is managed in England, many of your own sons dislike it as well as we. Especially in these particulars :

" 1 Its absoluteness ; being exercised by a sole authority in the breast of a particular Diocesan, acting all in his own name, without commission or warrant from any other. Sir Francis Bacon, who was highly for the Church of England, tells us the Bishop gives orders alone, excommunicates alone, and affirms it to be without example in all good government ; for kings and monarchs have their counsellors ; the courts of King's Bench, Common Pleas and Exchequer, have many Judges ; and the Chancellor hath the assistance of twelve Masters of Chancery. I am assured that the Scripture warrant is directed to a *number ;* ' *Dic Ecclesiæ,*' tell the church

" 2. The authority and power of discipline is generally managed by delegation or deputation of lay-persons, as Chancellors, Officials, Registers, Sumners, Canonicals, etc , choosing such as helps in government rather than the clergy: which the Lord

Verulam affirms to be contrary to all rules of good government, for offices of confidence and skill cannot be exercised by deputies. The confidence and trust being personal and inherent cannot be transposed to an ignorant and unqualified lay-person more than such can be deputed to preach the Word and administer the sacraments.

" 3. The English church-discipline is turned into a mere money-matter and the use of Christ's keys is made mercenary, punishing the purses and not afflicting the consciences of the delinquents; as a great man of the church, in a sermon preached at one of the Universities, told them—*Claves Christi pulsant erumenas, non verberant conscientias.* And Hickringale assures us from his certain knowledge that guineas will procure absolution from Doctors Commons without any confession or show of repentance; yea, without a sight of the guilty party. A more bare-faced practice than that of the Romish churches who always use confession and penance for a cloak."

If such are the imperfections of discipline at the fountain-head, it may be imagined what are the practices where there is no discipline at all.

Beverly's *History and Present State of Virginia*, published this year, says of the Dissenters in that province:

" They have no more than five conventicles amongst them; namely, three small meetings of Quakers and two of Presbyterians. 'Tis observed that those counties where the Presbyterian meetings are, produce very mean tobacco and, for that reason, can't get an orthodox minister to stay amongst them."

Does Mr. Beverly refer to Accomack? If so, he evidently is not aware that the Rev. Thomas Teackle preached on the Eastern Shore for thirty-nine years —a longer period than any other " orthodox " clergyman in the colony. Nor does he seem to know of the large estates there owned by both the " orthodox " Teackle and the Dissenter Makemie. Or does the new historian speak only of the " conventicles " in Princess Anne county supplied by Rev. Josias Mackie? On one point he is certainly posted—the ambition of the clergy to secure parishes where their salary of sixteen thousand pounds of tobacco per annum shall be of the very best quality!

In the mean while, our minister watches for the temporal advancement of the sister-provinces as well as for their spiritual good. This year he publishes in England a little book with the following title: *A Plain and Friendly Perswasive to the Inhabitants of Virginia and Maryland for Promoting Towns and Cohabitation. By a Well-Wisher to both Governments. London. Printed by John Humphreys, in Bartholomew Lane. 1705.** Absent in body, his heart is still in America.

In the preamble to an act passed by the Virginia Assembly in 1699 providing for a revisal of the laws, the province is styled "His Majestie's ancient and great colony and dominion." My father thinks this the first official record of the term "Ancient Dominion." One of the first instances of its use in all literature is in the inscription this year of Mr. Makemie's little book: "Dedicated to his excellency Major Edward Nott, Her Majesty's Governor of the Ancient Dominion of Virginia."

This new governor is a decided improvement upon the immoral, irascible, lovesick Nicholson, now withdrawn. The latter "true son, or rather, nursing-father of the church of England in America," as he has been called by the Philadelphia clergyman Talbot,† has of late been involved in constant strife with Commissary Blair and the vestries, and has played the tyrant as despotically toward his Church as toward his lady-love Miss Burwell. The mild character of the

---

* One copy extant, in the library at Harvard.
† Anderson's *Colonial Church*, ii. 236

present incumbent is an encouraging contrast. Mr.
Makemie thus gracefully addresses the new governor.

"May it please your excellency, There is nothing more seasonable for allaying the heats and curing the animosities both in
the ecclesiastical and political body of the present constitution of
Virginia (whereby the conduct of public affairs there has been
greatly retarded of late and a great deal of time and many opportunities lost of advancing and improving a noble country)
than a new Governor invested with so large a stock of temper
and unbiased interest as your Excellency, by an universal character, is represented to be.

"As Queen Elizabeth was the original discoverer and founder
of this ancient and noble colony of Virginia, from whom it de-
rives its name; so it is to be hoped that our present Majesty will
be the founder of ports, towns and cohabitation, by recommending the same to your Excellency's care and conduct in promoting
that which will be the glory and only improvement of that country, and, if accomplished, will be a perpetual monument to the
praise of your Excellency, in conquering all such difficulties as
have been too mighty for former governors, whose attempts of
this nature have proved ineffectual and abortive.

"As our Plantations abroad, and especially Virginia, have long
groaned under perhaps a worse character than it now deserves,
which created no small prejudice and aversion in the breasts of
many against transportation to those colonies; so nothing would
more effectually wipe off such scandalous imputations than by
promoting and encouraging education and virtue, checking and
discountenancing vice or immorality in all, from the highest to
the lowest, by the example of a severe and virtuous conversation
in Governors and councillors, and promoting a reformation of
manners, in putting all our penal laws in due execution, encouraging the strictest justice in all our Judicatories, and in
propagating the true knowledge of the Christian religion to
all pagans, whether Indians or Negroes; all which has been
lamentably neglected, even by such as have pretended to the
highest pitch of zeal.

"Your Excellency has a fair opportunity put into your hands
for laying such obligations on the inhabitants of Virginia as they
have not yet had experience of, and advancing the honor and
interest of our present Sovereign, and laying a lasting foundation
for promoting and facilitating the trade of England to that colony

and giving a copy to all our neighbor Plantations. And that this may be the real effect of your Excellency's government, is and shall be the unfeigned desire and prayer of—Your most humble and most obedient servant."

I quote this dedication entire to show how Mr. Makemie is able to use a secular theme for advancing the honor of his Master. Managing very skillfully to get the ear of governor and queen, while pressing the direct purpose of a temporal measure, he does not forget to magnify his office as a minister of truth and righteousness.

The attempts heretofore made in Virginia and Maryland to legislate towns into existence have mostly failed. Mr. Makemie speaks of "the beginnings of towns at Williamsburg, Hampton and Norfolk," and tells of some little commerce, "particularly in Norfolk town, at Elizabeth River, who carry on a small trade with the whole bay." Our minister owns a house and lot down there, and Mr. Mackie, our other Scotch-Irish minister-merchant, shares in the trade. In our own county, out of the seven or eight made by act of Assembly, we have only the most humble pretensions to villages at Snow Hill and Rehoboth. The largest in Maryland is our capital, containing only forty or fifty houses. Of this village the *Sot-Weed Factor* writes:

> " To try the cause then fully bent,
> Up to Annapolis I went;
> A City situate on a Plain,
> Where scarce a House will keep out Rain;
> The Buildings, framed with Cyprus rare,
> Resembles much our Southwark Fair;
> But Stranger here will scarcely meet
> With Market-place, Exchange or Street;
> And if the Truth I may report,
> 'Tis not so large as Tottenham Court.

> St. Mary's once was in repute,
> Now, here the Judges try the Suit
> And Lawyers twice a year dispute;
> As oft the Bench most gravely meet,
> Some to get Drunk and some to eat
> A swinging share of Country Treat."

Mr. Makemie considers the present a " happy juncture " for bringing the people closer together into villages. The English authorities have been lately urging it upon the Maryland Council. Our pastor says:

"The trading part of England, of whom you have had a former jealousy and suspicion of their aversion to towns, are now for them. The Government of England recommends it to your determination."

In this *Perswasive* the author describes the beautiful country lying contiguous to the Chesapeake and portrays its advantages for agriculture, manufactures and commerce. To develop these he pleads for enterprising towns, and he exhorts the people to arm themselves against all dividing debates and to work toward this one great interest. Of its opposers he says:

" Let the brute beasts check them, who generally resort together in droves. I'll send them to the fishes of the sea, who swim together in shoals. The very fowls of the air do flock together. All these concur to upbraid our folly "

Two years ago (1703) the eccentric Czar of Russia, defying the rigors of the North and the malarious marshes of the Neva, laid the foundations of his intended capital, and is determined that the new town of St. Petersburg shall be a great city. Our minister seems possessed of no less enterprise.

While he is writing this little book, Mr. Makemie is prosecuting far more important plans. The excitements of the great war in Europe and the brilliant campaigns of Peterborough in Spain do not divert his efforts; nor do the triumphs of the Whigs in the Parliamentary elections, nor the Jacobite High-Church cry that "the Church is in danger," and the proclamation of the queen against these scandalous and seditious clamors; nor the continued strife in Ireland about Presbyterian marriages; nor the agitation of a union between England and Scotland, and the bad feeling accompanying it. None of these things move him or dampen his purpose.

During these negotiations for a supply of ministers, shall we not think of him as looking to the North and conferring with brethren of the Scotch Church of whom he had said, while speaking of their tenet of predestination :

"I do profess myself fully of their sentiments in this and all other doctrines of faith, and in God's strength shall never swerve nor prevaricate " ?

Shall he remain a year in Europe without again walking the floors of the university which he entered just thirty years ago, and again worshiping in the churches which have been baptized since then with the blood of martyrs? My friend Mary, the Scotch lassie, seems often to see him standing reverently by the grave of John Knox, or by the monument to the eighteen thousand in Grey Friars' churchyard, or by the waters of Blednock where Margaret Wilson died. And shall he not run up to Borthwick and talk with Mr. Trail about the Pocomoke and the scenes around the old plantation of Brother's Love? Mr. Trail is now sixty-four years of age, was married four years ago to his second wife, Jean Murray, and is still roused up to solemn duties, I suppose, by the mysterious calls at his room door and on the head of his bed. No other men in Europe can talk as intelligently about the needs of our great field as these two.

The little girls, Betty and Anne, watch the glistening Sound of Pocomoke for their father's sail. Naomi, with her assistants, manages the large estate and awaits his coming. On the 7th of March she and James Kemp get judgment in the Accomack court against John Haskins for the amount paid in his behalf last year. The same case is still before the court on April 4 and June 6 in the name of these same attorneys of Mr. Makemie (67). Perhaps Madam Tabitha Hill anticipates his arrival with anxiety no less intense than the rest of us. So, too, the Rev. Alexander Adams of Stepney and the Rev. Robert Keith of Coventry.

Mr. Makemie's diplomacy is rewarded with success. The claims of America have been ably represented, and the ministers of London have agreed to undertake the support of two missionaries for two years, after which time it is expected that they shall secure a maintenance and settle; then the association engages to send out two more upon the same terms (68). With his knowledge of the work and of the workmen needed, it is not to be feared that Mr. Makemie has made any mistake in his selection of men. Whether they be from Scotland or Ireland, we may be sure of staunch Presbyterians. Of the former there can be no suspicion, and this very year the Synod of Ulster again puts itself unanimously upon record as follows:

"Such ministers as are to be licensed shall subscribe the Westminster Confession, and promise to adhere to the doctrine, discipline and government therein contained; as also those that are licensed and have not subscribed, are to be obliged to subscribe before they are ordained."

And now the son of Donegal again bids farewell to the scenes of his youth—probably a final farewell. The castle, the mill and the cottage fade from view; the voices of the Ulster Makemies die out upon the ear. He goes not, as once he did, a young man, to an unknown land and strange faces: he sails away, a weatherbeaten voyager, to wife and children and a church which he has planted and watered. With him are two young men. Were the ancient Argonauts returning to Iolchus more proud of their golden treasure than was Mr. Makemie when entering the Chesapeake with these "itinerants" consecrated to the gospel-work in Maryland?

Rehoboth, Snow Hill, Monokin and Rockawalkin are glad, for John Hampton and George Macnish are here with their leader, and the Presbyterian heart again is cheered and grateful to almighty God. The new church is certainly to be built at Rehoboth, and another just as certainly at Monokin. English, Scotch and Scotch-Irish crowd about the three ministers to hear the news from the fatherland. Yes, and the Huguenots too; for Mr. Makemie will know of the condition of their friends in Ireland and in London and the latest aspects of the struggle in France. Our pioneer talks of forming a Presbytery and bringing the scattered churches and ministers into complete organization for aggressive work. The primitive bishop remembers that he is a presbyter too.

The jealousy of the Churchmen toward our cause is not decreasing. In Philadelphia, Talbot writes:

" There is a new meeting-house built for Andrews almost finished, which I am afraid will draw away great part of the Church, if there be not the greatest care taken of it."*

Does this desire to have it *taken care of* prompt the intrigue for extending the authority of Lord Cornbury over Pennsylvania? Talbot seems to distrust George Keith's prophecy of two or three years ago—that " the Presbyterians are not like to increase here." We are reminded of the complaint of a writer ten years ago, nearer our own latitudes—that "the dissenters deluded many Churchmen by extemporary prayers and preachments."†

The Rev. Robert Keith of Coventry and the Rev. Alexander Adams of Stepney are not pleased with the outlook in Somerset. The Quakers still tithe the meanest tobacco,‡ and Presbyterian conventicles and Presbyterian ministers are too many and too popular. Something must be done. Though Commissary Bray was defeated in the year 1700 in his attempt to force the Prayer-Book upon all places of public worship, and though in 1702 the Toleration Act was definitely incorporated in the code of Maryland as a condition precedent to the Establishment, yet to give all these conventicles the protection of law will never do. And may not Governor Seymour even yet be brought around to play into the hands of the Church? To close the mouths of these newly-imported itinerants would be a crushing blow upon the author of *Truths in a True Light*, who therein shows too plainly the weaknesses of Prelacy.

It is understood that these dissenting preachers are expecting at the first court in November to put them-

* Gillett, i. 24.   † Hill's *Sketches*, p 72.   ‡ Bishop Hawks, p. 80.

20

selves and their churches formally under the shield of
the Act of Toleration.   The law must be retarded and
tested, think the reverend rectors.   The two clerical
plotters put their heads together and await their
opportunity.   Would not John Hewett, who lived
here for twenty years before their day, preaching the
gospel, marrying the early colonists and baptizing his
Indian converts, have scorned such machinations?

On the 14th of November the court meets at Dividing Creek.   The tobacco is gathered in, the colonists
are at leisure, and the court-house hill is full of men
talking about the conflict between the preachers.
Yonder, document in hand, stand the two sagacious
rectors.   Yonder dismounts Mr. Macnish, familiar from
birth with the aggressions of Prelacy and knowing that
he has little favor to expect at its hands.   But the sturdy young Scotchman is here to assert his rights.

From the Nanticoke to the " Divisional Line," from
the bayside to the Sinepuxent beach, appear the grand
jurors.

The licensed ordinary on the court-house premises,
flowing with the fire-waters, is doing a thriving trade.

The following justices take their seats upon the
bench: Captain John West, John Cornish, Thomas
Newbold, Captain John Franklin, Captain Charles
Ballard and Joseph Venables.

On the land of Judge Venables, up on the Wicomico,
stands our Rockawalkin church.

The justices, the clerk, the sheriff and the crier are
all sworn, and subscribe their signatures to the Abju-
ration and Test.   Every court must be purged of all
possibility of sympathy with Popery.   There is much
swearing in these days.

Amid a great deal of other business, an order is made for Captain John Franklin and the Quaker John Goddin to supervise the repairing of "the great bridge of Pocomoke River" at Snow Hill. Also that no one shall drive or catch a horse or horses upon the said bridge. Direction is given that publication be made of this order "at the churches and meeting-houses at Snow Hill and on the seaside."

But there is more important business than bridging rivers or protecting life and property. The Rev. Robert Keith is impatient to offer a momentous petition from his vestry, and the Rev. Alexander Adams is waiting to back it with his influence. The Dissenters must be circumvented. For yonder stands the Scotchman ready to qualify. He must be anticipated with the following piece of chicanery:

"To the worshipful the Commissioners of Somerset County, the Address of the Vestry of the Parish of Coventry, humbly sheweth that—Whereas we have good ground to believe that Mr. Francis Mackemmy and others his assistants are intended to address your worships on account of a Toleration granted to Dissenters for preaching and building meeting-houses and doing what else is incumbent on them as such, and we, duly considering the import of the matter, humbly desire that the whole as to premises be remitted to his Excellency the Governor of this Province and the Honorable Council of State thereof, by them to be considered, ordered and determined as they may think fit; and that nothing be done in the premises until warrant and order be obtained from them, as to the whole premises or any part thereof; and the same presented to your worships in open Court, or to the Vestry of the said Parish and the remnant Vestrys therein concerned. This our humble desire we offer without any presumption of disobedience to the laws, whereof we find ourselves not competent judges. May it therefore please your worships seriously to consider the matter above represented, and to grant our desire according to Justice; and your petitioners will ever pray &c. Signed per order John Keith, pro Vestry."

No "presumption of disobedience to the laws" forsooth! None of your enactments for the establishment of Episcopacy in Maryland could gain the royal assent until you had distinctly embodied the Toleration Act of William and Mary. What is there uncertain or indefinite in the law? Instead of the place of worship being registered, as in England, in the court of the bishop or archdeacon or at the county sessions, does not our Maryland law clearly prescribe that the meeting-houses shall be recorded in the county courts? Where is there one word about the vexatious delay of sending up these cases to governor and Council, the latter very often not in session, as is the case now? What possible excuse for this manœuvre but to intimidate the Dissenters and outlaw our ministers?

These reverend plotters had shrewdly anticipated the following document :

"To the Justices of the worshipful Court of the County of Somerset now sitting, the petition of George Macnish humbly showeth—That your petitioner craveth that the usual oaths according to law tendered to, and to be taken by, Dissenting ministers and preachers may be tendered to your petitioner. And your petitioner shall in bounden duty pray &c.
"GEORGE McNISH."

Here was respect for law and for its officials. His people are helping to support Mr. Keith and Mr. Adams, paying the forty pounds per poll and obeying the Act of Establishment. This is not enough; our ministers must be silenced, and we must receive the ordinances at the hands of these rectors or not at all! Both parties are heard, but the majority of the Bench are Episcopalians and the governor is an Episcopalian, and there is some plausibility in the claim that he is the representative of the ecclesiastical headship of the queen; and the plea to the jurisdiction overpowers the worshipful judges. The following record is made:

"The petitions aforesaid being read in open Court, worshipful Judges having heard and deliberately considered the premises on both sides, it having reference to his Excellency for result in Ecclesiastical matters &c., he being here Representative in Chief, of Church and State, allow the said Vestry's petition to have its final result and determination by his said Excellency and Honorable Council of State as prayed for. Notwithstanding the said McNish in decent manner did require (he being a Dissenter from the Church of England) that he might be dignified as by law in this county to preach, offering to take the Oaths and subscribe the Declaration, nevertheless the worshipful Court hath resolved as aforesaid."

The rectors triumph. Macnish and Hampton are not to be "dignified" with even the grudging permit of the Establishment Act: their rights are held in abeyance at the will of ecclesiastical tricksters. It is no surprise to those who have come from amid the persecutions of Scotland, Ireland and England, but our Presbyterian population need not be expected longer to repress their rising indignation. The insolence and the profligacy of the "Maryland parsons" are growing worse and worse, so that even the government at Annapolis is beginning to show impatience. We have reason to hope that Governor Seymour will not truckle to the humors of the busy rectors, and that this "reference" will have no worse result than that of delay.

It will be noticed that the petition is aimed primarily against Mr. Makemie. The man who brought the Virginia government to an official recognition of the Toleration Act is not likely to permit it to lapse in Maryland.

No less persistent than Prelacy itself is Grandmother Tabitha in her efforts to harass our pioneer. She means that he shall have no peace in his management of the Custis property and the Custis children. The testator had served with Mr. Makemie in a former executorship and knew well his ability and honesty, but she continues to question both. On the 4th of December, to meet her cavils and completely satisfy the law, an order is made by the Accomack court for securities. There is no difficulty in finding them. Not merely to secure the estate against imaginary depredations, but to protect him from her frequent accusations, he offers the following strong array: Ralph Custis, John Parker, George Parker, Perry Leatherberry and James Alexander. It will be noticed that a near relative of the deceased and of the orphans heads the list. Perfectly willing to conform to all requirements of law, Mr. Makemie is not to be worried out of the executorship. The sloop Tabitha still sails our waters, less troublesome to her master than her aged namesake!

On the same day Mr. Makemie and Naomi sign their names to a conveyance of land. Thus we constantly find him a man of affairs, an industrious citizen, as well as the founder of a church. This 4th day of December, 1705, is the first date of his appearance in court since his return from Europe. Meanwhile, through our poor postal facilities, through chance travelers and occasional sloops and ketches, the correspondence continues with regard to the formation of a Presbytery. Twenty-two years of his American life passed away, the hope long deferred seems at last to approach its consummation.

CHAPTER XXVII.

A. D. 1706.

" You suffer yourselves to be imposed upon and know little more of Presbyterians but misrepresentations and calumnies thrown upon them by malicious, ignorant and ill-minded men, as if they were monsters and most insufferable in Church and State "—MAKEMIE.

M R. ROBERT KEITH, clerk, and Mr. Alexander Adams, clerk, are greatly elated at the success of their strategy. Wherever Mr. Macnish and Mr Hampton officiate in the sacred office, they lay themselves open to prosecution by any malicious person; and there are those who exult in the continued humiliation.

Mr. Makemie holds his Barbadoes and Virginia certificates, and comes over the line when he pleases. The thrust aimed at him in the petition of the parsons does not intimidate him. It continues to be our delight to have him, Naomi and the two little girls occasionally with us at the wigwam in the pines. This evening I heard Matchacoopah teaching the children to count in the dialect of the Nanticokes:

" *Nick-quit*, one; *na-eez*, two; *nis-(whu)*, three; *yaugh-(whu)*, four; *nup-pai-a*, five; *noquuttah*, six; *my-gay-wah*, seven; *tzah*, eight, *papa-conque*, nine; *mittah*, ten; *ahtz-ickquit*, eleven; *ahtz-na-eez*, twelve; *ahtz-whuo*, thirteen; *ahtz-yaugh*, fourteen; *ahtz-uppayah*, fifteen; *ahtz-aquuttah*, sixteen; *ahtz-magaywah*, seventeen; *ahtz-wah,* eighteen; *ahtz-pap-a-conque,* nineteen; *nee-e-smittah,* twenty; *nee-qua-nick-qmt,* twenty-one; *supoocks-kay,* thirty; *yaugh-pook-kay,* forty, *nup-pay-e-pooksqua,* fifty; *nequuttah-epooksquah,* sixty; *ma-ah-wa-epooksquah,* seventy; *tzah-epooksquah,* eighty; *papa-conque-epooksquah,* ninety; *wcembakipana,* a hundred; *neez-akipana,* two hundred; *nis-wâkipana,* three hundred; *yaugh-wah-kipana,* four hundred; *nuppay-a-tashakipana,* five hundred; *nuquuttah-tashakipana,* six hundred; *may-gah-wah-tashakipana,* seven hundred; *tzah-tashakipana,* eight hundred; *papa-conque-tashaki-pana,* nine hundred; *muttah-tashakipana,* a thousand."

Shall the Presbyterian ministry thus increase in numbers from the first who came over in 1683 to thousands in the far future? or shall they be crushed out before the devices of Keith and Adams? While thinking of the new preachers, whose lips the High Churchmen are trying to close, we listen very attentively to Mr. Makemie's words:

"Where there is no ministry, or unfaithful watchmen, sin and iniquity abound and irreligion prevails For ministers of Christ should not only stand in the gap to keep off the imminent and threatened judgments of Heaven from their people and flock by prayer and pleading; but should always be standing in the gap to keep out an inundation of sin and profane irregularities in life by their plain and free doctrines, their fervent prayers and frequent supplications, their seasonable and bold reproofs, by their instructing and exemplary lives, endeavoring by all means to engage their hearers to lives becoming the Gospel of Christ." *

Thus Mr. Makemie himself stands in the gap Nor are Mr. Macnish and Mr. Hampton disposed to forfeit any rights by inaction On the 8th of January they appear together before the court at Dividing Creek

* Makemie's New York sermon.

and file another application. This petition covers the
entire case, the law and the reasons, and there are
some of us who do not fail to detect the legal knowledge and tact of Mr. Makemie in the model paper.
The same justices are again upon the bench—West,
Cornish, Newbold, Franklin, Ballard and Venables:

" To the worshipful Court of Somerset County, in the Province
of Maryland, the petition of George McNish and John Hampton
most humbly showeth—That,

" Whereas there is an Act of Parliament made in the first year
of the reign of King William and Queen Mary, intituled an Act
for Exempting their Majesties' Protestant subjects, dissenting
from the Church of England, from the penalties of certain laws;
and—

" Whereas, by the express words of the said law, we are required to tender to the Justices of the Peace at the General or
Quarter Sessions of the County Town, parts or division where we
live, to take the Oath of Allegiance, take or subscribe the Declarations, and declare our approbation of and subscribe the Articles
of Religion made the thirteenth year of the reign of Queen Elizabeth, excepting such as are excepted in said Act; and—

" Whereas we, in ready compliance with said law, have already
attended and tendered ourselves to take the said oath and perform everything required in said law; we do humbly tender
ourselves again to your worships as the proper Court held by the
Justices of the Peace for this county, empowered and required to
administer such oaths, and for receiving such subscriptions as are
enjoined in said Act of Parliament;—

" We, therefore, your humble petitioners pray that, by a further
consideration of said law, we may be admitted to do our duty in
complying with said law, which we are ready to do, seeing all
Dissenters in all her Majesty's dominions have in this manner
qualified themselves; And your petitioners as in duty bound
shall always pray."

Nearly two months since the former application, the
two law-abiding young men again ask the recognition
of their rights; but no answer has yet come from Annapolis, and the judges still hesitate. Prelacy in the

ascendant, a majority of the justices its adherents, the rectors still have their way. Oh for a William Stevens now upon the bench! Another disgraceful record is added to the history of our county Here it is:

" The aforesaid Petition being read and by the worshipful Court considered, that whereas a petition from Coventry Parish and another from said Macnish, was in November Court last to this Court preferred and the same referred to his Excellency and Hon. Council for result; it is this day likewise by the worshipful Justices again ordered that said Hampton and Macnish petition be continued till the aforesaid result be returned."

Thus those appointed to enforce the law defeat its operation. While the rights of our ministers are denied them, the Rev. Robert Keith, clergyman, purchases this year his four hundred and forty-six acres south of Dividing Creek, near enough to the courthouse to watch and manipulate the ecclesiastical proceedings of our justices. This is the plantation formerly owned by that William Morris who denounced Mr. Makemie with such horrible profanity at Rehoboth in 1691. Over the " marks " of the two sons of the drunken blasphemer the land is now deeded to the " Maryland parson " before Justices John Franklin and William Fasset The land was originally owned by Colonel Stevens under the name of " Suffolk." Where the former enemy of Makemie lived and grew besotted and broke God's Sabbaths and learned to curse the God of quick and dead, Mr. Keith will now have opportunity to prosecute his crusades against the Presbyterians.

Madam Tabitha Hill continues as vexatious and persistent as the mosquitoes of the Pocomoke. Now and then she gets the better of our minister, and we all have our laugh.   Having himself given ample security for his duties in the Custis estate, he feels the need of some protection against *her* mismanagement, and on the 5th of February he asks an order of the Accomack court for the enforcement of a former order that she shall render an account of her appropriations and expenditures in said estate or pay a fine of five hundred pounds.   The records are examined, and on the next day the court returns the answer that no such order can be found.   Mr. Makemie is positive that the order was made, but through the neglect of the clerk he suffers a temporary defeat, and Madam Tabitha sails off as gayly as the sloop Tabitha before the high winds of the Chesapeake.

My father watches all these things which identify our minister with the current life of contemporaries. On the 7th of the same month (February) he has a suit pending before the same court against John Poulson, but Mr. Makemie fails to appear, and the case is dismissed.   On the 13th of January a writ had been issued by our own presiding judge, Captain John West, against Francis Makemie and *Anne his wife*, executors of Edmund Custis, late agent of Daniel Lewis of London, the suit being brought by Captain William Whittington.   On the 16th of March our pastor appears at Dividing Creek and gives special bail for his appearance for trial in June.   He takes no advantage of the error in the name of his wife.   What a vexatious responsibility is this managing of estates for other people !

A few days before, during this same month, the following order was issued by the governor from Annapolis:

"By his Excellency the Governor, March the 13th 1706, ordered then that the worshipful Justices of Somerset County take the Oaths of the Dissenting ministers according to the Act of Parliament of the first of King William and Queen Mary exempting her Majesty's Protestant subjects from certain penalties etc. Signed per order, W. Bladen, Clerk of Council. Indorsed to Somerset Court."

The new State-House across the bay has just been completed; it is a neat brick building in the form of an oblong square. Entering the hall, you see, opposite the door, the judge's seat, and on each side of this hall are jury-rooms. On the wall above the judge's seat hangs a full-length portrait of Queen Anne presenting a printed charter of the little city of Annapolis. In this room our General Assembly henceforth holds its sessions and legislates for both Church and State. Surmounting the building is a handsome cupola surrounded by a balustrade and furnished with seats for those who desire from this elevation to enjoy the attractive scenery. Here the beauty and chivalry of our colonial capital gather in the evening, exchange their courtesies, talk of the last ball, trace the bright Severn to the sea, and breathe the refreshing breezes which blow from the salt waters beyond.

Not far away is the armory, with its large hall, seats all around it, and its walls covered with the arms of the period. Here is another portrait of Her Gracious Majesty. From the ceiling hangs a wooden chandelier, gilt and shining, which at times throws its light over the dancers. For this is the ball-room, where, arrayed in the last costumes from Europe, our great officials and our aristocratic society gather to while away the hours in the pursuit of pleasure. Those who have spent the day in forming laws for the gov-

ernment of the Church of the living God here pass
their evenings quaffing their goblets of wine and rum
and practicing their devotions to Terpsichore.*

In one of the apartments the governor and Council
hold their sessions, and from this room has issued the
order for the "dignifying" of our ministers "as by law
in this county to preach."

South of the State-House is the academy of King
William, a plain edifice, the only school-building in
the province; for the scheme of Governor Nicholson
to establish public schools in every county has failed.
Of our native Marylanders, there are more that sign
their marks than write their names.

Not far from the Capitol stands the only brick
church in the colony. Built by public taxes, it is a
monument to the churchly zeal of the most immoral
of our governors. Our government, taking the Episcopal Church upon its hands, is finding that it has
adopted a very wayward, grasping, unmanageable
ward. Not satisfied with exacting a state support
largely paid by Dissenters, it would cheat them out
of every franchise, deny them the benefits of the toleration proviso of 1702, worry the Quakers, persecute
the Papists, outlaw the Presbyterian ministry and
keep society in a ferment. The Assembly finds it
necessary to re-enact the law of toleration this year,
but even in doing this it has been so influenced by
the High-Church party that it has managed to empha-
size the penal clauses more than its principles of religious freedom. Did our Somerset troubles with the two
belligerent rectors help to bring about the re-enactment of a statute plain and intelligible enough before?

* The annals of Annapolis.

The June court approaches, and it is known that an important order has arrived from governor and Council. Nearly a year has elapsed since the "itinerants" came to America, and full seven months have passed since their first formal application for license was made and evaded. What now will our opposers do? Will they be ready with other intrigues? Will they too far provoke the governor who repulsed Bray and Hewetson, and who is growing disgusted with the immorality of the clergy?

Of course the Presbyterian colonists await the action of this court with intense solicitude. William invites me to accompany him to Dividing Creek; so, mounting my· beach-pony, I ride bravely by his side. Our women are very quiet about public affairs until blows are aimed at their ministers and their Saviour. Our little Francis, the young Marylander, rides behind his papa, representing the interest of coming generations in the events of to-day.

> " Here stately pines unite their whisp'ring heads,
>   And with a solemn gloom embrown the glades;
>   See! there a green savannah opens wide,
>   Through which smooth streams in wanton mazes glide;
>   Thick-branching shrubs o'erhang the silver streams,
>   Which scarcely deign to admit the solar beams " (69).

This ought to be the clime of peace and holy concord.

While in the last few weeks the Duke of Marlborough has been winning the great victory of Ramilies and is driving the French out of the Netherlands, and while the High-Church Tories are still doing all they can to obstruct these glorious triumphs; while the union between England and Scotland is approaching consummation and the Episcopal Jacobites of the North are trying to defeat it, clinging still to the hope of a return to the throne of a scion of the persecuting Stuarts, it does seem lamentable that this same High Church intolerance should have crossed the deep and kindled its flames of passion and hate within sight of our forest court-houses.

June is a soft, gentle month upon the Eastern Shore, and the companies of riders are saluted on all sides with the hum of insects and the carol of birds.

> " On every tree behold a tuneful throng,
>   The vocal valleys echo to their song.
>   But what is he who, perched above the rest,
>   Pours out such various music from his breast ?—
>   His breast, whose plumes a cheerful white display;
>   His quivering wings are dressed in sober gray.
>   Sure, all the Muses this their bird inspire,
>   And he alone is equal to the choir
>   Of warbling songsters who around him play
>   While, echo-like, he answers every lay.
>   The chirping lark now sings with sprightly note .
>   Responsive to her strain *he* shapes his throat;
>   Now the poor widow'd turtle wails her mate,
>   While in soft sounds *he* coos to mourn his fate.
>   Oh, sweet musician, thou dost far excel
>   The soothing song of pleasing Philomel !
>   Sweet is her song, but in few notes confined;
>   But thine, thou mimic of the feathery kind,
>   Runs through all notes   Thou only know'st them all,
>   At once the copy and the original."

We had started early that we might call by Mrs. Mary Edgar's, formerly Mrs. Rounds, and also carry some wheaten bread and some medicine to the cabin of our friend Matchacoopah, whose Askimmekonson bride lies sick. His corn-patch is growing well, and he is collecting some of the white man's comforts about his home.

It is the twelfth day of the Indians' Fawn Moon—so named because at this time the deer bring forth their young. Our Presbyterian preachers are promptly on the ground. Mr. Makemie has business of his own, in addition to his deep interest in his two " assistants." Yesterday a deed was executed by himself and his wife conveying his two hundred and fifty acres of land down on Pitts Creek to Mr. Isaac Piper, one of his elders.* This is part of the tract called " Fookes's Choice," formerly owned by Mrs. Makemie's father, half of which was sold to Andrew Alexander in 1695 Mr. Piper's purchase is called " Convoy," and is described as about five miles from the Pocomoke and near the divisional line between Virginia and Maryland.† Ministers love to see staunch Presbyterians making their homes near the churches.

To-morrow Mr. Makemie will withdraw the former plea in the suit of Daniel Lewis of London against the executors of the Custis estate, and he and " *his wife Amy*," as they now have it, will confess judgment. Our minister has examined the claim, and recognizes its justice.

At this court a man called William White, *alias* Whitt, *alias* Watson, is charged with stealing horses down in Virginia and riding them up over our Pocomoke ferry and concealing them by help of his accomplice, Rice Morgan. A man is also suing for the recovery of papers which he had been induced to sign after being made drunk on boiled cider.

* Mr. Piper was a member of Presbytery in 1712.
† Where the old Pitts Creek church now stands.

But the chief interest of this session of court centres upon the petition of George Macnish and John Hampton. The same justices are upon the bench as at the time of previous applications. Our preachers come armed with the order of the governor, of March last, and that order is so definite that there can be no further evasion. The two rectors have exhausted their strategy, and must submit. They have accomplished two things—long delay and the attendant ill-feeling—and have pilloried their names upon the court records for the contempt of future centuries. Upon his plantation of Suffolk, the rector of Coventry Parish may ruminate over his disgraceful device, while our ministers, protected by law, go abroad bearing the messages of salvation. The records of last November, of January and of to-day will form a fit epitaph for these intolerant clergymen :

" This day appeared Mr John Hampton and Mr. George Macnish and exhibited an order from his Excellency the Governor and Honorable Council for their qualification to preach in this county, In obedience thereunto this Court did administer the Oath appointed per Act of Parliament to the said Hampton and Macnish who did comply therewith and did likewise subscribe the Declaration ; whereupon this Court did allow that the aforesaid Hampton and Macnish should preach at the meeting-house near Mr. Edgar's, the meeting-house at the head of Monokin, the meeting-house at Snow Hill, and the meeting-house on Mr. Joseph Venables' land as per the Dissenting preachers required " (70).

So closes this disagreeable business, and we all ride home in the evening, enjoying the scenes and sounds of Nature far more than in the morning. Thank God that we have had a Seymour for governor rather than a Cornbury! This reminds me that the Venerable Society for the Propagation of the Gospel in Foreign

Parts, who sent out Robert Keith and Alexander Adams, have this very year been proclaiming their gratitude for the queen's favor, which, they say in their report,

" has had very good effects abroad, by influencing and exciting the governors and inhabitants to build several new churches and even to convert some of the meeting-houses of the Quakers and other sectaries into houses of worship according to the Church of England " *

Now the queen's cousin, the profligate Cornbury— "that noble patron of the Church," as he has been called—may congratulate himself in the emphatic approval of the Venerable Society upon his church-stealing and parsonage-stealing and his base treatment of Mr. Hubbard. Shall we not expect them next to pronounce their eulogies upon William White, the Pocomoke horsethief?

Last October died the youthful Hubbard, defrauded of his rights to the last and under the ban of the governor's displeasure. By the same high-handed measures, unquestionably, would the rectors of Coventry and Stepney have been glad to drive out our ministers and appropriate our Somerset churches. This year Mr. Cotton Mather testifies that the people of Jamaica have adorned the doctrine of God their Saviour by a most laudable silence and wonderful patience under their wrongs.†

Well understanding the spirit of our opposers, Mr. Makemie shows his characteristic good sense in having our new church at Rehoboth built upon his own lots. The fee-simple in a private person, not even a Lord Cornbury could take possession and "convert it

* Webster, p 84   † Letter to London ministers.

into a house of worship according to the Church of England." It is fortunate to have a minister who has law-books in his study and legal knowledge in his head.

To future generations it will look strange that the savages can more easily obtain justice in the courts than our ministers. This year three white men commit depredations upon the cabin of our old acquaintance, Matchacoopah. The crime seems to have been perpetrated without provocation, perhaps while the men were drunk. The owner is absent in the woods, and on returning he finds the wigwam in flames and sees three men mounting their horses and hastening away. One of them he recognizes as Charles Innis. Hurrying to the burning cabin, Matchacoopah rescues his sick wife, already scorched by the flames.

All that he had in the house, his furniture and provisions for the winter, were destroyed—ten bushels of corn, two bushels of dried roasted corn (or corn dried in the sun), one new streaked white blanket, one gun, two chests, a shirt, three brass kettles, twenty-one arm's lengths of *roenoke,* four Indian belts, twenty bowls, one raw doeskin, besides spook-baskets and mats for their bed. These items we record as sworn to on the trial, in order to give a glimpse into the cabin of a Nanticoke of to-day.*

On the 4th of December, Innis is brought to trial, and is bound over to keep the peace until the case shall be tried before the provincial court at Annapolis. In all crimes where life has been endangered, or where life or limb is the penalty, the upper court alone has

---

* Somerset records, 1706. The item "bowls" uncertain; seems rather to be "boles."

jurisdiction. This is a serious matter for Innis, and it
is to be hoped that the two accomplices may also be
discovered and brought to trial. There are no offences
which the court at Dividing Creek is more ready to
punish than wrongs against the Indians.

Says Matchacoopah of our colonists,

"Some *wee-eet* (good), some *mat-tit* (bad); but the
good whites are stronger than the bad whites."

So may it ever be—in Church and in State! And
now our friend Matchacoopah has his name immortalized upon the public records.

The obstructions raised in the way of the young
"assistants" have not prevented Mr. Makemie from
pushing forward his plan for a thorough organization
of the Presbyterian system in America. The forerunner of Trail, Davis, Thomas Wilson, John Wilson, Josias
Mackie, Nathaniel Taylor, and bringing over two more
helpers last year no less sound, he has hoped to see
the blessed results of these long years of waiting
moulded and compacted for future enlargement. Our
churches have been without any central bond of
union. There has been too little to distinguish them
from the Independency which Mr. Makemie does not
approve. Kind and tolerant to all who hold the
fundamentals of Christianity, he loves Presbyterianism and wishes to see it established upon its own
distinctive basis. There are enough ministers now
to form an efficient Presbytery of a thorough Scotch
type.

Mr. Andrews and Mr. Makemie have become warm
friends, and the strong personality of our Scotch-
Irish pioneer is likely to impress itself so deeply upon
the younger man that the latter shall grow as stout a

Presbyterian as any.   The fact that the yearly sessions of Presbytery shall continue to be held in his new church in Philadelphia cannot fail to enlist his sympathies and admiration more and more for our scriptural forms.

And so it is arranged.   The selection of place is good, for several reasons: It is central; it is the nearest colony where perfect religious freedom is enjoyed. The visits of Lord Cornbury and the efforts of the Episcopalians to secure him for governor and thereby bring an ecclesiastical despotism to Philadelphia have failed.   There the Presbytery will be free and untrammeled, for the following law still prevails in Pennsylvania :

"All persons living in this province, who confess and acknowledge one Almighty and Eternal God to be the Creator, Upholder and Ruler of the world, and that hold themselves obliged in conscience to live peaceably and justly in civil society, shall in no ways be molested or prejudiced for their religious persuasion or practice in matters of faith and worship; nor shall they be compelled, at any time, to frequent or maintain any religious worship, place or ministry, whatever."

Besides these reasons for selecting Philadelphia, it is also probable that the influence of the Presbytery there held will gradually reach those churches in the Jerseys and on Long Island, and perhaps in New England, where there is strong Presbyterian sentiment, and finally bring them into union with us, a beacon to light them into safe harbor after a while.

We recall again George Keith's prophecy of three years ago : "They have here a Presbyterian meeting and minister, one called Andrews; but they are not like to increase." Would it not astonish the prophet to see, before three years have passed, that new church

on High street [now Market], a goodly congregation
assembled, and the vigorous young Presbytery in session ?   There our ministers meet and organize and deliberate upon the interests of Christ's kingdom on this
vast continent.   Widely to the north and south and
west the thinly-populated country and its unexplored
regions stretch away, while here at the gate stands this
heroic band, sending forth our scriptural system of
doctrine and of church-government to the New
World and the new century   Prelacy looks on from
the one side, prognosticating failure; Quakerism looks
on from the other, averring that it is only of men
and Babylonish.   There sits Mr. Makemie in the moderator's chair, rejoicing in the final fulfillment of hope
long deferred, triumphant at last.   Here, successfully
planted, is a primitive Presbytery composed of primitive bishops.

In addition to the usual oversight of churches and
ministers, it is decided that sermons shall be preached
at each annual meeting by two ministers upon texts
previously assigned, these sermons to be subject to
criticism by the rest of the brethren.   The Epistle to
the Hebrews is to be expounded in regular order.
The first and second verses are assigned respectively
to Mr. Makemie and to Mr. John Wilson.   They are
inclined to put Mr. Makemie first in everything.   My
father says that it was in this way after apostolic days
that in the Church, composed wholly of coequal Presbyters, certain men of natural gifts and influence were
gradually advanced to precedence, until finally, in the
corruptions of the times, those who were only moder-
ators at first, *primi inter pares*, began to grasp at permanent power and became transformed into diocesan

bishops. There is no danger of this from the author of *Truths in a True Light.*

When Presbytery adjourns, it is with the understanding that the moderator and Mr. Hampton and Mr. Andrews meet in Freehold in the Jerseys for the purpose of examining and ordaining the candidate, Mr. John Boyd. The arrangement suits our ministers very well, as Mr. Makemie and Mr. Hampton are expecting to make a journey to New York, and probably to Boston. It will give our organizer an opportunity to confer with the Dissenters along the way and learn what suitable material may be found ready for moulding into the Presbytery now established. His broad plans comprise all the colonies; and why should not the same comprehensive management which has succeeded in bringing Virginia, Maryland and Pennsylvania under this one court of the Lord be able in course of time to include the other provinces?

During the Christmas holidays the three ministers meet at Freehold—a village full of memories of the dark days of Scotland's agonies. Mr. Walter Ker, banished from his native land in 1685, is still there, and can talk with Mr. Makemie of the times of persecution in Lanarkshire aggravated by the malignant curate Joseph Clelland, then as zealous against Presbyterians as the Somerset rectors of to-day.* There too he will meet with John Foreman, John Henderson, John Foord, and other sturdy old exiles. Not to be satisfied with any but the purest Presbyterianism, as soon as a Presbytery is formed they look at once to this authoritative court for a minister.

For a long while immigration to East Jersey has

* Walter Ker was the ancestor of the Somerset Kers

27

been largely from New England. These Independents preponderating in numbers, all compromises between Presbyterianism and Independency have necessarily inclined to the advantage of the latter. Thus most of the congregations have been formed. But these Scotchmen have as positive grounds for opposition to Independency as to Prelacy. We learn that the probationer Boyd is a Scotchman.*

In the church known as "The Scotch Meeting-House" they proceed to "the trials" of the young man. Those of us who know the moderator can have no doubt of the thoroughness of the work. The subject assigned as the "common head"—*De regimine Ecclesiæ*—seems very appropriate at this juncture, when the government of our American Church is assuming its permanent form. Again we seem to see in it the hand of Mr. Makemie. Twenty-five years ago, when the Presbytery of Laggan was selecting subjects for himself and Mr. Alexander Marshall, *De regimine Ecclesiæ contra Erastianos* was the one assigned to the latter. America is no less interested in such questions to-day than Ireland was then.

On Friday, Mr. Boyd preaches from the twelfth verse of the first chapter of John: "For as many as received him, to them gave he power to become the sons of God, even to them that believe on his name." He defends his thesis presented in the morning, is examined upon the languages, and is questioned by the brethren as they think fit. All his parts of trial are sustained, and his ordination is appointed for the approaching Sabbath, the 29th.

We can imagine the enthusiastic assembling of the

* Hodge, p. 78; name of church, p. 71.

people from the town and the country around on God's
holy day to hear the sermons and witness the ceremonies.   When Cornbury came into power over this
colony, four years ago, he ordered that the Prayer-
Book be used in the churches, that the sacraments
be administered only by persons episcopally ordained,
and that all ministers without ordination of that sort
report themselves to the Bishop of London.*   I do
not think that Mr. Boyd is likely to report to that
high functionary for apostolic virtue, appreciating, far
higher than anything the bishop can confer, the laying
on of the hands of the Presbytery in true apostolic
form and the certificate of ordination which they
give him on Monday.   The indignation of the governor may be expected.   Cornbury might himself
have learned something valuable from our young
minister's common head, *De regimine Ecclesiæ.*

So goes out the eventful year 1706, wearing in its
last days as a coronal the first purely Presbyterian
ordination in the New World—harbinger, we hope,
of many yet to be (71).

* Webster, p. 88.

CHAPTER XXVIII.

A. D. 1707.

"Was there ever a time wherein more occasion was given to all enemies of our holy religion to reproach and ridicule Christianity than now, while we observe such a contradiction between the lives and the pretenses of the professors of this age?"—MAKEMIE

WITH little Francis at our side, William and I talk of our absent pastor. My husband has lately been by the Makemie mill at Assawaman, where its wheels constantly roll beneath the eaves of the Episcopal church on the hill. Our pioneer's large business, whether of milling, merchandise, farming, commerce or settling estates, is all left promptly behind whenever the voice of the Master is heard calling to the gospel field. The new church at Rehoboth, the new church at Monokin and the successful Presbytery in Philadelphia all tell of a spirit of religious enterprise as practical and energetic as that which he has shown in the management of his secular affairs

William startles me by saying that he has been thinking of late that Mr. Makemie seems to be striving to have all his plans so far advanced that his own removal may not interfere with their assured triumph. What put that into William's head? Yet, when I reflect, it does look as if he had been working very assiduously since his return from Europe that all his designs may be brought toward a certainty of consummation. Is he feeling that the time is hastening when these interests must be handed over to Mr. Macnish and Mr. Hampton ? Is this the reason that he has taken Mr. Hampton with him upon this long journey of exploration and of conference with those like-minded to the north? What could we do without him ?

Brother John and my Huguenot sister-in-law, with their little Francis, come in to spend the evening. Seeing the sadness on my brow, the sweet singer of the Vincennes seeks to arouse us all with one of the lighter songs of the Troubadour Peter Vidal :

> " Thy breeze is blowing on my cheeks,
>   O land of lyre and lance !
> In every gush to me it speaks
>   Of her I love and France
> 'Twas there I sang and won renown,
>   'Twas there my heart I gave
> Unto the dame whose cruel frown
>   Me forth an exile drave.
> How pleasant every breeze that leaves
>   The land of lyre and lance !
> How welcome every voice that weaves
>   A tale of her and France !"

Thus many an exile breathes again in imagination the airs of the fatherland. Soon will Margaret be chanting one of the solemn hymns of Marot Perhaps this very evening the blue-eyed Peggy is humming a tune of Ulster to her cluster of little ones— children of the father who once lay almost starving under the walls of Derry, and who used to send his rhymes of devotion to the maiden across the sea. Over yonder, in another log nursery, Mary, the Scotch mother, still rosy-cheeked, is probably singing one of the psalms of old Rouse, while her native-born Amer-

ican husband builds the needed cradle from the section
of a hollow tree, timing his strokes to the chords of the
music.   Before the day is done they will all be teaching their boys and girls from the Catechism of Mr.
Makemie.   So grows the household in the wilderness.

Through the open door I hear the voice of Assateague Weegnonah telling our boys the Nanticoke
names for the household's constituent parts:

"*Wahocki*, a man; *acquahique*, a woman; *nups-soh-
soh*, a husband; *nee-ee-wah*, wife; *now-oze*, father;
nick, mother; *awauntit*, a child; *wahocki-awauntit*, a
boy; *peekquah*, a girl; *nucks-quah*, a son; *huntawn*, a
daughter; *nee-ee-mat*, a brother; *nimps*, an older sister; *neighsum*, a younger sister."

Meanwhile, Mr. Makemie and Mr. Hampton are
preaching in East Jersey and laboring to extend the
boundaries of the new Presbytery.   At Woodbridge
there are staunch Presbyterians ready to fall in at once
with the great movement, but they are impeded by an
element of New Englanders who prefer the Independent way, and who, all over that country, have the
advantage of first settlement and of organizations
working hitherto under their system.   Here again
our minister hears the familiar accent of old Scotland
—the voices of those transported from the prisons of
Edinburgh, Glasgow and Stirling in 1685, who had
listened, during that terrible voyage of suffering and
death, to the earnest tones of the Rev. Archibald Riddel, whose wife and many others had found a watery
grave before they reached the shore   They now listen
to a minister no less firm to his convictions, no less
ready to go to prison for the truth, than was Riddel
himself when he lay for years in the Bass, near Edin-

burgh, rather than promise to preach no more. Mr. Makemie's sermon is from the text, " Now consider this, ye that forget God, lest I tear you in pieces and there be none to deliver. Ps. L. 22." *

Mr. Makemie's preaching is largely expository; and the more doctrinal, the more practical.

The ministers are also in Newark, at the house of Mr. Jasper Crane, conferring with him, Mr. Samuel Melyen and others in reference to the interests of our Church. For this they will be called to account ere long; the spies of the government will be trying to hatch treason against Church and State out of this friendly conversation. Finally, the travelers pass over to the little town of New York. They are now under the shadow of the castle of Lord Cornbury himself.

Here there is a Reformed Dutch church, also one of French Huguenots. A small circle of Presbyterians are in the habit of meeting together in private houses for reading the Scriptures and for prayer and praise. They are true men and tried. One of these, a lawyer of talents and growing influence, Mr. David Jamison, was imprisoned for his religion in Europe and brought to this country and sold into servitude for a term of years. I hear also of Captain John Theobalds, John Vanhorn, a merchant, Anthony Young and William Jackson, both of the latter also banished from Scotland for devotion to Christ and Presbyterianism.† Among such as these, our missionaries find congenial spirits and warm welcomes.

Mr. Makemie and Mr. Hampton are passing publicly through the provinces, having nothing to conceal. On Friday, the 17th of January, Mr. Jackson

* So he tells us in New York sermon.   † Webster, p. 302.

waits on the governor and tells him that two ministers from the South are in the town and would like to speak with him. They well know the character of Lord Cornbury, and are determined that nothing covert or clandestine shall be charged against them. Under some sudden impulse of clemency or of diplomacy, the governor sends back an invitation for them to dine with him. Is it for the purpose of learning their designs and taking the measure of the men? Is it to make friends to the southward in the hope of extending his authority in that direction, according to the plans of the Episcopalians of Pennsylvania and Maryland?

Our pioneer sits at the table of the grandson of the Earl of Clarendon, the cousin of Queen Anne. Is it any higher honor than to be entertained at the houses of Stevens, Jenkins, King and other settlers of the Eastern Shore, with characters far less impeachable than that of the governor of New York? But our minister observes the Bible injunction to honor the powers that be. Of the magistrate or ruler he declares here in New York:

"The subject oweth allegiance, loyalty and obedience to his just and lawful commands, for he is the minister of God for good; and this is due by virtue of a divine command and appointment"

Therefore there is no hesitation in Mr. Makemie's submitting himself unto governors and paying them the respect due their lofty station. Lord Cornbury treats them very courteously, "being willing," he says, "to show what civility I could to men of that character." *

* Letter to commissioners of plantations, October 14

Anxious to hear the gospel from Makemie's lips, the few Presbyterians apply to both the Dutch and the French for the use of their churches; deterred by fear of Cornbury, this request is denied. It is said that Mr Young made application to the governor for permission for them to preach in the Dutch church and was refused. Strangely enough, Lord Cornbury denies that any such application was made. Our ministers, intending to hurry on their way, had not expected to preach, had not mentioned it to the governor, and had nothing to do with these applications; but, thinking themselves protected by their certificates from courts of record in Barbadoes, Virginia and Maryland, they are ready to proclaim the gospel whenever opportunity offers and wherever the people provide a place.

Finally, it is decided to hold worship with open doors at the house of William Jackson, on Pearl street. There Mr. Makemie preaches to a small congregation and baptizes a babe. In the audience is a servant of Cornbury's, "one of Cæsar's household." To that little audience, who had been driven from their homes and churches in Europe, it is a precious privilege to hear the truth once more in the tones of their native heaths, and to bring the child and have it consecrated to God in the arms of one of their own faith. Who shall envy the little band of exiles the rare privilege? No one knows what is coming, nor dreams that the ecclesiastical despotism which has been defeated upon the fields of Scotland is now to make a desperate stand in the streets of New York. This is the less to be expected when we remember that the charter granted to this province by that bigoted Papist the Duke of York guarantees:

" Persons which profess in godlyness Jesus Christ shall at all times have and fully enjoy their judgments and consciences in matters of religion."

Let it be known too that there is upon the statute-book a law as follows:

" No person or persons, which profess faith in God by Jesus Christ his only Son, shall at any time be any way molested, punished, disturbed, disquieted, or called in question, for any difference of opinion or matter of religious concernment, who do not under that pretence distuib the civil peace of the province. And all and every such person and persons may from time to time and at all times hereafter freely have and fully enjoy his or their religion, persuasion and judgment in matters of conscience and religion throughout all this province, and there worship according to their respective persuasions, without being hindered or molested."

Protected by such laws and by his certificates, Mr. Makemie speaks upon another verse of the same psalm from which he had preached at Woodbridge: "To him that ordereth his conversation aright will I show the salvation of God." We have heard him at Rehoboth preach both morning and afternoon from this text. His New York audience, listening to but few sermons since they left the old country, will not complain of the length. About this he says:

" When you are informed I designed it for two discourses, you need not be amazed at its bulk, beyond the new mode of preaching."

Mr. Makemie has not failed to notice the disposition of a degenerate age to cut down into but an hour or two the three- or four-hour sermons of the days of the martyrs.

This discourse is as full of Scripture as was Peter's on the day of Pentecost. The introduction holds up the Bible as a clear looking-glass in which we may behold the sinner's condition and needs and find a universal guide for faith and conduct. The psalm is briefly outlined and expounded, and then he says:

"The promise annexed as the improvement and application in part of the foregoing doctrine, is my text."

Attention is called to its two parts ·

"First, A large, comprehensive, rich and enriching promise, assured and manifested, 'I will show the salvation of God.' Second, The person particularly described to whom the promise is made, 'To him that ordereth his conversation aright.'"

Mr. Makemie analyzes everything. He shows four points in the promise—the manifestation, "I will show;" the thing promised, salvation; a distinguishing account of this salvation magnifying the promise, it is the salvation of God, and the Promiser, God.

Having fully "opened the words," he raises this proposition—that a well-ordered conversation is the only way to eternal salvation:

"Not the meritorious, procuring cause, for that were to assert downright Popish merit, in derogation to free grace and the efficacious merits of our Redeemer. But I assert and maintain it, for all adult believers, to be the pathway to the kingdom of Heaven—the *via regni*, though not *causa regnandi.*"

His theme is to be handled upon the following method What is presupposed by an orderly walk and conversation? What a well-ordered conversation is or wherein it consists; reasons why a well-ordered conversation is highly necessary as the way of salvation; what is necessary and requisite for promoting and advancing this well-ordered conversation; what usually and ordinarily hinders and obstructs it, and a practical application: first, for information; second, for exhortation; third, for consolation. This sermon is most fitting to time and place in its earnest protests against the laxness of the times.

Mr. Makemie himself said of the discourse:

"I am now committing it to the public view of all, that both you and they may try it at the bar of Scripture, law and reason, and impartially determine whether it contains anything favoring of pernicious doctrine and principles; anything to the disturbance of the Church of England and the government. If I had been thoroughly acquainted with New York and the irregularities thereof, which I was afterward an eye and ear witness of, I could not have fixed on a more suitable doctrine; which must be purely attributed to the divine Providence."

Yea, and if our minister had known all about the base character and profligate life of Lord Cornbury, he could not have proclaimed a message of more withering rebuke to that "noble patron of the church." *

Mr. Makemie remains with his friends in New York Monday, January 20, unconscious of having committed any crime in preaching the gospel to the destitute (72). On Tuesday he crosses over to Long Island, expecting the next day to preach at Newtown, where Mr. Hampton had preached on the Sabbath. This town, formerly called Middlebury, was settled by Independents; but, like most of the towns on this end of the island, there are Presbyterians among them who are glad to welcome ministers of their own persuasion. Those unfamiliar with the distinctive differences sometimes speak of them as Independents, sometimes as Presbyterians.

Meanwhile, there is excitement in New York.

* For the character of Cornbury, see Smith's *History of New York,* i 190–194.

Word has been carried to the castle that a veritable conventicle has been gathered on Pearl street—that the strolling preacher from the South has held worship in a private house with over five persons and administered baptism; and of course there is no telling what treasonable plots have been hatched. Worse still, these men have been preaching previously in His Lordship's province of East Jersey, and there, where His Lordship has undertaken to see that none shall preach except under authority from the Bishop of London, these fanatics have actually presumed to ordain young men to the ministry! Now they are persisting in their contempt for his will, and are pursuing their high-handed course under the eaves of Fort Anne. It must be stopped! The following warrant is hurried off upon their tracks:

" Whereas I am informed that one Mackennan and one Hampton, two Presbyterian preachers who lately came to this city, have taken it upon them to preach in a private house without having obtained my license for so doing, which is directly contrary to the known laws of England; And being likewise informed that they are gone into Long Island with intent there to spread their pernicious doctrine and principles, to the great disturbance of the Church by law established, and of the government of this province; You are therefore hereby required and commanded to take into your custody the bodies of the said Makennan and Hampton and them to bring with all convenient speed before me at Fort Anne in New York. Given under my hand, at Fort Anne, this 21st day of January, 1707.

" CORNBURY."

It must again be stated that there is no " Church by law established" in the province of New York, and that all pretensions that way are sheer, shameless usurpation. The only statute upon which that claim is based was passed in 1693, and about this law Mr.

Makemie makes the following uncontrovertible statements ·

"1. This law is not general, for the whole government, but for four counties where there are nine. 2. It was made upon the motion and application of sundry Dissenters on Long Island who are yet alive, who expected another benefit by it than they have since been treated with. 3. It was made by an Assembly who were generally Dissenters and who are so to this day. 4. There is not any mention of the Church of England, or the mode or manner of the Church of England's worship, government or ceremonies, in all the law; without which I cannot imagine they have an establishment 5. Every sufficient Protestant minister, duly called according to the directions of said law, has a right hereunto and none else, and that Dissenters, for whom this law was originally designed, are deemed and called ministers and men in holy orders, is plain from the express words of the Act of Toleration. 6 It is observable, at the time this law was made, there was not a Church-of-England clergyman in all that country, and for some time after. 7. By the last clause of the law, all former agreements made between ministers and people were confirmed and ratified; and all such were then, and are to this day, Dutch, French and British Dissenters."

It is clear that the "good sufficient Protestant minister" mentioned in this law of 1693 had no more reference to the Church of England than to any other Church. Governor Fletcher had at once tried to fasten his own meaning upon it—that it was made for the sole benefit of Prelacy; but in 1695 the Assembly interpreted the act to mean otherwise, and to authorize churches "to call a Dissenting Protestant minister; and that he is to be paid and maintained as the act directs."

Nevertheless, under their own false and violent construction of the law, the governors have continued their tyrannical course for imposing a repulsive ecclesiastical system and its extortions upon an unwilling people. Notwithstanding Vescy's success in building up Trinity church, and the influence of the government there and elsewhere, Mr. Makemie testifies that even yet only one out of twenty of the population is Episcopal.

The warrant is directed to the high sheriff of Queen's county or his deputy. The sheriff—Thomas Cardale—is one of the worst men in the county, well known to be a fellow of low and mean character (73). This is not the first time he has been the willing tool of the oppressor. In 1702 he had in custody the Quaker preacher Samuel Bownas for nearly a year, under charge of speaking disparagingly of the Church of England. George Keith, who is still harassing his former fellow-religionists in England,* instigated the usurpations of Cornbury and set on foot the prosecution. The grand jury refused to find a bill and were browbeaten by the presiding judge, but, says Bownas, "the other Justices, being mostly Presbyterians, cared nothing." One of them said.

"The judge frets because he cannot have his way of you, and the Governor is disgusted, he expecting to have made considerable advantage by it." †

Cardale was also fit instrument in the ejectment of the Dissenters of Jamaica, on Long Island, from their church and parsonage, holding the keys against the rightful owners and seizing the glebe, dividing it into lots and leasing them out for the support of ecclesiastical buccaneers ‡

This is the man who serves Cornbury's warrant on our two ministers at Newtown on Tuesday evening.

* Anderson's *Colonial Church*, iii. 232   † Bownas's Journal.
‡ Macdonald's *History of the Jamaica Church, in loco.*

It being late, the prisoners are permitted to spend the night with their friends on their parole. The next day, instead of taking them directly to New York, Cardale and his deputy, Stephen Luff, carry them seven miles out of the way around by Jamaica, and remain there over Wednesday night "As if they were to be carried about in triumph to be insulted over as exemplary criminals, and put to further charge," says Mr. Makemie. There is indeed little doubt but it is done as a defiance to the Presbyterians of Jamaica, adding new insult to former injuries. Here our ministers remain all night, shut up in the church as prisoners

This puts new emphasis upon the church-stealing of the past. Yonder stands the handsome parsonage of which the Dissenters had reason to be so proud, and in which Mr. Makemie and Mr. Hampton have a right to be entertained as honored guests to-night, but it is in possession of the intruder, the Rev. Mr. Urquhart. While speaking of the pretended Act of Establishment, Mr. Makemie says:

" None.have any right unto, or should have any benefit by this Act, but he that is called by twelve men chosen by the free votes of the people of the county ; which Mr. Urquhart of Jamaica never had by any vote of the majority. Therefore he has as great a right to the salary there, as he has to the meeting-house, with the house and land he lives upon, of which the proprietors have been ousted with violence, without all legal process or ejectment; and being of fifteen hundred pounds value. It is a matter of satisfaction that this practice is singular and not yet made a precedent of , though Newtown is threatened by the same parson."

Two years ago this clergyman, Urquhart, and the Rev. Mr. Thomas, clergyman at Hempstead, wrote thus in a joint-letter to the Venerable Propagation Society :

" The ancient settlers have transplanted themselves from New England, and do still keep a close correspondence and are buoyed up by schismatical instruction from that interest, which occasions all the disturbance and opposition we meet with in our parishes. They have hitherto been used to a Dissenting ministry, and they still support one at Jamaica, which has a most pestilential influence over our people who from their cradles were disaffected to conformity."

What damaging admissions!   And yet, in the face of this righteous opposition from the large majority of the people, Mr. Urquhart is willing to occupy the pulpit and parsonage properly belonging to the present young pastor, Mr. Francis Goodhue!   Near by is the grave of Hubbard, whose life, perhaps, was shortened by the persecutions of Cardale and Cornbury.   Before the year closes, Mr. Goodhue also will be where the wicked no more can trouble (73).

Last year Cotton Mather thus described Jamaica :

"A town consisting of considerably above a hundred families, and exemplary for all Christian knowledge and goodness, and a church with a worthy pastor in it.   About half a score of families (and of meaner character) in this town declared for the Church of England, and thereupon a minister of their profession was sent them, one Urquhart."

After describing the seizure of church and parsonage, he adds :

" If such things proceed, that noble Society for the Propagation of Religion in America will greatly wound religion and their own reputation also."

In the midst of these scenes Mr. Makemie and Mr. Hampton sleep on Wednesday night.   Around them

28

are eloquent reminders of what they may expect at the hands of Lord Cornbury.

About noon on Thursday the prisoners reach New York under escort of these minions of tyranny. They are brought into the council-chamber about three or four o'clock It has been two full days since their arrest but a few miles away.

"How dare you take upon you to preach in my government without my license?"

Such is the rude salutation of the governor. Our minister is not to be intimidated To prevent misrepresentation, Mr. Makemie tells us that the conference "was very soon committed unto writing." He answers:

"We have liberty from an Act of Parliament, made the first year of the reign of King William and Queen Mary, which gave us liberty, with which law we have complied."

Lord Cornbury. "None shall preach in my government without my license."

Mr. Makemie. "If the law for liberty, My Lord, had directed us to any particular persons in authority for license, we would readily have observed the same; but we cannot find any directions in said Act of Parliament, therefore could not take notice thereof."

Lord C. "That law does not extend to the American Plantations, but only to England."

Mr. M. "My Lord, I humbly conceive it is not a limited or local Act, and am well assured it extends to other Plantations of the Queen's dominions, which is evident from Certificates from Courts of Record of Virginia and Maryland, certifying we have complied with said law."

The certificates are produced and read, but the governor persists:

"I know it is local and limited, for I was at the making thereof."

Mr. M. "Your Excellency might be at the making thereof, but we are well assured there is no such limiting clause therein, as is in Local Acts, and we desire the law may be produced to determine this point."

The governor, turning to the attorney, Mr. Bekely, asks him:

" Is it not so, Mr. Attorney?"

. *Attorney.* "Yes, it is local, My Lord."

Mr. M. "I desire the Law may be produced; for I am morally persuaded there is no limitation or restriction in the Law to England, Wales and Berwick on Tweed; for it extends to sundry Plantations of the Queen's dominions, as Barbadoes, Virginia and Maryland; which was evident from the Certificates produced, which we could not have obtained, if the Act of Parliament had not extended to the Plantations. And I presume that New York is a part of Her Majesty's dominions, and sundry ministers on the East end of Long Island have complied with said Law and qualified themselves at Court by complying with the directions of said Law, and have no license from Your Lordship."

Lord C. "Yes, New York is of Her Majesty's dominions; but the Act of Toleration does not extend to the Plantations by its own intrinsic virtue, or any intention of the Legislators, but only by Her Majesty's Royal instructions signified unto me; and that is from her prerogative and clemency. The Courts which have qualified those men are in error, and I shall check them for it."

Mr. M. "If the law extends to the Plantations any manner of way; whether by the Queen's prerogative, clemency or otherwise; our certificates are a demonstration that we have complied therewith."

Lord C. "These Certificates were only for Virginia and Maryland; they do not extend to New York."

Mr. M. "We presume, My Lord, our Certificates do extend as far as the Law extends , for we are directed by the Act of Parliament to qualify ourselves in the places where we live, which we have done; and the same Law directs us to take Certificates of our qualification, which we have accordingly done; and these Certificates are not to certify to such *as behold us taking our qualification,* being performed in the face of the country, at a public court; but our Certificates must be to satisfy others abroad in the world who saw it not nor heard anything of it—otherwise it would be needless. And the Law which obliges us to take a Certificate, must allow said Certificate to have a credit and reputation in Her Majesty's dominions—otherwise it is to no purpose."

The governor takes refuge in a rude retort.

"That Act of Parliament was made against strolling preachers, and you are such and shall not preach in my government."

Mr. M. "There is not one word, My Lord, mentioned in any part of the Law against traveling or *strolling* preachers, as Your Excellency is pleased to call them. We are to judge that to be the true end of the Law, which is specified in the Preamble thereof, which is, for the satisfaction of scrupulous consciences and uniting the subjects of England in interest and affection. And it is well known, My Lord, to all, that Quakers who also have liberty by this Law, have few or no fixed teachers but are chiefly taught by such as travel, and it is known to all that such are sent forth by the Yearly Meeting at London, and travel and teach over the Plantations and are not molested."

Lord C. "I have troubled some of them and will trouble them more."

Mr. M "We hear, My Lord, one of them was prosecuted at Jamaica, but it was not for traveling or teaching, but for particulars in teaching, for which he suffered." *

Lord C "You shall not spread your pernicious doctrines here!"

Mr. M. "As to our doctrines, My Lord, we have our Confession of Faith, which is known to the Christian world, and I challenge all the clergy of York to show us any false or pernicious doctrines therein! Yea, with those exceptions specified in the Law, we are able to make it appear that they are in all doctrinal articles of faith agreeable to the established doctrines of the Church of England."

Lord C. "There is one thing wanting in your Certificates, and that is, signing the Articles of the Church of England."

Mr. M. "That is the Clerk's omission, My Lord, for which we are no way accountable. If we had not complied with the whole Law, in all the parts thereof, we could not have had Certificates pursuant to said Act of Parliament. And Your Lordship may be assured we have done nothing in complying with said Law but what we are still ready to perform, if Your Lordship require it; and that ten times over. As to the Articles of Religion, I have

* Bownas. Charged with speaking disrespectfully of the Church of England in reference to baptism.

a copy in my pocket and am ready at all times to sign, with those exceptions specified in the Law."

Lord C. "You preached in a private house not certified according to Act of Parliament."

Mr. M. "There were endeavors used for my preaching in a more public place, and—though without my knowledge—Your Lordship's permission was demanded for my preaching in the Dutch church; and being denied, we were under a necessity of assembling for public worship in a private house, which we did in as public a manner as possible, with open doors. And we are directed to certify the same to the next Quarter Sessions, which cannot be done until the Quarter Sessions come in course—for the Law binds no one to impossibilities; and if we do not certify to the next Quarter Sessions, we shall be culpable but not till then. For it is evident, My Lord, that this Act of Parliament was made and passed the royal assent May 24th. It being some time before the Quarter Sessions came in course, all ministers in England continued to preach without one day's cessation or forbearance; and we hope the practice of England shall be a precedent for America."

Lord C. "None shall preach in my government without my license, as the Queen has signified to me by her royal instructions."

Mr M "Whatever direction the Queen's Instructions may be to Your Lordship, they can be no rule or law to us, nor any particular persons who never saw, and perhaps never shall see them; for promulgation is the life of the law."

The experience that Mr. Makemie has had in the courts of Accomack and Somerset has not been in vain.

Lord C. "You must give bond and security for your good behavior, and also bond and security to preach no more in my government."

Mr. M. "As to our behavior, though we have no way broke it, endeavoring always so to live as to keep a conscience void of offence toward God and man, yet if His Lordship required it, we would give security for our behavior; but to give bond and security to preach no more in Your Excellency's government, if invited and desired by any people, we neither can nor dare do."

Lord C. "Then you must go to gaol."

The spirit of the covenanting times was upon our
minister.   He answers :

"We are neither ashamed nor afraid of what we have done!
We have complied and are ready still to comply with the Act of
Parliament, which we hope will protect us at last.   It will be un-
accountable to England to hear that Jews who openly blaspheme
the name of the Lord Jesus Christ and disown the whole Christian religion ; Quakers, who disown the fundamental doctrines
of the Church of England and both sacraments ; Lutherans and
all others, are tolerated in Your Lordship's government, and
only we, who have complied and are still ready to comply with
the Act of Toleration, and are nearest to and likest the Church
of England of any Dissenters, should be hindered, and that only
in the Government of New York and the Jerseys.   This will appear strange indeed."

Lord C. "You must blame the Queen for that."

Mr. M. "We do not, neither have we any reason to blame
Her Majesty, for she molests none, neither countenances or encourages any who do; and has given frequent assurances, and
of late in her Gracious speech to her Parliament, That she would
inviolably maintain the Toleration."

Our champion is not to be placed in the false position
of disloyalty to his queen.   He alludes to her words at
the close of the session of 1702 :

" I shall be very careful to preserve and maintain the Act of
Toleration and to set the minds of all my people at quiet "*

While the governor writes an order transferring the
prisoners from the custody of Cardale to that of Ebenezer Wilson, sheriff of New York, Mr. Hampton, who
had hitherto remained silent, asks a license of His
Lordship   It is refused   Mr. Makemie moves that
the Law of Toleration be produced and examined to
see if it is local and limited, offering to pay the attorney
for a copy of the limiting clause.   Says our pastor :

" Everything relating hereunto was declined and disregarded."

* Knight, v 114.

Said Lord Cornbury, with a sneer worthy of the brutal Jeffreys :

"You, sir, know law ?"

Mr. M. "I do not, My Lord, pretend to know law , but I pretend to know this particular law, having had sundry disputes thereon."

His own experience and the long contest provoked by Robert Keith and Alexander Adams had given him abundant opportunity to study its provisions

Our two ministers become prisoners of state in the house of the sheriff A copy of the governor's order of commitment, frequently asked for, is not given them until Saturday.   It is as follows :

"You are hereby required and commanded to take into your custody the bodies of Francis Makemie and John Hampton and them safely keep until further orders ; and for so doing this shall be your warrant. Given under my hand and seal this 23rd day of Jan 1707.

"CORNBURY '

Mr. Makemie's demand for a copy of the *mittimus* shows his purpose to contest the legality of the proceedings at every step.   He thus dissects the paper:

"First ; It is granted and signed by the supreme authority, and not by any sworn officers appointed and authorized by law for commitment of offenders.   The supreme authority of England have not put any such power into practice without a special act of Parliament empowering them so to do ; and that only upon necessity and emergent occasions Second ; Here is no mention of the Queen's name or authority ; which must be acknowledged as a novelty not easily understood.   Third ; There is not the least shadow of a crime or suspicion of a crime alleged Fourth , This *mittimus* is erroneous in conclusion ; which should be, 'Until they are delivered by due course of law,' and not, 'Until further orders,' which is condemned by law and lawyers as insufficient."

Thus, under sheer usurpation of ecclesiastical power and under a commitment illegal in form, these two

Presbyterian ministers go to prison. Our pioneer and his young friend take their places by the side of the old Scotch and Scotch-Irish worthies as sufferers in defence of civil and religious liberty. Well does Mr. Makemie remember when, under the spite of Bishop Leslie, his beloved pastor, John Drummond, and three others lay in confinement at Lifford for six years, and the later days when Mr. William Trail and others of the Presbytery of Laggan endured the same oppression under High Churchmen. Deliberately facing these possibilities when first devoting himself to the ministry, he is not the man to waver when the hour of trial comes.

Determined to exhaust all legal remedies, a respectful petition is sent, under the signatures of the two and by the hands of the sheriff, asking His Lordship that they be permitted to know their crime, not hinted in the *mittimus*, and praying that, as

" strangers on our journey to New England, above four hundred miles from our habitations, we may be allowed a speedy trial according to law."

No written answer is condescended, and it is only after several days that the verbal answer is returned through the sheriff:

" 1. Lord Cornbury did admire they should petition to know their crime, he having so often told them. 2. If they take the right way, they may have a trial."

They challenge a trial and inquire the way from both sheriff and attorney-general. Nothing is learned, and the imprisonment continues. Mr. Makemie says:

"They resolved to arm themselves with patience, until they

could obtain a writ of *Habeas Corpus* from the Hon. Roger Mompesson, Esq , Chief-Justice, who lived in another Government and could sign no such Writ until he came into the Government of New York."

The chief-justice is in New Jersey, and will not be in New York before his March term. Says our pastor :

"In the mean time, The Quarter Sessions for the city and county of New York being in course; and being still absolute strangers to the Constitution of New York, and being ready to manifest their readiness in complying with the Act of Toleration in all things; they addressed Lord Cornbury by the following Petition :

"The humble petition of Francis Makemie and John Hampton most humbly sheweth—That whereas Your Lordship is pleased not to allow our Certificates from Courts of Record in Virginia and Maryland to reach Your Excellency's Government; Therefore we being Your Lordship's prisoners, must humbly pray we may be admitted in the custody of the Sheriff to apply ourselves to the Quarter Sessions, that we may there offer ourselves to qualification as the Law directs, which we are again ready to do , we being resolved to reside in Your Lordship's Government. And we Your Excellency's most humble petitioners, and afflicted prisoners, as in duty bound, shall always pray."

Of course the petitioners do not contemplate a permanent residence, but only through the months necessary for the full settlement of these difficulties and for the vindication of the rights of their Church Mr. Makemie had already argued, while before Cornbury, that the law is satisfied by applying to the *first Quarter Sessions in course after preaching.*

The governor spurns the petition and browbeats the messenger—another touch of the spirit of Jeffreys. This is done under the technical quibble that no names are signed to the petition Then says Mr. Makemie :

"We resolved to trouble His Excellency with no more petitions."

Two weeks had now passed, when, on the 5th of February, the following was sent directly to the Quarter Sessions. I give the paper because of the attorney's pretence with regard to it, and because it is another step leading up to the first great trial for religious liberty on the continent of America:

"Whereas your petitioners are Protestant ministers dissenting from the Church of England, who have Certificates from Courts of Record of Virginia and Maryland, certifying we have taken the oaths and performed all such qualifications as are required in an Act of Toleration made the first year of King William and Queen Mary for liberty of Their Majesties' Protestant and Dissenting subjects, which Certificates His Excellency Lord Cornbury is not pleased to allow to extend to his government, We therefore, Your Worships' humble petitioners, pray we may be admitted to appear in the custody of the Sheriff at the bar of your Court, to qualify ourselves again according to the particular directions of said Act of Toleration; which in obedience to the Law we are always ready to do."

This paper, duly signed, passed from hand to hand among the justices, but was not allowed to be read in open court The attorney pronounced it a libel on Lord Cornbury, and instructed them that it was not their business to administer the qualifications. Where is there the shadow of libel on the governor? Amid all these wrongs, it is remarkable that our ministers remained so self-possessed as not once to speak evil of dignities.

In the second section of the Toleration Act it is positively provided that

"All and every person and persons already convicted or *prosecuted in order to conviction*, that shall take the said oaths and subscribe the declaration, shall be henceforth exempt and discharged."

Such is the arbitrary disregard of all law by Lord Cornbury and his subservient officials.

At the same court application is formally made that the house of William Jackson, on Pearl street, be recorded as henceforth a regular place of worship. These petitions, kept in hand for two days with the law read and explained, were both rejected. This, too, notwithstanding the fact that the same court had lately recorded a Quaker meeting-house upon similar petition and under these same provisions of law! It is evident that tyranny is determined to crush Presbyterianism if it can.

After weeks more of illegal imprisonment, they hear that the chief-justice has reached New York to preside at the March assizes. Mr. Regniere, a practicing lawyer, and a son-in-law of Colonel Markham, deputy governor of Pennsylvania, has been retained by Mr. Makemie to undertake the defence. Through him application is made for writ of *habeas corpus.* The illegal *mittimus* of Lord Cornbury is attached to the petition, and, as this *mittimus* alleges no crime against the prisoners, it is supposed that they will be immediately discharged. And now two pieces of arrant wrong are perpetrated—one by the sheriff, and the other by the sheriff and the governor together.

In the presence of three witnesses, the sheriff refuses to take any step for securing the writ of *habeas corpus* until the ministers have paid him twelve "pieces-of-eight" for their illegal commitment, and as much more for executing the present writ.* The money is paid, and a receipt for it is asked and refused!

* A "piece-of-eight" was equal to about one dollar; twenty-four dollars in all.

Meanwhile, the governor promptly substitutes another warrant, thereby plainly admitting the illegality of the former, and confessing that these victims of his despotic will have suffered six weeks of unlawful imprisonment. This second sudden warrant, of precisely the same date with the writ of *habeas corpus*, is as follows ·

"You are hereby required and commanded to take into your custody the bodies of Francis Makemie and John Hampton, pretended Dissenting ministers, for preaching in this province without qualifying themselves according to an Act of Parliament made at Westminster in the first year of the reign of our late Sovereign Lord and Lady, King William and Queen Mary, and also without my License first obtained, and them safely to keep till they shall be discharged by due course of law. And for so doing this shall be your sufficient warrant. Given under my hand and seal this 8th day of March, 1707.
"CORNBURY."

This late warrant is thus criticised by Mr. Makemie:

"It is observable that it is granted and signed by the supreme authority (the Governor) without mentioning the Queen's name or authority. And the supposed crime is double, 1st, Preaching in New York Government without complying with the qualifications of the Act of Parliament made in the first year of William and Mary, whereas Lord Cornbury had read in January their Certificates, both from Virginia and Maryland, certifying their qualification according to said Act of Parliament. 2d, Preaching without License being first obtained of Lord Cornbury; whereby it is plain that complying with the Law is not esteemed sufficient without a License."

My father says that a lawyer will appreciate these strictures. Let it be remembered, too, that when the second *mittimus* was written they had complied with the Toleration Act even in New York by tendering themselves to the Quarter Sessions to take the lawful oaths. It is noticeable that the governor here confesses what he previously so emphatically denied—that the Toleration Act *is* in force in New York.

The *habeas corpus* is granted on Saturday, and commands that they be brought before the chief-justice "immediately upon receiving the writ;" but it is not executed until Monday. Sheriff and governor are evidently in collusion in these delays. On Monday they are before Mompesson, and are discharged upon their recognizances to appear for trial at the next day's sitting. Dr. John Johnstone and Mr. William Jackson become their bail in a bond for twenty pounds, and Mr. Makemie himself for forty pounds. This Dr. Johnstone is a Scotchman who came over in 1685 in the ship in which died his father-in-law, George Scott of Pitlochie, his mother-in-law and many others. Knowing what imprisonment and oppression mean, having learned it well in the days of Claverhouse and Dalziel, the doctor witnesses with indignation this high-handed attempt to introduce the same persecutions upon these Western shores.

On Tuesday, March 11, the accused are arraigned for trial. The attorney drops Mr. Hampton out of the prosecution. Mr. Makemie says:

"For reasons best known to himself, though both equally guilty of the same crime, of preaching a sermon in the Government of New York, and having suffered equally by imprisonment."

Now our pioneer stands alone, the cause of American and Presbyterian liberty embodied in one man.

Says our pastor:

"To such as knew the Grand Jury, they plainly appeared to be chosen on purpose to find a presentment."

While some of them were utter novices in such proceedings, several of them were of the bench of justices who at the late Quarter Sessions had prejudged the case and refused to let the ministers qualify. One of them, who at that time was inclined to grant their petitions, "was threatened as to his trade and business."

Four of Mr. Makemie's hearers—Captain Theobalds, Mr. John Vanhorn, Mr. Anthony Young and Harris, the governor's coachman—testify that "they heard no unsound doctrine nor anything against the Government." There is little else of importance before the grand jury, but their action in this case is withheld for four days—until Friday, the last day of the court, when they know it will be impossible for the accused to secure a hearing. Evidently, the prosecuting attorney is manipulating the business to please his master. This first indictment of the kind in America ought to be preserved :

"The Jurors of our Sovereign Lady the Queen upon their oath do present that Francis Makemie, late of the province of Virginia, Gentleman, pretending himself to be a Protestant Dissenting Minister and Preacher, and contemning and endeavoring to subvert the supremacy, jurisdiction and authority of our now Lady and Queen in ecclesiastical affairs, the 22nd day of January and fifth year of the Queen's reign, to wit, at the Southward of the City of New York, did privately and unlawfully take upon him to preach and teach, and did preach and teach divers of Her Majesty's liege subjects within the said City, to wit, at the dwelling-house of one William Jackson, situated in the ward aforesaid, privately and unlawfully then and there met and assembled together, to above the number of five persons at one time, under the pretence of divine worship, without any leave or license by him the said Francis first had and obtained according to law for the same, in great derogation of the Royal authority and prerogative of Our Lady the Queen, and to the evil example of all others in like case offending against the peace of Our Lady, her crown and dignity.

"And the Jurors aforesaid upon their oath aforesaid, do further

present that the said Francis Makemic afterward, to wit, the
22nd day of January in the year aforesaid, at the city and ward
aforesaid, and at the dwelling-house of the said William Jackson,
did privately and unlawfully assemble and gather together divers
of Her Majesty's subjects unknown, and did then and there voluntarily and unlawfully use other rites, ceremonies, form and
manner of Divine worship than what are contained in a certain
Book of Common Prayer, and administration of the sacraments
and of other rites and ceremonies of the Church of England,
against the form of the statute in that case made and provided,
and against the peace of Our Lady the Queen, her crown and
dignity.

"And the Jurors aforesaid do further present that the said
Francis Makemie afterward, to wit, the 22nd day of January, in
the fifth year aforesaid, being then, and now is, a person not
qualified by law to preach, teach and officiate in any congregation or assembly for religious worship at the City aforesaid, to
wit, at the Southward of the City, at the aforesaid dwelling-house
of the said William Jackson, situate in the said ward, did take
upon himself to preach, teach and officiate, and then and there
did preach, teach and officiate in a congregation, assembly, conventicle and meeting, not permitted or allowed by law, under
color or excuse of religion, in other manner than according to
the liturgy and practice of the Church of England. At which
conventicle, meeting and assembly, were five persons or more
assembled together, against the form of the statute in that case
made and provided, against the peace of Our Lady the Queen,
her crown and dignity."

Such is this memorable document.

Let it be noted again that "the statute in that case
made and provided" is an utter assumption of the
sycophantic jury—that there is no enactment upon
the statute-book of New York establishing the
Church of England or making it incumbent upon
anybody to observe its forms. Into the hands of
this jury had been put the explanatory act of 1695
declaring that the act of 1693 was meant as much for
the protection and maintenance of the worship and
churches of Dissenters as any other. It must pro-

voke a righteous indignation to hear this packed jury saying upon their oaths and in the form of law that this meeting of godly men, where that noble sermon was preached and the little child was baptized in the name of the Holy Trinity, amid the solemn service of prayer and song, was "under pretence of Divine worship," "under color or excuse of religion."

So ends the first part in this drama. The case is deferred until the June term, and Mr. Makemie is released under bond and security to return at that date, at great sacrifice of time and money, to stand trial. Forfeiture of bond would cost him far less than the expense of the long journey and the suit, and I have no doubt but Lord Cornbury thinks that this will be the end of the matter, and that he will be troubled no more by Mr. Makemie and the Presbyterians. We may safely prophesy that the governor has again mistaken the spirit of the man.

CHAPTER XXIX.

A. D. 1707 (Continued).

"I hope it will be no crime for *Losers* to speak, in telling the World what we have suffered on sundry accounts; not only by Imprisonment and the exorbitant expensive prosecution; and besides great loss of time, many diminutive reproaches upon our Reputations by a Set of men who could reach by their Short Horns to no higher degree of Persecution. And all this for Preaching one Sermon."—MAKEMIE.

MORE than four months has Mr. Makemie been absent from the banks of the Pocomoke I think that Mr. Robert Keith and Mr. Alexander Adams are not a little elated at the turn matters have taken, learning that the certificates which they contested in Maryland have not been honored in New York, and that the possessors of these certificates have been held in durance vile. They would like it well, and admire Cornbury only the more, if the Northern prison had remained permanently closed upon the two Dissenters.

This infamous prosecution has not made some of us Marylanders feel any more kindly toward New York and what has been called the "Crown Requisitions," begun in 1692 for the defence of that colony against the French and Indians.

Mr. Makemie is fully abreast of all the questions of the day, and he well says of his treatment in that province:

29

" What the consequence of such practices, if persisted in, will
prove to such a place where men and money are so wanting for
the defence of New York, both by sea and land, which not many
years since—by demands of men and money from the neighboring colonies on the continent—was represented as their own barrier and frontier, I leave to thinking men and considering politi-
cians to answer."

Little Betty and Anne are again longing to see their
father and talking of the bad men who are keeping him
away   Amid the fragrance of the spring flowers along
the marshes, they launch their little sloops of bark on
the waters of Houlston's Creek and tell them to sail
away and bring papa home

Says Matchacoopah :

" *Waaks* (the fox) of the North would keep in his
den *ah-whap-pawn-top* (the eagle) of the Pocomoke."

Meanwhile, the church at Snow Hill raises a subscription in tobacco and makes out a formal pastoral
call to be presented to one of these prisoners at the
approaching Presbytery. The spendthrift cousin of
the queen cannot, with all his prisons, alienate the
heart of the little village from Mr. Hampton. The
Spences and the Fassitts and the Whites will be
only the prouder of the young man who has proved
himself worthy to stand by the side of the founder of
these churches.

In his Catechism, Mr. Makemie had taught that
" people are to maintain their ministers." In his reply
to George Keith he says :

" What narrow and niggardly souls those people have who
would allow no more to the ministry of the Gospel than common
charity obliges them to give to the most common beggar that
goes from door to door, even a necessary competency and ali-
ment ; whereas ministers should have such a maintenance as
may not be necessitated to entangle and incumber themselves

with secular affairs, and be diverted from their holy office and ministerial calling ; and further, they ought to have such an honorable allowance as they may not only live answerable to their station but be able to maintain duties to hospitality."

The two years during which the London ministers agree to support "the itinerants" are nearly out, and Snow Hill church, as taught by her founder, is moving laudably to secure and support a settled pastor.

While these important events have been occurring in our own country, the union between England and Scotland is finally consummated, and in the latter the rights of the Presbyterian Church have received a permanent guarantee. The queen thus addresses the General Assembly :

"We take this opportunity of renewing to you our assurance that you shall have our protection in the free enjoyment of all the rights and privileges that by law you are possessed of."

The Archbishop of Canterbury has declared that:

"He believes the Church of Scotland to be as true a Protestant Church as that of England." *

In comparison with this, how contemptible the spirit of Cornbury and of the rectors of Coventry and Stepney! The danger to the Scotch Church is henceforth not so much from without as within, the mercenary Prelatists, who played the persecutor as long as they could, now conforming and subscribing to the Confession of Faith which they hate.

Our Presbytery is to meet in Philadelphia on the 22d of March—only two weeks after adjournment of court—and Mr. Makemie remains North, working for the Master. To reach home and return would occupy

* Carstare's *State Papers*, p. 760 ; Hetherington, p. 320.

almost the entire fortnight on the road Cornbury's protracted *hospitality* has prevented the intended visit to Boston.   However anxiously our pioneer desires to be with his family, he is ready to sacrifice his business and his pleasure for the sake of the Church.

The establishment of the first American Presbytery has been signalized by persecutions, but in the providence of God these persecutions of the moderator are helping his grand purpose forward, attracting the attention of the Presbyterians scattered through the Jerseys and on Long Island, enlisting their sympathies, reviving old memories, awakening their Church-attachments, and preparing for a general banding together in the years to come. Few in numbers, mingled with Independents, grown accustomed to the looser system of ecclesiastical government, it needs some such shock to arouse their dormant Presbyterian sentiment and cause them to move forward to complete organization.

How glad the brethren are to meet their acknowledged leader in Philadelphia !   At the opening of the Presbytery the ministers John Wilson, Jedediah Andrews, Nathaniel Taylor and George Macnish, and Elders Joseph Yard, William Smith, John Gardener and James Stoddard, are present   Mr. Wilson is elected moderator, and Mr. Macnish clerk.   A letter is read from Mr. Samuel Davis excusing himself for not attending the former and the present meetings of Presbytery, but his reasons are not sustained.   Those now present do not feel disposed to proceed with business until Mr. Makemie arrives from the North, and they adjourn over to Tuesday, the 25th, four o'clock P. M. At that time Mr Makemie, Mr. Hampton and Mr.

Boyd appear, coming from the jurisdiction of Lord Cornbury, and our pastor and Mr. Wilson preach, according to appointment, on the first and second verses of the first chapter of Hebrews. These discourses are approved.

Mr. Wilson is directed to write a letter to Mr. Davis requiring him to be present at the next meeting. The enactments of the youthful Presbytery are already not simply advisory, but authoritative.

Letters from Snow Hill church are read to the Presbytery, and the following action is taken:

"Whereas the aforesaid people do by their representatives and letters earnestly address the Presbytery for their joynt concurrence and assistance in prosecuting their call to Mr. John Hampton, that he may undertake the work of the Ministry among them as their settled and proper Minister and Pastor, Ordered by the Presbytery that the call be sent to Mr Hampton by the foresaid people, and also the other paper containing their subscriptions for his encouragement to undertake the work of the Ministry among them, be given to Mr Hampton to peruse and consider."

The pastor-elect having considered the call and made certain statements to the Presbytery, action is taken as follows:

"Whereas Mr. Hampton, after his receiving the call to him from the people at Snow Hill, gave several satisfactory reasons why he could not at this time comply with it; The said Mr. Hampton may have the call and the paper of subscription continued in his hands for his further perusal till the next Presbytery. Ordered further, in this affair, that a letter be sent in the name of the Presbytery to the people of Snow Hill, to encourage their endeavors for a settled Minister among them, and that Mr. Nathaniel Taylor write the letter expressing the mind of the Presbytery."

Their elder, Mr. William Smith, will bring this letter back to the little church to cheer them in their laudable efforts to put their church-relations upon a sound Presbyterian footing. From the brave village up the Pocomoke comes the first formal pastoral call known upon the American records.*

Our peninsular churches still look to the land of staunch Presbyterianism for ministers. On Wednesday, Mr. Makemie is directed to write to Mr. Alexander Coldin of Oxam, Scotland, to urge him to accept an invitation from our people about Lewes, and Mr. Wilson is appointed to write to Mr. Coldin's Presbytery. Mr Andrews and Mr. Boyd, having been made a committee on the day before to prepare overtures bearing upon the interests of religion in the various congregations, proposed the following, which were considered and adopted:

"1. That every minister, in the respective congregations, read and comment upon a chapter of the Bible every Lord's day, as discretion and circumstances of time, place &c., will admit. 2. That it be recommended to every minister of the Presbytery to set on foot and encourage private Christian societies. 3. That every minister of the Presbytery supply neighboring desolate places where a minister is wanting and opportunity of doing good offers"

Two things here are worthy of notice. The first overture proves that Independency is to have little influence in moulding our Presbyterian usages. Presbyterianism is determined to honor the Bible with a prominent place in the public services of the sanctuary. Our Scotch and Scotch-Irish ministry excel in expounding the word of God, and they call those who oppose it "dumb readers." The second point worthy to be remembered is the marked evangelistic spirit, as proved in the third overture. God's workmen are to

* See records   Published by the Presbyterian Board of Publication,

go out from the present centres and carry the gospel to destitute regions. However weak and feeble our churches, they must share the bread of life with starving souls around them. The mother-Presbytery is a missionary Presbytery.

After appointing Mr. Andrews to preach at the next meeting on the first clause of the third verse of the first chapter of Hebrews, and Mr. Taylor on the second clause, the Presbytery adjourns to convene in Philadelphia on the first Tuesday of April, 1708. Thus in that stronghold of Quakerism, which has sent its propagandists to convert the Eastern Shore to their mystic faith, our vigorous Presbytery sits down as in a permanent place of assembling. The transaction of business at these meetings moves on as smoothly as at St. Johnstown or in Edinburgh.

Everything from Mr. Makemie's lips or pen is growing more precious daily, and I want to preserve a letter written by his hand from the midst of these historic scenes. Two days after Presbytery adjourns, while awaiting conveyance southward, the friendly missive is addressed on the 28th to the Rev. Benjamin Colman, pastor of the Brattle Street church, Boston :

"R'D BROTHER, Since our imprisonment, we have commenced a correspondence with our r'd brethren of the ministry at Boston, which we hope, according to our intention, has been communicated to you all, whose sympathizing concurrence I cannot doubt in our expensive struggle for asserting our liberty against the powerful invasion of L'd Cornbury, which is not yet over. I need not tell you of a pick'd jury ; and the penal laws are invading our American sanctuary without the least regard to toleration ; which should justly alarm us all.

"I hope Mr. Campbell, to whom I direct this for the more safe conveyance, has shown or informed you what I wrote last. We are so far upon our return home ; tho' I must return for a final trial, which will be very troublesome and expensive. And we only had liberty to attend a meeting of ministers we had formerly appointed here, and were only seven in number at first but expect a growing number.

"Our design is to meet yearly, and oftener if necessary, to consult the most proper measures for advancing religion and propagating Christianity in our various stations, and to maintain such a correspondence as may conduce to the improvement of our ministerial abilities, by prescribing texts to be preached on by two of our number at every meeting, which performance is subjected to the censure of our brethren. Our subject is Paul's Epistle to the Hebrews. I and another began and performed our parts on vs. 1 and 2. The 3rd is prescribed to Mr. Andrews and another.

"If my friends write, direct to Mr. John Yard at Philadelphia, to be directed to me in Virginia. Pardon, sir, this diversion from—

Your humble servn't, and brother in the Work of the Gospel—

" FRANCIS MAKEMIE." *

The travel homeward is tedious and wearisome— down to New Castle to Mr. Wilson's congregation, thence across the peninsula to the Chesapeake, there to await some chance sloop down the bay to the Patuxent, and then another chance ketch over to the Eastern Shore. What joy it brings to all this country when at last we hear of his arrival on the Pocomoke and listen again to his eloquent words at Rehoboth!

During her husband's long absences in Europe and elsewhere, Naomi has grown accustomed to the management of his large estate—the store at the plantation, the mill at Assawaman, the sloops, the extensive landed interests. The women of America learn to be strong in time of need. Weaklings do not make heroes of husbands and children. Now thirty-nine years of age, Naomi is a sensible business-woman equal to the many emergencies of colonial life. And

* Neill's *Terra Mariæ*, p. 195; Colman papers, Boston.

yet the wife and the little girls sorely miss the loved one while away, and no heart but theirs and his and the Saviour's can ever know all the sacrifice in these long separations.

We feel prouder of this hero of Accomack, now that he has suffered bonds for the gospel's sake and means to return like Regulus into the hands of his enemies. A promise to preach no more in New York and the Jerseys will at any moment save him from the conflict; but no! with him there is no compromise. It is gratifying to see the leading men of our county gathering about him and volunteering to sign to the authorities in New York the strongest testimonials to the purity of his character as a citizen and a man of God. These testimonials he will carry back with him, " signed by some of the best quality of the most contiguous county," he says, in order to rebut any attempt to impeach his integrity.

I have been thinking of Mr. Makemie's own words in the sermon for which he suffers persecution :

" To whom much is given, of them is much required; much knowledge calls for much obedience; a strong faith, the more fruit, the higher our station or calling is, the more shining and exemplary should our lives be, the more grace God bestows on us, the more obedience will he require at our hands. Therefore it is not sufficient that we do as much as others do, that we are as holy and righteous as our neighbors; but is our walk and life suitable to the obligations we are under to God's gifts and graces bestowed on us, and answerable to the calling and station we are placed in of God ?"

The great Head of the Church had exalted this preacher into a position of prominence before the whole land. How pleasant to know that his grand life and spotless reputation will stand the scrutiny of every eye !

The conduct of his persecutors has been even more despicable than we had supposed.   Our pastor says:

"I cannot omit a true and strange story I lately heard of; That, during the imprisonment, either to find out a crime, none being specified in the *mittimus*, or to aggravate our imaginary faults, an order was given to Major Sandford of East Jersey to put sundry persons upon examination and their oaths, to discover what discourse we had with sundry of our friends at the house of Mr. Jasper Crane in Newarktown in East Jersey where Mr. Samuel Melyen, Mr. Crane, and another, gave their depositions before Major Sandford; but they found nothing to their purpose. The practice is not to be outdone, yea, scarcely paralleled by the Spanish Inquisition; for no men are safe in their most private conversations if most intimate friends can be compelled upon oath to betray one another's secrets.   If this is agreeable to the English Constitution and privileges, I confess we have been hitherto in the dark."

June is approaching, and into the power of such enemies our minister is firmly resolved to return. We see again the wisdom of God in putting means into the hands of this good man.   Were he poor, it would be impossible for him to fight the heavy conflict through.   Nothing compels his going.   Cornbury is very willing for the matter to rest where it is —the champion of Presbyterianism worried out of his government and the policy of suppression triumphant. When the Southern preacher boldly reappears to contest usurped authority, the governor and his minions will be only the more embittered.   As Mr. Makemie bids his friends farewell and turns northward, we think of Paul's journey from Miletus to Jerusalem, Luther's departure for the Diet at Worms, and the fearless defiance of tyranny when John Knox enters council-chamber and palace nor fears the face of man.

Our pioneer is not looking very well.   He takes one

of his servants with him, to be a help on the journey. The soft Maryland May is verging on toward the summer hours. Matchacoopah's *ah-seeque* (the crane) stands in the marshes watching for the little *kosh-kik-ene-suk* (the perch), *uck-quack* (the raven) croaks in the pines, and *ah-whap-pawn-top* (the eagle) leaves his nest and flies steadily up the coast. *Ah-skoke* and *oh-kaush-kip* (the snake and the lizard) sun themselves in *pamp-tuck-koik* (the woods). The eagle soars in his flight.

On Tuesday, June 3, the court sits in New York, and the defendant is promptly present, to the disappointment, unquestionably, of the authorities He is ordered to plead to-morrow On Wednesday he formally enters the plea of " Not guilty." Now follows some skirmishing with the prosecuting attorney, who proposes to introduce a copy of the queen's instructions in place of the original document. The governor is out of the city, and has left this paper certified under his signature Mr Makemie at first objects, but he sees that the attorney is likely to use this as a pretext to postpone the case until the next term Our minister then moves that he also may have a copy, and declares he

"cannot but wonder of what service these Instructions, which are no law, can do Mr Attorney, seeing the Presentment runs upon Statutes and Act of Parliament. He expects to have a trial before a Court who are judges of law and not of private instructions."

On Friday, the 6th, the petit jury is called and sworn. Mr. Makemie proves by Mr. Young that one of them has prejudged the case. This Huguenot is set aside, Mr Makemie sharply remarking:

"I am amazed to find one who was so lately dragooned out of France for his religion and delivered out of the galley, so soon prove a persecutor of the same religion for preaching a sermon in this city."

The doctrine of religious toleration is poorly understood. It is a sad fact that many who have suffered severely and have fled from great wrongs in Europe have become no less uncharitable and cruel to others as soon as the opportunity of power is given them. This must always be the result of the claim of the civil government to punish heresy.

There are several other French Protestants on the jury. I will record the whole panel, as a roll of honor: John Shepherd, Thomas Ives, Joseph Wright, Thomas Wooden, Joseph Robinson, Bartholomew Laronex, Andrew Lauron, Humphrey Perkins, William Horswell, Thomas Carrell, Thomas Baynex and Charles Cromline.

The queen's instructions—so often denied to the defendant, but admitted in evidence and found to be in precisely the words given by King William to a former governor—were as follows.

"And you are to permit a Liberty of Conscience to all Persons (except Papists) so they be contented with a quiet and peaceable enjoyment of it, not giving offence or scandal to the Government.

"You are not to permit any Minister coming from England to Preach in your Government without a Certificate from the Right Reverend, the Bishop of London; Nor any other Minister, coming from any other part or place, without first obtaining leave from you, our Governor."

The attorney being about to have four of Mr. Makemie's hearers sworn to prove the fact of the preaching, the defendant frankly said:

"The swearing of these four gentlemen as evidences will but

give a needless trouble and take up the time of the Court. I will own to the matter of fact as to my preaching, and more than these gentlemen can declare upon oath , for I have done nothing therein that I am ashamed or afraid of, but I will answer and own it, not only before this bar, but before the tribunal of God's final Judgment."

Attorney. "You own that you preached a sermon and baptized a child at Mr. William Jackson's ?"

Mr. M. "I did."

Att. "How many hearers had you ?"

Mr. M. "I have other work to do, Mr. Attorney, than number my auditory when I am about to preach to them."

Att. "Were there more than five hearing you ?"

Mr. M. "Yes, and five to that."

Att. "Did you use the rites and ceremonies enjoined by and prescribed in the Book of Common Prayer by the Church of England ?"

Mr. M. "No, I never did, nor ever will, till I am better satisfied in my conscience !"

The answer was bold and ringing, spoken with all the brave dignity of Presbyterian dissent.

Att. "Did you ask leave, or acquaint My Lord Cornbury with your preaching at York, when you dined with him ?"

Mr. M. "I did not know of my preaching at York when I dined with His Excellency ; no, not for some days after. When we came to York, we had not the least intention or design of preaching here but stopped at York purely to pay our respects to the Governor, which we did , but being afterward called and invited to preach, as I was a minister of the Gospel I durst not deny preaching ; and I hope I never shall, when it is wanting and desired."

Att. "Did you acquaint My Lord Cornbury with the place of your preaching ?"

Mr. M. "As soon as I determined to preach, leave was asked though not by me ; for it was the people's business, and not mine, to provide a place for me to preach in. I would have been admitted to preach in the Dutch Church, but they were afraid of offending Lord Cornbury. Anthony Young went to the Governor to have his leave or permission for my preaching in the Dutch Church, though all this was done without so much as my knowledge. But My Lord opposing and denying it, I was under the necessity of preaching where I did, in a private house, though in a public manner and with open doors."

It already begins to be manifest that the attorney is meeting no weakling in this defendant. But he proceeds to contend for the several parts of the indictment, arguing the supremacy of the queen in ecclesiastical affairs from old statutes of the reign of Henry VIII, and claiming that this same supremacy lodges by delegation in the governor. Then he pleads the statutes of Elizabeth and Charles for uniformity, and parades the penal laws against conventicles. After discussing these at some length and making a great deal of the queen's instructions, he says:

"Gentlemen of the Jury, the matter of fact is plainly confessed by the defendant, and I have proved it to be repugnant to the Queen's Instructions and sundry acts of Parliament, therefore I do not doubt but you will find for the Queen."

Mr. James Regniere and Mr. William Nicoll follow in defence, analyzing the indictment and showing that there has been no violation of law. These retained lawyers are supported in a strong speech by Mr. David Jamison, a Presbyterian and one of the ablest men in the province, a volunteer counsel for Mr. Makemie. He said:

"We do not come here to oppose or call in question the Queen's supremacy and Prerogative, but are willing to pay all due respect and deference thereunto. We cannot see that her instructions to Lord Cornbury are a law to anybody else but to His Lordship. In New York we have no established religion. On the East-end of Nassau or Long Island are, and always have been, Independent Ministers; * the French have their own way

* Jamison knew the difference between Presbyterianism and Independency, and the distinction is here made in the presence of the founder of American Presbyterianism. This is conclusive as to the

and Ministers, and the Dutch in like manner. The very Jews and Quakers have the free exercise of their religion. When we did set about erecting a Church of England congregation in this town and obtained a charter for the same of Governor Fletcher, although we were desirous to have the National Worship amongst us, yet was it the care of these members who promoted it, to get such clauses inserted in it as should secure the liberty of the Dutch and French congregations from our successors. And in an Act of Assembly made for its encouragement, the like care and precaution was had. This province has not been much more than forty years in the possession of the Crown of England, and is made up chiefly of foreigners and Dissenters ; and persecution would not only tend to disuniting us all in interest and affection, but depopulate and weaken our strength and discourage all such adventurers for the future. Therefore as this prosecution is the first of this nature or sort ever in this province, so I hope it will be the last."

This was the man who had helped to secure the planting of the Episcopal Church in New York. How different the spirit of those who would now gladly drive everything else out of the province!

Another champion of liberty takes the floor, Mr. Makemie himself asking and obtaining permission to speak. I give his own words:

"I am amazed to find Mr. Attorney so much changed in his opinion ; for when I was before My Lord Cornbury, who told us the Act of Toleration was limited and local and extended not to the Plantations, Mr. Attorney was pleased to confirm it by asserting the same thing, and went a little further by producing an argument to strengthen his opinion, That the Penal Laws of England did not extend to the Plantations, and the Act of Toleration was made to take off the edge of the Penal Laws ; therefore the Toleration does not extend hither. But we find soon after, by an Indictment, both the Penal Laws and Toleration reach hither—and all their penalties too!"

Chief-Justice. "Gentlemen, do not trouble the Court with what discourse passed between you before My Lord or at any other time ; but speak to the point."

claims of Hempstead, Jamaica, etc., to be the birthplace of the American Presbyterian Church.

Mr. Makemie's opening had been very adroit, showing that the prosecution has changed front since the
arrest, and letting the jury know that the governor
himself has testified to the righteousness of the theory
of the defence. Our minister is not to be cheated out
of his advantage by the interruption of the court:

" May it please Your Honor, I hope to make it appear that it
is to the point, and what was Mr. Attorney's argument then, is
now mine. For whatever opinion I was of, while an absolute
stranger to New York and its Constitution, yet since I have informed myself thoroughly with the Constitution of this place, I
am entirely of Mr. Attorney's opinion, and hope he will be of the
same still.

"As to the Indictment, to return to the particulars thereof, first
I am charged with contemning and endeavoring to subvert the
supremacy of the Queen in Ecclesiastical affairs. As to the
Queen's supremacy about Ecclesiastical persons and things, we
allow and believe that she has as large a supremacy as in the
Word of God is allowed to any Christian kings and princes. Our
Confession of Faith which will compare with any in the world,
and is universally known to the Christian world, is very full in
that matter."

The standards of his Church in hand, he stands and
reads:

"God, the Supreme Lord and King of all the world, hath ordained Civil Magistrates to be, under him, over the people, for
his own glory and the public good. It is the duty of people to
pray for Magistrates, to honor their persons, to obey their lawful
commands, and to be subject to their authority for conscience,
sake."

Thus the Confession of Faith, proudly quoted and
its worth boldly asserted before the courts of New
York, is shown to be not such a dangerous or treasonable book, after all. He proceeds:

" I cannot learn one argument or one word from all the quoted
Statutes that preaching a sermon is the least contempt or over-

throw of the supremacy. And I hope it is not unknown to any that the oath of supremacy has been abolished by law ever since the Revolution, and consequently the subjects of the government must be delivered from some obligation thereby. How far this will be considered to extend, I leave to the Judges to determine

"As to my preaching without license first obtained from Lord Cornbury, which is asserted to be against law, I cannot hear from any law yet produced that Lord Cornbury has any power or directions to grant license to any Dissenters, or that any of them are under obligations to take license from His Lordship, before they preach or after. Mr. Attorney pretends no law, unless he concludes the Queen's Instructions to be a law or to have the force of law That they have no force of law, has been abundantly proved. Neither am I any way culpable even from the Queen's Instructions which are produced in Court; for they consist of two parts, or rather two distinct Instructions, not relating at all to the same persons.

" In the first, His Excellency is required to permit liberty of conscience to all persons except Papists. This liberty is allowed to Dissenters, which we claim by virtue of this Instruction. Here is no license mentioned or required. Permission is a negative act, and implies no more than this—You shall so allow it, as not to hinder, molest or disquiet them, but rather protect them in it. Papists being particularly expressed, it cannot be applied to the Church of England. Therefore, Dissenters are intended by this Instruction, and no other. If this permission is granted us, according to the express words thereof, we desire no more. It cannot be esteemed by any that imprisoning and punishing us at such a rate for preaching one sermon is permitting us liberty of conscience.

" The two paragraphs, though joined together in this copy, are at a considerable distance from one another in the original—as we really found it so in a copy of instructions to a former Governor. As the former concerns Dissenters, so this is intended for the clergy of the Church of England , who by their Constitution are under strict obligations to take license or certificate from their Ordinary; and such as come to the Plantations acknowledge the Bishop of London as such No Dissenter, either in England or anywhere else in the Queen's dominion, ever took or was ever under any obligation to take any license from the Queens or Kings of England, or any other person or persons whatsoever— until a method has of late been erected and forced into practice in New York. If our liberty either depended on a license from the

Bishops of England or the Governors of America, we should
soon be depiived of our libeity of conscience secuied to us by
law and by repeated resolutions of our present sovereign and
giacious Queen inviolably to maintain the Toleration; which
she is pleased to signify in her royal Instiuctions to all her Governors abroad, and which we are the more assured of from the
Instructions produced in this Court. As the first clause of this
second instruction cannot be applied to any other Ministers but
of the Church of England, so the latter clause can be understood of no other but the same soit. Mr. Sharp, now Chaplain
at Fort Anne, came from Maryland. He being a Minister of the
Church of England and enjoying a considerable benefice thereby, was obliged to comply with the Constitution of his own
Chuich and take a license from Lord Cornbury if none could
be produced from the Bishop of London. All this is foreign to
us, and not at all required of any Dissenter in Europe or
America.

"But it has already been made appear that these Instructions
cannot have the foice of law to bind the subject to obedience,
seeing that Promulgation, which is the life of the law, has never
yet accompanied these Instructions. So if this be Mr. Attorney's
law we have broke, I hope you, Gentlemen of the Jury, cannot
but find that we aie no way culpable thereby.

"As to the last part of the Indictment concerning the Penal
Laws or the Sundry Statutes against Conventicles, they never
were designed nor intended by our English Legislators for
America or any of the Plantations thereof. They are limited
and local Acts, all of them restiicted to England, Wales and
Berwick upon Tweed, as is manifest fiom the express words.
Neither have they ever been put in execution in any of the Plantations until now. Yea, in England, Wales and Berwick upon
Tweed, for which they were calculated and made, they have not
been executed these twenty years past. When they were put in
the most strict and rigorous execution in England, which was
about the last of the reign of King Charles II, the Dissenters
of America lived very quiet, even in such Plantations where the
Church of England has a full and formal Establishment. What
is more, the Roman Catholics, who aie excluded from all benefit of the Act of Toleration, cannot be touched in America by
these Penal Laws.

"If the Penal Laws of England do not extend to those Plantations where the Church of England has a legal Establishment, it
cannot be imagined that they can take place where there is no

particular persuasion established by law and where consequently all persuasions are upon an equal bottom of liberty. This I find to be the case with New York, where there is not one Act of Assembly wherein the name or manner of worship of the Church of England is so much as expressed. Where there is no legal Establishment or any penalties or restrictions on the liberty of any Dissenters, there is no room for any Toleration. In New York government all persuasions are upon an equal level of liberty. This is confirmed to all Dissenters, except Papists, and allowed by an Act of Assembly already read in open Court. And if Jews who openly blaspheme the Lord Jesus, Quakers and Lutherans and all other persuasions are allowed in this government, it is matter of wonder and I can know no reason why we only should be put to molestation as we are by my present prosecution. Is it because we are Protestants? Is it because we are likest the Established Church of England of any Dissenters? Is it because we are the most considerable body of Protestants in the Queen's dominions? Is it because we have now, since the Union, a National Establishment in Great Britain as nighly related and annexed unto the Crown as the Church of England itself? Sure such proceedings, when known, will and must be a prodigy in England!"

In taking the floor again, the attorney began by saying:

"There has been so much delivered and by so many, it is impossible for any man to answer all that has been offered."

Mr. M. "I verily believe it *is* impossible for Mr. Attorney to answer what has been said. It is a great truth which Mr. Attorney asserts!"

Our minister's readiness in debate may be seen in his prompt answer to the attorney's triumphant boast that he can produce one statute not local or limited, but reaching to all the royal dominions. He quotes from the Act of Uniformity made in the first year of Elizabeth and containing the words:

"Or other place within this realm of England, Wales and the Marches of the same, and other the Queen's dominions."

Mr. M. "I hope to make it appear that this Act does no way affect the Plantations and far less affect Dissenters ; therefore is altogether foreign to our present purpose. For, *First*, That Act of Parliament was made in the first year of the reign of Elizabeth and consequently before any Plantation had a being or was thought of, and so could have no relation to them at all. *Second*, All over the Act, and in sundry places thereof, it is directed to Ministers and Parsons or Vicars in Cathedrals, Parish-Churches, Private Chapels, or Oratorios ; and not a word, in the whole Act, of Dissenters or Conventicles. For, *Third*, At that time, when this Act was made, there were not, strictly and properly speaking, any number of Dissenters in England who held separate meetings from the public and established worship. There were those however in the Church of England who always, from the beginning of the Reformation, scrupled the use of all the Common Prayer and omitted some ceremonies, which was and is to-day the grounds of the separation , and it was to oblige such to a uniformity in public worship. As soon as the Act was made and put in execution, with all its penalties, many were discouraged and others cast out of the Church for nonconformity. This really made the separation, and all the mischiefs of the separation are originally owing to this Act. As soon as the separation was made, they could not touch Dissenters by the penalties of this Act and therefore were under the necessity of making new Acts of Parliament in the following reigns for punishing separated Dissenters ; all which were limited and local in express words, and never designed to pursue persecuted persons to an American wilderness. *Fourth*, I am able to make it appear that, if this Act of Uniformity were strictly put in execution, the most of the clergy of the Church of England would fall under its lashes and penalties ; for none of them are to use any other Rite, Ceremony or open Prayer but what is mentioned and set forth in the said Book of Common Prayer. But it is well known that the most valuable men in that Church use another public prayer than is in that book ; and all such persons, being in communion with the Church of England, are alone liable to be prosecuted upon this Statute.

" Mr. Attorney affirms that giving and taking license is very common and universal. I am well assured that there never was, neither is to this day, any such practice in any Plantation in America. There are but few persons as yet in York Government that have licenses. Besides the two Dutch Ministers who differ upon Long Island, and it is said that licenses are the cause of their difference, there is but one English Nonconformist Minister in all the government who has taken license. It is certain that Mr. Dubois and sundry others of the Dutch Churches have no license, neither will submit to any such as are granted."

Mr. Makemie's stock of historical and general information is too great for the attorney. The latter, seeing that the jury are impressed, now claims that they shall bring in a special verdict as to the simple fact of preaching, already admitted by the defendant, and leave the question of crime wholly to the judges. Mr. Makemie promptly objects:

"May it please Your Honors; I am a stranger who live four hundred miles from this place, and it is known to the whole country what intolerable trouble I have been put to already, and we cannot consent to a special verdict, for that is only to increase my trouble, multiply my charge, and give me further delay. It is a known truth in law that strangers are to be favored always with expedition in justice and it does no way approve of delays. If this should be allowed, no man's innocence is able to protect him. If I am cleared, I should suffer more in charges at last than if I were really guilty of many Penal Laws of England.

"As to the Jury's judging of law, and my confessing the fact, I cannot see one point of the law to be judged. For that the Penal Laws are local and limited is owned on all sides; and Penal Laws are strictly to be taken and interpreted, and not allowed to the ruin of the subject to extend or be interpreted beyond the plain and strict sense of the words. It is also true that we have confessed preaching a sermon at the house of Mr. William Jackson with all the true circumstances, but we have not owned this to be a crime or repugnant to any law or inconsistent with any of the Queen's Instructions yet produced. Neither has Mr Attorney made anything of this yet to appear."

Att. "These gentlemen acknowledge and say that the Ministers of the Church of England are to take licenses and are obliged so to do. If so, the Dissenters should also; otherwise they must expect more favor and liberty than the Ministers of the Church of England."

Mr. M. "The case is very different; for it is the opinion and constitution of the Church of England that, notwithstanding their ordination, they are not to preach or officiate as Ministers until they procure or have a license from their Bishop or Ordinary, which no Dissenting Minister is concerned with ; and their clergy voluntarily and freely bring themselves under an oath of Canonical obedience to their Ordinary If he require them to take licenses or anything else, they are sworn to submit thereunto. Finally, there is a great reason why Ministers of the Church of England should submit to license but we should not ; because it is only *bare liberty* which Dissenters have, but *they* have not only liberty but a considerable *maintenance also*, without which I never knew any of them value liberty only. Dissenters having liberty only without any maintenance from the government, are not under any obligations, nor is it required of them, to take license of any."

The chief-justice, not being clear in his mind how far unpublished instructions may go in having the force of law, and also as to the point raised by Mr. Makemie that the oath of supremacy is abolished in England, tells the jury that he prefers a special verdict, but that they may do as they please about it

The Presbyterian parson has puzzled the New York attorney and the New York Bench. They are not left long in suspense. The jury soon returns, and finds the defendant " Not guilty "!

Lord Cornbury's judges are dissatisfied, and begin to demand reasons for the verdict. The chief-justice instructs them that they may choose whether they will or will not give their reasons. The foreman answers that the defendant *has transgressed no law*. On the next day, Saturday, June 7, Mr. Makemie is discharged, but ordered to pay all the costs. To this he righteously objects.

"It is an hard case that an innocent person, and one found so upon trial and by law, and suffering so much already, and not only innocently but for doing good, should pay so severe fees at last."

Finally, he signifies his willingness to pay all legal fees to the court and other officers who have not been endeavoring to secure his conviction, but he protests against rewarding his prosecutors for their zeal against him :

"This will be nothing else than hiring our enemies to ruin us."

No argument is permitted, and there is no appeal. Then Mr. Makemie asks that, as a stranger, he may not be left to the arbitrary demands of officers, but that the bill may be examined in open court. The chief-justice declines to have anything to do with it, and refers it to Justice Milward, one of his assistants, who is to tax the bill after due notice of time and place given to defendant or his attorney. This notice was not given, and, instead of abating anything from the heavy charges, others are added. The exorbitant bill is paid to the last farthing, and then a receipt for the money is refused !

I give the items of cost, as preserved by Mr. Makemie :

" To Thomas Cardale, Sheriff of Queen's County, for ap, rehending and bringing us before Lord Cornbury at Fort Anne—four pounds, one shilling. To charges at Jamaica, whither we were carried out of our way—twelve shillings To expenses at White Hall Tavern, while attending Lord Cornbury's leisure, besides what sundry friends spent—two shillings, three pence. To Ebenezer Wilson, High Sheriff, for commitment to his house—four pounds, one shilling To the same for accommodation (board &c. at his house during imprisonment,—thirteen pounds, five shillings, six pence. To the same for extraordinary expenses during the time of our imprisonment—six pounds To the same for a copy of the Panel—five shillings, six pence. To the same for Return and *Habeas Corpus*—four pounds, one shilling. To the same for fees after trial—one pound, ten shillings."

Thus the fees of the two sheriffs amounted to thirty-three pounds, sixteen shillings !

Other officers of the court he paid as follows :

" To the Chief-Justice when we gave recognizance—one pound, sixteen shillings. To the same, after the first term—eighteen shillings. To the Judge—one pound. To Judge Milward, for taxing the bill of cost I think—twelve shillings. To Mr. Secretary for fees—five pounds, twelve shillings, six pence. To the Crier and Under Sheriff—ten shillings. To Mr. Attorney for the Queen, though cleared—twelve pounds, twelve shillings, six pence !"

This last is the greatest outrage of all, compelling a man pronounced innocent to pay the lawyer who strove to convict him and failed ! In addition to all this must be added the expenses incurred by himself:

"To my charges in returning with my man from Virginia, both by land and water, to attend trial at New York—twelve pounds, six shillings, six pence. To Mr Regniere—nine pounds, nineteen shillings, nine pence. To Mr. Nichol—four pounds, two shillings."

Here is a sum-total of eighty-one pounds, four shillings, nine pence, wrested from a person, says Mr. Makemie,

"who is not only innocent, but for doing good, as was determined by the trial ; and for complying with the most solemn obligations of duty both to God and the souls of men. In addition to which, besides loss of time and absence from my family and concerns, I might have justly charged twelve pounds more money, by being necessitated to make my escape, both by land and water, to New England, from Officers with new Precepts ; whereby a whole Sabbath was profaned in seeking to apprehend me."

Thereby hangs another story. Of course, among the better class of people in New York and the country adjoining, there was great rejoicing over Mr. Makemie's triumphant vindication ; but while he walked under the shadow of Fort Anne as the successful champion of the rights of conscience against the will of a tyrant, there were those who hated and watched him.

While the suit was pending, the sermon which was Cornbury's pretext for the great wrong had been published in Boston, its dedication to those who had heard it being dated March 3, five days before the writ of *habeas corpus* was obtained. In the sheriff's own house, during imprisonment, the weary days had been occupied in writing it out for publication, and thence it passed to the printers (74).

This sermon was now in circulation and inflaming his enemies only the more. They feel its publication to be a challenge and defiance, and sinners are certainly aroused, though probably not in the way contemplated by Mr. Makemie when he said:

"That this Discourse may be blessed of God to awaken sinners to reflect on and detect the irregularities of their past lives and furnish any with prevailing considerations to a more universal conformity to the rules of the Gospel, is and shall be the desire of him who is a well-wisher to immortal souls."

On Sabbath our minister preached in the Huguenot church, the late trial attracting no little attention to the preacher. The governor and his sycophantic Churchmen feel their defeat, and something must be done. The pretended Establishment is threatened! An uproar like that of which the counsel Nichol spoke as prevailing at Ephesus because of a dreaded loss of gain, rages around Fort Anne. Says Mr. Makemie:

"Preaching in a private house was a crime; and preaching since, after being declared not guilty in a legal trial, in a public Church allowed by law to the French, is since resented as a greater crime by some high-flown sparks, pretended sons of the Church, who with a great deal of unbounded fury declared that if such things were allowed, their Church was ruined! Which is language of the same nature of those high-fliers in England who were declared by a vote of the House of Lords enemies to the Queen and Government for suggesting that the Church was in danger from the liberty or Toleration of Dissenters." *

Lord Cornbury's venom rankles against the man who is checking his arbitrary will. Another pretext for persecution must be found. The governor's life, private and official, supplies a tempting target to satire, and early in the year there appeared in print a severe excoriation under the title of *Forget and Forgive.* This philippic was never read or seen by Mr. Makemie until he was in prison, but it now serves the purpose of Cornbury and his party to charge the authorship of the pamphlet upon the minister. Another prosecution is ordered, the officers are commanded to make the arrest; search is made everywhere; but the intended victim has friends, information is given, and he is safely on his way to New England. Soon he reaches Boston, whither he started six months ago.

Mr. Makemie is now among friends. By the slow exchanges of the day, occasional communications from his hand have come hither in reference to the great interests of Christ's kingdom. In his former loneliness in the American desert he had sought fellowship of thought and counsel with the strong men in these regions, doctrinally the same, differing only in views of church government. Twenty-three years ago letters

* Knight, v. 170. The term "highfliers" is this year used by the secretary for Ireland, himself a Churchman, and applied to High-Church Tories (Reid, ii 527).

and other courtesies had begun to pass between him and Increase Mather, the ablest man then on the American continent. In the old Puritan way, the name "Increase" had been given because of "the increase of every sort wherewith God favored the country about the time of his nativity." Born on American soil, he has also breathed the air of Mr. Makemie's own native isle, having taken his Master's degree at Trinity College, Dublin, in 1658. President of Harvard College seventeen years, now sixty-eight of age, he is found by our minister still adding to his stores of learning by sixteen hours of daily study. He may sit by the old man and read his book of *Illustrious Providences*, published the year after our pioneer's arrival on the Pocomoke and while he was writing the letters from Elizabeth River. The advocate of liberty against Lord Cornbury will find a warm sympathizer in him who stood foremost in Massachusetts against the tyranny of Sir Edmund Andros, and who said of oppressions not dissimilar :

"The Foxes were now made the administrators of justice to the Poultry."

Mr. Makemie will also visit the great Mather's greater son, his copastor in the North church, now already famous at forty years of age. Cotton Mather will entertain him with his wonderful readiness of wit and unexampled erudition, and may possibly admit to him, as he has admitted to others, that in the late witchcraft frenzy he "went too far" The scholarly host will not be averse to any compliment he may see fit to bestow upon that ponderous book *The Magnalia,* issued five years ago and over the publication of which he had passed through "so many prayers and cares and tears and resignations." The visits must not be too extended, for over the study-door are the suggestive words " Be Short." The New England poet Benjamin Thomson well says of him, " Play is his toil and work his recreation."

Our pastor will probably meet the preacher-poet Nicholas Noyes of Salem, who was likewise carried away with the terrible delusion, but now humbly confesses the great wrong and goes about trying to make reparation for his course against the poor old witches.

Of course, Mr. Makemie will talk face to face with his correspondent the eloquent Benjamin Colman, and will tell him further of the work of the gospel to the southward, and of the prospects of the infant Presbytery, now composed of the sacred number of seven. Perhaps his friend will read to him his poem *Elijah's Translation*, published this year, or his gifted little daughter Jane may entertain him with some of her youthful rhymes and question him about his own little girls far away in the Virginia land

Perhaps, too, our minister will listen to some of the last of those wonderful theological lectures of Rev. Samuel Willard in the South church, or perhaps he will stand among the mourners at the funeral of this great man and hear his colleague pronounce him " for so long a time the light, joy and glory of the place;" for this year closes for ever his two hundred and fifty lectures on the Assembly's Catechism. It will be a delight to Mr. Makemie to find our doctrinal standards so honored by the grander intellects of New England

So pass the weeks among these giants of Congregationalism.   Here had been published the *Answer to Keith* under the endorsement of Willard, the Mathers and others.   Here, too, has been issued the New York sermon.   Mr. Makemie appears among these men as one not unknown—the brave representative of the Scotch and Scotch-Irish Presbyterianism of the continent.   There he is, hundreds of miles from home, with New York between, bristling with warrants and false accusations.   Mr. Makemie is not willing to relinquish his plans for extending and compacting our ecclesiastical system northward from Philadelphia, but the policy of Lord Cornbury stands directly across his way.

Another attempt is made to influence the governor by conciliatory means.   Under date of July 28, Mr. Makemie thus addresses him from Boston:

"May it please Your Lordship; I must humbly beg leave to represent to Your Excellency my just astonishment at the information received from sundry hands since my arrival in these Colonies, and after so long and so expensive a confinement, so deliberate and fair a trial before Judges of Your Lordship's appointment and by a jury chosen by your own Sheriff on purpose to try the matter.   I have been legally cleared, and found guilty of no crime, for preaching a sermon at New York, though my innocence protected not from intolerable expense.

"I am informed, may it please Your Excellency, there are orders and directions given to sundry officers in the Jerseys for apprehending me, and a design of giving me fresh trouble at New York.

"If I were assured of the true cause of Your Lordship's repeated resentments against me, I doubt not but my innocence would not only effectually justify me, but remove those impressions imposed on Your Lordship by some persons about you.

"And as to my preaching; being found at the trial against no law nor any ways inconsistent with Her Majesty's Instructions produced there; and considering the solemn obligations I am under, both to God and the souls of men, to embrace all opportunities for exercising those ministerial gifts vouchsafed from Heaven, to whom I do appeal that I have no other end besides the glory of God and the eternal good of precious souls; I must assure myself Your Lordship insists not on this now as a crime, especially in New York Government where all Protestants are upon an equal level of liberty and there is no legal Establishment for any particular Persuasion.

"I hear I am charged with the Jersey Paper, called, *Forget and Forgive.* Though the proving a negative in my just vindication be a hard task and not an usual undertaking, yet I doubt not but the thing itself [will clear me], the matter it contains being foreign to me; the time of its publication, being so soon spread abroad after my arrival. I am well assured that none dare legally accuse me, while the authors smile at Your Lordship's mistake and imposition, whose informers deserve to be stigmatized with the severest marks of Your Lordship's displeasure, and the authors will find a time to confront my sworn accusers with perjury. And besides that, I never saw it till about the last of February.

"We have suffered greatly in our reputations, and particularly by being branded with the character of Jesuits; though my universal known reputation in Europe and America, makes me easy under such invidious imputations. I have been represented to Your Lordship as being factious in the Government, both of Virginia and Maryland. I have peaceably lived in Virginia, and I brought from Maryland a certificate of my past reputation, signed by some of the best quality of the most contiguous county, ready to be produced at the Trial, if there had been occasion for it. A copy of which I presume to inclose for Your Lordship's perusal and satisfaction.

"I beg leave to represent to Your Lordship my just concern at the sundry Precepts for apprehending me, both in York and Jerseys, as one of the greatest criminals, whereby I am prevented in performing my own ministerial duties to many in Your Lordship's Government of my own Persuasion who desire it. I shall patiently expect Your Lordship's commands and directions, in giving me an opportunity for vindicating myself in what is charged against me, and being always ready to comply with any qualification enjoined and required by law.

"I beg leave of Your Lordship to subscribe myself Your Excellency's most humble and most obedient servant."

While respectful, the letter abates nothing from the principles of law and liberty maintained in the trial.

He stands proudly upon his known character as a peer of the highest. The baseless accusations of perjured informers are treated with the scorn they deserve, and he challenges investigation and an opportunity to prove his innocence. But it is all done as by one who respects dignities and honors the law.

The opportunity for a fair vindication was not to be given This is not the plan of those who mean to keep so eloquent a heretic and so skillful an organizer out of New York and the Jerseys Cornbury has been disappointed in his attempts both upon Bownas and upon Makemie, and he wants no more judicial trials. Threatened incarceration, long delays, officers hungry for extortionate fees, the reiteration of unproved charges and base slanders,—these are better weapons.

Finally, Mr. Makemie opens his batteries upon this systematized tyranny. He *will* be heard. The whole disreputable procedure shall be held up to the execration of people everywhere. The press has served him well in the past, and he resolves to touch this mighty lever once more. He has carefully preserved the important documents in the case, and he draws up a full account of his treatment by the governor and his underlings, from the beginning through, and publishes it to the world, exposing the unholy prosecution in all its phases (75). He begins with the words:

"You have here a specimen of the clogs and fetters with which the liberty of Dissenters is entangled at New York and Jersey Governments beyond any places in Her Majesty's dominions"

He closes the merciless exposure with the significant sentence:

"A fair and legal decision cannot put an end to a controversy where the *same fact* is made criminal and a new Process violently designed and vigorously aimed at by such as nothing but the interposition of the authority of England will put a stop to."

This latter clause is the more significant from his publishing in the same pamphlet an Act of Parliament of the year 1700 for punishing governors who shall be found "guilty of oppressing any of His Majesty's subjects beyond the seas."

No answer is deigned by Lord Cornbury to Mr. Makemie's letter, and he reaches home as he can. But his injuries are not unnoted in the North. New York begins to be agitated with the voice of his wrongs, and to awake to the fact that their own sacred rights are in the grasp of a conscienceless usurper. Before the autumn has passed, the governor finds it necessary to undertake his own defence before his superiors in England. The violent blow aimed at Presbyterianism has proved a barren victory at last. In trying to crush the "strolling preacher" from the South, he did not know that he was arousing the same spirit which had overwhelmed his grandfather Clarendon and carried Clarendon's master to the block. Under date of October 14, we find him, with many misrepresentations, thus writing to the Right Honorable Lords Commissioners for Trade and Commerce:

" I trouble Your Lordships with these lines to acquaint you that on the 17th of January, 1707, a man of this town, one Jackson, came to acquaint me that two ministers were come to town, one from Virginia and one from Maryland, and that they desired to know when they might speak with me. I, being willing to show what civility I could to men of that character, ordered my man to tell Jackson that they should be welcome to come and dine with me. They came; and then I found, by the answers they gave to the questions I asked them, that one whose name is

Francis Mackensie is a Presbyterian Preacher settled in Virginia, the other, whose name is John Hampton, a young Presbyterian minister lately come to settle in Maryland. They dined with me and talked of indifferent matters   They pretended they were going toward Boston   They did not say one syllable to me of preaching here, nor did not ask leave to do it   They applied themselves to the Dutch minister for leave to preach in the Dutch church in this town; who told them he was very willing provided they could get my consent. They never came to me for it."

The governor prevaricates. Though the ministers did not themselves apply, yet, as seen in Mr. Makemie's testimony, Anthony Young did apply and was refused   The letter continues:

" They went likewise to the Elders of the French Church; they gave them the same answer the Dutch had. All this while they never applied themselves to me for leave, nor did they offer to qualify themselves as the law directs. But on the Monday following, I was informed that Mackensie had preached on the day before at the house of one Jackson, a shoemaker in this town; and that Hampton had preached on Long Island, and that Mackensie had gone over thither with intent to preach in all the towns in that island, having spread a report thereto that they had a commission from the Queen to preach all along this continent

" I was informed on the same day from New Jersey, that the same men had preached in several places in that province, and had ordained after their manner some young men who had preached without it among the Dissenters;* and that, when asked if they had leave from the Government, they said they had no need of leave from any Governor; that they had the Queen's authority for what they did. These reports, and the information I had from Long Island of their behavior there, induced me to send an order to the Sheriff of Queen's county to bring them to this place; which he did on the 23rd of January in the evening. The Attorney General was with me. I asked Mackensie how he came to preach in this Government without acquainting me with it, and without qualifying as the law re-

* Evidently Boyd at Freehold, indicating pretty certainly the place of the first Presbytery with which the present old presbyterial records open.

31

quires ? He told me he had qualified himself according to law in Virginia, and that, having done so, he would preach in any part of the Queen's dominions where he pleased ; that this province is a part of the Queen's dominions as well as Virginia, and that the license he had obtained there, was as good as any he could obtain here.

"I told him that Virginia was part of the Queen's dominions as well as this province, but that they are two different governments, and that no law or order of that province can take place in this, any more than any order or law of this province can take place in that, which no reasonable man would imagine could be allowed He told me he understood the law as well as any man, and was satisfied he had not offended against the law ; that the penal laws did not extend to, and were not enforced in America. To which the Attorney General replied that if the penal laws did not take place in America, neither did the Act of Toleration , 'nor is it proper,' said he, 'that it should, since the latter is no more than a suspension of the former.'

" Mackensie said that the Queen granted liberty of conscience to all her subjects without reserve. I told him he was so far in the right; that the Queen was graciously pleased to grant liberty of conscience to all her subjects except Papists ; that *he* might be a Papist, for all I knew, under pretence of being of another persuasion ; and that, therefore, it was necessary that he should have satisfied the Government what he was before he ventured to preach. He said he would qualify himself in any manner and would settle in this province. I told him that, whenever any of the people in either of the provinces under my government had desired leave to call a minister of their own persuasion, they had never been denied; but that I should be very cautious how I allowed a man so prone to bid defiance to Government as I found he was. He said he had done nothing he could not answer.

"So I ordered the High Sheriff of this city to take them into custody, and I directed the Attorney General to proceed against them as the law directs ; which he has done by preferring an indictment against Mackensie for preaching in this city without qualifying himself as the Act of Toleration directs The grand jury found the bill ; but the petit jury acquitted him. So he has gone toward New England, uttering many severe threats against me As I hope I have done nothing in this matter but what I was obliged in duty to do, especially since I think it is very plain by the Act of Toleration it was not intended to tolerate or allow strolling preachers, but only those persons who dissent from the Church of England should be at liberty to serve God after their own way in the several places of their abode, without being liable to the penalties of certain laws; so I entreat Your Lordships' protection against this malicious man who is well-known in Virginia and Maryland to be a disturber of the peace and quiet of all the places he comes into."

And yet at this very time Lord Cornbury had in hand the certificate of many leading citizens of Somerset county that this was not the case! It is pitiful to see the persecutor pleading for protection against his intended victim and trying to secure safety by perversion of the facts. He goes on trying to prejudice the minds of the English authorities against Mr. Makemie:

"He is a Jack-at-all-trades, he is a preacher, a doctor of physic, a merchant, an attorney, a counsellor at law, and, which is worst of all, a disturber of governments. I should have sent Your Lordships this account sooner, but I was willing to see the issue of the trial. I am, My Lords, Your Lordships' most faithful, humble servant."*

It will be noticed that the most flagrant circumstances of the case are here concealed. Nor is one word said of the queen's instructions, upon which the prosecution and Cornbury's claims of ecclesiastical authority were principally based. It is amusing to read the hard-pressed governor's caricatures of the pioneer, whose usefulness is not the less because he distributes both medicine and legal advice among a poor and primitive people. Evidently, the parson of the Pocomoke has frightened the cousin of Queen Anne until Lord Cornbury has become as censorious as Madam Tabitha Hill herself!

* Webster, p. 307.   Found in the Albany documents.

Before closing this chapter, I will anticipate certain events of the following years. In his *Narrative*, Mr. Makemie had said :

"Though the foregoing Trial has opened the eyes and undeceived most if not all at New York in this matter—for which they may thank a prison—so this is to enlighten, not only those abroad in the world, but also influence and direct the Assemblys of New York for the future , in not giving a handle to any to pervert their laws contrary to the intention of the Legislators, or in not confirming by subsequent Acts their unjust possessions "

Next year the Legislature took steps to prevent the recurrence of such infamous extortions upon those pronounced innocent by the courts. Cornbury grows more unpopular, parades the ramparts of Fort Anne dressed in women's clothes, and begins to exercise his tyranny upon ministers of the Establishment.* This despotism they had encouraged until it recoiled upon themselves. The home government finally removes him from office, and thereupon he is immediately arrested by his creditors and committed to the same prison where he had confined Makemie and Hampton for nearly two months. He had fallen into the pit which he had digged.†

While Presbyterianism has been fighting this battle for religious liberty upon American soil, the same war waxes hot in Ireland. The English government and their representative, the Earl of Pembroke, are doing what they can to protect Irish Dissenters in their rights, but the Anglican bishops and clergy are defeating these tolerant principles and enforcing the sacramental test. The old patriots of Derry and Ennis-

* Anderson's *Colonial Church*, iii. 300.

† Smith's *History of New York.* I have taken account of trial from Makemie's *Narrative*—one of the Force Tracts in my possession.

killen refuse to yield, and are deprived of their civil rights all over the kingdom. It is a kinsman of these who has stood firmly for liberty of conscience in America, and who finally drove Lord Cornbury from power.

The next time we saw Mr. Makemie in our new church at Rehoboth, he looked to me older and lacking something of his former vigor. It seemed strange to see our brave hero now walking with a cane and appearing to lean upon it at times, the black camlet cloak hanging about him loosely. Was this a suggestion of advancing years and of a vacancy ere long?*

I am wondering if Mr. Makemie, during his sojourn in New England, saw the bright little four-year-old Jonathan Edwards, son of the godly father and queenly mother at Winsor, Connecticut. Did our minister smile upon the tiny one-year-old Benjamin Franklin in Boston? Did he meet with the Yale graduate of two years ago, Jonathan Dickinson, now twenty years old and just moving to Elizabethtown, New Jersey? and did our pioneer leave his blessing upon the sprightly young man? And, thinking of the children, I follow once more our minister in his former trip across the ocean to seek for ministers for the New World, and wonder if he sought them among the babies Gilbert and William in the house of the Episcopal clergyman William Tennent of Antrim, the first born in 1703 and the other in 1705?

* Cloak and cane mentioned in his will, the latter "fixed" in Boston.

CHAPTER XXX.

A. D. 1708.

" How unspeakably transporting must it be, when we come to a Dying Bed, to look back and see we have lived the Life of the Right-eous, and have a well-grounded hope we shall die the death of the Righteous !"—MAKEMIE

ROBERT KING, now nineteen years old, has come over from his sister's, Mrs. Mary Jenkins, and takes our little Francis and the two Makemie girls for a stroll along the Pocomoke. Matchacoopah joins the little group, and I hear the children again trying to learn the language of the Nanticokes. He has been telling of their great king Winikako up on the Chop-tank, and speaks of him as *ah-quak* (the sun) in *moose-sac-quit* (the sky).

" What is your word for ' sick ' ?" was asked.

" *Huntoimip.*"

" For ' kill ' ?"

" *Nepoictow.*"

" What is the word for ' dead man ' ?"

" *Tsee-ep,*" dwelling upon the last syllable solemnly. The same is their word for " ghost "

" What do you call the place where the dead are deposited ?"

" *Mutz-uck-cumpq* "

" What is the name of the house where you keep their bones after the flesh has all crumbled away ?"

"Sometimes *mantokump;* sometimes *chio-ca-son.*
There the bad white men would have sent my *nee-
ee-wah* (wife) with their cruel *tunt* (the fire)." *

"What do you call the grave?"

Why did the children's minds still think of these
sadder things?

The Indian answered,

"*Wawsko.*"

"And what is your word for death?"

"Sometimes *unguelack;* sometimes *ewashawaak.*"

The Indian's voice was drear and weird.

The sweet childish tones answered:

"But religion makes all this pleasant and cheerful.
What is your word for religion?"

"*Lap-poi-o-wees.*"

"When war is over, what is your word for peace?"

"*E-wee-ni-tu.*"

While I have been preserving some fragments of
this strange dialect to go on sounding in concert with
the waves of the sea and the sighs of the pines far
into the future years, it may not be amiss to introduce
my last chapter with such words as touch the destiny
of every race, savage and civilized, and the synonyms
of which will never cease along these shores.

I thought then, as I have thought often since, of
Mr. Makemie's words:

" Whatever are our tossings by Divine Providence here, it will
afford abundant consolation in all ups and downs by prosperity
and adversity, in sickness and health, that we have made conscience of our former ways both toward God and toward our
neighbor. Sure nothing can be more desirable and comfortable

* The manuscript vocabulary of Mr. Murray, taken in 1792, says:
" Winikako's body was preserved and kept in a *chiocason*-house;
seventy years dead."

than the testimony of a good conscience, which is a continual feast, that we have walked blamelessly in all manner of conversation; especially at the hour of death when that grim king of terrors looks us in the face." *

Since his long contest in the North, we all feel the moral grandeur of Mr. Makemie's character more than ever. Undoubtedly the prominence there given him by his persecutors and his brave stand for the rights of our Church will go farther than anything else to attract and weld together the scattered Presbyterian elements. He is as attentive to business as ever. I hear of one more suit brought by him down in Accomack, through his friend and attorney Andrew Hamilton, against Thomas Bonnewell His training in these courts, his settlement of the Anderson and Custis estates, and all the attendant worriment from Madam Tabitha Hill, were long fitting him, as we did not dream, for his mission before the chief-justice of New York A well-rounded, practical man, of clear judgment, sound sense and gentlemanly bearing, prepared for all the emergencies of a new country and a population made up of various nationalities, he is pre-eminently the man for the times Managing African slaves, employing Indian servants, helping indentured refugees, superintending his large business interests, mingling with the lower classes and unabashed at the table of governors,—he need not be greatly offended at Cornbury's epithet, "Jack-at-all-trades." No one could add "master of none"

I love to keep in mind the picture of him as I saw him this spring walking with his little daughters around the new church at Rehoboth, built upon his

* New York sermon.

own land, and viewing the loved American sanctuary
and its grounds. Was there the look of triumph in his
blue eyes and over the fine forehead while he thought
of the full achievement of noble purposes? This
finished structure, a second and larger forest-temple,
in sight of his first landing-place a quarter of a century ago; Mr. Macnish preaching up at Rockawalkin,
and also in another new church at Monokin; Mr.
Hampton about to be installed at Snow Hill; the
mother-Presbytery thoroughly organized and reaching out on all sides for wider acquisitions of numbers
and influence,—well might he be glad of heart and
glory in the Sceptre which had prospered him. Is
there an expression upon his face as upon the face of
Simeon when he said, "Now lettest thou thy servant
depart in peace"?

How rapidly the time has flown, like fish-hawk or
eagle over Eastern Shore streams! Mary, the rosy
Scotch lassie, Peggy, the blue-eyed maid of Ulster,
Margaret, the sweet singer of the Vincennes, and the
writer of this journal too, are beginning to look very
matronly, our nurseries well stocked with a mingling
of races and our heads already streaking with gray.
Even Naomi, the bright Virginia girl, is forty years
old. To put away the sadder thoughts that force
themselves upon the spring-time which is abroad
by forest and river, I ask my Huguenot sister-in-law
to sing me a song of the Troubadours, and, behold!
she has just sung an *elegy* by Aymerie of Beauvoir:

> "Sanchez is dead! Ah! woe is me!
> I cannot sing for sighing;
> Or if I do, alas! 'twill be
> As sings the swan in dying.

"With mournful tears mine eyes are dim,
    My heart is pierced with sorrow;
The dirge I weave to-day for him
    Will serve for me to-morrow.

"I weep not for the good and brave,
    For he is blest in heaven;
But all I've buried in the grave—
    To that my plaints are given."

To cheer our minds Henry Hudson comes upon the scene, a new book in hand, published this year. The Quakers have always been a choice subject of ridicule to our incorrigible wit, and he is now delighted while he reads of the experience of the sotweed factor in dealing with these perfectionists:

"To this intent with Guide before,
I tript it to the Eastern Shore.
While riding near a Sandy Bay,
I met a Quaker Yea and Nay;
A Pious Conscientious Rogue
As e'er wore Bonnet or a Brogue,
Who neither Swore nor kept his Word
But cheated in the Fear of God;
And when his Debts he would not pay,
By Light within he ran away.
With this sly Zealot soon I struck
A Bargain for my English Truck,
Agreeing for ten thousand weight
Of Sot-weed good and fit for freight,
Broad Oronoko bright and sound,
The growth and product of his ground,
In Cask that should contain complete
Five hundred of Tobacco neat.
The Contract thus between us made,
Not well acquainted with the Trade,
My Goods I trusted to the Cheat
Whose crop was then aboard the Fleet;
And going to receive my own,
I found the Bird already flown!

> Cursing this execrable Slave,
> This mean pretended Godly Knave,
> On dire Revenge and Justice bent,
> I instantly to Counsel went,
> Unto an ambidexter Quack,
> Who learnedly had got the Knack
> Of giving Glisters, making Pills,
> Of filling Bonds and forging Wills,
> And with a stock of Impudence,
> Supply'd his want of Wit and Sense" (76).

"One of our colony's Jack-at-all-trades : see the late epistle of Lord Cornbury," was the reader's comment.

The " pettifogger doctor " is bribed, and the factor worse off than ever

"A severe satire," said William, "but from such contemporary burlesques some hints of truth may sometimes be obtained. The doctrine of perfection will always invite satire. Of his old opponent Mr. Makemie well says, ' Actions are a better demonstration of a work of grace than all Keith's vainboasting language, which can be esteemed nothing else than a crying up and preaching himself instead of Christ.' "

"Where now is George Keith ?" some one asked.

"In England, settled as rector of Edburton, enjoying a good maintenance and upsetting his old flings at the ' mercenary ' Presbyterians. His late fellow-mystics he continues to lash, only last year preaching and publishing a sermon against ' the fundamental error of the Quakers that the light within them, and within every man, is sufficient to their salvation without anything else, whereby, as to themselves, they make void and destroy all revealed religion.' " *

* Anderson's *Colonial Church*, iii 232.

Thus Mr. Makemie's opposers change and vacillate, while the doctrines and principles which he has planted remain as staunch and firmly rooted as the sturdy coast-oaks which bear and beat back the stormy north-easters.

Meanwhile, another effort is made by the Established Church to stay the progress of our cause in this county, evidently inspired by our other Keith, the vigilant Robert, rector of Coventry Parish, a fair specimen of the Scotch prelatic clergy. On the 9th of June, at Dividing Creek, Captain John West, Captain John Franklin, Captain Charles Ballard, Mr. Joseph Venables and Mr Joseph Gray being upon the bench, the following petition is presented:

" To the Worshipful Court of Somerset County, the petition of Moses Fenton and Pierce Bray sheweth that, in obedience to an Act of Parliament made the first year of King William and Queen Mary establishing the liberty of Protestant Dissenters, we in humble manner certifie to this Court that the new meeting-house lately built at Rehoboth Town, is one of the fixed places for the public service or worship of God by Protestant Dissenters, and Your Worships are in humble manner prayed to direct your Clerk to record the same and give certificate thereof to any who will require it, for which we are ready to pay the fee specified in the last paragraph of said Act of Parliament, and the petitioners as in duty bound shall always pray &c."

Mr. Makemie has already made arrangements for the transfer to the church of the land on which the meeting-house is built, as will appear hereafter, and he wishes the elders to put our rights upon a thoroughly legal footing. The question is discussed by the judges, and the majority—Franklin, Venables and Ballard—decide to grant the petition, West and Gray entering their dissent with the following reasons:

" This same thing concerning the Church built at Rehoboth

Town by Dissenting Protestants was layed before the Governor and Councill and no final result has been returned to this Court since concerning the premises."*

Thus it will be seen that there is still a party which is disposed to enforce the policy of the rectors and keep our ministers outlawed and our churches closed through official delays.

On the next day the following order is recorded:

" This day, viz., the 10th of June, 1708, ordered that the new meeting-house built by Protestant Dissenters at Rehoboth Town in Somerset County in the Province of Maryland, be and hereby is appointed to be a house for the worship of Almighty God in, the minister thereunto appointed having qualified himself as law required. Entered per order

" ALEX. HALL, *Clerk.*"

So that matter is settled, and we believe that this second temple, built upon the birthplace of our American Presbyterianism, is registered on high upon more enduring records by the great Head of the Church himself.

On the same day with the preceding order the following paper was also presented:

" To the Worshipful, the Judge and Justices of the Court of Somerset, humbly sheweth, That, whereas divers persons in and about Monokin, of the Presbyterian Interest and Persuasion, have built a meeting-house for the public exercise of their religious worship, and haid by Monokin Bridges, and being willing to satisfy the law according to Act of Parliament in petitioning the County Court where a meeting-house is or shall be erected that it may be put on public record; In compliance therefore with the end and design of the law in such case, your petitioner in name of the persons foresaid do request that house foresaid may be legally recorded as law wills   And your petitioner shall pray &c.

" *June 10th, 1708.*   GEORGE MCNISH."

*The author has failed to find any such reference with regard to Rehoboth on the Somerset records.

The court unanimously orders that the record be made. I suppose that the scruples of Justices West and Gray are satisfied by the fact that the governor and the Council had directed that the old church at Monokin should be recorded two years ago.

This very year Governor Seymour and the Legislature are so shocked by the increasing immorality of the clergy in the Maryland Establishment that they are trying to devise a court of laymen to take cognizance of these errors and suppress the debauchery of these "Successors of the Apostles." So the Virginia Assembly had been compelled to take action with regard to their licentious ministry in 1632:

"Ministers shall not give themselves to excesse in drinkinge or ryott, spending their time idelie by day or by night playinge at dice, cards, or any other unlawful game."

There stands the telltale law upon the statutes of the Old Dominion for ever.

The admirers of Episcopacy are alarmed at the proposed interposition of our provincial authorities, and clamor against the remedy proposed. The lay-element among the judges reminds them painfully of our Presbyterian church-courts, and they resist it bitterly as

"a Presbyterian form of ministers and ruling lay Elders; and as laying a foundation for the introduction of a Presbyterian form of Church-government in the Church of England in Maryland, as well as subversion of the Canons of the Church which give the Bishop alone power to pronounce sentence." *

The prevailing profligacy of the clergy and all the widening corruptions are preferred by these Churchmen to anything that even looks like Presbyterianism!

* Bishop Hawks's *Maryland*, p 130, archives at Fulham.

Thus the restraints enacted by the Assembly are defeated, and the disgrace continues. Well may Mr. Makemie say,

"It is too notorious how our Christian religion is evil spoken of by the pernicious ways of its followers and professors."

I find myself tarrying in my history, my pen almost refusing to go on. I am inclined to speak of the great contemporary wars in Europe; the heroic struggle of Charles XII. of Sweden against Czar Peter; the great victories at Oudenard and Lille by Marlborough and the allies over Louis of France; of the appointment to the government of Ireland of the firm friend of the Presbyterians, the Earl of Wharton, with the young man Joseph Addison as his secretary; while all the wit of Dean Swift is arrayed against the rights of the Irish Dissenters. I might delay with the details of local history—the vote of Assembly to form a town of fifty acres in Sinepuxent Neck, on the land of John Walton called "Neighborhood"—an enactment defeated by the veto of the governor; or I might tell of the trial of our mischievous friend Henry Hudson at Dividing Creek on a charge of wronging the red men.

Under date of April 2, the week preceding the appointed meeting of Presbytery, appears this record:

"Articles of agreement between Her Majesty and ye friendly Indians read in Court on a complaint made by King Daniel and some of their great men, concerning ye burning of their cornfields and fencing, and other enormities by some done. Being demanded of the Court here if they knew any of them, they replied Henry Hudson was one and that John Dennis could inform the Court more fully. Wherefore ordered by the Court here that the Clerk issue out a Summons for Henry Hudson to appear June Court next and answer the complaint aforesaid;

and that John Dennis be summoned on part of the Indians to appear the next June Court to inform the Court to the best of his knowledge concerning the premises."

The jolly Henry is in trouble at last. But, knowing the determination of our courts to protect the children of the forest, our friend is too wise to let the matter come to trial without a compromise with the King of the Pocomokes; so, on the 11th of the Fawn Moon— the next day after the recording of Rehoboth and Monokin—the following action was taken:

"This day the plaintiff, the Indians, appeared and the defendant Henry Hudson; and the defendant being interrogated by the Worshipful Court, replyed he did light a fire but not with any design to do any damage to the Indians. Whereupon the Indians being demanded what damages they had sustained by the fire, replyed they were satisfied and had agreed with the said Hudson. Wherefore the Court dismissed the said Hudson, he paying the fees become due according to law."

Says Matchacoopah,
· " *Weesauce pattin* (the wise eel) slipped out of *mannote* (the basket)."

We feel no little pride that these original owners of the woods and streams of the Eastern Shore have never failed of redress from our county authorities whenever they please to seek it. Nor are we less proud that Mr. Makemie has plead for an apostolic zeal "in propagating the true knowledge of the Christian Religion to all Pagans, whether Indians or Negroes."

While the Episcopal Church in Maryland is virtually an anarchy and threatened with lay supervision, our own ecclesiastical system is in full and symmetrical exercise. It seems to me one of the noblest sights in our primitive history, these heroes of the cross, on horseback and in rude sloops, starting out through the wilderness, exposed to all the hardships of weather or want, going to the appointed meeting, intent upon the Master's business. In a letter to the ministers of Connecticut this year they thus speak:

"Through the good providence of our Lord Jesus Christ assisting us, we the ministers of the Gospel of the Presbyterian persuasion, in this province and those adjacent, taking into our serious consideration the case and circumstances of our holy religion in these parts, have, to our great toil and labor and great difficulty to divers of us, by reason of our great distance from one another, formed ourselves into a Presbytery, annually to be convened, for the furthering and promoting the true interest of religion and godliness."

This spring they fail to meet at the time set, the first Tuesday of April. Probably the feeble health of their recognized leader, *primus inter pares*, caused the postponement. They meet on the 18th of May, but still he is not there Mr. Davis, now for twenty-four years on this peninsula, is elected moderator. Six ministers and three elders are present Cohanzy, in West Jersey, seeks Presbyterial oversight, and Woodbridge and Amboy are moving too, Woodbridge church asking help in relieving itself from an Independent minister. A letter is sent to Monokin and Wicomico "exciting them to their duty to pay what they promise to Mr. Macnish," and also one to the people of Snow Hill "requiring their faithfulness and care in collecting the tobacco promised by subscription to Mr. Hampton" Mr. Davis and Mr. Macnish are appointed to "inaugurate" the latter This duty has since been performed by Mr. Macnish, Mr. Davis not attending. Thus, at Snow Hill, on the banks of the little Pocomoke, with the Indian canoes still ploughing

32

its waters, for the first time on this continent has a
pastor been installed under Presbyterial authority
Here, too, the first published book of Mr. Makemie
will be useful in training our youthful charges. In
his answer to George Keith he says:

"In my Catechism for young ones, I lay down the several
duties of ministers and people."

Everything reminds me of something the pioneer
has said or written. Now I recall his testimony in
his reply to the carping Quaker:

"I have upon all occasions publicly taught, and do and shall
in the strength of Jesus Christ, firmly believe and that *unto the
end*, the illuminating, sanctifying, mortifying, quickening opera
tions of the Holy Spirit of God in the heart of every believer, in
restoring the corrupted soul to the forfeited image of God."

I remember, too, his ringing appeal, in his *Perswasive*, for advancing both the material and the religious
interests of the two sister-colonies:

"Now at length put on a public spirit; combine with harmoni-
ous and united counsels, avoiding partiality, waiving self-interest
or causing it to truckle to the common good; arm yourself against
all dividing debates and smother or stifle all heats in your public
consultations; and look upon this as the happy juncture and
period for commencing the happiness of Virginia and Maryland."

Again I think of his brave and self-sacrificing defence of soul-liberty until he shakes to their foundations the usurpations of Cornbury:

"We cannot, we dare not, be silent at this juncture but are
bound to let both Europe and America know the first prosecution
of this kind that ever was in America; which we hope, from the
merits of the case, manner and proceeding and its unsuccessful-
ness, will never be drawn into precedent in our quiet and peaceable wilderness."

Now I remember, in his pastoral to the people of Barbadoes, his emphatic endorsement of the Calvinistic theology of the land of Wishart and Knox and its tenet of election and reprobation:

"Though I owe not my birth but a part of my education only to that kingdom, yet having read many of their books, heard several of their ministers, for several years, on all doctrines of the Christian religion, and having always with me their Confession of Faith, their Catechisms, with many sound and excellent Treatises; I do profess myself fully of their sentiments in this and all other doctrines of faith, and in God's strength shall never swerve nor prevaricate!"

At last the time has come when to such memorable words I am to add parts of another document, full of his deep heart-interest in his friends and of manly care for his loved ones, showing his appreciation of high Christian culture, evidencing to the end his business-like ways and administrative skill, proving his undying love for his favorite Rehoboth and his estimate of Philadelphia as a predestined centre of wide Presbyterian influence, embodying his gratitude to the divine Giver of all his possessions, and putting upon record, as a testimony to future generations, his calm personal trust in the glorious Saviour whose name he had preached from Barbadoes to Boston.

For some while we saw that his health was failing, but we remembered his recovery from "tedious illness" seventeen years ago, and hoped on. He knew what was coming better than we. The Maryland spring-time brought no relief. On the 27th of April, three weeks before the Presbytery met, there was a gathering of friends at his house—a business-call as well as one of friendship. These were Elizabeth Davis, Elizabeth Price, John Parker of Mattapani,

Andrew Hamilton, Tully Robinson and John Lewis. The latter are prominent citizens in the colony, and in their presence he thus testifies in contemplation of what soon may be:

"In the name of God amen. I, Francis Makemie, of the county of Accomack, in Her Majesty's dominion of Virginia, being weak and infirm of body but in perfect soundness of mind and memory, and sensible of the universal frailty of life and an approaching dissolution by death, and desirous to settle that estate which God in his bounty hath been pleased to bestow upon me and for preventing future differences which may arise concerning the same, committing my body to ye dust decently to be interred and my immortal soul to an Almighty and Most Merciful God in hopes of a glorious and blessed resurrection unto eternal Salvation through the efficacy of the powerful merits of the Lord Jesus Christ, our blessed and glorious Redeemer; I do hereby revoke, make null and void all wills and testaments heretofore by me made, and do make, constitute and ordain this to be my last will and testament in manner and form following."

To his "kinsman" William Boggs * he gives a negro man named "Jupiter." To his own wife and two daughters he gives forty books apiece, to be selected from his English library by Naomi; the survivor to have them all. To Mr. Andrew Hamilton, the attorney and friend, he bequeaths all his law-books The remainder of his thousand volumes he wills to Mr. Andrews of the First church of Philadelphia and his successors "of the Presbyterian or Independent persuasion," the books to be put upon record and remain as "a constant library for ye use of foresaid minister or ministers successively for ever." † To Mr. Andrews he also leaves his black camlet cloak and his "new cane bought and fixed at Boston."

* Tradition says Mr. Makemie's nephew. Many descendants of the name are found in Accomack.

† Where are these books ?

To his daughter Elizabeth he bequeaths eight hundred and fifty acres of land on the south part and contiguous to Sykes's Island; also two hundred acres of swamp called "Dumfreece," "near Pocomoke Bridges;" also either the marshes on the south side of Crooked Creek or the marshes promised in exchange therefor by Samuel Sandford; also his lots at Onancock.

To his daughter Anne he gives one hundred and seventy-four acres on Watts's Island; also three hundred and fifty acres on the south side of Matchatank Creek; also one hundred and fifty acres, part of the land once owned by James Howker; also the "lot where ye smith's shop was built on ye townland at Onancock, commonly called Scarborough Town."

His lot and house "at ye town in Princess Anne county on ye Eastern Branch of Elizabeth River," also his "lot and house or frame of a house in the new town on Wormley's Creek called Urbanna," also his "lot joining to ye new Meeting-House lot in Pocomoke Town called Rehoboth," are to be sold by the executrix and the proceeds to go into the estate. Naomi is empowered

"to make over and alienate that lot on which ye meeting-house is built in as ample a manner to all intents and purposes as shall be required for ye ends and uses of a Presbyterian Congregation as if I were personally present, and to their successors for ever; and none else but to such of ye same persuasion in matters of religion."

His "water and grist mill at Assawaman" is Naomi's for life, to be kept in good repair, and at her death to belong to the two daughters.

His twelve hundred and sixty acres on Smith's Island are left to Elizabeth and Anne. His negro slaves and all the rest of his estate, real and personal, are given to wife and daughters, to be equally divided between them, and to revert to the longest liver. If his children have no issue, all the property left in this will is entailed upon his

"youngest sister Anne Makemie of ye kingdom of Ireland and the two eldest sons of brothers John and Robert Makemie, both of ye name of Francis."

An exact inventory of his estate is to be taken and put upon record. No division of property is to be made until all debts are paid. Mr. Andrew Hamilton, Captain John Watts, Mr. Robert Pitt and Mr. James Kemp, his " trusty and good friends," are named as advisers in the settlement of the estate, in taking the inventory and appraising and dividing. Now his heart is laid bare still more:

"I do constitute, appoint and ordain my dear and well-beloved wife Naomi Makemie my Executrix of this my last will and testament, committing to her and her only the guardianship and tutorship of my aforesaid children whilst in minority, during her natural life. And in case of ye death of my dear wife before this will is proved and executed, or ye arrival of my said daughters Elizabeth and Anne Makemie at age, I do constitute, appoint and ordain the Honorable Col. Francis Jenkins of Somerset county in Maryland and Mary Jenkins his lady and beloved consort Executors of this will and guardians to my said children during their minority and till marriage; charging all persons concerned, in ye presence of Almighty and Omniscient God, to give and allow my said children a sober, virtuous and religious education, either here or elsewhere, as in Britain, New England or Philadelphia; and that no other person or persons, courts or judicatories whatsoever, besides my Executrix or Executors nominated and appointed and whom they shall appoint in case of the mortality of Executors already appointed, shall have any power to intermediate with my said estate, real or personal, or the tutory or guardianship of my said children without incurring ye penalty of the Statute of Wards and Liveries and thereby liable to an action of Trespass. My will and pleasure is that, in case of my wife marrying, she have power and authority, if she apprehend it requisite or necessary, either before or after marriage, to relinquish her Executorship and commit ye same with relation to her children's estate and guardianship unto ye trust, care and management of Col. Francis Jenkins and his lady."*

While few in either Europe or America are taught to write or to read, we see the good man's appreciation of the culture of the female mind and his anxiety that this shall consist of something higher than mere outward or secular accomplishments. Scotland leads the world in her system of parochial schools, and in her care that its benefits shall not be narrowed to either sex. The dying father's views and hopes are as broad as Scotland's.

The weak and infirm body of the good man grows more frail as spring passes into summer. The sea-breeze that blows from ocean to bay brings no return of the rich, warm complexion which once, with brown hair and eyes of blue, formed our ideal of handsome manhood.

Dr. Charles Barrett comes and goes,† and there is no improvement. The decline is not rapid, but sure. Mr. William Coman takes charge of the house and assists the family while the feebleness increases. Need

---

* Colonel Jenkins died within a year or two after Makemie. His widow married Mr. Makemie's successor at Rehoboth, the Rev. John Henry, and afterward the Rev John Hampton. Her old broken tombstone lies now on the ground, under a tree, on the Jenkins property, just below Rehoboth. She died in 1744, seventy years old, lacking three days. Her brother married Anne Makemie.

† Accomack records: "To Dr. Charles Barrett for means and visits in Mr. Makemie's last sickness—five pounds. To Mr. William Coman for funeral and trouble of his house in Mr. Makemie's sickness—twelve pounds."

I say that there is sadness along our many little rivers, throughout our inland churches and over to the seaboard? Rehoboth is under deep shadows. So the days pass on hopelessly toward midsummer.* The founder of the American Presbyterian Church is going away.

Our little Francis wonders at the general sorrow, and weeps in sympathy with an anxiety not fully understood. The negroes wander around the premises at Houlston's Creek, watching the windows and waiting in silence. Indian Peter wonders if the Good Spirit is going to take away the great *werowance*† of the Christians.

Shall I go on?

One evening Peggy of Ulster and her husband were sitting with William and myself in front of the "wigwam in the pines," talking of our sick pastor, when a strange, weird, hollow, rushing sound seemed to pass directly over our heads and the whole atmosphere seemed to tremble with sighs. Did not the pine trees moan and the cypresses, fringed with crape, bow earthward as if awaiting a storm? And yet the sky was cloudless and the stars were bright, and no passing terror could be seen. But we sat as if under a spell, and nature, tremulous and in dread, seemed to feel it too. Was it funeral music or dying groans that filled the air and hurried through the sky, past Rehoboth and down the river toward the west and the south? Our breath was almost taken away and our hearts almost ceased to beat, and we sat dumb until that mysterious rushing

---

* Will probated "August ye 4th 1708" Died not long before.

† Name for chieftain among the Powhatan tribes, of which the Accomack Indians were a part.

dirge had wailed itself into the distance.   Then whispered my friend,

"It is the Banshee! It follows our families over the sea It is the harbinger of death."*

Now, on one of these days, while the good man rested and his eyes looked from the window westward to where the blue of the sound and the blue of the sky meet and mingle, golden ripples upon the azure of the waters and golden cloudlets upon the azure of the heavens, by and by his eyes partly close, and the watchers believe that the weary one is sleeping.   I try to follow his vision, and there seems to come before him—perhaps upon the bosom of a flowing river, or out yonder far away—something which I hardly dare to tell, and yet something without which my story would be incomplete.

Only a few months appear to glide away, when to his side, there by the plantation grave, one of his darling daughters—yes, it is Betty—seems to come smilingly and lovingly, dressed for the tomb and for heaven, and to lie down fondly near her father's bosom.   Mother and sister would fain detain her, but she wearies for the strong embraces she once knew; and she turns away from the fatherless home and seeks again the lost companionship.   Then is heard a voice like that which once wept on the plains of Bethlehem: "Call me not Naomi; call me Mara; for the Almighty hath dealt very bitterly with me" (77).

*Old people tell us that something like this actually occurred just before the death of "Parson Wallace," an Irish minister buried at Dover. People at Poplartown who heard it were much startled, but the parson assured them that it always followed his family, that it foreboded his approaching end, and that they need have no fears for themselves.

Still the eyes of the invalid are out upon the waters
—waters bearing ever onward ; and a day comes—
twenty years, thirty years, from now?—when the beloved wife also weans from all things earthly, sees no
more the flowers of yellow and of blue in the marshes
where the blackbirds build, and is willing to lie down
by the side of her father, her husband and her
child (78).

The years pass on—many years in the estimates of
earth, not long as it looks from the borders of eternity—and the younger daughter, now an old woman
white-haired and bowed, far on yonder amid the vast
results of her father's labors, interested in the new
Western nation and the growing Church, finally lays
down the weight of years and is gathered to her
loved ones in the same country burial-ground.   Then
there are none left of the blood of Makemie; but the
name lives and scatters fragrance and beauty through
all the far centuries.

Still the blue eyes rest upon the distant vistas, and
he looks upon another child of his, which does not
wax old nor die.   It appears as a fertile vine planted
by God's hand between the two beautiful bays, sending out its living branches to all points of the compass.
The Long Island and New Jersey churches lift the
Presbyterian banner and fall into line with Rehoboth.
Others follow all over the land.   New Presbyteries are
formed, and a Synod ere long.

Still the pioneer gazes out upon the waters, and his
face brightens.   God's presence shines like the She-
china   Glorious refreshings descend, and souls are
flocking to Christ   God is preparing the Church for
grander expansion.

But, alas! clouds arc seen rising over the ark. There is contention, there is sundering. Good men are at variance, and the seamless robe is torn. The heart of the dying man is troubled. But Jehovah has not forsaken Brighter days dawn again, and, lo! the two Synods are one.

Meanwhile, the son of Donegal seems to see thousands of his fellow-countrymen coming from Ulster, spreading through Pennsylvania, up the Virginia valley and on into Carolina Knowing in other days of blessed revivals in Ireland, they welcome now the fruits of the American Pentecost with grateful hearts. In the track of orthodoxy follow able, earnest preachers, and the tide-waters of Makemie's adopted province, and the regions beyond, begin to blossom as the rose. For now is heard the eloquent voice of another apostle of Presbyterianism—one born upon the same peninsula where the Church was first planted, one who had been won to Christ at the same early age as himself.[*]

And now, out yonder upon the stream of time, there seems to be the noise of conflict, the battle-cry of freedom A mighty republic is born. Once he had said of this " medley and mixture of nations,"

" Heats and animosities and separate interests, backed with pride and envy, will keep them asunder from ever uniting under a single head."

But there have been great changes. No king nor bishop rules the state. The people are sovereign No favored Church domineers. The soul-freedom for which he contended in New York has triumphed.

[*] Samuel Davies, born in Delaware in 1723, and converted when fifteen years old

The successors of Robert Keith and Alexander Adams are no longer in power. Presbyterianism has filled the army and the councils of the nation with heroes. Just one hundred years from the time Makemie set foot upon American soil, peace is proclaimed, independence achieved (1683–1783). The contest won, the Church nerves herself for grander victories.

It is amid the calm that follows in the state and amid the gladness of the young republic, and while the Church is renewing her youth like the eagles', that the younger daughter, having lived to witness the triumph of her father's principles, comes cheerfully and lies down to sleep with the kindred dust (79).

As the century dies there arise before him new Pentecostal visions. Revivals go on brightening the years. The vine is throwing out its prolific branches everywhere. A new missionary spirit seizes and sways the energies of Zion. Frontiers and foreign heathendom are conquered for Christ. Another instrumentality comes into action, claiming the *children* for the Master—Sunday-schools singing the praises of Jesus. The air is full of youthful voices well attuned. The dying man, converted on the hills of Donegal at fifteen years of age, seems to be a boy again, and to mingle his voice with theirs in the juvenile choruses.

Colleges and divinity schools dot the broad land, north and south and east and west. Great agencies are set in motion for educating God's worthy poor for the ministry, for the dissemination of religious literature, and for evangelizing our own continent and all lands.

He who had plead in vain for the gathering of our scattered population into towns, sees the Chesapeake bordered with large cities, the commerce of its shores, along which the Tabitha sailed, swelling to millions. Yes, and great cities up and down the coast, and far out westward to another ocean; and the spires of Presbyterian temples are in them all.

A great Protestant empire fills the vast future. Error rises and falls, but the truth brought over from Ulster lives on. Quakerism, whose early extravagances he was called to combat in its fanatical attempts to break down the visible Church and her visible ordinances, he sees fade away from the Lower Peninsula, until its past existence is indicated only by a graveyard here and there.*

But hark! The nation groans, and there are strife and rending. There has been sin, and the Church has shared the sin. The face of our founder is turned to the wall. But again dawn the days of peace and unity, the dark chasm yawning no more, Christians drawing nearer to one another and massing their influence for advancing the common cause, the times of harsh judgments and of persecution for ever passed away, all churches loving one another more and more and bidding one another Godspeed in proclaiming the one glorious gospel, the great Presbyterian brotherhood, with its own rents healed, leading in the paths of charity and purity and universal kindliness.

A smile settles upon the fading face as in rapt vision he watches the streams that flow away from the valley of the Pocomoke on toward the ocean of eternal love. The skill of Dr. Barrett is no longer needed, for the

---

*A hill between Snow Hill and Berlin is called the "Old Quaker Burying-Ground"—the only monument of the sect in those counties where George Fox and Story and Keith and Chalkley once preached.

great Physician has his case in hand and is about to remove him to more healthful climes. In the bright midsummer hours, while the illustrious Marlborough is gaining the famous victory in Flanders, another triumph is celebrated upon the banks of our sunny sound, and the victor of grace divine has gone up on high.

The twenty-five years of busy life in "the American wilderness" are over—a quarter of a century momentous in the annals of time.

On the plantation where his happy wedded years have been spent—the Anderson property which looks out to the "mother of waters"—we bury him (80). Prominent men from both provinces are there, for, whatever the differences of religious belief, all recognize him as a man of mark and worth, a citizen of great value in a country like this. Mr Macnish and Mr. Hampton feel bereaved as of a father. Rehoboth and Snow Hill and Monokin and Wicomico, and the seaboard outposts on up to Lewes, are sighing in unison with the perpetual requiems of the pines. The loved voice will be heard along these shores no more. The blue eyes sleep within an honored grave. Two little girls go out there daily to talk of papa and to weep. Shall not the children of our Church through the ages learn to think of him as their father too, and long to remember their Creator in the days of their youth as he did?

Matchacoopah comes to our wigwam in the pines, bringing us a white flower from the Pocomoke Strand, and says, "*Matt-whu-saw-so waap-pay-u mat-ah-ki-ween* (the brave white chieftain) sends you this!"

APPENDIX.

1. Page 11. *Assateague, Sinepuxent.*—The first mention of this neck of land found by me upon the Somerset records is under date of June 10, 1697, as follows: "Ordered that William Fausett be joined overseer for Seny Puxone with John Freeman."

The lower end of the neck—called "Genezer" and containing two thousand acres—was granted to Edwin Wale (Whaley ?) and Charles Ratcliff in 1679, and divided between the two in 1681; the former was living there in 1679. Another tract northward was granted to Francis Jenkins in 1678, and contained fifteen hundred acres. On this the old patents mention an *Indian field*. Farther up is a tract called "Neighborhood," patented by William Walton in 1679. Still northward is a tract of two thousand acres patented by Colonel William Stevens in 1679. In this patent the bay is called "New Haven," and the Thoroughfare is mentioned.

I find a patent on Selby's Bay as early as 1656, and one north of the Pocomoke, called "Auquintica," patented to George Wale in 1658. Our histories are mistaken in saying there were no settlements on the lower Eastern Shore until after 1660. They were few in number, however.

2. Page 18. *Language of the Nanticokes.*—Not far from the mouth of the Pocomoke are large banks of shells, marking the site of an old Indian village, and now called "Shell Town." Here Smith probably traded for the "puddle water." In all that country good drinking-water is very rare.

The Eastern-Shore Indians have faded from the earth, and so, I thought, had their language too. Smith speaks of them as "of another language from the rest, and very rude." Heckewelder describes them as speaking a dialect of the Lenni Lenapes. Accidentally I came upon a manuscript in possession of the American Philosophical Society, Philadelphia, a transcript of which is now before me, and from which I take the words used in my book. I cannot express my delight in recovering the dead language of a dead tribe—sounds once familiar to Makemie's ear.

The manuscript has the following heading ·

"Taken at Locust-Neck Town, the remains of an ancient Indian town on Goose Creek, Choptank River, in Dorset, Maryland. Five wigwams and a board house with a glass window now form the whole that is left of the Nanticoke tribe, which was a hundred years since numerous and powerful. Many of them migrated to the Six Nations within my memory about twenty-five years since. These words were principally taken from a squaw called Mrs. Mulberry, the widow of the late chief, who was called Colonel—no king having succeeded their famous Winikako who died seventy-five years since.

"Taken by Mr. Murray of Maryland. See his letter of Sept. 18, 1792."

The manuscript is among the papers contributed to the society's collection by Thomas Jefferson Mrs. Mulberry's true name was Weningominsk.

3 Page 19. *The Indians.*—Captain Smith says: " The people of these rivers are of little stature." It is a singular fact that the inhabitants of the peninsula are now noticeably of smaller stature and features than the average elsewhere.

4 Page 20. *Colonel William Stevens.*—About a mile above the town of Rehoboth is the farm, the old cellar and the foundation of the house still visible. There is the tombstone of Stevens, yet legible, lying flat on the ground.

We learn the nativity and parentage of Colonel Stevens from the following memorandum on the Somerset records

" Richard Stevens, brother to William Stevens of Somerset county in ye Province of Maryland, was youngest son of John Stevens of Lebourn in ye Parish of Buckingham in England, died at the house of his brother William aforesaid, ye 22d day of April 1667, and was buried at his plantation called Rehoboth in ye county and province aforesaid in America ye 25th day of April 1667."

This record enables us to trace the origin of the name of Buckingham church.

There was another William Stevens contemporaneously in Accomack.

5. Page 23. *Governor Stone.*—See Bozman's *History of Maryland* (ii. 32), where the pamphlet published in 1655 by the Catholic Langford calls Stone "a zealous Protestant and generally known to have been always zealously affected to the Parliament."

Says Bozman (ii. 354): "There are strong grounds to believe that the majority of the members of this Assembly of 1649 were Protestants, if not Protestants of the Puritanic order."

6. Page 24. *The majority Protestants.*—See Rev. Ethan Allen's *Maryland Toleration;* also McMahon's *History of Maryland.* Of reputable historians, only the Catholic McSherry would have it otherwise.

7. Page 26. *Rev. Matthew Hill.*—My description of Hill is almost *verbatim* from Calamy's *Nonconformists' Memorial.* See also Neill's *Terra Mariæ*, p. 139. I am unable to discover the "new troubles" which caused him to leave—probably the agitations under Coode.

8. Page 27. *The grand jurors.*—Somerset records, 1672. The foreman, David Brown, afterward bequeathed five hundred pounds to Glasgow University. The other jurors were Robert Hart, Marcum Thomas, Thomas Covington, James Dashiell, Benjamin Cottman, Levin Denwood, Richard Ackworth, John Dorman, William Woodgate, Richard Davis, Alexander Draper, Peter Dorotey, Robert Houlston, Thomas Davis, Thomas Roe, Cornelius Johnson, John Bozman, John Williams, Richard Tull and Philip Askew

I have been inclined to claim Mr. Maddux for a Presbyterian, because of the tradition that the Eastern-Shore family of that name were originally of our Church. The name is still frequently pronounced *as spelled in the record.* In the same year (1672, December 30) the records show the marriage of John Bishop and Mary Bowen by Robert Maddux, clerk. The latter was the title for minister.

9. Page 29. *Naomi.*—In Accomack records, in an affidavit taken December 3, 1717, Naomi's age is given at "49 years or thereabouts." Hence we adopt 1668 as date of birth.

10. Page 35. *Hominy.*—Not thus in the Nanticoke dialect, however, so far as I know. Roger Williams gives this as the Indian term in the North.

11. Page 36. *Scotch martyrs.*—An old volume, out of print, entitled *A Cloud of Witnesses for the Royal Prerogatives of Jesus Christ.* See also Wodrow, *passim.*

12. Page 39. *Toleration.*—McMahon, p. 215; more fully, *Neill's Founders of Maryland*, p. 148, etc. Also Neill's *Terra Mariæ* for following facts.

13. Page 41. *John Coode.*—Bishop Hawks's *Ecclesiastical Contributions* (ii. 63): "When we next meet with Coode, he is in holy orders, offering a striking illustration of the facility with which, in

that day, vice that deserved a prison could figure in these unfortunate colonies clad in the robes of a priest."

14. Page 42. *A woman indicted* —Accomack records, December 16, 1678, Mr. Anderson is named as "intermarrying with Mary, Widow of John Renny" In March, 1669, Mrs. Mary Renny, wife of John Renny, was indicted for "execrable cursing, blasphemies and wicked speaking" I find no record of prosecution following. Perhaps it was, after all, only some harsh words against the Established Church !

These records supply a full inventory of her wardrobe in 1703.

15 Page 46. *Traduced clergymen.*—Records of Northampton and Accomack—among the oldest in America. See also Bishop Meade's *Old Churches and Families of Virginia*, also Neill's *Colonial Clergy*. The court records furnish interesting data as to history, customs and manners.

16. Page 49. *The lad Makemie.*—Reid's *History of the Presbyterian Church in Ireland*, ii. 266, etc., for next paragraph, Reid, ii. 303; for description of ancient Ramelton, Reid, i. 117.

17. *Makemie before Presbytery* —Reid, ii 342. "In the year 1675 he was enrolled as student in the University of Glasgow as Franciscus Makemius, Scoto-Hyburnus." See Wodrow and Hetherington for cruelties of those years in Scotland; Reid, ii. ch. xviii , for history in Ireland.

In answer to questions addressed to Professor Thomas Witherow of Magee College, Derry, author of *Historical and Literary Memoirs of the Presbyterian Church in Ireland*; and other valuable works, I received the following reply under date of May 28, 1880 :

"DEAR SIR In answer to your letter of 11th inst I beg to say—

"1. That the 'Meeting,' or Presbytery, of Laggan in 1681 covered a district which, if we leave out the Presbytery of Limivady, was about coextensive with all the Presbyteries now comprised in the modern Synod of Derry and Omagh--viz , Derry, Glendermot, Letterkenny, Strabane, Raphoe, Omagh and Donegal.

"2. The following were the ministers of Laggan in 1680—viz. Robert Rule, Derry ; John Hart, Taboyn ; William Liston, Letterkenny ; Robert Campbell, Ray ; James Alexander, Raphoe ; John Hamilton, Donagheady ; Robert Craighead, Donaughmore; Thomas Drummond, Ramelton ; David Brown, Urney , James Tailzior, or Taylor, Glendermot; Robert Wilson, Strabane , William Trail, Lifford ; William Hampton, Burt ; Adam White, Ardstraw ; Samuel Haliday, Omagh ; William Henry, Drumholm; John Rowatt, Cappagh, Thomas Wilson, Killebegs; Fannet congregation, vacant, Enniskillen, vacant.

"3. I know nothing of Makemie's descent or the true spelling of the name. It is understood that the Presbyterians of the North-west were all from Scotland, with few exceptions.

"4. Tradition points out the spot on the shore of Lough Swilly where his father's house once stood.

"5. The notices of Makemie on the minute-book are as follows:

"Page 223: '*St. Johnstown, Jan. 28, 1680.*—Mr. Francis Mckemy comes with a recommendation from Mr. Thomas Drummond to the Meeting. Messrs. John Hart and Robert Rule are appointed to speak privately to him and inquire into his reading and progress in his studies.'

"Page 232. '*St. Johnstown, May 19, 1680.*—Mr. Francis Mckemy presents a petition from the people of Ramullan in prosecution of their former call to James Tailzior and promise £30 of yearly maintenance, and are content that his only preaching place be at Ramullan and say that the people of Clondevaddock have consented to this.'

"Page 234, same meeting: 'The Meeting appoint Messrs Robt. Campbell and William Liston to speak to Francis Mckemy and Alex. Marshall, and to inquire about their studies and encourage them in these and to make report to the Meeting.'

"Page 236: '*St. Johnstown, July 7, 1680.*—Mr. Francis M. kemy and Alex. Marshall are recommended to the brethren that are to be at Raigh communion, to speak to them about their studies and knowledge in the body of Divinity, and also the brethren are to call them to account for afterward from time to time until they be satisfied and clear to present this business to the Meeting.'

"Page 238: 'Mr. Francis Mackemy presents a petition from Killigarvan in prosecution of their call to Mr. James Tailzior'

"Page 240: '*St. Johnstown, August 11, 1680.*—Mr. Francis Mackemy from Ramullan likewise desires an answer to that people's petition about Mr. James Tailzior.'

"Page 241: 'Messrs. John Heart and Robt. Campbell to take some inspection and oversight of Mr. Alex. Marshall's studies; and Messrs. Thomas Drummond and Wm. Liston to do the like to Mr. Francis M. Kemy.

"Page 243: '*Sept. 29, 1680.*—Mr. Wm. Liston reports that Mr. Francis Mackemy desires some more time and that he is diligent, &c.'

"Page 247 '*Decem. 29, 1680.*—Col. Stevens from Maryland beside Virginia his desire of a godly minister is presented to us, The Meeting will consider it seriously and do what they can in it. Mr. John Heart is to write to Mr. William Keyes about this, and Mr. Robt. Rule to the M'gs of Route and Tyrone, and Mr. William Trail to the Meetings of Down and Antrim.'

"Page 253 : '*St. Johnstown, March 9, 1681*—Upon the good report we get of Mr. Francis Mackemy and Mr. Alex. Marshall the Mg think fit to put them upon trials in order to their being licentiated to preach, and they name 1 Tim 1. 5 to Francis Mackemy and Titus 2. 11 to Mr. Alex. Marshall as texts for their private homilies.'

"Page 255 : '*St. Johnstown, April 20, 1681.*—Messrs. Alex. Marshall upon Tit. 2. 11, 12, and Francis Mackemy upon 1 Tim. 1 : 5, delivered their private homilies and were approved. The Mg appoint Math. xi : 28 to Mr. Francis Mackemy and Romans viii. 6 to Mr. Alex. Marshall as texts for their private homilies at the next Meeting, and also the common-heads De Antichristo to Mr. Francis Mackemy and De regimine Ecclesiae contra Erastianos to Mr. Alex. Marshall.'

"Page 257 : '*St. Johnstown, May 25, 1681.*—Mr. Francis Mackemy delivered his private homily on Mat. xi. 20, and is approven. Both he and Mr Alex. Marshall are to give in their theses (which they do), and at the next Meeting they are to have their common-head and are to sustain their disputes.'

"This is the last entry in the minutes of Laggan regarding Makemie. A few weeks after, four ministers of the Presbytery were sent to jail for keeping a fast. Whether they met as a Presbytery afterward, I cannot say ; but if they did, no minutes are preserved from July, 1681, till after 1689. For this reason nothing is known of the date of Makemie's ordination or the circumstances under which he left the country. In the preceding extracts you have all the original information in regard to him now known to exist in Ireland.

"I remain, dear sir, very faithfully yours, etc."

18. Page 59. *George Fox.*—Extract from Fox's journal (pp. 461, etc.), giving his work in Somerset county. "The 12th day of the 12th month (1672) we set forward in our boat, and, traveling by night, we ran our boat on ground in a creek near Monaco River. There we were fain to stay till morning, till the tide came and lifted her off. In the meantime, sitting in an open boat and the weather being bitter cold, some had like to have lost the use of their hands, they were so frozen and benumbed. In the

morning, when the tide set the boat afloat, we got to land and made a good fire, at which we warmed ourselves well, and then took boat and passed about ten miles farther to a Friend's house, where next day we had a precious meeting, at which some of the place were I went after meeting to a Friend's about four miles off, at the head of Anamessy River where, the day following, the Judge of the county and a Justice with him came to me and were very loving and much satisfied with Friends' order

"The next day we had a large meeting at the Justice's in his barn, for his house could not hold the company. There were several of the great folks of that country, and among the rest an opposer, but all was preserved quiet and well. A precious meeting it was; the people were much affected with the truth, blessed be the Lord! We went the next day to see Capt. Colbourn, a Justice of the Peace, and there we had some service Then, returning again, we had a very glorious meeting at the Justice's where we met before, to which came many people of account in the world, magistrates, officers and others It was a large meeting, and the power of God was much felt; so that the people were generally well satisfied and taken with the truth, and, there being several merchants and masters of ships from New England, the truth was spread abroad, blessed be the Lord!

"A day or two after, we traveled about sixteen miles through the woods and bogs heading Anamessy River and Amaroco River, part of which we went over in a canoe, and came to Manaoke to a Friendly woman's house, where on the 24th of the 12th month we had a large meeting in a barn. . . . After this we passed over the river Wiccacomaco and through many bad watery swamps and marshy way and came to James Jones', a Friend and a Justice of the Peace, where we had a large and very glorious meeting, praised be the Lord God! Then, passing over the water in a boat, we took horse and traveled about twenty-four miles through woods and troublesome swamps, and came to another Justice's house, where we had a very large meeting, much people and many of considerable account being present; and the living presence of the Lord was amongst us, praised for ever be his holy name!

"This was the 3d of the first month 1673 The 5th of the same we had another living and heavenly meeting, at which divers Justices with their wives and many others were; amongst whom we had very good service for the Lord, blessed be his holy name! At this meeting was a woman that lived at Anamessy, who had been many years in trouble of mind, and sometimes would sit moping near two months together, or hardly speak or mind anything. When I heard of her, I was moved of the Lord to go to her and tell her, That salvation was come to her house. After I had spoken of the word of life to her and entreated the Lord for her, she mended, went up and down with us to meetings, and is since well, blessed be the Lord!

"We left Anamessy the 7th of the First month, and, passing by water about fifty miles, came to a Friendly woman's house at Hungar River. We had very rough weather and were in great danger, for the boat had liked to have been turned over. But through the good providence of God we got safely thither, praised be his name! At this place we had a meeting Amongst the people were two Papists, a man and woman, the man was very tender, and the woman confessed to the truth. I had no Friend with me but Robert Widders, the rest having dispersed themselves into several parts of the country in the service of the truth.

"So soon as the wind would permit, we passed from hence about forty miles by water, rowing most part of the way, and came to the head of little Choptank to Dr. Winsmore's, a Justice of the Peace lately convinced Here we met with some Friends with whom we staid awhile, and then went on by land and water, and had a large meeting abroad, for the house we were at could not receive the people Divers of the magistrates and their wives were present; and a good meeting it was, blessed be the Lord who is making his name known in that wilderness country!

"We went from thence to William Stephens', where we met with those friends that had been traveling in other parts; and were much refreshed in the Lord together when we imparted to each other the good service we had in the Lord's work, and the prosperity and spreading of the truth in the places where we traveled. John Cartwright and another Friend had been at Virginia, where were great desires in people after the truth; and, being now returned, they staid a little with us here and then set forward to Barbadoes. Before we left this place we had a glorious meeting, at which were many people; amongst others the Judge of that country, three Justices of the Peace, and the High Sheriff and their wives. Of the Indians was one called their Emperor, an Indian King, and their speaker, who sat very attentive and carried themselves very lovingly. An establishing settling meeting it was. This was the 23d day of the First month

"The 24th we went by water ten miles to the Indian town

where this Emperor dwelt, whom I had acquainted before with my coming and desired to get their kings and councils together. In the morning the Emperor came himself and led me to the town; where they were generally come together, their speaker and other officers being with them, and the old Empress sat among them. They sat very grave and sober, and were all very attentive beyond many called Christians. I had some with us that could interpret to them. We had a very good meeting with them, and of considerable service it was; for it gave them a good esteem of truth and Friends, blessed be God!

"After this we had meetings in several parts of that country; one at William Stephens', which was a general meeting once a month, another at Tredhaven Creek, another at Wye, another at Reconow Creek, and another at Thomas Taylor's in the Island of Kent Most of these were large, there being many people at them, and divers of the most considerable in the world's account. The Lord's power and living presence was with us and plenteously manifested among the people, by which their hearts were tendered and opened to receive the truth which had a good savor amongst them, blessed be the Lord God over all for ever!"

On the Somerset records of 1672 is an order for building a bridge over Dividing Creek for "a convenient road to the greatest seat of the Indians." Hence I prefer to locate the old emperor's town up the river, above Colonel Stevens's. Perhaps, however, it was at Shell Town.

19. Page 69. *Commissioners of Somerset county.*—" Cæcilius, Absolute Lord and Proprietary of the Provinces of Maryland and Avalon, Lord Baron of Baltimore, &c., To Stephen Horsey, William Stevens, William Thorne, James Jones, George Johnson, John Winder, Henry Boston and John White, Gent., greeting.

" Know ye that we, for the ease and benefit of the people of our Province and more exact administration of justice, have erected, and do by these presents erect, all that tract of land within our Province of Maryland, bounded on the South with a line drawn East from Watkin's Point (being the North Point of that bay into which the river Wighco, formerly called Wighcocomoco, afterwards Pocomoke, and now Wighcocomoco again, doth fall exclusively) to the ocean-sea on the East, Nanticoke river on the North, and the sound of Chesapeake bay on the West, into a county by the name of Somerset county in honor of our dear sister the Lady Mary Somerset; and for the great trust and confidence we have in your fidelitys, circumspections, providences and wisdoms, have constituted, ordained and appointed, and do by these presents constitute, ordain and appoint, you, Stephen Horsey, William Stevens, William Thorne, James Jones, John Winder, Henry Boston, George Johnson, and John White, Gent., Commissioners jointly and severally to keep the peace in Somerset county aforesaid, and to keep and cause to be kept all laws and orders made for the good and conservation of the peace, and for the quiet rule and government of the people, in all and every the articles of the same, and to chastise and punish all persons offending the form of any the laws and orders of this our Province, or any of them in Somerset county aforesaid, as according to the form of these laws and orders shall be fit to be done

"We have also constituted and ordained you and every four or more of you, with you the said Stephen Horsey, William Stevens and William Thorne (unless some one of our Council be present) are always to be our Commissioners to inquire by the oath of good and lawful men of your county aforesaid, as to all manner of felonies, witchcrafts, enchantments, sorceries, magic arts, trespasses, forestallings, ingrossings and extortions whatever of all and singular other misdeeds and offenses of which Justices of the Peace in England may or ought lawfully to inquire, by whomsoever done or perpetrated or which hereafter shall happen to be done or perpetrated in the county against the laws and orders of this our Province ; provided you proceed not in any of the cases aforesaid to take life or members, but that in every such case you send your prisoners with their indictments and the whole matter before you to our Justices of our Provincial Court next to be holden of this our Province, whensoever or wheresoever to be holden, there to be tried.

"And further we do hereby authorize you to issue writs, processes, arrests, and attachments, to hold plea of, hear and determine and, after judgment, execution to award in all causes civil whatever, in account real or personal, where the thing in action doth not exceed the value of 3000 lbs weight of tobacco, according to the laws, orders and reasonable customs made and used in this our Province of Maryland In which causes civil so to be tried, we do constitute, ordain and appoint you the said Stephen Horsey, William Stevens and William Thorne, or either of you, to be our Judge as aforesaid, unless some one of our Council be there in Court

"And therefore we command you that you diligently intend the keeping of the peace, laws and orders, and all and singular other the premises, and at certain days and places which you or any such four or more of you as is aforesaid, shall in that behalf appoint, ye make inquiries upon the premises and perform and fulfill the same in form aforesaid; doing therein that which in justice pertaineth, according to the laws, orders and reasonable customs of this our Province, saving to us the amercements and other things to us belonging.

"And we command the Sheriff of your said county for the time being, by virtue of these presents, that at certain days and places which you or any such four or more of you as aforesaid, agreeth and make known to him, to give his attendance on you and, if need require, to cause to come before you or any such four or more of you aforesaid, such and as many good and lawful men of your county, by whom the truth in the premises may be the better known and inquired of.

"And lastly we have appointed Edmund Beauchamp Clerk and Keeper of the Records of proceedings in this your County Court, and therefore you shall cause to be brought before you at the said days and places the writs, precepts, process and indictments, to your Court and jurisdiction belonging, that the same may be inspected and by due course determined as aforesaid.

"Given under the great seal of this Province of Maryland, the two and twentieth of August, in the five and thirtieth year of our dominion over the said Province, and in the year of our Lord one thousand six hundred and sixty-six. Whereof our dear son Charles Calvert Esq. is our Lieutenant General, Chief Governor and Chief Justice of our said Province of Maryland."

From Somerset records, 1666. Spelling modernized

20. Page 80 —*Mackemie's appearance* —In her will Makemie's daughter, Madam Anne Holden, leaves the portraits of her father and mother to Samuel Wilson. Dr. Balch came into possession of these valuable memorials, and they were afterward burned with his house and library. Irreparable loss! Will not the owners of such treasures hasten to deposit them in the fire-proof rooms of the Presbyterian Historical Society? My descriptions of the personal appearance of Makemie are drawn from the memories of the picture by a daughter of Dr. Balch still living.

21. Page 89 *Johnny-cake.*—We had thought that the word "jonakin" belonged peculiarly to the Southern slave-vocabulary, but here we find it becoming classic in Boston two centuries ago. The extract is taken from the prologue to Thomson's long poem on King Philip's War, called "New England's Crisis."

22. Page 92 *The Richardsons.*—I do not know who these

Richardsons were. David is found on the Somerset records marrying a couple in 1680, and Robert in 1681. The clerk may have made two of but one. My only reason for speaking of them as Episcopalians is because there was a clergyman by that name preaching in Northampton previous to 1676 who was displaced on account of not being regularly ordained (Meade's *Old Churches*, i. 258). Perhaps he passed up into Maryland.

23. Page 94. *Virginia bells.*—So says the humorous author of the "Sot-Weed Factor."

24. Page 100 *The Indians.*—The old patent mentions the Indian field. The writer exercises some license in locating these particular Indians here. The Somerset records mention them by name as patenting one thousand acres somewhere on the seaboard in 1713 and selling a part of the tract to John Burton in 1736. It was called "Auquexeme."

25. Page 101. *Burley.*—Where Berlin now stands, and the present Presbyterian church; the site also of the old cemetery where stood the former brick church, and where Charles Tennent and many of the fathers are sleeping, the hill on which the explorers are singing. Undoubtedly, "Burley" is the original for "Berlin."

26. Page 102. *Buckingham.*—I fail to find any clue to the date of the organization of the ancient Buckingham church. At the point described in the text, near Poplar Town, it was first built, on the Buckingham tract, and thence deriving its name, thus pointing back to the native shire of Judge Stevens. Some are inclined to claim that this was the meeting-house described in the sheriff's report of 1697 as "on the road going up along the seaside."

27. Page 106. *From Patapsco to Annapolis.*—An anachronism, but I cannot deny myself the pleasure of quoting now and then from this old Maryland poem, published in volume ii of *The Gentleman's Magazine*, and called "A Journey from Patapsco in Maryland to Annapolis, April 4th, 1730" (Neill's *Terra Mariæ*, 239).

28. Page 111. *Letter to Increase Mather.*—This autograph letter addressed to Increase Mather of Boston under date of "Elizabeth River, Va., 22 July, 1684," is still preserved in the library of the Massachusetts Historical Society, and, with two others to be quoted hereafter, determines the true spelling of his name—Makemie.

29. Page 113. *William Trail.*—Here I touch upon facts hitherto undreamed of in our histories.

My researches in tracing Mr. Trail were exciting and protracted. In notes taken on Somerset records of 1689 I had jotted down the name of Trail for the sake of contemporaneous history, supposing him to be a Church-of-England clergyman, and thought no more of it until, while afterward reading Reid's account of the persecutions of the minister of Lifford, it occurred to me that I had the name somewhere among my notes. Again searching the records, I found several items about the Maryland Trail as hereafter given—among others, his purchase of a farm on the Pocomoke in 1686.

At once I wrote to Professor Witherow of Derry for whatever he knew of Trail. Among other facts was his dropping out of European history *during these very years of his apparent sojourn in Maryland.*

Dr. Killen, the continuator of Reid, wrote me: "It appears to me that you are quite correct in your views with respect to the Rev. William Trail. After leaving Lifford he seems to have made his way to America. On hearing of the success of the English Revolution and of the re-establishment of Presbytery in Scotland, he returned there and became a parish minister in his native country."

After supplying me other interesting facts about William Trail, hereafter embodied in my narrative, Dr. Robert Anderson of Glasgow tells me: "After this [his release] he went to Maryland and returned at the Revolution."

The identification is complete.

Finally, my friend Mr W. H. Brown of Princess Anne, Maryland, who has assisted me so materially, put the history back to the very year in which the Presbytery of Laggan signified their purpose to emigrate, discovering the record of marriage performed by Trail in 1684, as given in the text.

Hitherto the first historical notice of Samuel Davis was of his living at Lewes in 1692—evidently a mistake as to locality. I found the Somerset records mentioning him frequently prior to that: the first mention a marriage solemnized by him during this same year of 1684. We know nothing of the antecedents of Davis. Dr. Hodge thinks he was from Ireland.

I have no authority for the arrival of the three ministers on the same ship. The first mention I could find of Thomas Wilson on Somerset records is 1691, when he had evidently been in the country some while. I put his arrival in 1684 because of the expressed purpose of his Presbytery at that date. Professor Witherow gives me the following items from the minutes of Laggan:

" 1674, August 17 : Mr. Henry of Donegal instructed by Presb to name Mr. Wilson to the Killybegs people as suitable. 1676, January 11 : Thomas Wilson appointed to supply Killybegs. August 19 : Credentials received in his favor from Route Presbytery. 1677, October 10 : Killybegs promises to support Mr. Wilson better. 1678, July 3 : Wilson is asked to attend Presbytery and give an account of his ministry, as the people cannot be induced to come to tell how they supported him. November 13 : Killybegs has paid him only twelve pounds a year for last two years. No prospect for improvement. 1681 No word of his removal from Killybegs up to the point in this year where the minutes break off (July 13). When the minutes resume, in 1691, no word of Killybegs and Wilson. I suspect he was starved out. Presbyterianism has now no adherents in Killybegs, on the western coast of Donegal."

30. Page 125. *The Spences.*—Spence's *Letters*, p. 80. In Somerset records 1691 is a deposition giving the age of Adam Spence then as twenty-nine. The records show a David and an Anne Spence living in Wicomico Hundred in 1666, the year the county was organized, and children born to them as follows, David, 1666; Alexander, 1669; John, 1672; James, 1675; Anne, 1677.

In Scotland, Samuel Spence is heavily fined in 1680 (Wodrow, iii. 179). William Spence, secretary to the duke of Argyle, is barbarously tortured in 1684 and 1685 (Wodrow, iv. 95).

31. Page 133. *The Counties.*—St Mary's, a settlement rather than a county, but left a county by carving others out of it · Anne Arundel, organized 1650; Calvert, 1654; Charles, 1658; Baltimore, about 1659, Kent settled like St. Mary's, but left a county by forming others around it: Talbot, 1651, Somerset, 1666; Dorchester, about 1669; Cecil, 1674

32 Page 137. *Trail's purchase.*—Somerset records, Liber M. A., fol. 815. After careful inquiry, I think it is the farm now known as Riggins's Landing

33. Page 143 *The mysterious calls.*—This mystery in the life of Mr. Trail has been furnished me by Rev. Robert Anderson, D. D., Glasgow, Scotland · part of the superstition of the times.

34. Page 163. *Tomb of William Stevens.*—The ancient tomb is still there and legible, flat upon the ground, in the orchard of the old Stevens plantation, about a mile above Rehoboth. The brick foundation of the family mansion is seen some thirty to fifty yards from the grave.

35. Page 171. *Makemie's return to the Eastern Shore.*—Hence,

but without direct authority, I date Mr Makemie's return to the Shore at about this time. Evidently, from the first record-notice of him in 1690, he had been back some while. The probability of Mr. Trail's leaving may also have had something to do with Makemie's return.

36. Page 172. *James and Romanism.*—This is true. In a captured letter, now in the Royal Irish Academy, written this very year (1689) to the pope, James says : " The only source of all these rebellions against us is that we embraced the Catholic faith, and do not disown ; but that to spread the same, not only in our three kingdoms, but over all the dispersed colonies of our subjects in America, was our determination.

37. Page 173. *For character of Virginia clergymen,* see Bishop Meade's *Old Churches,* i. 162, and so forth ; Bishop Hawks's *Maryland Contributions,* p 63; Anderson's *History of the Colonial Church*—all Episcopal authorities.

38. Page 176. *Ninian Beall.*—McMahon (p. 237) gives a list of leaders signing terms of surrender at Matapony on the part of the Associators : John Coode, Henry Jowles, John Campbell, Kenelm Cheseldine, *Ninian Beall,* Humphrey Warring, Nehemiah Blakiston, John Turlinge, Richard Clouds.

39. Page 177. *Annie Laurie.*—Composed by Douglas of Finland in honor of Miss Laurie of Maxwelton in 1688, or near that date.

40. Page 185. *The regicide Whalley.*—I put this mystery in my story of the times because of a singular tradition yet prevailing and written out by a descendant of Mr. Wale as long ago as 1769. The document is as follows

"As most men wish to know something of their ancestors, and as I have from authentic documents and direct tradition a number of facts relative to my ancestor Edward Whalley, otherwise Edward Middleton, ye regicide, I desire to set down here ye facts concerning his life and death in Maryland.

" Edward Whaley was born in Northampton, England, about 1615, and married Elizabeth Middleton ; soon after he joined ye rebellion under Oliver Cromwell, and was one of ye judges yt condemned king Charles ye first, and at ye restoration of Charles ye second (anno domini 1660) he fled to America with many of his misguided companions , he went to Connecticut, and there lived in concealment until ye reward offered by ye Crown of England made his residence amongst ye Yankees unsafe, and he then came to Virginia in 1681, where two of his wife's brothers met him with his family. He then traveled up to ye province of

Maryland, and settled first at ye mouth of ye Pocomoke river, but finding yt too public a place, he came to Sinepuxent, a neck of land open to ye Atlantic Ocean, where Colonel Stephen was surveying, and bought a tract of land from him and called it Genezar it contained 22 hundred acres, south end of Sinepuxent, and made a settlement on ye Southern extremity and called it South Point, to which place he brought his family about 1687 in ye name of Edward Middleton; his own name he made not public until after this date, after ye revolution in England (in ye yeare of our Lord 1688) when he let his name be seen in public papers and had ye lands patented in his own name. He brought with him from ye province of Virginia six children, three Sonnes and three daughters. He had one daughter, ye wife of his companion Goffe, in England. His sonnes were John, Nathaniel and Elias, his daughters were Rachel, Elizabeth and Bridget. Nathaniel Whaley married and settled in Maryland ; John Whaley went to ye province of Delaware and settled, and his family afterward removed away from ye province to ye south. Elias Whaley married Sarah Peel, daughter of Col. Francis Peel, and died leaving one darter, Leah Whaley, and she married Thomas Robins, 2nd of ye name, and died leaving one son, Thomas Robins, 3rd of ye name, ye deponent. Edward Whaley's darters all married. Rachel married Mr. Reckliffe, Elizabeth married William Turvale, and Bridgit married Ebenezer Franklin. Col Whaley lived to an advanced age and was blind for many years before his death ; he died in ye yeare of our Lord 1718, æt. 103 years. His will and yt of his sonne Elias we have in ye records. His descendants are living here in ye province but hold to ye established church, for ye which they ever pray ye divine protection. So died Whalley the regicide. Had he received yt due to him, he would have suffered and died on ye scaffold as did many of his traitorous companions. Vivet rex !

" THOMAS ROBINS,
" 3rd of ye name.

" JULY 8th, in the year of our Lord, 1769 "

This same tradition is in the Whalley family spoken of as removing to the South, now living in South Carolina, and until recently without communication with the Maryland branch.

Of the regicide Whalley, who was in New England with Goffe and Dixwell, no record of death remains, and the last authentic mention of him there is in a letter of Goffe's in 1674: "I do not apprehend the near approach of his death more now (save only he is much older) than I did two years ago."

President Stiles of Yale, writing in 1794, says: "It has always been in public fame that of the two judges at Hadley one died there and was buried in the minister's cellar, but which this was was never said; and that the other, to escape Randolph's dangerous researches, disappeared and was supposed to be gone off to the West toward Virginia, and was heard of no more. This I perfectly remember to have been the current story in my youth." Again he says: "The story of one going off to the westward after the other's death at Hadley is spread all over New England, and is as trite at Rhode Island at this day (1794) as at New Haven and Hadley."

In New Haven, near the grave of the third regicide, Dixwell, are two stones, one marked "M. G." and supposed to mean "William Goffe," the other marked "E. W." and supposed to mean "Edward Whalley." But by strong arguments this tomb has been claimed for others. A Maryland tradition asserts that it was erected to prevent further pursuit.

The following items, gathered by me from the Somerset records, prove the Robins paper wrong in several respects.

(1) A record of marriages and births: "Edward Wale and Elizabeth Ratcliffe were married at Pocomoke by Mr. William Stevens, one of His Lordship's Justices of the Peace for ye county, 29th of January, 1669. John, son of Edward and Elizabeth his wife, was born at Pocomoke, Dec. 2nd 1669; Sarah, at Pocomoke, Feb. 4th 1671; Charles at Pocomoke, Jan. 26th 1674; Elizabeth at Pocomoke August 25th 1677; George at Sinepuxan Feb. 20th 1679; Bridget, same place, Oct. 8th 1681; William, same place, Decem. 26th 1683; Nathaniel, same place, April 8th 1686; Rachel, same place, Novem. 15th 1688; Elias, same place, June 28th 1691."

(2) Parcel of land north of the Pocomoke, called Auquintica, patented by George Wale in 1658; another part in 1668, and conveyed to Edward Wale, and by him to Thomas Newbold in 1678.

(3) Tract of land "near ye heads of ye branches of Assateague river" patented by Edward Wale and Charles Ratcliff in 1679. The Genezer tract the same year.

(4) Deed in 1680 of tract called "Assatcague Fields," patented by Edward Wale in 1678.

(5) I find Edward Wale on the grand jury in 1696, when the regicide would have been over eighty years old.

This Edward Wale was certainly in the county as early as 1669; date of marriage five years before the last definite mention of the regicide in New England—1674. The other dates and items prove that he could not have been Major-General Whalley, as claimed by the Robins paper. But may not all these interesting facts, dates and traditions be harmonized by the hypothesis that Edward Wale of the county records and of the Robins paper was the son of the regicide, and that his father joined him in Sinepuxent?

In his *Memoirs of the House of Cromwell*, Mark Noble says that, besides Mrs. Frances Goffe and a son John, there were born to the regicide other children, of whose career *nothing is known*. An authority quoted by E. D. Neill gives the names of the other children as Mary, Judith, Henry *and Edward*, the latter two by his second wife, Mary Middleton. Mrs. Goffe writes to her husband in 1662 · "My brother John is gone across the sea, I know not whither" (Hutchinson's *History of Massachusetts*, p 534).

During these years I find frequent mention of Middletons on the Accomack records. In 1667, December 16, Thomas Middleton was convicted of "mutinous behavior" and ordered to receive thirty lashes on his bare back, In 1683 is a deposition of his daughter Bridget, twenty-two years old—the same name as one of Edward Wale's daughters.

In the registry of marks of cattle on Somerset records, June 10, 1681, Edward Wale's name is spelled *Wali*, showing that it was pronounced as two syllables

The Whaley and Robins families still live on the Eastern Shore and trace their descent as above. I give these striking traditions for what they are worth, neither defending nor controverting them

41. Page 187. *Words from Makemie's Answer to Keith's Libel on his Catechism.*—From this *Libel* and *Answer* we gather our only knowledge of the Catechism Oh that a copy of the little book might yet be found! Every expedient has been tried by the present writer to secure a thorough search of the old libraries and garrets of the Lower Peninsula, but as yet in vain The date and the place of publication are unknown We only know that it was in the hands of the people at the time of Keith's visit to Somerset, in 1691.

42. Page 190. *Makemie on Accomack records.*—These two are the earliest notices of Makemie yet found on the Accomack records The Finny trial was known to Spence and others When I discovered his assessments for this year and the following years, I hoped that I was about to trace him by these tax-lists back to his first settlement on the Shore , but what was my disappoint-

ment to find that back of 1690 no tax-lists were put upon record.

We have not been able to find *anywhere* any mention of Makemie after his letter to Mather in 1685 up till the present year. Unfortunately, most of the Somerset records between those dates have been destroyed—a disappointing hiatus. Certainly he had returned to the Eastern Shore before 1690. I have chosen to place his removal near the time of the Virginia troubles and of Trail's departure for Europe.

Mr. Finney was afterward (1720) the second husband of Mrs. Makemie's sister Comfort. The fish-hawk's nest and other features of the scenery are from my own view of the Matchatank in 1880.

43. Page 193. *Makemie's marriage.*—The date of marriage cannot be ascertained. From the Accomack records we see that his home in 1690 was at Matchatank. His answer to Keith is dated 1692, and speaks of the Quakers being "at my house at Poccomok" the year previous. Between these two dates—1690 and 1691—he seems to have changed his home to Mr. Anderson's or near it. This is my only reason for placing his marriage at this time. Hill says it occurred "about the latter part of the year 1697 or the beginning of 1698," but gives no authority. Those are the years during which we know nothing of Makemie. Hill is a zealous *guesser*.

44. Page 194. *Profanity punished*—The following affidavit was discovered by myself in 1880, putting back the record-evidence of Rehoboth church seventeen years and proving that "the *new* church" of Makemie's will was the second there built (Somerset records 1687–1691, fol. 90). The Maryland Legislature having lately passed a law for the punishment of profanity, and arrests having been made and no little excitement caused thereby, I was thinking of history repeating itself, and therefore reading with some interest the old prosecution of two centuries ago, when
• I was startled by dropping upon the names of Makemie and the church, used in the affidavit for locating the crime and verifying dates. Like many of my discoveries, it has been used freely by others without credit.

The affidavit is made by Dr. John Vigerous before Justices Francis Jenkins, Thomas Newbold and George Layfield, as follows :

"Memorandum. That upon the second of this present April, anno 1691, there being a funeral sermon preached at Rehoboth church by Mr. Francis Mackemy, minister, toward night on the day aforesaid, William Morris came over to the house of Mr Edmund Howard near Rehoboth town. The said Morris began to curse and swear several oaths against the said Mackemy, calling him fool and loggerhead and puppy with other ill language, saying, —— him, he could preach a better sermon than that fool could do upon such a subject as death. At last the said Morris laid down to sleep. In the night he got up again, I did judge it to be about twelve or one o'clock. The said Morris proceeded much after the aforesaid language with many horrible oaths," etc.

These oaths and blasphemies against "Christ our Judge" I need not transcribe. For these he was prosecuted, not for his denunciations of Makemie. His repeating the words "the last enemy that shall be destroyed is death" among his blasphemies causes the supposition that this was the preacher's text.

45. Page 203. *Makemie ill*—We cannot tell what the ailment was, but under date of July 26, 1692, in the preface of his *Answer to Keith*, Mr. Makemie says: "If any should censure me for my tediousness in answering, I had finished it a year ago, but by reason of my tedious affliction not transcribed until now."

Mr. Makemie left his English books to wife and daughters at his death, and two volumes of Flavel are in the widow's inventory—probably her husband's

46. Page 205. *His will.*—This ingot of gold was unearthed by my friend and helper, William H. Brown, deputy clerk of Somerset court, following closely upon my own discovery of the Morris affidavit. The latter proved the existence of a church at Rehoboth in 1691 ; this valuable paper proved the presence of two other Presbyterian ministers in the county the same year. So far as I know, this is the only mention of Thomas Wilson on the records.

The will is witnessed by Adrian W. Marshall, John Vigerous, William Robbeson, Alexander Cillock and Robert Nearn (Somerset records 1690–1692, fol 94, 95)

47 Page 208. *William Boggs*—Accomack records, Feb. 21, 1692. In Makemie's will he remembers his "kinsman William Boggs." A descendant of this Boggs in Accomack tells me that his ancestor was "the *nephew* of old parson Makemie and came with him from Ireland."

48. Page 212.—*The commissioners to lay out parishes* were as follows : Matapony : Thomas Purnell, Henry Hall, William Stevenson and Richard Holland ; Pocomoke : John Cornish, John Starret, Alexander Maddux, William Noble ; Annamessex · William Colburn, William Planner, Thomas Dixon, —— Hall ;

Monokin Arnold Elzey, Richard Chambers, Richard Whitty, John Strawbridge, Mony · George Betts, John Law, John Renshaw and John White, Wicomico. Daniel Hast, William Elgate, William Alexander and Matthew Wallis; Nanticoke. Robert Collier, James Weatherby, John Round and William Piper. It does not necessarily follow that all of these were Episcopalians.

49 Page 225.—*This is the last assessment* in the Accomack records against Mr. Makemie.

These lists mention the taxpayer's name, and opposite it the number of tithables, thus:

"Francis Makemie ... ... 3"

This is the uniform way throughout the lists. This year alone it is different from all others, thus·

"At Mr. Makemie's ... ... 3"

Was he at this time out of that province, and only his tithables (servants) living there? In the lists for the next two years (1694 and 1695) he is not mentioned at all. Had he removed across the line? After 1695 no lists are put on record.

I have an idea that for a while Mr. Makemie was making his home at Rehoboth. His *Answer to Keith* is dated thus: "At Rehoboth in Pocomok Maryland, This 26 July 1692." The will of Galbraith speaks of him (August, 1691) as "minister of the Gospel at Rehoboth Town." A note given this year (1693) to Mr. Makemie is for corn to be delivered "at the mill at Rehoboth." None of these things are, of course, conclusive, but, taken in connection with the fact of his owning property there and his apparent absence from Virginia, there is some probability in the supposition. Did his "tedious affliction" cause him to move up nearer to a physician—Dr. Vigerous?

50. Page 239 *The court-house.*—Still known as "Court-House Hill," about five miles above Pocomoke City. I cannot find where the former court-house stood. The first point designated for holding court was on the 10th of January, 1666, "at the house of Thomas Pool at Mannakin." In January, 1667, it was ordered that a site be selected and a court-house built at "the most convenient place." January 12, 1688, it "was ordered that the Clerk draw a conveyance for the ten acres of land, where the court-house now is, from Andrew Whittington to two commissioners." November 14 of the same year (1688) agreement was made with William Venable, joiner, to new-roof the house and make other changes. This is all I know until the new house is ordered, as in the text.

51. Page 239. *Thomas Fookes.*—In 1674 the will of Thomas

Fookes or Fowkes is recorded; in it his wife Amy is mentioned, and his "trusty and esteemed friend" William Anderson also, the "right and lawful heirs" of the latter to hold the reversion of certain lands.

In 1678 the nuncupative will of Mrs. Amy Fookes is proved, appointing William Anderson administrator, saying he has been a "dutiful son to her" and giving his daughters Naomi and Comfort each three cows and calves.

My idea is that the Thomas Fookes of the text was a son of the above maker of the will, the second husband of Mr. Anderson's mother.

52. Page 243. *Answer to Keith.*—Two copies of this book are in existence—one in the library of the Old South church, Boston, the other in the library of the Massachusetts Historical Society. The title is as follows :

AN ANSWER

TO

GEORGE KEITH'S LIBEL

AGAINST A

CATECHISM, Published by Francis Makemie.

To which is Added, by way of *Postscript*, A Brief Narrative of a Late Difference among the *Quakers*, begun at *Philadelphia*

BOSTON :

Printed by Benjamin Harris, at the Sign of the BIBLE, over-against the *Blew-Anchor*

MDCXCIII.

53 Page 267. *Weavers*—McMahon, p. 275, note; names of weavers are from Somerset records In 1709 a writer (*British Empire in America*) says: "There is little or no woolen manufacture followed by any of the inhabitants except what is done in Somerset county."

54. Page 271. *Indian town*—Town mentioned in Somerset records. On Herman's map (1670) it is located up the river, apparently on both sides. In 1698 the Quaker preacher Chalkley was at George Truitt's, in the vicinity of Snow Hill, and speaks of an "Indian town not far from his house." Was not Askim-

mekonson the locality above Snow Hill, north of the river, known as "Indian Town" to this day?

The customs and the facts upon which the imaginary speech is based are drawn partly from Bozman's *Maryland*, but more especially from the best account we have of the Nanticokes, in a book published in 1819: *Historical Account of the Indian Nations who once inhabited Pennsylvania and the Neighboring States. By Rev. John Heckewelder of Bethlehem.*

When the Nanticokes finally left the Peninsula, our author speaks of seeing them passing up through Bethlehem bearing the bones of their dead. They are said to have faded away very rapidly.

In the manuscript of Mr. Murray in the Philadelphia Society, from which I take specimens of dialect (1792), is the following note: "Wynicaco, the last king crowned of the Nanticoke tribe. He died at past 80 years since. His body was preserved and very formally kept in a Quacason house—Chiacason house, 70 years dead."

55. Page 279. *Thomas Wilson.*—I have no idea what had become of this Thomas Wilson (see Appendix 29); he had evidently either died or left the county. Nor do I know who Rev. James Breekin is. His is a Scotch name—perhaps a Presbyterian—but quite a number of superfluous Scotch curates were coming over about this time, and he may have been one of them. He is mentioned again hereafter in his testimony on Layfield's marriage.

56. Page 279. *The churches.*—A mystery I cannot solve. There is record-evidence of a church at Rehoboth and Mr. Makemie preaching there in 1691. Is the old public road from Morumsco, passing Rehoboth, crossing the river at Stevens's Ferry, running over toward Selby's Bay, thence up the coast, the road described as "going up along the seaside"? The whole county is described in the older patents—even the lands north and west of the Pocomoke—as "on the seaboard," distinguishing this from the Western Shore. An order of court in 1705 that "no one drive or catch a horse or horses upon the great bridge on Pocomoke river" is directed to be published "at the churches and meeting-houses at Snow Hill and on the seaside." The bridge was at Snow Hill, and the publication seemed to be designed partly for those who should use it from "the seaside."

Was there a Dissenters' meeting-house nearer the coast than Pitts's Creek or Snow Hill? Was it Buckingham? Was it at St. Martin's? My father told me, when a boy, of an old tradition that there was once a Presbyterian church where St Martin's Episcopal church now is. (See Appendix 70.)

57. Page 284. *Mr Davis.*—Affidavit on Somerset records for next year (1698). This is the last notice I could find of Mr Davis in Maryland. He speaks here of going to Hoarkil (Lewes), the next we hear of him (a blank till 1706) he is living at Lewes. When Hampton came over, Snow Hill was vacant. If Davis had been in the county in 1698, he would probably have been a witness at Layfield's trial.

58. Pages 288 and 312 "*Truths in a True Light.*"—So is the little book dated—Barbadoes, December 28, 1697—but its title-page shows that it was not put in print until two years afterward. We know of but one copy in existence, that in the library of Harvard. From that my transcript is taken. The title is as follows :

TRUTHS

IN A TRUE LIGHT;

OR,

A PASTORAL LETTER

TO THE

REFORMED PROTESTANTS

IN

BARBADOES.

Vindicating the Non-Conformists from the Misrepresentations
commonly made of them in that Island and
in other places;

AND

Demonstrating, that they are indeed the truest and soundest
part of the Church of

ENGLAND

From Francis Makemie, Minister
of the Gospel.

2 PET 3 : 17.

*Beloved, seeing ye know these things before, beware .   Lest ye fall
from your own steadfastness*

EDINBURGH.

Printed by the Successors of Andrew Anderson.

1699

59 Page 301. *Plantation bequeathed to Makemie.*—This is now the Miles farm, near the mouth of Holden's Creek. Madam Holden (Anne Makemie) in after-years built a residence at the eastern end of the estate—now the Fletcher farm—and died there. In her will she speaks of the "Westernmost part *where I formerly lived*"—*i. e.*, the Miles tract, where was the old homestead and burial-ground

60. Page 308 *The arrest in 1699.*—I do not vouch for this arrest and trial of Makemie. Dr. Miller's *Memoir of Rodgers* (p. 90) states it positively. Foote's *Sketches* (p. 48) says "We have only strong conjectural evidence, besides tradition, of his being called before legal tribunals in Virginia."

I place it in the present year for reasons appearing in the text —the date of the Virginia Toleration Act and of Makemie's qualifying under it.

61 Page 309. *Church-buildings.*—This shows that at this date there were no church-buildings in Accomack, while there were several in Somerset, and had been for some while, as shown before.

62 Page 316 *The name perpetuated.*—In various forms the name, both Francis and Makemie, is very common on the Peninsula. It is frequently hidden under such perversions as "Kimma," etc.

In 1880 I was riding over the Makemie tract, south of the Matchatank, when I met a Mr. Boggs, a descendant of our pioneer's nephew, who volunteered to take me across the creek to "talk traditions" with his mother. While speaking enthusiastically of "old parson Makemie," suddenly she pointed to a house within sight and said, "Why, yonder within a month has been born a little girl whose middle name is Makemie." Thus the name lives on.

63 Page 342. *John Wilson* seems to have been at New Castle as early as 1686 (Webster, p. 311).

64. Page 351. *The Jamaica church.*—Careful reading of Dr. McDonald's *History of the Jamaica Church* must convince any one of the author's failure to prove it the oldest Presbyterian church in America. No doubt a church of Dissenters was there long before Makemie's landing at Rehoboth, but, by the author's own showing, it was in no true sense Presbyterian. My statement in the text is a fair summing up of the case.

On p. 70, Dr. McDonald shows from documents that in 1686 a Mr. Prudden had been "for ten years discharging the work of a minister according to the way of ye churches in New England "

Prudden is a zealous Congregationalist, and, dissatisfied with the Presbyterian elements in his flock, proposes to organize an unmixed Congregational church. The author argues that Prudden's Congregationalism was the obstacle to collecting his salary, but we find that the church in 1691, *acceding to his own terms* (p 79), agrees to pay arrearages and increase his salary. Had not Congregationalism triumphed?

So with the author's other arguments. They show that there were Presbyterians in Jamaica, which no one denies; but, instead of proving that it was a Presbyterian church in any true sense of that term, they prove directly the reverse.

Dr. McDonald must have felt that he fails to make out his case, for he says on p 145 "Mr McNish may therefore be regarded as the father of the Presbyterian church on Long Island. . . . He may be with equal propriety be regarded as the father of Presbyterianism *in its distinctive form* in New York."

But Mr. McNish did not settle in Long Island until 1711—five years after Makemie had organized the Presbytery in Philadelphia, a quarter of a century after four Presbyterian ministers had lived and preached on the Eastern Shore of Maryland! The Presbyterianism of Long Island went to our Lower Peninsula to find a father.

65 Page 356 *Makemie's children.*—I find it impossible to discover the ages of Makemie's children. The first mention found of Elizabeth is in the will of Mr. Anderson, dated this year (1703). We know that the Makemies had no children when Mr. Anderson's will was made (1698). The older daughter was born within those five years.

66. Page 370, *Maryland Indians.*—Matahocka's cabin at Onancock is mentioned on the Accomack records as early as 1678 in connection with the annual fair held near it. Morumsco James is mentioned on Somerset records of current dates.

67. Page 393. *Makemie's return in 1705* —His business being managed by Mrs. Makemie and Mr. Kemp certainly as late as June 6, we infer that Dr. Hill is mistaken in saying that Makemie returned "late in March."

68 Page 393. *Help from London.—Records of the Presbyterian Church* (p. 16). A letter addressed by Presbytery to Sir Edward Harrison in May, 1709, says: "The negotiations begun and encouraged by a fund in the time when our worthy friend Mr. McKemie, now deceased, was with you, for evangelizing these colonies, was a business exceedingly acceptable to a multitude

* Published by the Presbyterian Board.

of people, and was likely to have been of great service if continued."

On p. 20, in a letter of September, 1710, to the Presbytery of Dublin, they say · "Our late dear Brother Mr. Francis McKemie prevailed with the ministers of London to undertake the support of two itinerants for the space of two years, and after that time to send two more upon the same condition, allowing the former to settle, which, if accomplished, had proved of more than credible advantage to these parts, considering how far scattered most of the inhabitants be."

The latter letter of 1710 settles positively the comparative ages of the Accomack and Somerset churches · "In all Virginia there is but one small congregation, at Elizabeth River, and some few families favoring our way in Rappahannock and York. In Maryland, only four."

Dr. Hill, with usual recklessness, represents Mr Makemie himself to have been sent out by these London ministers !

69 Page 408. *A Maryland poem.*—An anachronism. These and other verses in the chapter are from a beautiful Maryland poem published twenty-four years afterward in the *Gentleman's Magazine* "A Journey from Patapsco to Annapolis, April 4th 1730" (Neill's *Terra Mariæ*, p. 239)

70 Page 411. *The First church.*—"Near Mr. Edgar's." This is generally supposed to be the old Pitts's Creek church, but after years of effort I am as far as ever from settling the question definitely.

In 1684, James Round secured a warrant for five hundred acres of land to be located "on the seaboard." Two hundred were located on St. Martin's River, on the coast, not far below the Delaware line, and the tract was called in the old patent "South Benfleet," now Benefit It was in the neighborhood of Wrixam and Ambrose White, and other Presbyterians After ward the remaining three hundred acres were patented (1686) "in the Pocomoke" and called "Good Success," on the opposite side of the river from Pocomoke City and about a mile above, now the Melvin property and lands adjacent

Mrs. Mary Rounds, widow of the patentee, marrying John Edgar, both these tracts became his. The St. Martin's tract was deeded by Edgar and wife to a Mr. Cropper in 1704. Somewhere between that date and 1707, Edgar died, for then we find the widow making a deed to the Pocomoke tract

In the patents both of these tracts are described as " on the seaboard," although the latter is at the same time described as

north-west of the Pocomoke, and is almost as near to the Chesapeake as to the Atlantic. All Somerset county (Somerset, Worcester and Wicomico) was at that time spoken of as "on the
seaboard," as appears from many old patents and from the commission from Baltimore to Stevens to encourage the settlement
of "the seaboard."

This Pocomoke tract of Edgar's is about seven miles from
both Pitts's Creek and Rehoboth, and seven miles was "near" in
those days of scattered population and long distances. I do not
think that Rehoboth church is meant, 1. Because it would better
have been designated by the name of the town than by a plantation so far away; 2. Because Rehoboth church is recorded
under its own name two years afterward, when it is stated that
application had been made some time before and referred to
Annapolis, 3. Mr. Makemie considered his Barbadoes and Virginia certificates sufficient protection, as we shall find, in New
York.

There is a tradition—inveterate and hard to ignore—that the
first Makemie meeting-house was built where Pocomoke City
(formerly New Town) now is. This was the old Stevens ferry,
at one time also called "Meeting-House Landing." It is said that
the church was first erected here to accommodate all the people
on both sides of the river, who, while there was but one church,
could best meet at the ferry. After this the traditions differ, one
asserting that the church of cypress logs was torn down by the
Episcopalians before completed and thrown into the river at
night—that the logs floated to Rehoboth and there were drawn
on shore and the house built. Another tradition affirms that the
logs were collected at the ferry and put together again, the Presbyterians remaining by the building night and day, armed, until
it was under roof and safe.

An old gentleman still living told me that when a boy, near
the beginning of the present century, he saw the roof and other
remains of what was called "the old Presbyterian meeting-
house." Persons still older, now dead, told relatives yet living
that they used to attend, not far from the middle of the last century, what was even then called "the old Makemie church," located definitely upon a lot near the river in Pocomoke City. I
have found it impossible to rebut these traditions so wonderfully
fortified. Only one fact seems directly to conflict. history and
the records give no indication of such hostility of the Episcopalians on the Eastern Shore at that early date.

To strengthen these traditions, we have but lately discovered the true locality of "Mr. Edgar's," and find it to be within a mile of the place where this stubborn tradition located the first church, locating it there without any knowledge that the Edgar plantation was so near! And yet traditions are not always decisive. There are traditions just as strong and inveterate that the first church was at Snow Hill; and that it was at Rehoboth. My opinion is that several churches were built very near the same time—perhaps the same year. For reasons appearing all through the text, my belief is that Rehoboth will always maintain its claim to priority.

Another reason hard to rebut is found in the words of Rev. Samuel McMaster, Anne Makemie's pastor, copied by Spence (*Letters*, p. 97) from McMaster's autograph: "The first congregation which worshiped at Rehoboth, consisted of English Dissenters. A few families migrated from England, their consciences not suffering them to comply with the Establishment there existing, and settled near the mouth of Pocomoke River and the adjacent parts—some on the east, and some on the west, side of the river—and formed themselves into a religious society for the public worship of God. A house for public worship was built on the west side of the river, at a place called 'Rehoboth'"

A comma after the word "congregation" is alone needed to make the assertion positive that the first place of worship was Rehoboth. But, besides this, we know that the chief early settlements had been in that part of the county, and with this in mind, and the early prominence of Rehoboth, the inference is unavoidable that McMaster was speaking of the first organization in the county.

71. Page 419 *First meeting of Presbytery.*—It is impossible to ascertain positively the date of the first meeting of Presbytery. In his introduction to the old records Dr. Engles says "Judging from the first date which appears on page 3 of these records, it must have been about the beginning of the year 1705." This cannot be, for Makemie and "his assistants" did not reach America until in the summer at the earliest.

Hill thinks it was in 1705, Webster believes it was probably in September, 1706, both consider the meeting with which the records open to have been an adjourned meeting at Freehold for the special purpose of ordaining Boyd. Hodge expresses no opinion as to date. Gillett leaves it uncertain as between 1705 and 1706. Foote thinks it not likely to have been organized until after the qualification of Macnish and Hampton, which was in June, 1706.

This latter is my own opinion, as embodied in the text, for I have no idea that these ministers and their leader would have been absent from Maryland while their licensure and its momentous issues were still in doubt and needing constant vigilance. I put it toward the close of the year because of a probability that the ministers taking part in the adjourned meeting would have the two meetings near together, so as to obviate the necessity of another hard trip home and back again.

The mutilated records do not make it certain that the meeting with which they now begin and the ordination occurred at Freehold, but Cornbury's letter charging Makemie and Hampton with ordaining young men in New Jersey leaves no doubt as to place. The old manuscript minutes begin abruptly at the top of the third page, and are as follows.

"De regimine ecclesiæ, which being heard was approved of and sustained. He gave in also his thesis to be considered of against next sederunt.

"Sederunt 2nd 10 bris 27. Post preces sederunt Mr. Francis Makemie Moderator, Messrs. Jedediah Andrews and John Hampton, Ministers.

"Mr. John Boyd performed the other parts of his trial, viz., preached a popular sermon on John 1 12; defended his thesis; gave satisfaction as to his skill in the languages; and answered to extemporary questions; all which were approved of and sustained.

"Appointed his ordination to be on the next Lord's Day, the 29th inst., which was accordingly performed in the public meeting-house of this place before a numerous assembly; and the next day he had the certificate of his ordination."

72. Page 428. *The New York sermon* —There is some confusion of dates as to the time of preaching. The Force tract containing the narrative believed to be written by Mr. Makemie himself states that the sermon was preached on the 20th, and the other dates hang along upon that. But the 20th was Monday, and evidently the preaching was on Sunday, which was the 19th. Undoubtedly, the author mistook the day of the month. So Cornbury says: "On the Monday following, I was informed that Makemie had preached *the day before.*"

73. Page 433. *Persecutions of Cardale.*—Webster, p 85. In 1711, Colonel Heathcote declares: "Many of the instruments made use of to settle the church in Jamaica were of warm tempers, and, if report is true, indifferent in their morals. One Mr. Cardale, a transient person and of very indifferent reputation,

was recommended and made high sheriff of the county, and the settling of the church was left in a great measure to his care and conduct." Smith, the historian, calls him "one Cardwell, a mean fellow." Thomson in his *History of Long Island* says that he sustained a despicable character and was afterward thrown into prison, and there hanged himself.

74. Page 473. *The Sermon* was issued under the following title:

A GOOD CONVERSATION.

A

SERMON.

PREACHED AT THE CITY

OF

NEW YORK.

Jan. 19th, 1706-7

By Francis Makemie, Minister of the Gospel of Christ.

MATT. 5 : 11.—Blessed are ye when men shall revile you and persecute you and shall say all manner of evil against you falsely for my name's sake.

ACTS 5 29—Then Peter and the other Apostles answered and said, We ought to obey God rather than men

Preces et lachrymæ sunt arma Ecclesiæ.

BOSTON in N. E.

Printed by B Green for Benj. Eliot

Sold at his Shop, 1707

75. Page 479. *Makemie's account of his prosecution.*—The title-page is as follows, from one of the Force tracts :

A

NARRATIVE

OF A NEW AND UNUSUAL

AMERICAN

IMPRISONMENT

OF TWO

PRESBYTERIAN MINISTERS:

AND PROSECUTION OF

MR. FRANCIS MAKEMIE,

ONE OF THEM FOR PREACHING ONE SERMON AT THE
CITY OF NEW YORK.

BY A LEARNER OF LAW AND LOVER OF LIBERTY.

PRINTED FOR THE PUBLISHER: 1707

This tract was republished in 1755, and was used in the cause
of American liberty (Webster, p. 307).

76. Page 490. "*The Sot-Weed Factor*"—The full title of this
early Maryland poem is as follows ·

THE

SOT-WEED FACTOR;

OR, A VOYAGE TO

MARYLAND.

A

SATYR

IN WHICH IS DESCRIBED

The Laws, Government, Courts and Constitutions of the Country, and
also the Buildings, Feasts, Frolics, Entertainments and
Drunken Humors of the Inhabitants of that
Part of America.

IN BURLESQUE VERSE.

BY EBEN COOK, GENT.

LONDON:

Printed and Sold by D. Bragg, at the Raven in Pater Noster-Row,
1708   (Price 6d.)

My copy is a *fac-simile* reprint fiom the first edition, one of Shea's *Early Southern Tracts*, 1865

77. Page 505 *Elizabeth Makemie* —Elizabeth, the oldei daughter, died the same year with her father. On the Accomack records, dated October 6, 1708, is this entiy "This day Madam Naomie Makemie petitioned this Court for Administration on the Estate of Elizabeth Makemie, her daughter, late deceased, she dying intestate, which was by the Court granted, she giving Bond and Security as the Law diiects," etc. John Brandhurst and Hill Drummond were the secuiities.

78. Page 506. *The widow of Makemie* —On the 7th of April, 1709, a document is recorded beginning as follows "We the subscribers did on the day of date hereof inventory sundry goods and several negroes which upon view of William Anderson's will was wholly left and bequeathed, according to our judgment, to Naomi Makemie, now Naomi Kemp, daughter of the said Anderson," etc.

Here we learn that Mrs Makemie had married again in less than a year after her husband's death. The iecords show that rich widows married rapidly in those days. This James Kemp was one of the "trusty and good friends" named in Mr Makemie's will "to be aiding, advising and assisting my aforesaid executrix in ye management of my estate." He had also been included in the power of attorney given Mrs Makemie by her husband during his absence in Europe (1704–1705)

On the 5th of October, 1709, an inventory of Elizabeth Makemie's estate is presented by Naomi Kemp. Another of the same estate (Elizabeth's) is piesented May 4, 1710, by James Keimp, as follows "Negro girls Hannah, £22, Sarah, £24; Sue, £12; Kate, £12, Negro boys, Adam, £9, Toby, £7"

Under date of December 3, 1717, is a "deposition of Naomy Kemp aged 49 years or thereabouts."

On the 7th November, 1721, the will of James Kemp is probated by Naomi Kemp, executrix—again a widow. The will is pioved by Mrs. Comfoit Finney and Anne Makemie. Comfort's first husband, Elias Taylor, had died in May, 1717, and in 1720 she had married William Finney, whom Mr Makemie had sued for fifteen bushels of wheat in 1690—the first mention of our pioneer on the county iecords

Kemp's will gives cows and calves and negroes to his "kinsman James Wishart." To "sister Mary the wife of Thomas Wishart of Princess Anne county in Virginia 200 acres of land lying and being in ye said county at Back Bay known and so-called." Remainder of estate "to my loving wife Naomi Kemp."

Rev. Josias Mackie owned a farm on Back Bay, and in his will, dated 1716, November 7, and probated the 16th, he leaves bequests to John Wishart.

In an inventory of Kemp's estate presented by Naomi, September 14, 1723, are the following books, which I take to have been Makemie's. "Pool's *Annotations on the Bible*, 1 pound five pence; one sermon book by Flavel, 8 shillings; two other books by same, 13 shillings, twenty-four old books, 3 pounds."

On September 27, 1728, is recorded a survey to lay out the land of Naomi Kemp south of Matchatank Creek, the tract purchased from Robert Hutchinson by Makemie in 1693. This is the last mention I have been able to find of Mrs. Makemie. She was then sixty years old. Her sister Comfort died in the year 1732. William Boggs, the "kinsman" of Mr. Makemie's will, and named in the land-grant of 1692, died in 1718, an inventory of his estate appearing that year.

79 Page 508. *Makemie's younger daughter.*—Reliable tradition affirms that Anne Makemie first married a Mr. Blair. Since hearing of this I have had no opportunity for verifying it from the records. Her second husband was Robert King, born in 1689, son of Robert King and brother of Mrs. Mary Jenkins, the wife of Colonel Jenkins and warm friend of Makemie. Mrs. Jenkins afterward married the Rev. John Henry, Mr. Makemie's successor at Rehoboth, by whom she left two sons, Robert Jenkins Henry and John Henry, both men of prominence. After Mr. Henry's death his widow married the Rev. John Hampton. Lying flat on the ground in the wreck of a graveyard on the Jenkins plantation, a mile below Rehoboth, is an old crumbling stone on which I deciphered these words: "Under this stone lyeth the body of Madam Mary Hampton who departed this life the 19th of Oct. 1744, Aged 70 years wanting three days."

On the Accomack records is the will of Robert King, dated May 30, 1753, with several later codicils, and finally probated by his wife, Anne, May 9, 1755. How long they had been married I cannot discover. He speaks of a former wife and her children, Nehemiah and Robert, the latter deceased; of his two grandsons, Thomas and Robert Jenkins King; of his "deceased sister, Mary Hampton," and her two sons; of "my granddaughter Mary Barns" and of "my niece Elizabeth Dashiel, wife of Charles Dashiel." He refers to his wife's "home-plantation in Accomack " and her " Matchatank plantation," thus certainly identifying his wife, Anne, with Anne Makemie.

The widow next marries George Holden, clerk of the county court. The records show them husband and wife in 1765, and there is also recorded a deed signed by himself alone in 1760. They had evidently married between these two dates. He was a widower with an only son, of his own name.

On the 14th of September, 1768, Holden makes the following will: " In the name of God amen. George Holden of the county of Accomack in Virginia do ordain this my last will and testament. Whereas, I promised my wife Anne that, if she should consent to dock the entail of the lands at Matchatank of which she was seized as tenant in fee tail at the time of our marriage, and having docked the same, and got the fee simple thereof in me and my heirs; that she should, in case she survived me, enjoy and possess the said lands for and during the term of her natural life, and receive the whole profits thereof to her own use without impeachment of waste; therefore, in order to comply with the same promise and engagement, do hereby devise and bequeath the same to the said Anne and her assigns for and during the term of her natural life without impeachment of or for any manner of waste. As witness my hand this 14th day of Sept. 1768. Written by my own hand."

Such docking of entail explains why Makemie's lands, on failure of issue by his daughters, never came into possession of relatives in Ireland, according to his will. We could have wished otherwise.

Holden probably died in 1774, the above will being probated that year "on the motion of George Holden only son and heir at law to the said testator."

Anne Makemie was for the third and last time a widow. Tradition represents her to have been very patriotic during the Revolution, and in frequent danger from British gunboats. This patriotism appears in three deeds dated June 26, 1787, in one of which she gives twenty-five acres of land to Joseph Boggs " for and in consideration of the natural affection that she bears to the said Joseph, and that the said Joseph will vote at the annual elections for the most wise and discreet men who have proved themselves real friends of the American Independence, to represent the county of Accomack." For like consideration a second deed gives twenty-five acres to John Milbourn, and a third deed gives four hundred acres—the "tract of land lying on Matchatank known by the name of Fookes's Neck "—to John, Francis and Joseph Boggs.

35

Very old and decrepit, she died between the 15th of November, 1787, and the 29th of January, 1788—her will made on the former date, and probated on the latter. In her will she mentions her "deceased husband King." Among other bequests are these: "I give the two pictures of Father and Mother to Samuel Wilson," "I give to the Rev. Jacob Ker the sum of twenty pounds. I give to the Rev. Samuel McMaster the sum of forty-six pounds, a mahogany desk, a bed and furniture, and a negro woman called Keziah and her children," "I give and devise to John Milligan and Mary Milbourn all the land and plantation where I live, John Milligan to have the old part where I formerly lived being the Westernmost part of the land; and Mary Milbourn the Easternmost part of the land where I now live;" "I give fifty pounds to the good poor of my neighborhood to be given and disposed of at the discretion of William Selby;" "I give one hundred pounds to the Pitts Creek Congregation to be disposed of by the Session for the support of a minister." The executors are Dr. William Williams, Colonel William Selby, Elijah Milbourn and the Rev. Samuel McMaster.

The "old part" of the land, where she "formerly lived," is the present Miles farm, near the mouth of Holden's Creek—evidently the site of the Anderson and Makemie homestead.

Under date of April 16, 1789, is a recorded settlement between the executors of Madam Holden and "George Corbin on behalf of John Perrin Executor of George Holden Junior, deceased, who was the Executor of George Holden Senior."

The last of Makemie's children had not even a stepson to survive her long.

Upon the records is an inventory of Mrs. Holden dated September 29, 1789—very long, and containing the names of seventy-eight negroes, also mentioning the *mahogany desk* left to the Rev. Samuel McMaster, and appraised at six pounds. This desk was left by him to his son, Samuel McMaster, Esq., after whose death it was purchased at the vendue by the late John B. White. In the year 1883 it came into possession of the author—a venerable old piece of furniture, the only known relic of the Makemie family.

80. Page 510 *Makemie's grave identified.*—The plantation where the pioneer lived and died is well known, stretching along the south bank of Holden's Creek, formerly Houlston's, in Accomack county, from Jenkins's bridge to Pocomoke Sound. On this large tract of land, bequeathed by his father-in-law, are two old graveyards, about two miles apart—one on the upper or east-

ern farm, one on the lower or western. That one or the other of these is the Anderson and Makemie burial-ground there has never been a doubt. But *which* of these ?

On page 302 of the text, and throughout Anderson's will, is seen his anxiety to preserve the said Pocomoke plantation in regular descent—the old English pride to found and perpetuate family estates. In the colonies of Virginia and Maryland there were few public cemeteries ; on these family estates were the household graveyards, where the bones of the testator and of his far posterity were to sleep together and be protected by kindred hands from profanation for ever. A generous pride and pathetic dream !

Mr. Anderson shared all this. Having no sons, Pocomoke and Matchatank are bequeathed to his first-born, Naomi, and "Son Makemie." "If Naomi should become mother of more than one child, the most worthy of blood is to have Pocomoke " "In case Naomi dies childless, after her and her husband's natural lives on it, my other granddaughters are to have it as co-heirs among them, giving them liberty to sell each of their parts to each other," but most positively to no one "out of the family." The Makemies are bound to keep this home-plantation in thorough repair, just as the testator left it. So he passed away, doing all that could be done by testamentary precision and the laws of primogeniture to conserve that estate to his descendants. There Makemie lived through the ten years following, and there died— *his* favorite home also. There Naomi lived until at least twenty years after. There Anne Makemie lived through three marriages and a third widowhood until 1787, and there died upon the same plantation. There, unquestionably, they were all buried.

But the main difficulty in the traditionary evidence was the conflict with regard to the *two* graveyards on the same large tract—the eastern one on what is now the Fletcher farm, and the western on the Miles farm. An examination of the will of Anne Makemie (Madam Holden) began to solve the difficulty : "I give and devise to John Milligan and Mary Milbourn all the land and plantation where I live ; John Milligan to have *the old part where I formerly lived, being the westernmost part of the land;* and Mary Milbourn the easternmost part of the land *where I now live.*" The Milligan devise was near the mouth of the creek, at Pocomoke Sound—the present Miles farm. This was "*the old part,*" where her father and grandfather had lived and died. There would be the family burial-ground, and certainly not two miles away, on the new part (now the Fletcher farm) improved

by her after their death.   Tradition is correct, however, in pointing to the beautiful site at Jenkins's bridge as her last place of
residence and the scene of her death

During the summer of 1879 my friend Dr. J. T. B. McMaster
of Pocomoke City, a grandson of Madam Holden's pastor, accompanied me to the house, near Jenkins's bridge, of Mrs. Charlotte Corbin, a lady then seventy years old, from whom we hoped
to gain important information.   It was our glad surprise to find
that her maiden-name was Milligan—a niece of John Milligan
of the will—and that she had grown up from childhood on "the
old part" of the farm, associating with those who had known
Madam Holden well   The Holden negroes used to amuse young
Charlotte by imitating the *peculiar sneeze* of the old lady, and
our informant and her companions used to dig about the old
family mansion for the silver and gold said to have been buried
as a protection from the British   Another tradition asserts that
the bequest was made to Milligan because of his prompt bravery
in assembling the neighbors and driving off an English gunboat
steering for the rich widow's.

Mrs. Corbin told us that the old family graveyard was surrounded by a *brick wall,* around the top of which she used to
run in play when a barefoot girl ; that the tombstones were already becoming badly broken and the fragments carried off for
whetstones ; that there was then no difference of opinion in the
community as to this being the place where Madam Holden and
her forefathers were buried, and this too during the lifetime of
hundreds of those who knew the deceased personally ; that the
present graveyard had grown around the eastern corner of the
wall, outside of it ; that the old family burying-ground, therefore,
lies west of the present graveyard, and *just where the cattle-pen
and stables now are,* and that she, our informant, remembered
when this act of desecration was deliberately perpetrated

Thus directed, we hastened down to "the old part" and with
our hoes removed the surface-earth in search for some vestige of
that brick wall.   Sure enough, just as Mrs. Corbin described, we
struck upon the foundation below the ground, followed its angles
and found it enclosing the cattle-pen !   Entering the pen and
digging below the accumulations, we came upon indications of
graves covered with old English bricks laid edgewise

Our informant told us of a negro woman, Aunt Peggy Milligan, considerably older than herself, of remarkable intelligence
and entirely trustworthy, who has since been interviewed by Dr.
McMaster.   Besides confirming in every particular the state-

ments of Mrs. Corbin, whose birth she distinctly remembers, thus placing her own birth very near the time of Anne Makemie's death, Aunt Peggy testified very clearly and definitely in addition that the low brick wall surrounding the graves was surmounted originally with a wooden fence, as is sometimes still seen in that section ; that it was the only graveyard with a brick enclosure in all that neighborhood ; that everybody knew it was the burial-ground of Madam Holden's family , that the graveyard at the Fletcher farm is of considerably later date and only used as such after the death of Madam Holden.

Thus the documentary, the traditional and the oral living testimony all agree, both circumstantially and directly, and with an accumulative force that is perfectly conclusive. How fortunate to find those living witnesses just when we did !

We now know where our Makemie sleeps. "Committing my body to ye dust decently to be interred," but now alas the sacrilege and the desecration ! It cannot hurt *him*. So sleeps the dust of John Calvin, under almost equal neglect.

LIST OF AUTHORITIES.

A Cloud of Witnesses for the Royal Prerogatives of Jesus Christ. (Scotch pamphlet. Out of print.)

Annals of Annapolis. (Out of print.)

Annals of the American Pulpit. By William B. Sprague, D D Robert Carter & Bros , New York

Annals of Philadelphia By J F. Watson Philadelphia · J B. Lippincott Company

Bacon's Laws of Maryland.

British Empire in America. Oldmixon 1707. (Out of print)

Character of the Province of Maryland. By George Alsop. Edited by J G Shea. New York: Wm. Gowans. 1869 (Out of print)

Constitutional History of England. By Henry Hallam New York ; Harper & Brothers 1851

Constitutional History of the Presbyterian Church in the United States of America. Charles Hodge. Philadelphia Presbyterian Board. 1851.

Contributions to the Ecclesiastical History of the United States Bishop Hawks New York J. S Taylor 1839 (Out of print)

Conversations, Discussions and Anecdotes of Thomas Story. Philadelphia : Zell. 1860.

Court Records of Accomack County, Virginia.

Court Records of Somerset County, Maryland

Derry and Enniskillen in the Year 1689 Prof. Thomas Witherow Belfast : William Mullen 1876

Diary of John Evelyn Edited by Wm Bray London · Warne & Co 1818

Early Religious History of Maryland. Rev B F Brown. Baltimore : Innes & Co. 1876

Founders of Maryland. Edward D. Neill Albany: John Munsell. 1876

General History of Virginia. Capt John Smith

Historical and Literary Memorials of Presbyterianism in Ireland Prof. Thomas Witherow London and Belfast · Wm Mullen & Son. 1879

Historical View of the Government of Maryland   John V. L. McMahon. Baltimore   1831.   (Out of print.)

History, Manners and Customs of the Indian Nations   John Hecke-welder.   Philadelphia: Pennsylvania Historical Society.   1876.

History of American Literature.   Moses C. Tyler   New York   G P. Putnam's Sons   1879.

History of the Church of England in the Colonies.   James S. M. Anderson   London: Rivingtons.   1856.

History of the Church of Scotland   W M Hetherington   New York: Carters.   1870

History of England.   T. B. Macaulay   Philadelphia.   J B Lippincott Company   1879.

History of the Colony and Ancient Dominion of Virginia.   Charles Campbell   Philadelphia: J. B. Lippincott Company.   1860

History of Maryland.   John L Bozman.   Baltimore: Lucas & Deaver. 1837.   (Out of print.)

History of Maryland.   James McSherry.   Baltimore: Murphy   1849.

History of Maryland.   J. Thomas Scharf   Baltimore.   John B. Piet. 1879.

History of My Own Times   Bishop Gilbert Burnet.   Oxford.   1823

History of New Sweden   Israel Acrelius.   Philadelphia: Pennsylvania Historical Society.   1876

History of New York   William Smith

History of the Presbyterian Church in Ireland   James S Reid.   Continued by Killan   Belfast: Wm Mullen   1867

History of the Presbyterian Church in America.   Richard Webster. Philadelphia.   J M. Wilson.   1857.   (Out of print.)

History of the Presbyterian Church in the United States of America. E H Gillett   Philadelphia   Presbyterian Board.   1864

History and Present State of Virginia   Robert Beverley   London. 1705   Reprint, Richmond   1855

History of the Rise, Progress, Genius and Character of American Presbyterianism.   William Hill   Washington City: J Gideon   1839 (Out of print.)

History of the Sufferings of the Church of Scotland   Robert Wodrow Glasgow.   Blackie, Fullerton & Co.   1828.   (Out of print.)

History of the United States.   George Bancroft   Boston: Little, Brown & Co   1852.

Journal of George Fox   Philadelphia. Friends' Bookstore.

Journal of George Keith.   Reprint by Episcopal Historical Society. (Very scarce.)

Journal of Samuel Bownas.   (Out of print.)

Journal of Thomas Chalkley   Philadelphia: Friends' Bookstore. 1875.

Leah and Rachel: the Two Fruitful Sisters Virginia and Maryland John Hammond   Force's Historical Tracts.   (Out of print.)

Letters on the Early History of the Presbyterian Church in America. Irving Spence. Philadelphia: Henry Perkins. 1838 (Out of print.)

Makemie's A Good Conversation : A Sermon Preached at the City of New York Collections of New York Historical Society. 1870.

Makemie's Answer to George Keith's Libel against his Catechism. Two copies Library of Massachusetts Historical Society and of the Old South Church, Boston.

Makemie's Narrative of a New and Unusual American Imprisonment. Force's Historical Tracts.

Makemie's Perswasive for Promoting Towns. Library of Harvard University.

Makemie's Truths in a True Light. Library of Harvard University

Manuscripts of the American Philosophical Society. Philadelphia. (Transcripts)

Minute-Book of the old Laggan Presbytery (Transcripts.)

Nonconformists' Memorial. Edmund Calamy. London : Button & Co 1802 (Out of print)

Notes on the Virginia Colonial Clergy. Edward D Neill. Philadelphia. 1877

Old Churches, Ministers and Families of Virginia. Bishop Meade. Philadelphia: J. B. Lippincott Company. 1878.

Pennsylvania Historical Magazine.

Popular History of England Charles Knight. New York : Lovell. 1878

Provincial Records of Maryland.

Records of the Presbyterian Church. Philadelphia: Presbyterian Board.

Reports of Pennsylvania Historical Society.

Reports of New York Historical Society.

Report of Commissioners on the Boundary-Line of Maryland and Virginia. Valuable ancient maps Richmond 1873. (Out of print.)

Sketches of Virginia, Historical and Biographical. William Henry Foote. Philadelphia Martien. 1850 (Out of print)

Sot-Weed Factor. Eben Cooke, Gent London. 1708 Reprint Shea's Southern Tracts, No 2. (Out of print)

Terra Mariæ Edward D Neill. Philadelphia: J. B. Lippincott Company 1867

Two Centuries of the History of the Presbyterian Church of Jamaica, Long Island. J. M Macdonald New York Carters. 1862. (Out of print.)

Troubadours, Their Loves and their Lyrics. John Rutherford London Smith, Elder & Co 1873.

Who were the Early Settlers of Maryland? Rev. Ethan Allen. Baltimore. (Out of print.)

INDEX.

ACCOMACK COUNTY settled 44; clergy and churches, 45, 46; Quakers, 45, 46; their petition to settle in Maryland, 55; Onancock, 84; Makemie's home, 171, 190, 371.

Adams, Rev. Alexander, 378; vs Macnish, 396, 403.

Anderson, William, home and family, 42; dies, 298; will, 299; grave, 303; widow dies, 364.

Andrews, Rev. Jedediah, 295; ordained, 342, 358; church built, 377, 396; Presbytery, 415, 452, 497; Makemie's will, 500.

Authorities, List of, 551–553

Barbadoes, 286; pastoral to, 312

Baxter, Rev. Richard, before Jeffreys, 128; dies, 202.

Beall, Colonel Ninian, arrival, 25; nativity, etc., 176; services honored, 309

Bermudas, early Presbyterianism, 146.

Blair, Commissary, 227; college, 226; "sort like Presbyterians," 348.

Boyd, Rev. John, 417.

Bray, Dr. Thomas, commissary, 265, 305, 311, 321, 340, 360, 378.

Bray, Pierce, Elder, 337.

Brechin, Rev. James, 278, 283.

Buckingham plantation, 101.

Burley plantation (Berlin), 99.

Cabot, Sebastian, Maryland beaches, 10

Colonial prices in tobacco, 116, 117, 158, 164, 165, 257, 274, 368.

Coode, John, plotting rebellion, 40, character, 41, 136; in revolution, 173; plotting again, 265.

Copley, Governor Lionel, 208, 210, 230, 236.

Cornbury, Lord, 349; character, 350; prosecutes Bownas, 349; Jamaica outrage, 351; in Philadelphia, 358; tyranny approved, 412; persecutes Makemie, 429, etc.; letter in self-defence, 480; imprisoned, 484.

Davis, Rev. Samuel, in Maryland, 112; marriage by, 114; visit from Keith, 200; receives bequest, 205; recording marriages, 278; Layfield's marriage, 283; moderator of Presbytery, 497.

Dashiel, James, 209

Drummond, Rev. Thomas, Makemie's pastor, 49; imprisoned, 49; vouches for Makemie, 50.

Dryden, John, 240

Duke of York, cruelty, 32, 67; becomes king, 123.

Eagle Wing and cargo, 69.

Edgar, Mrs Mary, or Mrs. Round, plantation, 254, 537.

Elizabeth River, Virginia, Congregationalists there, 109; Makemie, 109, etc.; Mackie, 222, 273.

Fasset, William, 404.

Fox, George, in Somerset, 57–59; journal, Appendix No. 18; dies, 196

Franklin, John, 276, 393, 397, 403, 408, 492.

Franklin's creek, 276.

Freehold, New Jersey, Presbytery, 417.

Galbraith, John, will of, 205.

Hampton, Rev. John, 394, 403, 408, 424, 450, 498.
Hart, Rev. John, 51, 53, 62
Hewett, Rev John, Indian baptism and marriage, 60, elected burgess, 209; on school-board, 266; record of marriages, 278
Hill, Rev Matthew, First Presbyterian minister in Maryland, 25.
Huguenots, 37, 127, 139, 167, 182, 314
Indians, Eastern Shore of Virginia, 43, 44; Eastern Shore of Maryland, 18, 19, hear George Fox, 59; baptism, 60, "our confederates," 68; King Daniel, 80; in court, 235, 255; laws concerning, 238, 297; town, 270; origin of Nanticokes, 271, money, 328, first pale-faces, 329, dialect, 18, 383, 401, 422, 483; Matchacoopah in court, 413; King Daniel *vs* Hudson, 495
Jamaica, Long Island, 350, 432
Jenkins, Colonel Francis, and wife, 79, 84, 167; Catholic insult, 181; judge, 209; commissioner, 238; executors and guardians, 502
Jones, James, Justice, 72; Quaker, Appendix No. 18.
Keith, George, Quaker, in Somerset, 196; visits Makemie, 198; at Snow Hill, 199, schism, 217, joins Episcopalians, 305; in "holy orders," 318, missionary, 349, 358, returns to Europe, 374; rector of Edburton, 491
Keith, Rev. Robert, opposes Macnish, 396, 403; his home, 404
Ker, Walter, 417
King, Robert, born, 176.
Laggan, country of the, 47, Presbytery, 33, 48; about to emigrate, 103.
Layfield, George, marriage, 224, 283; prosecuted, 292; dies, 365
Londonderry, siege, young Presbyterians close the gates, 161; heroic defence, 168.
Loyola, patron saint of Maryland, 90, festival, 135.

Mackie, Rev Josias, nativity, 222; at Elizabeth River, 222, 273
Macnish, Rev. George, arrives, 394; applies for license, 396, 403; licensed, 408; in Presbytery, 415, 452, 497; on Long Island, 536
Maddux, Rev Robert, First Somerset preacher, 27.
Makemie, Rev. Francis, nativity, 48; boyhood's haunts, 49; conversion, 50, 86, in Scotland, 50; probationer, 50, trial-sermons, 52; hears of Maryland, 53, preaches at Burt, 61; ordained, 70, arrives in Maryland, 77; described, 79, 80, Scriptures honored, 80; family religion, 85; between extremes, 88; deplores dissensions, 91; on baptism, 107; at Elizabeth River, Virginia, 109, etc.; autographs, 111, 124; on Prelacy, 160; in Accomack, 171, 190; describes the country, 178; Catechism, 186, 356; taxed to support Prelacy, 190, marries, 192, funeral sermon, 193, visited by Keith, 196; sickness, 203; receives legacy, 205; answers Keith, 214, 243; in Philadelphia, 215; land-owner, 190, 207, 222, 225, 301, 348, 362, 390, 410, 412, 501, on High Churchmen, 231; salary, 235, Pocomoke trader, 239; on lax doctrine, 257, on heaven, 262; on colonial schools, 266, the Trinity, 279, in Barbadoes, 287; Bible in business, 290; practical preaching, 293; Quakers questioned, 304, on uniformity, 307, arrested in Virginia, 308; preaching-places recorded, 309; pastoral to Barbadoes, 312; doctrine of election, 313; his own lawyer, 314; on liturgies, 324, will of Custis, 332; mill built, 335, 361; troubles with Mrs. Hill, 336, 347, 400, 404, saints' perseverance, 337, bishops, 338; his children, 356, 370, 501, 504,

505, church discipline, 361, 386; intends for Europe, 362; house and furniture, 371; store, 375; library, 375, 500; slaves, 376; in Europe, 377; scenes there, 380, 391; his *Perswasive*, 388; address to Governor Nott, 389, secures helpers, 393; "in the gap," 402, first Presbytery, 414; at Freehold, 417; at Woodbridge, 422; at Newark, 423; at Cornbury's table, 424; sermon, 426; arrested, imprisoned, indicted, 429–448; at Presbytery, 452; letter to Coleman, 455; at home, 456, returns, and tried in New York, 458–472, his speech, 463; in Boston, 474; letter to Cornbury, 477; his *Narrative*, 479; his will, 499, death and grave, 510.

Maryland charter, 22, toleration. 13, 22; law of 1649, 23, rebellion, 38, described by Governor Culpeper, 40, Quakers, 56; St. Mary's, 131, Church Establishment, 210, 241, 251, 263, 265, 291, 297, 309, 310, 321, 340, 343, Governor Copley, 208, 210, 230, 236, Governor Nicholson, 240, 263, 296, 297, 320, 388; disease and scarcity, 242, 250, 261; Annapolis, 243, 390; first post-route, 252, wild game, 275; Governor Blakiston, 296; capitol burnt, 310; population, 166, 339; Governor Loyd, 341; Act of Toleration, 344, capitol again burnt, 368, slavery, 378; Governor Seymour, 378; "Maryland parsons," 359, 379, 386, 395, 399, new State-house, 406, only brick church, 407.

Mather, Cotton, 243, 412, 433, 475.

Mather, Increase, 111, 124, 243, 475

Monokin church, 86, 125, 394, 408, 493, 497

Nicholson, Sir Francis, governor of Maryland, 240, 263; transferred to Virginia, 296, charac-

ter, 297; love-affair, 320, displaced, 388.

Oyster, first mention in American history, 96, 370.

Penn, William, grant of province, 67; comes to America, 67; conference with Lord Baltimore, 69; liberty of worship, 339; Episcopacy, 340; disgusted, 358.

Philadelphia laid out, 67; Makemie first Presbyterian minister there, 215; Quaker schism, 216; first Episcopal minister, 252; first Congregational minister, 295; first Presbyterian pastor, 295; first Presbyterian church, 377, 396; first Presbytery, 415; second Presbytery, 412; third Presbytery, 497

Pitts's Creek church, 94, 537.

Pocomoke River, first mention, 17; battle, 19; described, 19, 22, 268.

Quakers in Accomack 45, 46; settling Somerset, 55; wrongs in Maryland, 56, Fox in Somerset, 57; extremes, 88, hat in Somerset court, 181; schism in Philadelphia, 216, Thomas Story, 216, 259; officials, 239; loyal to James, 241, 249; Thomas Chalkley, 294, Samuel Bownas, 349; lonely graveyard, 509

Rehoboth plantation, 73; congregation, 78; religious centre, 92, 145; town, 83, importance, 105; mill, 151, 240; prison, 336, first record of church, 194; new church, 386; recorded, 492; ground given by Makemie, 501.

Riddel, Rev Alexander, 422

Rule, Rev. Robert, superintends Makemie's studies, 51; to confer about Stevens's application, 53

Scarborough, Colonel Edmund, settling Somerset, 55; raid upon Somerset, 57, against the Assateagues, 332

Seymour, Governor, wants no commissary, 378, order to Somerset court, 406; disgusted with clergy, 490.

Snow Hill church, 86, 124; town, 135, 201, 268, 390; parish, 212; bridge, 239; pastoral call, 450; presbyterial letter, 497; installation, 498.

Somerset county settled, 55; Scarborough's irruption, 57; organized, 71; towns, 84, 104, 134, 390, 495; defence, 181; election, 209; parishes, 212; thanksgiving, 223; cattle, 226; courthouse, 238, 253, 256; manufactures, 267; churches, 279; fruit, 352; ague, 354; parochial libraries, 360.

Stevens, Colonel William, nativity, 20; writes to Laggan Presbytery, 33; vindicates Indians, 69; children, 79; tolerant, 92, 145; deputy-lieutenant, 105; will, 159; dies, 153; tomb, 163; widow marries, 224; she dies, 267; niece marries, 283.

Taylor, Rev. Nathaniel, in Maryland, 182.

Teackle, Rev. William, 45, 46, 165, 202, 251.

Trail, Rev. William, to confer about Stevens's letter, 53; before the Council, 63; nativity, 64; in prison, 66; burnt in effigy, 66, in Somerset, 112; marriage by,

115; his father, 120, his home, 136; mystery, 143, petition, 165; returns to Scotland, 179; member of Assembly, 186, wife rejoins him, 193; he marries again, 342; at Borthwick, 392

Virginia, college founded, 226, 229; education, 227; Prelacy, 253, character of clergy, 172, 253, 264, college commencement, 319; population, 339; first peaches, 342; college burnt, 368; slavery, 377; Dissenters, 109, 387; Governor Effingham, 171; Governor Nicholson, 296, 297, 320, 388; Governor Nott, 387, 389.

Wale, Edward, 96, 184.

Walker, governor of Derry, stolen honors, 183; dies, 184.

Whalley, Major-General, 97, 184.

White, Ambrose, 100.

White, Father, Jesuit, 90.

Whittington, Captain William, 209, 238.

Wicomico church, 86, 125, 479.

Wilson, Ephraim, sheriff, 230.

Wilson, Rev. Thomas, 112, 125, 205, 279

Witchcraft, 72, 73, 158, 208.

Woodbridge, New Jersey, Makemie there, 422.

Woodbridge, Rev. Benjamin, in Philadelphia, 295.

THE END.

Milton Keynes UK
Ingram Content Group UK Ltd.
UKHW020624171024
2222UKWH00012B/33

9 781016 109086